TRADE NEGOTIATIONS IN THE TOKYO ROUND

William R. Cline, Noboru Kawanabe,
T.O.M. Kronsjö, and Thomas Williams

TRADE NEGOTIATIONS IN THE TOKYO ROUND

A Quantitative Assessment

THE BROOKINGS INSTITUTION
Washington, D.C.

Copyright © 1978 by
THE BROOKINGS INSTITUTION
1775 Massachusetts Avenue, N.W., Washington, D.C. 20036

Library of Congress Cataloging in Publication Data:

Cline, William R
    Trade negotiations in the Tokyo Round.

    Includes bibliographical references and index.
    1. Tokyo Round, 1973–1977.   2. Contracting Parties
to the General Agreement on Tariffs and Trade.
3. Tariff.   4. Nontariff trade barriers.   I. Title.
HF1721.C52   382.1   77-91799
ISBN 0-8157-1472-6

9 8 7 6 5 4 3 2 1

THE BROOKINGS INSTITUTION is an independent organization devoted to nonpartisan research, education, and publication in economics, government, foreign policy, and the social sciences generally. Its principal purposes are to aid in the development of sound public policies and to promote public understanding of issues of national importance.

The Institution was founded on December 8, 1927, to merge the activities of the Institute for Government Research, founded in 1916, the Institute of Economics, founded in 1922, and the Robert Brookings Graduate School of Economics and Government, founded in 1924.

The Board of Trustees is responsible for the general administration of the Institution, while the immediate direction of the policies, program, and staff is vested in the President, assisted by an advisory committee of the officers and staff. The by-laws of the Institution state: "It is the function of the Trustees to make possible the conduct of scientific research, and publication, under the most favorable conditions, and to safeguard the independence of the research staff in the pursuit of their studies and in the publication of the results of such studies. It is not a part of their function to determine, control, or influence the conduct of particular investigations or the conclusions reached."

The President bears final responsibility for the decision to publish a manuscript as a Brookings book. In reaching his judgment on the competence, accuracy, and objectivity of each study, the President is advised by the director of the appropriate research program and weighs the views of a panel of expert outside readers who report to him in confidence on the quality of the work. Publication of a work signifies that it is deemed a competent treatment worthy of public consideration but does not imply endorsement of conclusions or recommendations.

The Institution maintains its position of neutrality on issues of public policy in order to safeguard the intellectual freedom of the staff. Hence interpretations or conclusions in Brookings publications should be understood to be solely those of the authors and should not be attributed to the Institution, to its trustees, officers, or other staff members, or to the organizations that support its research.

Foreword

THE DYNAMISM of the international economy in the postwar period owes much to freer trade. Within Europe, trade barriers were eliminated among members of the European Economic Community and the European Free Trade Association. A series of multilateral negotiations under the General Agreement on Tariffs and Trade (GATT), especially the ambitious 1963–67 Kennedy Round, successively and substantially reduced barriers from their crippling levels of the 1930s. The current GATT negotiations in Geneva, named the Tokyo Round after the city in which they began in 1973, represent another phase in the process. This time, in addition to tariffs, nontariff barriers to trade are at stake as well.

The Tokyo Round has been slow, like the Kennedy Round before it. Changes in national administrations and unresolved issues involving the extent to which trade in industrial goods and agricultural commodities should be liberalized have contributed to delay. More recently, worldwide recession has heightened the fear that unemployment might be worsened by increased imports and thus has intensified demands for protection. Yet the political leaders of the principal negotiating countries have committed themselves, in a series of economic summit meetings, to a successful and expeditious conclusion of the negotiations. Although prospects for timely completion improved in 1977, the negotiations could well last through 1979, when U.S. negotiating authority expires.

In this book the authors seek to quantify the prospective economic effects of trade liberalization in the Tokyo Round. Their estimates include calculations of the economic benefits, trade changes, employment effects, and exchange-rate effects of alternative tariff-cutting proposals under consideration in the negotiations. They present similar estimates for the effects of lowering nontariff barriers to agricultural trade and barriers to trade affecting government procurement, and estimate the impact that liberalization in the Tokyo Round could have on the exports of the developing countries. The results provide a basis for assessing the economic effect of future trade liberalization generally and thus constitute a guide to the effects to be expected under specific alternative outcomes of the Tokyo Round itself in view of the negotiating positions of the principal parties. The estimates suggest that much is to be gained and little lost from thoroughgoing liberalization: the economic benefits of lower prices, investment stimulus, and greater economies of scale are likely to be substantial, whereas the labor adjustment costs and trade balance disruptions are likely to be slight.

William R. Cline is a senior fellow in the Brookings Foreign Policy Studies program. When the study was prepared, Noboru Kawanabe, T. O. M. Kronsjö, and Thomas Williams were Brookings research associate, senior fellow, and research associate, respectively. Kawanabe and Kronsjö have since rejoined the faculties of Kobe University of Commerce and the University of Birmingham, respectively; Williams now teaches at Brandeis University.

For helpful comments at various stages in the study, the authors thank Robert E. Baldwin, Richard Blackhurst, Geza Feketekuty, Edward R. Fried, Harry Grubert, Anne O. Krueger, John M. Leddy, Fred Sanderson, Robert M. Stern, Philip H. Trezise, and Larry J. Wipf. For computational assistance in the preparation of chapter 7 and appendix H, respectively, they thank A. B. M. Azizul Islam and Louanne Sawyer. The manuscript was edited by Robert L. Faherty, checked for factual accuracy by Penelope S. Harpold, and typed by Delores Burton. The index was prepared by Florence Robinson.

The study was financed by the Sumitomo Foundation, the Rockefeller Brothers Fund, and the Bureau of International Labor Affairs of the U.S. Department of Labor. The views presented in this book are the authors' alone and should not be ascribed to the persons or organizations whose assistance is acknowledged above, or to the trustees, officers, or other staff members of the Brookings Institution.

BRUCE K. MAC LAURY
President

November 1977
Washington, D.C.

Contents

Text Tables

Appendix Tables

Text Figures

Appendix Figures

TRADE NEGOTIATIONS IN THE TOKYO ROUND

CHAPTER ONE

Introduction

SINCE World War II, Europe, Japan, and the United States have dramatically reduced their protective barriers against imports through a succession of trade negotiations conducted within the General Agreement on Tariffs and Trade (GATT). International trade has grown at an unprecedented pace in these three decades, in part because of this continuous process of world trade liberalization and the related movements toward economic integration in Europe, which resulted in the total elimination of tariffs within a major trading region.

This study examines the present state of trade protection and the economic effects of future trade liberalization. We estimate the changes in trade flows, welfare benefits, employment, and exchange rates that could be expected from alternative types of liberalization of remaining tariff and nontariff barriers to trade. The study carries out these estimates for the United States, the European Economic Community (EEC), Japan, Canada, Austria, Finland, Norway, Sweden, Switzerland, Australia, and New Zealand. In addition, it considers prospective effects of the trade negotiations on the exports of the developing countries. The study therefore represents a comprehensive assessment of existing protection and the economic impact of trade liberalization for the industrial Western economies and for the Third World.

The immediate motivation for this study comes from the Tokyo Round of Multilateral Trade Negotiations. These negotiations, located in Geneva, have been in progress since 1974. A principal objective of the study is to provide a reliable basis for the evaluation of policy alternatives within the

1

Tokyo Round of negotiations, both by policymakers involved in the negotiations and by the informed public and legislatures that eventually will need to assess the significance of what the negotiations accomplish. A broader objective of the study is to assess the possibilities for economic gains through trade liberalization generally, whatever the particular bargains struck within the Tokyo Round.

The Tokyo Round, which was preceded by the modest Dillon Round in 1960–61 and the crucial Kennedy Round in 1964–67, represents a major step in the long succession of negotiations that, over the postwar period, have progressively liberalized international trade. It is named for the scene of its initiating meeting of ministers which occurred in September 1973. The Tokyo Round represents an ambitious effort to cut the remaining body of tariffs (averaging only 10 percent for the industrial countries) by as much as 60 percent and, at the same time, to liberalize the network of "nontariff barriers," which are also increasingly recognized as major impediments to trade.

As in the Kennedy Round, the trade negotiating authority of the United States has set the outside limit for the negotiating possibilities; maximum tariff-cutting authority under the Trade Act of 1974 allows 60 percent tariff cuts generally and the complete elimination of tariffs under 5 percent.[1] The act encourages the negotiation of reduced nontariff barrier protection; in this area, however, Congress must specifically approve any agreements negotiated. Also like the Kennedy Round, the Tokyo Round has been a slow process. The summit meeting agreement at Chateau de Rambouillet, France, in November 1975 set the end of 1977 as a deadline for completion of the negotiations, but that timetable has proved to be unrealistic. The ultimate deadline for completing the negotiations is December 1979, when U.S. negotiating authority under the Trade Act of 1974 expires.

Changes in administrations in the United States and other major countries, as well as in the commission of the EEC, have contributed to delays in the negotiations. The first three years of negotiations revealed continuing disagreement over the question of liberalizing agricultural trade (also an area of profound disagreement in the earlier Kennedy Round), and the lack of progress on agricultural issues slowed the pace of negotiations in other areas.

1. 88 Stat. 1982.

At the same time, conspicuous flare-ups of protectionism cast a shadow over the negotiations. In the United States, highly publicized protectionist pressures arose against imports of specialty steel, shoes, color television sets, and sugar. Under the Trade Act of 1974, producers seeking safeguards from import injury were able to petition the International Trade Commission for restrictive measures ranging from quotas and tariffs to adjustment assistance payments for displaced firms and workers. The recommendations advocating restrictions that the International Trade Commission made to the President posed a political dilemma for both the Ford and the Carter administrations. Both administrations were committed to free-trade policies in principle but were aware of the political dangers of seeming to ignore grievances of individual industries considering themselves to be the victims of import expansion (whether because of neutral market forces or because of practices by foreign suppliers which were deemed to be unfair). In Western Europe, administrative measures (such as pressures on major suppliers to apply "voluntary restraints" on their exports) have proliferated, principally against imports from Japan, as the European communities became alarmed over the deterioration of their trade balance with Japan. And throughout the industrial countries the recession of 1974–75, the worst since the Great Depression, aggravated the sensitivity of business and labor to competitive pressures from imports. As a consequence, within the four-year period following the meeting of ministers at Tokyo in September 1973, the multilateral trade negotiations became a locus for resisting new protectionist forces rather than a vehicle for reducing protection still further. Whether the multilateral negotiations in the Tokyo Round can return to the offensive and generate substantial new trade liberalization in addition to staving off rising protectionism remains to be seen.[2]

In any event, policymakers and the public should have at their disposal the most accurate possible evaluations of prospective effects of the trade negotiations. It is important to know the dimensions of the economic stakes in the negotiations. How large are the prospective savings to consumers and what savings are possible from reducing inefficient domestic

2. For a discussion of the individual protectionist pressures surfacing during this period, see Chamber of Commerce of the United States, International Group, "Implementation of the Trade Act: Major Developments in 1976," *Trade Negotiation Information Service,* special report (January 1977); and Richard J. Levine, "Controversy over Trade: Carter Must Decide Soon on Strengthening Import Curbs on Shoes, Sugar and TV Sets," *Wall Street Journal,* March 23, 1977.

production as the result of shifts in production to areas of comparative advantage? How large are other welfare gains from liberalization, including the resulting stimulus to investment and to technological change, the moderating influence on domestic inflation, and gains from increased exploitation of economies of scale? To what extent would alternative agreements provide "reciprocity" for the individual negotiating areas, raising each area's exports by amounts (or proportions) comparable to increases in imports? To what extent can the negotiating countries act together for their common gain, providing liberalization benefits for all, while avoiding serious adjustment difficulties for any individual country?

Analysis of the negotiations should provide important information to government, labor, business, and consumer groups that would be especially useful in deliberations about public policy. Policymakers should know the size of economic welfare benefits from liberalization, as well as the possible adjustment difficulties involved as regards labor and trade balance. Labor interests have serious reservations about possible unemployment which might result from further liberalization of imports, and they have a need for information on prospective employment gains from increased exports. Business and farming interests will wish to know about increased opportunities for exports and about products for which increases in imports are likely to be high. Consumer groups will be interested in the impact of liberalization on domestic prices.

These economic issues can usefully be examined with an analytical model that is capable of estimating the impact of alternative negotiation proposals on economic welfare, trade flows, exchange rates, and employment. In order to provide a balanced, multilateral view of the negotiations, a modeling effort should include calculations for all major countries participating in the negotiations. In this way the interests of each country may be taken into account in an overall assessment of the negotiations. In addition, it is desirable that the model be based on the greatest possible product detail, in order to obtain accurate results (especially for certain types of liberalization proposals) and to provide detailed estimates of interest to negotiators as well as to workers and firms in specific industries.

Surprisingly, work by governments in this area appears to be limited.[3]

---

3. Two private research efforts should, however, be mentioned. As discussed in appendix F, Robert E. Baldwin has conducted detailed calculations for the case of the United States, giving special attention to employment effects of liberalization. An-

Those countries that have the computational facilities and the analytical staff to conduct official analysis of this sort tend to focus their analyses on how the negotiating process would affect their own positions, and they keep the results confidential. These factors point to the potential usefulness of a "neutral" analysis. While a negotiating situation by definition implies an adversary procedure, its success depends on an awareness of the negotiators that all parties must benefit. This attitude can be strengthened by assessments that show not only how each country might be affected but also how the total gains could be maximized. The official entities (such as GATT) that might logically fit the role of "honest broker" in analysis face their own constraints, notably, the sensitive political problems involved in estimating the economic effects of one participant's proposals as opposed to those of another (especially in view of the unavoidable uncertainty associated with such quantitative estimates).[4]

These considerations lie behind the present study. It has been prepared by a multinational group of researchers under multinational financial support.[5] Its ongoing results have been made available in preliminary stages to several of the national delegations in the negotiations.[6]

The organization of the study parallels the major policy areas in the trade negotiations. Chapters 2 and 3 present our basic model of the tariff negotiations (discussing methodology and results, respectively). The tariff analysis examines twelve separate tariff-cutting formulas, computing

---

other study, by Deardorff, Stern, and Baum, presents a multilateral model with several methodological refinements, estimated for a single tariff formula (50 percent cut) using preaggregated data for broad product categories (twenty-two tradable goods). See Robert E. Baldwin, "Trade and Employment Effects in the United States of Multilateral Tariff Restrictions" (Washington, D.C., 1975; processed); and Alan V. Deardorff, Robert M. Stern, and Christopher F. Baum, "A Multi-Country Simulation of the Employment and Exchange-Rate Effects of Post-Kennedy Round Tariff Reductions" (University of Michigan, June 1976; processed).

4. Perhaps for these reasons, GATT has not undertaken the preparation of analytical models like those presented in this study. By contrast, the "descriptive" analytical work of GATT on profiles of existing tariffs is superb. See Contracting Parties to the General Agreement on Tariffs and Trade, *Basic Documentation for the Tariff Study: Summary by Industrial Product Categories* (Geneva, March 1974).

5. The authors are from U.S., Japanese, and British research institutions, and financial support came from the Sumitomo Foundation, the U.S. Department of Labor, and the Rockefeller Brothers Fund.

6. Analytical results that have been made available to negotiators include massive detailed estimates at the tariff-line level which are impossible to report in their entirety in a published volume.

trade, welfare, and employment effects for each. The calculations provide the basis for evaluating the main types of formulas which accomplish two key objectives: maximum economic welfare benefits from liberalization and "reciprocity" or balanced results from the viewpoint of individual participants. The twelve formulas examined span the range of major types of tariff-cutting proposals under consideration in the negotiations during 1975 and early 1976.

Chapters 4 and 5 conduct quantitative estimates of the trade and welfare effects of liberalizing agricultural quotas and "variable levy" nontariff barriers. Chapter 6 reports estimates by earlier studies of the trade effects of liberalizing another important barrier, discrimination in government procurement. The chapter also discusses in qualitative terms the issues involved in the negotiations over other major nontariff barriers.

Chapter 7 investigates the importance of trade liberalization among the industrial countries as regards the export opportunitites of the developing countries. It also examines the specific question of whether the developing countries should advocate deep cuts in tariff and nontariff barriers on a "most-favored-nation" (across-the-board) basis, or whether the interests of the developing countries would be better served by the maintenance of current protection by the industrial countries in order to guarantee the special advantages provided to developing countries by duty-free entry under "tariff preference" schemes.

Chapter 8 sets forth the principal conclusions in detail. The appendixes report detailed aspects of the analysis, including the traditional "average depth of tariff cut" approach, additional empirical analyses prepared for the case of Japan, and a special model designed to examine "optimal tariff reform."

In broad terms, the empirical results of this study show that there are major economic benefits to be derived from further trade liberalization, despite considerable success in reducing protection through previous rounds of trade negotiations. Lower tariffs would provide consumer savings on imported goods and would shift inefficient domestic production into activities with higher domestic productivity. Price reductions to consumers would be especially dramatic in the area of agricultural nontariff barriers. These "static" economic benefits would recur year after year and would grow along with the trade base. In addition, and what is probably more important, there would be economic benefits from increased exploitation of economies of scale associated with output expansion for increased exports, as well as from increased investment stimulated by the new export opportunities. Finally, freer trade should provide a competitive stimulus to technological advance as well as a moderating influence on import prices and, therefore, on domestic inflation. This should help achieve full employment in the trade-off between unemployment and inflation.

These various economic benefits may be achieved at very little cost in terms of labor adjustment or disturbances in trade balance. The total economic benefits completely dwarf the estimated labor adjustment costs. The number of jobs lost because of increased imports would be small, and adjustment would be facilitated by the gradual phasing in of liberalization over several years. On a net basis—that is, taking into account, the employment gains in export industries—the effect of trade liberalization on jobs would be negligible.

The search for a particular tariff-cutting formula achieved a breakthrough in September 1977, when the United States and the EEC agreed in principle on a compromise approach (see chapter 3). The compromise would mean an intermediate solution between the restrictive tariff-cutting proposals of the EEC and Japan and the liberal proposals of the United States and Canada. If applied with few exceptions, the formula implied by the agreement would achieve a fairly liberal outcome of the negotiations, on the basis of calculations in this study for a similar tariff-cutting approach. This result would represent a considerable achievement in view of the increasing protectionist sentiment in many industrial countries, largely associated with their high levels of domestic unemployment. Moreover, the economic benefits, employment, and trade effects would be relatively well balanced among the participants under the compromise approach.

The detailed calculations that lie behind these and other policy conclusions of this study necessarily require a number of methodological assumptions as well as reliance on particular statistical estimates of important building blocks such as import elasticities. Therefore, the specific estimates reported should not be interpreted as precise measurements. For purposes of drawing basic policy conclusions, however, the general magnitudes should be highly reliable. A special effort has been made to examine the sensitivity of the findings to the particular sets of import elasticities applied, and the test results indicate that the estimates are quite stable regardless of alternative elasticities used. Furthermore, in those parts of the study that overlap with other investigations (in particular, those by Baldwin and by Deardorff, Stern, and Baum cited above), the basic findings concerning the effects of liberalization on trade and employment are supported by similar results in these other studies.

Considered as a whole, the results document the potential for world economic gains through cooperative steps toward trade liberalization in the Tokyo Round. This evidence warrants special attention at a time when growing protectionist forces cast a shadow over the international trading system, threatening to reverse its impressive postwar strides toward liberalization.

CHAPTER TWO

A Model of Tariff Liberalization: Methodology and Data

THE INDUSTRIAL COUNTRIES have made remarkable progress toward reducing tariff protection in the postwar period. The Kennedy Round of trade negotiations in the early 1960s achieved especially important liberalization, cutting tariffs on manufactured products by an average of 35 percent.[1] The weight of remaining protection has shifted from tariffs toward nontariff barriers. Nevertheless, substantial room remains for liberalization in tariffs themselves. The average of tariffs on dutiable nonagricultural imports stands at 10.7 percent for eleven major industrial areas, as shown in table 2-1. Furthermore, the average tariff rises with the stage of processing, with very low tariffs on raw materials. The result of this well-known pattern of tariff escalation is that the "effective rates of protection," or tariffs expressed as fractions of value added after deducting intermediate inputs from product value, are much higher for manufacturing activities than would be expected on the basis of the relatively modest nominal

1. Ernest H. Preg, *Traders and Diplomats: An Analysis of the Kennedy Round of Negotiations under the General Agreement on Tariffs and Trade* (Brookings Institution, 1970), p. 12.

9

Table 2-1. *Average Tariff Rates for Eleven Industrial Countries, 1973*
Percent

Product category[a]	All imports					Dutiable items only				
	Total[b]	United States	Canada	Japan	EEC	Total[b]	United States	Canada	Japan	EEC
All products	6.2	7.1	6.7	6.3	4.2	10.7	8.9	14.2	11.2	9.0
Raw materials	1.5	2.3	0.4	3.8	0.3	5.7	4.4	6.3	10.6	3.5
Semifinished manufactures	6.6	6.0	10.6	6.2	5.9	10.5	9.5	14.5	8.9	9.9
Finished manufactures	9.4	9.0	6.7	12.0	8.9	11.3	9.5	14.2	12.5	9.2

Source: Contracting Parties to the General Agreement on Tariffs and Trade, *Basic Documentation for the Tariff Study: Summary by Industrial Product Categories* (Geneva, March 1974). Rates refer to weighted average no. 3; that is, weights based on importing-country values of imports from most-favored-nation suppliers.
a. Excludes agricultural products.
b. United States, Canada, Japan, EEC, Austria, Finland, Norway, Sweden, Switzerland, Australia, New Zealand.

tariff average of close to 10 percent.[2] Finally, tariff levels are considerably higher than the 10 percent average level in some important countries such as Canada (table 2-1).[3]

It is in the interest of all countries to reduce tariff protection in order to obtain cheaper sources of supply and to achieve the increased level of economic activity made possible by more efficient utilization of resources. Free trade permits these efficiency gains by allowing greater specialization according to each country's "comparative advantage."

In addition to static welfare gains through increased specialization, trade liberalization makes possible other important economic benefits. Greater exploitation of economies of scale becomes possible as firms increase the volume of output for exports. New export opportunities stimulate the rate of investment and therefore the growth rate. Greater stimulus to technological change occurs as increased competition from imports spurs domestic firms to adopt new techniques. Greater scope for the pursuit of macroeconomic policies favoring full employment becomes possible as the availability of imports at lower prices exerts a braking influence on the rate of domestic inflation. In view of these welfare gains, for all negotiating countries as a group, the most desirable result of negotiations will be the largest possible reduction in trade barriers.

2. Bela Balassa's study of effective protection using 1962 tariffs found that for the United States average effective protection was 20 percent compared with average nominal tariffs of only 11.6 percent. The corresponding averages were: 27.8 percent effective versus 15.5 percent nominal for the United Kingdom; 18.6 percent effective versus 11.9 percent nominal for the European Common Market; and 29.5 percent effective versus 16.2 percent nominal for Japan. Bela Balassa, "Tariff Protection in Industrial Countries: an Evaluation," *Journal of Political Economy*, vol. 73 (December 1965), p. 588. United Nations calculations using 1964 tariffs found that average nominal tariffs for four broad, successively higher stages of production for all industrial countries were: 4.6 percent, 7.9 percent, 16.2 percent, and 22.2 percent, respectively. The corresponding effective rates of protection for the highest three stages were: 22.6 percent, 29.7 percent, and 38.4 percent. *The Kennedy Round: Estimated Effects on Tariff Barriers*, UN Doc. TD/6/Rev. 1, 1968, p. 205. The relationship of average effective rates to average nominal rates is unlikely to have been changed much by tariff cuts in the Kennedy Round. Preeg, *Traders and Diplomats*, p. 235.

3. Referring to tariffs on dutiable items only. Note also that alternative weighting procedures can give much higher average tariffs. For example, the unweighted average of all U.S. tariffs on finished manufactures stands at 13.7 percent, whereas the average when weighting by imports in each category is only 9.5 percent. Contracting Parties to the General Agreement on Tariffs and Trade, *Basic Documentation for the Tariff Study: Summary by Industrial Product Categories* (Geneva, March 1974).

From the standpoint of any individual negotiating country, negotiation objectives will include the goal of reciprocity. Indeed, it is the desire that trade partners offer reciprocal tariff liberalization that necessitates trade negotiations in the first place. In the absence of this objective, individual countries could obtain the benefits of free trade by eliminating their own tariffs unilaterally. Reciprocal reductions by the other negotiating partners are necessary in order to ensure that a country's export opportunities expand along with the liberalization of its import market. Export expansion is important for three reasons: the full achievement of potential dynamic welfare gains from liberalization, the avoidance of substantial reductions in trade balance, and the attainment of balanced employment effects of liberalization.

With respect to welfare effects, the dynamic benefits related to economies of scale and stimulus to investment are linked to the expansion of exports. Negotiated agreements that fail to open up a country's export markets will forgo these sources of welfare gain for the country. Concerning trade balances, without a balanced expansion in both exports and imports, a country would have to anticipate a trade balance deterioration from liberalizing its own tariffs. Unless the country were running large balance-of-payments surpluses, trade balance deterioration would imply the need to resort to offsetting measures which could have economic costs. One such measure is devaluation, which would lead to a reduction in the country's terms of trade under the normal conditions of relatively elastic export supply in the country and abroad.[4] The existence of flexible exchange rates reduces potential adjustment costs because trade deficits need not be corrected by deflationary domestic policies causing unemployment and the loss of output. Nevertheless, flexible rates do not eliminate costs of adjustment because, generally, depreciation and terms of

---

4. See James E. Meade, *The Theory of International Economic Policy,* vol. I, *The Balance of Payments* (London: Oxford University Press, 1951), pp. 235–47. The question has recently been reformulated as a transfer problem in which the change in the terms of trade necessary to correct a trade balance deterioration depends on foreign and domestic marginal propensities to consume exportables, importables, and nontraded goods; see I. F. Pearce, "The Problem of the Balance of Payments," *International Economic Review,* vol. 2 (January 1961), pp. 1–28. Nevertheless, the "convention" remains that a trade balance decrease and a resulting exchange rate depreciation will cause a decline in the terms of trade; see Harry G. Johnson, "The Welfare Costs of Exchange Rate Stabilization," *Journal of Political Economy,* vol. 74 (October 1966), p. 514.

trade deterioration will follow the widening of a trade balance deficit under flexible rates. Furthermore, within the context of ongoing trade balance deficits attributable to trade surpluses run by the oil-exporting countries, the industrial countries have reason to watch their individual trade balances more closely than would have been the case in the absence of the rise in the price of oil beginning in 1973–74.

In addition to its impact on dynamic welfare gains and on the trade balance, reciprocity affects the employment implications of trade liberalization. One-sided liberalization could lead to losses of jobs in the liberalizing country because decreased employment in industries competing with imports would not be offset by increased employment in export industries. Of course, if the country depreciated its currency in order to offset the reduction in trade balance, there would be increased export jobs and additional jobs in import-competing sectors that would tend to offset the initial employment reduction associated with one-sided liberalization. In addition, macroeconomic effects might offset any employment loss. For example, with unilateral import liberalization, the resulting reduction in inflationary pressure (because of increased price competition from imports) might facilitate more expansionary policies (and thus more employment) for a government balancing the two objectives of full employment on the one hand and price stability on the other. However, to the extent that external balance already posed a constraint on expansionary measures, liberalization of imports without corresponding increases in exports could worsen, rather than alleviate, the macroeconomic obstacles to full employment. The dynamic effects of import liberalization in stimulating economic growth (through the impetus to both investment and technical change) could also cause an eventual increase in employment, even though the initial effect of import liberalization without corresponding export liberalization were to reduce employment.[5]

To recapitulate, significant tariff barriers remain despite past liberalization. Through the multilateral trade negotiations, countries may achieve static and dynamic welfare gains by reducing these barriers, and each

5. The fact that generalized, multilateral liberalization would shift production to countries having comparative advantage in each product suggests that the initial impact of liberalization for all countries would be a reduction in both labor and capital requirements for current levels of output, because of increased efficiency. The labor and capital resources released by increased efficiency would then be available for an increase in world output, with a resulting rise once again in the demand for labor.

country may seek to achieve a reciprocal or balanced outcome from the negotiations. The purpose of this chapter is to set forth the methodology used in a model constructed to estimate the various economic effects of tariff liberalization that comprise these welfare gains and aspects of reciprocity: the trade, welfare, exchange rate, and employment effects of liberalization. The chapter also describes the data base used for the calculations. The following chapter then reports the empirical results obtained from the model.

General Features of the Analysis

Before turning to the methodology applied, certain general features of the analysis warrant attention. First, the model includes estimates of the various economic effects for all of the principal countries participating in the negotiations. These estimates are essential to a central objective of this study, the examination of what would be a "balanced" or "reciprocal" result of the Tokyo Round of negotiations.[6]

Second, the analysis is based on extremely detailed data, permitting a much more accurate assessment of the effects of liberalization than would be possible using aggregate data.[7] In particular, to obtain precise results

6. The only other multilateral model of which we are aware is that by Alan V. Deardorff, Robert M. Stern, and Christopher F. Baum. That model is especially attractive from the theoretical standpoint because of its general equilibrium refinements. However, several aspects of the model limit its relevance for policy purposes. Its results are calculated for 1970, and enormous changes in the magnitude and composition of trade have occurred since then. Its use of aggregate categories probably introduces bias, especially if a harmonization tariff cut is involved (as discussed below). The model's supply assumptions would appear to bias upward the price effects and, more seriously, the employment effects of liberalization (as discussed below). The model also omits certain key effects, especially the substitution away from partner supply to outsider supply as tariffs decline around free-trade blocs. Alan V. Deardorff, Robert M. Stern, and Christopher F. Baum, "A Multi-Country Simulation of the Employment and Exchange-Rate Effects of Post-Kennedy Round Tariff Reductions" (University of Michigan, June 1976; processed).

7. Note, however, that for employment effects in the United States the study by Robert E. Baldwin provides far greater detail than does our model. The Baldwin study includes results by skill category and by state, for example. In addition, the basic calculations of that model are carried out at the tariff-line level, as are the estimates of our model. Robert E. Baldwin, "Trade and Employment Effects in the United States of Multilateral Tariff Restrictions" (Washington, D.C., 1975; processed).

for effects of alternative tariff-cutting formulas, it is necessary to use actual tariff-line data on tariffs and trade—rather than broader average tariffs for commodity groupings.[8] A formula applied to an average tariff can yield a quite different result from that obtained by applying the formula to actual individual line items with the trade effects then summed over all items in each commodity group.[9] The use of tariff-line data involves a massive effort of data manipulation, as described below. (The issues raised by combining these highly detailed trade and tariff data with import elasticities, or measures of the sensitivity of imports to import prices, derived from empirical estimates conducted for much broader categories, are examined later in this chapter in our discussion of elasticities.)

Third, the approach in this study is to examine short-run "impact" effects of trade liberalization. We do not seek to estimate longer run effects after the incorporation of Keynesian multiplier effects (which, in any event, will differ depending on the particular policy response chosen) or

8. By "tariff-line" we refer to the category to which the legally established tariff applies. There are approximately 5,000 detailed tariff-line categories for each of the industrial countries examined in this study.

9. As shown in appendix G, the use of preaggregated tariffs would cause a bias downward in estimates of import effects when harmonization tariff cuts are involved, whereby the percentage cut is larger for high tariffs than for low tariffs. Intuitively, this fact may be seen by considering the aggregation problem for a harmonization formula that would cut all high tariffs to the average tariff level in each broad group and leave alone all low tariffs. Calculations based on tariff-line commodity data would show an increase in imports for products with tariffs higher than the group average. However, a calculation using the group's average tariff to begin with would show no tariff cut whatsoever and therefore no increase in imports. Even when the tariff cut is "linear"—that is, a constant percentage cut of all tariffs regardless of their height—a small bias arises in the use of aggregate trade data and tariff averages (see appendix G).

Tests with a limited number of products suggest that preaggregation could bias downward the estimates of import increases by more than 10 percent. For example, when the harmonization tariff-cutting formula of the type suggested by the EEC (as discussed below) is applied to the four-digit Brussels Tariff Nomenclature (BTN) category 7315 (various types of alloy and high-carbon steel), the estimated increase in U.S. imports based on detailed estimates for all fifty-nine line items in the group is 11.1 percent higher than the estimate based on the average tariff and aggregate imports in the group. The corresponding difference between disaggregated and aggregated estimates for U.S. imports in BTN 2402 (tobacco products) is 10.8 percent. Moreover, estimates based on still broader aggregate categories and average tariffs would give a still greater downward bias to increased imports estimated under harmonization formulas.

after the introduction of general equilibrium effects. Our approach makes it possible to focus on the impact, other things being equal, of a trade-liberalization policy decision itself. As a separate step, however, we do examine the changes in exchange rates that would be required to offset the initial changes in trade balances resulting from liberalization. These exchange rate changes would eliminate any trade balance changes, and would reduce the magnitudes of changes in sectoral trade balances and employment; but they still would leave positive trade and employment effects in some sectors and negative effects in others.

It is necessary to make a number of working assumptions in order to apply our approach of examining short-run "impact" effects. One assumption is that idle capacity and unemployed labor exist within the relevant range for trade changes, so that, as export demand increases, it can be met through output expansion without raising prices and bidding factors of production away from other sectors.[10] Another assumption is that whatever small changes in aggregate monetary demand arise from changes in net trade balances are "accommodated" by a monetary policy that holds interest rates constant.[11]

Furthermore, in order to identify changes in employment resulting from trade effects of tariff liberalization, we must make two additional assumptions: (1) The level of domestic spending on the substitute for the import declines by the same amount as the increase in imports; (2) domestic spending on goods other than the import and the direct substitute for the import does not change (in other words, cross-price demand effects are zero with respect to these "third goods" and imports). The first of these two assumptions makes it possible to translate increased import value into estimates of reduced output of the import substitute and reduced employment in its production. The second assumption guarantees that employment does not decline in sectors other than that of the import

10. If labor is assumed to be transferable among sectors, then the assumption of existing unemployment of labor is necessary only for those countries in which net employment increases resulting from trade liberalization are identified (after deducting jobs lost to increased imports from extra jobs attributable to increased exports).

11. That is, suppose the measurements show increased net exports and employment for a country. These direct trade effects would tend to be frustrated by rising interest rates (and therefore declining investment) unless monetary authorities accommodated the rise in demand for money associated with the higher gross national product (GNP) caused by increased net exports, and expanded the money supply sufficiently to hold interest rates constant.

substitute as the result of a switching of consumption from these "third" goods to the purchase of imports as tariffs decline. Still another, related, assumption lying behind our procedure is that changes in net tax revenues resulting from changes in tariffs are offset. Private disposable income does not change, despite reduced tariffs, because other taxes are raised to offset reduced revenue from tariffs. (Otherwise, the change in disposable income would set off other changes in consumption, production, and employment.)[12]

It might be argued that, for trade balance effects in particular, an analysis of the short-run impact would be misleading for policy purposes. Generally, changes in trade balance are the result of macroeconomic policies. Therefore, it might be asked whether it is appropriate to sum up microeconomic estimates of liberalization effects in order to determine the macroeconomic effects on total trade and employment. For example, macroeconomic policies that cause expenditure to rise by an amount greater than production are considered to be the source of trade balance deficits in the "absorption approach" to analysis of the trade balance.[13] Similarly, the expansion of the domestic money supply at excessive rates when compared to foreign money supply causes a trade balance deficit according to the "monetary theory of the balance of payments," because citizens attempt to dispose of unwanted excess money balances by purchasing goods, thereby raising imports and reducing exports.[14] However, for purposes of measuring the specific impact of a particular policy decision, such as the reduction of tariffs by a given amount, it is appropriate to examine the initial impact based on the total of microeconomic trade responses, with the assumption that, other things being equal, this impact causes a deviation from the basic path of the trade balance set by preexisting macroeconomic policies. The fact that this initial impact may be offset subsequently by changes in macroeconomic conditions should

12. These various assumptions are analyzed in a detailed theoretical presentation by Robert E. Baldwin and Wayne E. Lewis, "U.S. Tariff Effects on Trade and Employment in Detailed SIC Industries" (paper prepared for the Conference on the Impact of International Trade and Investment on Employment, U.S. Department of Labor, held in Washington, D.C., December 2–3, 1976; University of Wisconsin, 1976; processed), appendix A.

13. Sidney S. Alexander, "Effects of Devaluation on a Trade Balance," *International Monetary Fund Staff Papers*, vol. 2 (April 1952), pp. 263–78.

14. Harry G. Johnson, "The Monetary Approach to Balance of Payments Theory," in Michael B. Connolly and Alexander K. Swoboda, eds., *International Trade and Money* (London: Allen and Unwin, 1973).

not be allowed to obscure the impact of the liberalization policy decision itself. On the contrary, the policy assessment should be broken down into parts, with the first step being the measurement of trade balance effects from tariff-cutting decisions, and the second step being an examination of the possible offsetting macroeconomic policies that might follow. We have followed this two-step procedure by calculating, first, the initial trade balance impact of liberalization and then, separately, the changes in exchange rates necessary to offset the initial changes in trade balance. The second, offsetting step could just as easily have been in the form of some other macroeconomic policy rather than the adjustment of exchange rates (change in fiscal or monetary policy), but, in the current situation of flexible exchange rates, the most likely macroeconomic adjustment to the impact of the trade balance effects of liberalization would be through a change in exchange rates.

Finally, the model presented in this chapter is designed to investigate the following policy questions: First, how large are the welfare benefits that can be obtained from further liberalization of tariffs? Second, of the major types or "families" of tariff-cutting formulas under consideration in the negotiations, which types are the most desirable—from the standpoints of overall welfare benefits, on the one hand, and of "balanced" or "reciprocal" outcomes, on the other? Third, what would be the main patterns of liberalization effects, under alternative tariff-cutting formulas, for each of the negotiating partners, and especially for the four major participants (the United States, Canada, Japan, and the EEC)? Answers to these questions are evaluated in chapter 3 on the basis of empirical results estimated using the model.

In addition, the results are elaborated further in subsequent chapters to address other policy questions. In particular, chapter 5 combines estimates of the trade and welfare effects of liberalizing nontariff barriers with the results for tariffs alone in chapter 3 to obtain an overview of the effects of comprehensive liberalization and to assess the relative importance of the two types of liberalization. Chapter 7 uses the detailed results lying behind the aggregate estimates of this chapter to examine the impact of multilateral trade liberalization on the exports of the developing countries. Finally, appendix H presents a linear programming model of "optimal tariff negotiations." This model uses the detailed results estimated for individual tariff formulas to determine optimal combinations of tariff-cutting rules for each country and major commodity group that will maximize welfare subject to constraints on the amounts by which trade balances may be allowed to deteriorate.

Methodology: General

This section treats the methodology used in the model of tariff negotiations in terms of the effects of tariff liberalization on trade, on welfare benefits, on free-trade blocs, on the so-called free-rider countries that do not reduce their own tariffs, on exchange rates, and on employment.

Trade Effects

The model of tariff negotiations first calculates, at the tariff-line level, the increase in imports of each commodity that would result from a proposed change in tariff. These increased imports are estimated for each of eleven industrial importing areas, with detail by supplier country. The calculation of increased imports in a given tariff category is based on the following method: The percentage of increase in import value[15] equals the percentage change in the import price to the consumer caused by the tariff reduction, multiplied by the "price elasticity of demand for imports." The percentage decline in the price of the import to the consumer equals the change in the tariff divided by unity plus the original tariff. For example, if the original tariff were 20 percent and it were cut in half to 10 percent, consumers would face a decline of 8.3 percent in the price. That is, originally they would have paid $1.20 for an item costing $1.00 without the tariff, and after the tariff cut they would pay only $1.10, giving a reduction of 0.10/1.20, or 8.3 percent, in consumer prices.

The price elasticity of import demand, for its part, represents the percentage change in demand for imports for each unit percentage change in the consumer price of the imports. Typically, statistical estimates of these elasticities range in the neighborhood of -0.5 to -3.0, meaning that a 10 percent decline in the prices of imports could cause a 5 percent to 30 percent increase in the volume of imports. As discussed below, we have based our calculations on the best available statistical estimates of import

15. Since world prices are assumed to remain constant (infinite elasticity of import supply), the percentage change in the value of imports also equals the percentage change in the physical volume of imports.

elasticities, including new estimates for Japan prepared in the present study.

In short, on the import side the model computes the increase in trade from tariff liberalization as follows: the base level of imports, times the import price elasticity, times the percentage change in consumer price (unity plus tariff) caused by the particular tariff reduction under consideration.

On the export side, the model merely adopts the mirror image of the import calculations: for every increase in one country's imports, there is a corresponding export increase by the country's suppliers. In fact, the model works with trade base data that specifically designate the individual suppliers of any given commodity. Therefore, when an importing country's increased imports are computed for a particular good coming from a specific country, the increase in imports represents an addition to the supplier country's exports. To determine the overall increase in exports for a country in a given product, these trade changes are summed up over all of the importing areas for the particular supplier and product in question.[16]

Our treatment of exports means that within the imports of any given country the existing shares of individual suppliers of any commodity will continue to apply to the extra imports induced by liberalization. The case of importing countries within a free-trade bloc is an exception to this rule, as discussed below. The treatment of exports reflects the fact that for a given commodity we apply a single import elasticity of demand to all existing suppliers. It also reflects our assumption that the elasticity of export supply for each existing supplier is equal to infinity; extra supply is assumed to be available at constant cost. Therefore, the export supply elasticity is identical for all suppliers, which is another condition for the constant shares of suppliers in increased imports resulting from liberalization.

The assumption of the model that export supply is infinitely elastic in the relevant range rests on the premise that all changes induced by trade liberalization will be small enough that export supply will be able to meet

16. Note that export totals are possible only at the four-digit BTN levels, because they require summing across various importing countries and the GATT data base used for the study has compatible import categories only at the four-digit BTN level. By contrast, a liberalizing country's import changes are compiled at the more detailed "tariff-line" level.

increased demand with no rise in the supply price. The assumption means that unit costs are constant rather than rising over the relevant range. This assumption would appear to be reasonable, especially in large countries such as the United States where exports represent a small fraction of production. Even in smaller, more open economies the assumption should be generally valid because, as shown in the empirical results described below, the magnitudes of trade changes are small relative to levels of domestic production.

The assumption of infinite elasticity of export supply is frequently applied in models of international trade.[17] Robert E. Baldwin and Wayne E. Lewis assume infinite elasticity of export supply in their study of effects of trade liberalization for the United States.[18] The few existing empirical estimates of export supply elasticities tend to confirm that these elasticities are high or infinite. Using simultaneous equation techniques, Stephen P. Magee estimated that the elasticity of supply of U.S. exports was 11.5 and the elasticity of supply of foreign exports to the United States was 8.5.[19] These elasticities are so high that, for practical purposes, they are close to infinity. For example, a 10 percent rise in the quantity of U.S. exports would require no price rise at all with an infinite export supply elasticity; it would cause a price rise of only 0.87 percent using an export elasticity of 11.5. More recent estimates by Morris Goldstein and Mohsin S. Kahn obtain an infinite supply elasticity for Japanese exports, and relatively high export supply elasticities of 5.0 for the United States and 4.6 for West Germany. The supply elasticities estimated for exports from smaller, more open economies are smaller, as would be expected (1.2 for Belgium, 1.1 for Italy).[20]

Overall it would appear that any bias contained in our results caused

17. See, for example, Sung Y. Kwack and George R. Schink, "A Disaggregated Quarterly Model of United States Trade and Capital Flows: Simulations and Tests of Policy Effectiveness," in Gary Fromm and Lawrence R. Klein, eds., *The Brookings Model: Perspective and Recent Developments* (Amsterdam: North-Holland, 1975), pp. 97–168.

18. Baldwin and Lewis, "U.S. Tariff Effects on Trade and Employment in Detailed SIC Industries," p. 1.

19. Stephen P. Magee, "Prices, Incomes, and Foreign Trade," in Peter B. Kenen, ed., *International Trade and Finance: Frontiers for Research* (Cambridge: Cambridge University Press, 1975), p. 204.

20. Morris Goldstein and Mohsin S. Kahn, "The Supply and Demand for Exports: A Simultaneous Approach," *Review of Economics and Statistics* (forthcoming).

by the assumption of infinitely elastic export supply will be very small.[21] The directions of change in estimates after eliminating any such bias would be as follows: First, the changes in values of trade resulting from liberalization would be smaller. Second, the volume increases in trade would be reduced by a greater degree, because changes in values of imports would incorporate increased world prices but changes in volume would not. Third, actual employment effects would be smaller than those estimated by our model, by amounts comparable to the smaller magnitudes for volume changes in world trade. Fourth, welfare effects from liberalization would be somewhat reduced, because of smaller changes in trade volumes and because increased world prices, reflecting higher world opportunity cost of extra supply, would erode part of the gains in consumer surplus obtained by reducing tariffs. Fifth, smaller countries would tend to have relatively greater reductions in estimated export gains from liberalization than larger countries, because smaller countries are likely to have lower export supply elasticities than larger countries. Sixth, conversely, with respect to static welfare gains, the benefits for large countries would be reduced relatively more than those for small countries, because supply prices facing the large countries would be more likely to be driven up by liberalization than those facing small countries. This last point reflects the possible phenomenon of a loss in terms of trade by large countries that reduce their tariffs below the "optimal" or "scientific" tariff levels relative to tariffs abroad. Once again, however, it seems likely that all of these adjustments would turn out to be extremely small, if the "true" export elasticities were known. The changes in trade resulting from liberalization are so small to begin with, relative to domestic output, that it is reasonable to expect that they could occur at constant costs and, therefore, with infinite elasticity of export supply over the relevant range. This conclusion is reinforced by the fact that trade changes would be phased

21. Consider the following typical magnitudes. With an average tariff of 10 percent, an average import elasticity on the order of -1.75, and a tariff cut of 60 percent, our model will predict increased import values and volumes on the order of 9.5 percent as the result of liberalization. Suppose that our infinite elasticity of export supply elasticity is replaced by an elasticity of 5 (based on the Goldstein-Kahn results). Then the 60 percent tariff cut will raise import values by only 8.5 percent, or by 11 percent less than our estimates of changes in values of trade. Import quantities will rise by only 7.07 percent, or by 26 percent less than our estimates of changes in import quantities.

in slowly, because tariff reductions would be staged over a period of at least five years.[22]

An important feature of the model is that it treats each product separately. There is no "cross-elasticity" causing an estimated change in the imports of one good when the tariff on a second good changes. Empirical estimates of cross-elasticities generally are not available. In order to consider the possible biases introduced by treating each product independently from all others, it is helpful to divide cross-product effects into two types: substitution among products in consumption, and cross-product effects derived from input-output relationships. In the case of substitution among similar goods, to the extent that a given class of substitutable products (for example, certain types of metals) tends to have similar tariff rates for all products in the class, the absence of specific attention to substitution among products will not cause a bias because the tariff change from a given tariff-cutting formula will affect substitutes equally. With no change in the relative prices of the substitutable products, there will be no incentive to substitute one for another. If tariffs vary, then biases will occur in estimates for individual products. However, the most detailed results reported in this volume are at levels of approximately twenty-one broad categories covering all trade (Brussels Tariff Nomenclature "sections"), and product substitution among these categories is likely to be quite low. Therefore, the sectoral results reported here are less likely to be biased than might be the case for the specific division of the trade

22. One attempt to incorporate less than infinitely elastic export supply into the analysis of the effects of trade liberalization should be noted. In their general equilibrium model of tariff negotiations, Deardorff, Stern, and Baum specify upward sloping supply curves for sectoral output, based on the assumption of fixed capital stock and full adjustment of output through variation in labor (in amounts necessary as determined by sectoral estimates of capital-labor substitutability based on constant-elasticity-of-substitution, or CES, production functions). This approach would appear to bias upward the magnitudes of price changes and, more seriously, employment changes resulting from liberalization. Forced to adjust inefficiently because of fixed capital, a sector would show a relatively large price increase from increased demand. And, with typically low elasticities of substitution between labor and capital as estimated in CES production functions, one would expect high percentage changes in employment to be predicted for small percentage changes in output, given the fact that the full burden of output adjustment in the model falls on labor. The key assumption of fixed capital would appear to be unrealistic, given the fact that trade changes would be phased in over periods of five years and more. Deardorff, Stern, and Baum, "A Multi-Country Simulation."

effects of liberalization among more detailed individual products within these broad categories.[23]

Any biases caused by omitting the calculation of input-output "cross-product" effects are also likely to be small. These biases, again, will be most pronounced at the detailed product level. For example, the model will show no change in the imports of cocoa beans when the tariff on chocolate declines and consumers begin buying foreign instead of domestic chocolate, even though domestic processors will have lower sales of chocolate and therefore lower imports of cocoa beans. At more aggregate levels, however, the intermediate effects tend to cancel each other out. Although increased imports of final goods will reduce the need for imports of intermediate inputs used in the domestic production of import substitutes, the increase of exports to other countries lowering their own tariffs will tend to cause increased import needs for intermediate inputs. Thus, if export and import changes from liberalization are in approximate balance, then the induced trade effects working through input-output relationships will also be in balance (unless, for some reason, the import intensity of inputs into export products differs substantially from that for inputs into the production of domestic import substitutes). Thus, for trade balance purposes, these intermediate effects will offset each other. In any event, because intermediate inputs represent only a fraction of gross output value (the relevant concept for changes in trade), and imported inputs in turn constitute only a fraction of total intermediate inputs, the trade effects of liberalization induced by intermediate input requirements will amount to only minor ripples compared to the direct trade effects, especially in largely self-sufficient countries such as the United States.[24]

23. These observations on greater reliability of final results at more aggregative levels do not mean that, in the derivation of the results, the initial use of aggregate data would be reliable. As discussed above, regardless of elasticities used, the use of preaggregated data on tariffs and trade would involve the loss of vital information necessary for unbiased estimates of trade effects, especially for harmonization formulas.

24. Although these indirect effects are likely to be minor, it should be noted that they will tend to run in the opposite direction from any overall effects on net trade balance measured for direct trade changes. Anticipating the results reported in chapter 3, the changes in direct trade balance from liberalization tend to be negative for the EEC and Canada, and positive for Japan and the United States. Thus, for the EEC and Canada the explicit introduction of trade effects on intermediate inputs would reduce the size of estimated trade deficits from trade liberalization, because the shifting of supply from domestic output to imports would permit the economizing

An important related question is that of the relationship of "tariff escalation" to the location of processing industries. The model used in this study deals with rates of nominal protection applied to full value of the product, rather than with rates of "effective protection," showing the protection as a percentage of value added and, therefore, the rate of protection on the economic activity of producing the final product, given the raw materials. Because raw materials tend to enter free or at low duties, the effective protection rates on processed manufactured goods can be much higher than their nominal tariff rates. That is, most of the protection applies to value added in the transformation activity rather than to the raw material inputs. Therefore, an alternative approach focusing on changes in rates of effective protection, and taking account of a domestic supply function for value added, could well arrive at larger estimates of import increases for processed goods (but, correspondingly, somewhat smaller estimates of increases in imports of raw materials) than those obtained in this study.[25] As a result, there may be two types of bias in the estimates obtained here. First, the sectoral composition of import increases for the industrial countries may understate import increases in processed goods and overstate import increases in raw materials. Second, for those countries specializing in exports of raw materials (such as Canada, Australia, New Zealand, and many developing countries), the estimates may understate export increases to be expected from liberalization. These countries are likely to make greater inroads into the export of processed goods than are estimated by our model, as tariff escalation declines and the location of processing activities moves from industrial importing areas to areas exporting raw materials.[26]

---

of imported intermediate inputs. Similarly, the estimated positive effects on trade balance for Japan would be somewhat reduced by incorporation of induced effects on intermediate products, because projected export increases would require increased imports of intermediate inputs. For the United States, where imported intermediate inputs are probably less important than in the other areas, adjustments incorporating intermediate inputs probably would have very little effect on the basic trade estimates.

25. In practice, an alternative approach of this type is not feasible. Estimates of current levels of effective protection at the detailed tariff-line level are not available; neither are empirical estimates of domestic supply functions for the corresponding sectoral supply of value added available.

26. Note that this tendency would give a net increase in trade balance to current exporters of raw materials above whatever trade balance results are estimated for them in this study. That is, as a group their decrease in exports of raw materials

Welfare Effects

The welfare effects calculated in this study are based on the traditional methodology for measuring welfare benefits from trade liberalization. That method captures the consumer benefits from lower prices of imports after liberalization. For the preexisting level of imports, any price reduction to the consumer merely represents a transfer away from government of tariff revenue formerly collected on the import and therefore no net gain to the country as a whole. But for the increase in imports, there is a net welfare gain equal to the domestic consumers' valuation of the extra imports minus the cost of extra imports at world price (excluding tariff). The standard approach in an evaluation of this sort, when price to the consumer changes, is to use an average between the original price and the final price. But these prices, respectively, are world price plus original tariff and world price plus final tariff. After subtracting out world price as the unit cost to the country of extra imports, the result is that the net welfare gain is merely the increase in import value times the average between the tariffs before and after liberalization. Thus, if imports of a commodity rise by $100 million as the result of cutting the tariff from 20 percent to 10 percent, the welfare gain is $15 million. That is, suppose the unit price without tariff is $100. Then, the unit value to consumers falls from $120 before liberalization to $110 after liberalization, giving an average unit price of $115. Subtracting the cost to the country at world price, or $100, there is a net welfare gain of $15 on each unit, or 15 percent of the import value at world prices. Therefore, the final welfare gain is 15 percent of the extra $100 million in imports.

Further elaboration of the welfare measurement is provided below in the algebraic presentation of the methodology. It is essential, however, to note a fundamental feature of the detailed welfare estimates: they are almost certainly far below the true welfare gains to be expected from liberalization. They represent "static efficiency" gains. Yet, the more important welfare gains from liberalization are the nontraditional effects described above: investment effects, increased economies of scale, outside stimulus to technical change for domestic firms, and output gains from macroeconomic policies made possible by a reduced rate of inflation (be-

---

would be more than offset by their increase in exports of processed goods, because the value of processed goods would contain the additional element of value added domestically in these countries.

cause of downward pressure on prices from increased import competition).

The development of a comprehensive methodology for measuring these effects remains an uncompleted task for researchers examining international trade.[27] However, on the basis of recent research on some of these nontraditional welfare effects in the case of the formation of the European Common Market, it is possible to estimate an order of magnitude for total welfare effects, given the measurement of static welfare gains (as discussed in chapter 3). For the more precise task of choosing among alternative proposals for liberalization (for example, alternative tariff-cutting formulas), it is necessary to assume that the measured static welfare gains provide a good guide to the relative magnitudes of total welfare effects of the various options for liberalization.[28]

Finally, we carry out calculations of the social cost of labor adjustment caused by increased imports. These estimates apply information on U.S. experience with the duration of unemployment of workers who have been affected by changes in trade. The labor adjustment costs are then compared with total welfare gains in order to obtain an evaluation of the order of magnitude of net welfare benefits from trade liberalization.

Free-Trade Blocs

The methods described above apply to importing areas that charge most-favored-nation tariffs for all suppliers. However, member countries

27. C. Fred Bergsten and William R. Cline, "Increasing International Economic Interdependence: The Implications for Research," *American Economic Review,* vol. 66 (May 1976), pp. 155–61.

28. It is reasonable to expect total welfare gains to be at least in the same rank order, by tariff-cutting formula, as static welfare gains. The static gains depend on the height of the tariff, the percentage tariff cut, and the increase in imports. Certain nontraditional welfare effects, such as gains from economies of scale and stimulus to new investment, should depend primarily on the size of increases in exports. Other nontraditional effects, such as the impetus to technical change and the anti-inflationary role of liberalization, should depend on the height of the tariff and the percentage tariff cut. Therefore, we would expect total welfare effects to be correlated both with static welfare effects and with the magnitude of trade creation. As will be seen in chapter 3, our estimates show a high correlation between the rankings of tariff formulas by size of import increase and rankings by amount of static welfare gain. There should be an even closer correlation of the rankings for static and total welfare effects because, on the basis of the above considerations, total welfare gains could be expressed as a function of both static welfare effects and size of import increase.

of the European Economic Community (EEC) and the European Free Trade Association (EFTA) allow free entry for each others' industrial goods (or will do so fully by 1977 in the case of trade between a country in one group and a country in the other group). The calculations must be adjusted to take this fact into account. Two basic adjustments are made. First, for a member of a free-trade bloc, the computation of increased imports under the "trade creation effect" discussed above is limited to imports from suppliers who are outside the bloc. It makes no sense to apply the calculations to imports from bloc partners because those imports already face free entry and there can be no further reduction in their price to consumers through trade liberalization. Another way of viewing this point is that, in principle, the standard calculation is applied, but the magnitude of the tariff change is zero, so that the resulting trade change is zero.

The second adjustment for trade bloc members is the introduction of a "trade substitution effect." This effect represents a shifting in the supply of even the prereform level of imports, away from partner suppliers within the free-trade bloc toward suppliers outside the bloc. This switching in source of supply occurs because, as the tariff wall around the bloc declines, the price of outsiders' goods falls relative to the (duty-free) price of partners' goods. It thus becomes more attractive to import from outside the bloc and less attractive to import from inside it. This substitution effect essentially represents an unwinding of "trade diversion" caused by the formation of the free-trade bloc in the first place—that is, the original shifting in favor of partners as the source of supply when the free-trade bloc was formed.

The net effect of the substitution adjustment is to raise the estimate of increased imports from nonbloc suppliers above the estimate that would result from the basic trade creation effect alone. For imports from partners, the result is to cause an unambiguous *decline* instead of an increase in imports. That is, there is no trade creation effect causing any increase in imports from partners, but there is a negative effect causing a decrease in those imports as the buying country shifts toward outsider supply.

The precise formulations of the trade calculations for "bloc" countries are presented below. The basic lines of analysis are the following. The preliberalization level of imports is "switched" away from bloc partner suppliers toward outside suppliers. The exact amount of their shift is computed by finding the change in the nonbloc share of total supply. The percentage change in the nonbloc suppliers' share depends on the percentage change in price for outsider goods caused by tariff reduction. It is the "elasticity of substitution" that determines precisely how much the percentage change in the nonbloc suppliers' share will be for a given percentage change in the ratio of outsider price (including tariff) to partner price (duty-free).

Once the percentage change in total nonbloc import share is calculated, the corresponding substitution effect for each individual outside supplier is obtained by allocating across all outside suppliers the total shift of preexisting imports toward outside suppliers. The individual allocation is based on the original share of each outside supplier in total outsider supply. For bloc partner suppliers, by contrast, a total decrease in imports is assigned, equal to the corresponding increase computed for total nonbloc supply. The decrease in total imports from partners is allotted across individual partner countries in proportion to each partner country's share in the preform total imports from bloc partners, for the commodity in question.

Finally, for nonbloc suppliers, the substitution effect is added to the trade creation effect, calculated in the original way applicable to all importing areas, to obtain the total change in imports of the bloc country from a particular nonbloc supplier. Again, for bloc suppliers the trade change is limited to the negative effect of trade substitution.

The welfare effect of liberalization also requires adjustment for the case where the importing country belongs to a free-trade bloc. For the component of increased imports from outsiders representing standard trade creation, the welfare effect is calculated as in the general case for nonbloc importers, as was described above. In addition, however, the bloc importer derives a welfare gain from shifting its preexisting imports away from bloc partners toward outsiders. This welfare gain arises in the following manner. Essentially, for each unit of imports shifted away from partner supply to outsider supply, the country saves an amount equal to the tariff. That is, partner suppliers can charge world price plus the tariff for their goods and still be competitive with outsider supply (since consumers pay no tariff on partner goods but must pay a tariff on goods from outside). Therefore, the country saves by shifting to cheaper outsider supply, and the amount of savings per unit is the tariff.

Once again, evaluation uses an average of "before and after" prices, so that the average between the original and the final tariff is applied to the amount of "trade substitution" to determine welfare gains from substitution. For example, if $100 million is switched from imports provided by bloc partners to imports provided by outside suppliers when the tariff wall falls from 20 percent to 10 percent, then the net welfare gain from the substitution effect is $15 million—that is, the average of the "before and after" tariffs (15 percent) multiplied by the amount of the trade shift. A fuller development of the measure is presented below.

Respending Effect

In addition to the trade effects described above, another important effect of liberalization involves the special situation of "rest-of-world" countries that benefit from improved access to markets in the liberalizing countries but do not reduce their own tariffs. These countries, basically the developing and the communist countries, are the "free riders." By long-established tradition under international trade rules, tariffs are applied on a "most-favored-nation" (MFN) basis. Thus, for example, if the United States cuts its tariff on goods from France in a trade negotiation, it also automatically cuts the tariff on the same goods from Brazil. In a reciprocal move, France will have cut some of its tariffs; Brazil, however, probably will have made no tariff concessions.

The overall impact of free-rider countries in a tariff negotiation is to build in a negative trade balance effect from liberalization for those negotiating countries that do reduce tariffs. That is, even if all of the Organisation for Economic Co-operation and Development (OECD) countries carry out liberalization that is reciprocal or balanced with respect to export and import effects considering only trade among themselves, the result would still be to induce a trade deficit for all of them in relation to those countries that do not reduce protection.

In the past, one approach to this problem has been to focus liberalization on products in which most trade takes place between the industrial countries actually liberalizing. But this approach requires numerous exemptions to general, across-the-board tariff-cutting formulas. Another approach could be to insist upon tariff reductions by countries usually unprepared to liberalize. But this alternative is unrealistic. The principle of "nonreciprocity" for less developed countries, the main group of free riders, is well established. And, if industrial countries insist on limiting liberalization to products for which the less developed countries will also reduce their tariffs, the result will be virtually no liberalization, even for the industrial countries. Another alternative might be to form a subgroup in GATT of members willing to undertake reciprocity while maintaining the most-favored-nation principle for other GATT members.[29]

A strong case may, however, be made that the fears about trade deficits caused by the free-rider problem are vastly exaggerated. The basic point that such fears ignore is that the developing and the communist countries have very little foreign exchange and they tend to "spend what they earn." For example, developing countries (LDCs) generally do not build up excess reserves when they obtain extra export earnings (as did Japan and Germany prior to the devaluation of the dollar). Instead, they relax a portion of their typically elaborate controls on imports and foreign exchange and increase their levels of vitally needed imports. Therefore, any extra earnings of foreign exchange by LDCs through the free-rider gains from a trade negotiation are almost certain to be "respent" almost immediately, increasing the exports of the industrial countries by approximately enough to offset the initial trade deficit caused by the free ride.

In reality, the effect on trade balance of liberalization with nonreciprocity for LDCs will be determined by the responding patterns of these countries. These responding patterns will depend on the propensities of LDCs to import from various countries. Since most of the imports of LDCs come from the industrial countries, these propensities will be high for responding on goods from industrial countries. The outcome for any individual industrial country will depend on its share of imports bought by LDCs and by the other free riders.

In order to obtain an accurate assessment of the trade effects of tariff liberalization for the industrial countries, then, it is necessary to add in extra exports of industrial countries caused by the responding effect for LDCs and other free-rider countries, including the communist countries.[30] The precise formulation of these calculations is specified below.

---

29. An approach suggested in Atlantic Council of the United States, *GATT Plus: A Proposal for Trade Reform* (Washington, D.C.: Atlantic Council, 1975).

30. This treatment assumes that the marginal propensity to spend extra export earnings is unity for developing countries. Implicitly, it assumes the same propensity is zero for industrial countries. In principle, it would be possible to introduce for the industrial countries a nonzero marginal propensity to import out of trade balance changes, and to compute a whole sequence of iterations of trade balance effects for the industrial countries. In practice, the information gained from this extension

Exchange Rate Effects

Once estimates are made of the effects of a given tariff-cutting formula on imports, direct exports, and exports induced by responding, it is possible to compute the exchange rate change that would be required to offset the corresponding initial impact of liberalization on the trade balance (exports minus imports). A country with a trade balance increase will appreciate in order to reestablish its preliberalization trade balance; a country with a trade balance reduction will depreciate. The amount of the exchange rate change will depend on the size of the trade balance change caused by liberalization, on the price elasticities of demand for imports and exports (assuming trade supply elasticities are infinite), and on the base level of imports and exports. These factors will determine the changes in the "effective" or "trade-weighted" exchange rates required to reestablish preliberalization trade balances.

Because all negotiating countries' trade-weighted exchange rates will be moving, the corresponding changes in each country's own "nominal" exchange rate with respect to an unchanging outside standard will depend on the movement of other countries' exchange rates as well as its own. For example, if a country's trade-weighted exchange rate should depreciate by 1 percent in order to restore the original trade balance, and if all of the country's trading partners depreciate their own nominal rates by a trade-weighted average of 0.25 percent, then the country in question would have to depreciate its nominal rate by 1.25 percent with respect to an outside standard. The precise calculations for these exchange rate changes are stated in the algebraic presentation below.

Employment Effects

Detailed calculations of the prospective impact of tariff liberalization on employment are made in the following way. The 1971 estimates of increased imports and increased exports at the four-digit BTN levels are multiplied by sectoral "job coefficients" relating the number of jobs per

---

would be insufficient to make the exercise worthwhile. It would be unreasonable to specify a nonzero propensity to spend extra foreign exchange earnings in the industrial countries in the absence of exchange rate change; and any policy information about exchange rate movements is more usefully explored in the direct examination of exchange rates, which we include below.

unit of gross output value. "Direct labor" job coefficients are applied for the United States, Japan, Canada, and the EEC. In addition, "total job coefficients" reflecting not only direct labor but also labor required to produce the necessary intermediate inputs are applied for the United States, Japan, and Canada.

This method assumes that, for any given trade change, there is a corresponding change that takes place fully on the side of production. Increased imports are treated as representing a decrease in domestic production by an amount equal to the increase in imports; increased exports are treated as causing an increase in production by the magnitude of the increase in exports. This approach tends to overstate the employment effects, on both the import and the export sides. The reason is that, in reality, a part of the trade change will represent changes in domestic consumption rather than production. Thus, an increase in imports will be accompanied by some increase in consumption and some decrease in production domestically, and the sum of these two changes will equal the rise in imports. Similarly, additional exports will be obtained in part from increased domestic output and in part from a reduction in consumption at home. In the absence of information on the appropriate division of the trade changes into consumption changes, on the one hand, and output changes, on the other, the method used here investigates the maximum possible employment change—namely, that based on the assumption that all of the change occurs on the side of production and none occurs on the side of consumption. As will be seen, even though the method tends to overestimate the resulting employment effects, the empirical results indicate very small employment changes as the result of tariff liberalization. More precise estimates incorporating an allocation of trade changes into consumption as well as production effects would yield still smaller estimates of employment effects, reinforcing the general conclusion that the changes are limited.

Updating of Results

A final methodological procedure requiring explanation concerns the updating of results. The basic set of GATT trade data prepared for the Tokyo Round negotiations refer to the base year 1971, although tariffs refer to 1973 (post-Kennedy Round). However, both nominal and real values of trade have grown enormously since 1971. Furthermore, 1971 was a disequilibrium year for the United States in particular, with a serious trade deficit and an overvalued exchange rate. Any calculations of the effect of liberalization based on 1971 data will tend to overstate the trade balance deterioration which may be expected by the United States from liberalization, because proportionate changes would be applied to an abnormally high import base and an abnormally low export base. Similarly, 1971-based results will overstate trade balance increases for Japan and Europe. Moreover, the 1972 data set subsequently prepared for negotiators in the Tokyo Round (after an extended period during which the sole GATT data base was for 1971) should be of little help, because in 1972 there was a worse disequilibrium (especially for the United States) than in 1971.

The procedure chosen for updating in this study uses OECD trade data available for 1974. These data are available in approximately twenty broad Standard International Trade Classification (SITC) categories. The category definitions are chosen so as to correspond as closely as possible to the twenty-one broad BTN categories, or sections. The OECD data for both 1971 and 1974 are used to obtain "expansion factors" for the trade base between the two years. A specific expansion factor is calculated for each broad commodity group, from each OECD supplier to each OECD importing country. For all non-OECD suppliers, a single rest-of-world expansion factor between the two years is calculated for each product group.

Once these expansion factors are obtained, they are applied to the 1971 results of the tariff-liberalization model aggregated to the level of the twenty-one broad BTN sections. The final result provides tariff-liberalization estimates based on 1974 trade levels.

Full details of the expansion procedure are presented in appendix B. (The appendix includes an analysis of the special treatment required for updating bloc importer results, to account for changes in suppliers' shares and corresponding changes in trade substitution effects.) Two aspects of the updating method, however, deserve emphasis at the outset. First, 1974 is a good year for specifying the analysis. It is much more an equilibrium year for trade balances among OECD members than was 1971. Because of the recession in 1975, the actual trade value magnitudes for 1974 are not far from those that would be obtained by using 1975 data, if these were available. Also, the main drawback of 1974 as a base year—radically increased oil prices—does not affect the results because the model wholly excludes petroleum, as a sector not affected by tariff negotiations. Even the other drawback of the year—abnormally high commodity prices —has little disturbing effect. For grains, the tariff analysis excludes the bulk of trade in any event, because they are mainly subject to nontariff barriers, which are treated in chapters 4 and 5. For tropical commodities, the analysis may overstate the longer run impact of tariff liberalization, but the results tend not to affect trade balance effects among the industrial countries themselves, nor the overall country trade balance effects once the respending effect is incorporated. In sum, 1974 is a good year for the trade base of the calculations.

A second major feature of the updating procedure is that it is quite detailed, involving some 8,000 individual expansion factors. Therefore, the overall 1974 expanded results should be reliable, although estimates for any single commodity group and supplier (especially a non-OECD supplier) could be subject to error.[31]

Finally, for the estimates of employment effects of tariff liberalization, a less-detailed updating procedure is applied. In the absence of data on the changes in labor productivity (expressed in current values per worker), it is not possible to use the detailed estimates of trade effects for 1974 to obtain corresponding estimates of employment for that year. Instead, the analysis of detailed employment effects must remain unadjusted on the basis of the 1971 estimates. Nevertheless, to correct for the biases inherent in using the 1971 base to assess overall employment effects, it is necessary to update at least the aggregate estimates for numbers of jobs displaced by additional imports and created through additional exports as the result of tariff liberalization. For this purpose, the following procedure is applied to the aggregate estimates of employment effects for 1971.

Since the estimates for aggregate employment effects are in physical terms (number of jobs), it is desirable to expand the results to 1974, using appropriate physical indexes. Therefore, we have used the physical

31. The alternative of expanding by single aggregative expansion factors would, of course, confront the problem that changes in the relative importance of product groups with differing degrees of protection would not be captured, nor would changing supplier composition. Both total trade creation and its allocation across suppliers (and therefore country export estimates) would be expected to be more biased by the use of single total expansion factors rather than by detailed product-supplier specific factors.

volume index of the *International Financial Statistics*.[32] The import index is applied to import-displaced jobs, and the export index is applied to export expansion jobs. The assumption is made that physical labor productivity remained constant between 1971 and 1974. Data to correct for changes in physical productivity are not available, and in any event cyclical disturbances in the period are likely to have distorted longer run trends in physical productivity. However, the assumption of constant physical productivity does tend to overstate slightly the change in the number of jobs for both export and import effects, for the 1974 base.

Methodology: Algebraic Statement

The following discussion restates the methodology used in the model of tariff negotiations in terms of specific equations. The reader unconcerned with these algebraic formulations of the methods described in more general terms above may wish to proceed directly to the next section, on data and elasticities.

Basic Direct Trade Effect Calculations

The following definitions are used for variables for a single "commodity" at the tariff-line level:

M_j = import value for country j (in dollars);
  0 = superscript for base period;
  1 = superscript for terminal period (postliberalization);
  η_j = price elasticity of import demand, for country j;
  t_j = most-favored nation (MFN) tariff rate for country j;
  T_j = $1 + t_j$ ("force of tariff");
  σ = quantity elasticity of substitution among alternative suppliers;
  M_{ij} = value of imports of buyer j from supplying country i;
TC, S = superscripts referring to "trade creation" and "substitution," respectively;
  Δ = change in variable.

32. The following physical expansion factors are used: United States—exports, 1.468, and imports, 1.171; Japan—exports, 1.314, and imports, 1.413; EEC (based on physical volume indexes for member countries weighted by 1971 shares in trade value)—exports, 1.2195, and imports, 1.324; Canada—exports, 1.204, and imports, 1.351. (For Canadian exports the terminal year is 1973, for which *International*

Using these definitions, the equations for computing the trade effects of tariff liberalization are presented below. These equations follow two alternative sets of calculations: one for importers that are not members of a free-trade area, and another for importers that belong to free-trade areas. The analysis treats the EEC and EFTA as a single, large free-trade area (designated B for bloc) since the two areas will have free trade in nonagricultural goods by 1977. The remaining countries are treated as nonbloc (NB) importers. For agricultural products, suppliers belonging to the bloc for the EEC are limited to members of the EEC itself.

For all importing countries, j, not belonging to the free-trade bloc, the basic equations are:

$$(1) \qquad \Delta M_{ij} = \Delta M_{ij}^{TC},$$

$$(2) \qquad \Delta M_{ij}^{TC} = \eta_j \dot{T}_j M_{ij}^0,$$

where the variable $\dot{T}_j$ refers to proportionate change in the variable T_j.

Equation 1 states that for nonbloc importer j, increased imports from source i are equal to the "trade creation" increase in imports from that source. In equation 2, this trade creation increase is given as equal to the base level of imports from the source, multiplied by the import elasticity of country j, multiplied by the proportionate change in the force of tariff $\dot{T}_j$, and hence the proportionate change in the price to the consumer. Note that $\dot{T}_j = \Delta t_j / (1 + t_j)$.

For importing countries belonging to the bloc, the corresponding equations are:

$$(3) \qquad \Delta M_{ij} = \Delta M_{ij}^{TC} + \Delta M_{ij}^{S},$$

$$(4) \qquad \Delta M_{ij}^{TC} = \eta_j \dot{T}_{ij} M_{ij}^0.$$

In equation 3 the term M_{ij}^{S} has been added to capture the effect of substitution among suppliers, i. This substitution term is discussed below. In equation 4 the trade creation effect is the same as before, except that the force of tariff term has an additional subscript, i, because the tariff is specific to supplier: it equals zero for bloc partners ($i \in B$) and the MFN tariff for nonbloc suppliers ($i \in NB$). Hence, the trade creation increase

Financial Statistics indicates a higher volume of exports than in 1974.) Calculated from International Monetary Fund, *International Financial Statistics*, vol. 28 (1975; selected issues), indexes 72 and 73.

in imports from bloc partners is zero. Thus, for example, the lowering of MFN tariffs by France will not increase imports from Germany, which already enjoys free entry.

The substitution term for bloc imports is:

$$(5) \qquad \Delta M_{ij}^S = \phi_{ij}^{NB} \phi_{Bj} \left(\frac{\phi_{Bj}^0 \sigma \dot{T}_{NBj}}{1 + \phi_{NBj}^0 \sigma \dot{T}_{NBj}} \right) M_j^0$$

for $i \in NB$, and

$$(6) \qquad \Delta M_{ij}^S = -\phi_{ij}^B \phi_{NBj}^0 \left(\frac{\phi_{Bj} \sigma \dot{T}_{NBj}}{1 + \phi_{NBj}^0 \sigma \dot{T}_{NBj}} \right) M_j^0$$

for $i \in B$.

The substitution term tells the change in bloc country j's imports from source i that are attributable to the shift in supplier composition of the *original* level of total imports, stemming from the fall in the relative price of nonbloc supply because of the reduction of the tariff wedge between the cost of imports entering free from partners and those entering under duty from nonbloc countries. In option 5, the supplier is not a bloc member, and it experiences an increase in sales to country j; equation 6 refers to suppliers within the bloc, for which the substitution effect is negative. In the equations, the additional terms refer to the following variables:

ϕ_{NBj}^0 = original share of nonbloc suppliers in country j's imports;

ϕ_{Bj}^0 = original share of bloc suppliers in country j's imports;

ϕ_{ij}^{NB} = original share of supplier i of the nonbloc group within total nonbloc supply to country j;

ϕ_{ij}^B = original share of supplier i of the bloc group within total bloc supply to country j;

$\dot{T}_{NBj}$ = proportional change in force of tariff facing nonbloc suppliers (and hence facing MFN tariff).

It can be noted that $\phi_{NBj}^0 + \phi_{Bj}^0 = 1$.

The increase in the value of bloc importer j's purchases from nonbloc suppliers in the filling of the prenegotiation level of import demand, caused by the substitution effect, may be written as:

$$(7) \qquad \Delta M_{NBj}^S = (\phi_{NBj}^1 - \phi_{NBj}^0) M_j^0,$$

where all terms are as before except that the term on the left side refers to increased purchases from all nonbloc suppliers in the aggregate (attributable to the substitution effect). That is, the change in purchases from all nonbloc suppliers equals the base level of total imports times the rise in the share of nonbloc supply in total supply (with regard solely to the substitution effect and to the preexisting import level).

In the following equations, λ is the ratio of the value of imports from nonbloc supply to that from bloc supply. Based on the response of this ratio to a change in relative price in view of the elasticity of substitution, we may write:

$$(8) \qquad \lambda_{j1} = \lambda_{j0}(1 + \sigma \dot{T}_{NBj}).$$

This equation follows from the fact that the proportional change in the relative price to consumers for nonbloc versus bloc goods is $\dot{T}_{NBj}$. For example, with a tariff of 10 percent, before liberalization the nonbloc price relative to the bloc price is $1.1/1$. If the tariff is eliminated, the terminal price ratio is $1/1$; the absolute change in the price ratio is $-0.1/1.1$; and the proportional change is $-0.1/1.1$ or $\dot{T}_{NBj}$. That is, within the subset of prior total imports, the ratio of nonbloc to bloc supply changes from its original level by a proportion equal to the elasticity of substitution multiplied by the proportionate change in the relative price. The elasticity of substitution used is the quantity elasticity, not the value elasticity (which is smaller in absolute value by unity). This is because the underlying import prices are not changing (only prices to consumer inclusive of tariff are changing), so that the proportionate change in import value in this case equals the proportionate change in import quantity.[33]

In order to obtain our equations 5 and 6 above for the substitution terms, we first use the relationship of λ_j to the share of nonbloc suppliers, ϕ_{NBj}, or:

$$(9) \qquad \lambda_j = \phi_{NBj}/(1 - \phi_{NBj}),$$
$$\phi_{NBj} = \lambda_j/(1 + \lambda_j).$$

33. By quantity elasticity of substitution we refer to the percentage change in the ratio of the quantity demanded of product A to that of product B when the price of A relative to that of B changes by 1 percent. By value elasticity of substitution we refer to the percentage change in the corresponding ratios of values rather than quantities. See, for example, Irving B. Kravis and Robert E. Lipsey, *Price Competitiveness in World Trade* (New York: National Bureau of Economic Research, 1971), pp. 130–33.

Then we may write:

$$(10) \quad (\phi_{NBj}^1 - \phi_{Bj}^0) = \left(\frac{\lambda_1}{1 + \lambda_1} - \frac{\lambda_0}{1 + \lambda_0} \right)$$

$$= \left[\frac{\left(\frac{\phi_{NBj}^0}{1 - \phi_{NBj}^0} \right)(1 + \sigma \dot{T}_{NBj})}{1 + \left(\frac{\phi_{NBj}^0}{1 - \phi_{NBj}^0} \right)(1 + \sigma \dot{T}_{NBj})} \right] - \left[\frac{\frac{\phi_{NBj}^0}{1 - \phi_{NBj}^0}}{1 + \frac{\phi_{NBj}^0}{1 - \phi_{NBj}^0}} \right].$$

Simplifying the final expression and then substituting into equation 7, we obtain:

$$(11) \quad\quad\quad \Delta M_{NBj}^S = \phi_{NBj}^0 \left(\frac{\phi_{Bj}^0 \sigma \dot{T}_{NBj}}{1 + \phi_{NBj}^0 \sigma \dot{T}_{NBj}} \right) M_j^0.$$

The value in equation 11 is the value of imports switched from bloc to nonbloc supply for importer *j*, within the subset of preexisting total imports into *j*. Therefore, multiplying this total value switched by an individual nonbloc supplier *i*'s share in nonbloc supply will yield the amount of imports shifted toward this individual supplier, which is given in equation 5 above. Similarly, the share of individual bloc supplier *i* in total bloc supply, multiplied by the total value of trade shifted, from equation 11, will constitute the value of trade shifted away from supplier *i* within the bloc, yielding the equation 6 above.

Traditional Welfare Gains from Import Liberalization

The welfare gains for nonbloc importers are represented in figure 2-1 (where SS = world supply, and P_w = world price). The welfare gains are calculated on the basis that, when the tariff falls from t_0 to t_1, there is an increase in consumer surplus by $A + C$. However, there is an offsetting decline in government revenue equal to C. At the same time, there is a new contribution to government revenue amounting to B. Therefore, the net welfare gain is the area $A + B$, or:

$$0.5(t_0 - t_1)\Delta M + t_1 \Delta M = \Delta M[0.5(t_0 + t_1)].$$

That is, the gain equals the increase in import value multiplied by the average of the tariffs before and after liberalization. This is the basic estimate for welfare gain following increased imports in a normal, nonbloc

Figure 2-1. *Welfare Gains from Tariff Liberalization: Import Demand Approach*

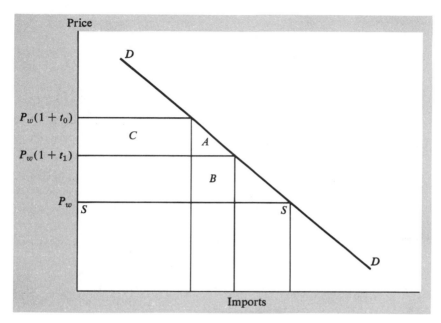

importing country; that is:

$$(12) \qquad\qquad W = \Delta M^{TC}[0.5(t_0 + t_1)],$$

where W is welfare gain, and ΔM^{TC} is the sum over all suppliers, i, for import increase (trade creation) in equation 2.

The above approach is based on the examination of the demand curve for imports, assuming an infinitely elastic supply curve for imports. A traditional alternative approach examines domestic supply and demand, treating imports as residual, as depicted in figure 2-2.

In figure 2-2, the world supply curve is horizontal at price 1.0; at the initial tariff of t_0, price to the consumer equals the world price plus the tariff $(1 + t_0)$. Domestic supply is at level Q_0 (point d on the domestic supply curve, SS). Domestic demand is at C_0 (point c on the demand curve, DD). The difference, distance dc (or Q_0C_0), comes from imports.[34]

---

34. When two points are named jointly, we refer to the distance of the line segment between them. When three or more points are named jointly, we refer to the area enclosed by them.

Figure 2-2. *Welfare Gains from Tariff Liberalization: Product Supply-Demand Approach, with Imports as Residual*

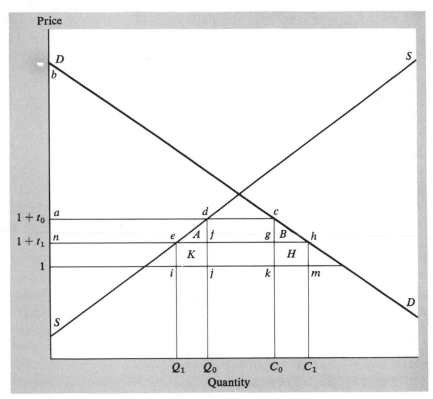

After the tariff falls to t_1, the new equilibrium level for domestic output is Q_1 (point e on the supply curve). The new level of demand is C_1 (point h on the demand curve), because demand is higher at the now-lower price of $1 + t_1$. Now the difference between domestic supply and demand, to be made up by imports, is the distance eh (or Q_1C_1). Imports have increased in two components: ef (to replace reduced domestic supply) and gh (to provide for extra consumption).

The first element of welfare gain derives from increased consumer surplus net of all transfers away from government and producers. Consumer surplus rises from triangle abc to triangle nbh. Of the increase, the trapezoid $nade$ is merely a transfer away from producer surplus. Rectangle $fdcg$ is a transfer away from government tariff revenue on the original level of imports. Thus, of the total increase in consumer surplus, only triangles *edf* and *gch* represent net gains to the economy; the remaining areas represent transfers to consumers away from producers and government.

The second element in welfare gain is government tariff revenue on the additional imports. This revenue appears as rectangles *iefj* and *kghm*. Total welfare gains, thus, are areas $A + B + H + K$. Measuring each of these four respective elements in a single equation, we have:

$$W = 0.5(t_0-t_1)(ef) + 0.5(t_0-t_1)(gh) + t_1(ef) + t_1(gh)$$
$$= 0.5(t_0 + t_1)(ef + gh).$$

Since $ef + gh$ equals total increase in imports, ΔM, this equation yields the same result as that derived from the previous approach dealing with a "derived" demand curve for imports directly (equation 12).

Bloc Importers: Welfare Gain

For bloc importers, the welfare gain from the net increase in total imports is the same as that given above. Bloc importers, however, also enjoy welfare gains from switching part of their preexisting imports away from expensive partner supply toward rest-of-world supply.

Define S as the value of imports "switched." Because of the reduction of imports from partners in this amount, there is a welfare loss of S (involving no consumer surplus matters, since partner price remains unchanged). This loss is more than offset by the gain from placing this expenditure of S on imports from the rest of world. Calling P_{NB} the unit price for nonbloc supply, the expenditure shifted will buy S/P_{NB} units of the good. Before liberalization, the nonbloc good sold for $P_{NB}(1 + t_0)$ to the consumer; after liberalization, it sells for $P_{NB}(1 + t_1)$. The appropriate valuation per unit to the consumer is therefore $P_{NB}(1 + \bar{t})$, where $\bar{t}$ is the average of t_0 and t_1. Therefore, the gross gain from increased imports from nonbloc suppliers, considering only trade substitution, is $[S/P_{NB}][P_{NB}(1 + \bar{t})]$. Canceling P_{NB} and netting out the welfare loss from reduction in imports from partners, the net welfare gain resulting from the substitution of nonbloc supply for partner supply is $S\bar{t}$.

From equation 11, the value of imports switched, S, is:

$$\Delta M_{NBj}^S = M_{NBj}^0 \frac{\phi_{Bj}^0 \sigma \dot{T}}{1 + \phi_{NBj}^0 \sigma \dot{T}},$$

where M_{NB}^0 is total preexisting imports from nonbloc supply. Thus, the estimate of the welfare effect from trade substitution is:

$$W_j^S = 0.5(t_0 + t_1) M_{NBj}^0 \psi,$$

where

$$\psi = \frac{\phi_{Bj}^0 \sigma \dot{T}_{NBj}}{1 + \phi_{NBj}^0 \sigma \dot{T}_{NBj}}.$$

Adding in the welfare effect from the trade creation increase in total import value, the total welfare gain for the bloc importer is:

$$(13) \qquad W_j = 0.5(t_0 + t_1)(\Delta M_j^{TC} + M_{NBj}^0 \psi).$$

Equivalently, the total welfare gain may be written:

$$(14) \qquad W_j = 0.5(t_0 + t_1) M_{NBj}^0 (\eta \dot{T} + \psi).$$

Respending Effect

Let ΔM_{ijk} be the increase of imports into industrial country j from a free-rider country i (in practical application, all countries other than the eleven industrial importing areas examined directly in this study). Let subscript k refer to product category k. Let ϕ_{ij} be the fraction of country i's total imports purchased in industrial country j (in 1971, the year for which the most recent data were available to the study).[35] Then, for industrial country j, the value of extra exports to free-rider countries caused by tariff liberalization is calculated as:

$$(15) \qquad \Delta X_j = \sum_i \phi_{ij} \sum_j \sum_k \Delta M_{ijk}.$$

That is, for each free-rider country i, there will be direct export increases totaling $\sum_j \sum_k \Delta M_{ijk}$. Of these export earnings, the fraction ϕ_{ij} will be respent on imports from country j—or, $\phi_{ij} \sum_j \sum_k \Delta M_{ijk}$ will be respent by free-rider country i in industrial country j. Summing up all free-rider countries, industrial country j can anticipate the extra total exports shown in equation 15. Unlike the calculations for direct trade effects of liberalization, the induced exports resulting from the respending effect cannot be broken down by commodity, because the coefficients for import propensities (ϕ_{ij}) are based on total import data rather than on data by commodity.

35. United Nations, Department of Economic and Social Affairs, *Yearbook of International Trade Statistics, 1970–71*, UN Doc. ST/STAT/SER.6/21, 1973.

Exchange Rate Effects

Given the estimates of changes in trade balance resulting from a particular tariff-cutting formula, it is possible to calculate the implied offsetting change in exchange rates that would be necessary to restore the initial trade balance. Assuming infinitely elastic supply for imports and exports, an appreciation in the trade-weighted exchange rate of a country by the fraction dR will cause a reduction in import value by (dR) $(\eta_m(M^0)$ and a reduction in export value by $(dR)(\eta_x)(X^0)$, where η_m and η_x are overall price elasticities of demand for imports and exports, respectively, and M^0 and X^0 are the base values of imports and exports, respectively. With a trade balance effect of B caused by tariff liberalization, the trade-weighted exchange rate should move by just enough to cause an offsetting change in the trade balance of $-B$. Therefore, the required change in the trade-weighted exchange rate for a given country will be as follows:

$$(16) \qquad dR = \frac{-B}{\eta_m M^0 + \eta_x X^{0}}.$$

Because η_m and η_x are both negative, a positive trade balance effect B will require an appreciation (positive dR) and a negative trade balance effect will require a depreciation (negative dR).

This method yields an estimate of the change in the trade-weighted exchange rate. In order to translate this change into a set of changes in nominal exchange rates from their original parities with respect to an unchanging outside standard, the following calculation is applied:

$$(17) \qquad \dot{R}^* = [I - \Phi]^{-1} \dot{R}^0,$$
$$ {}_{m x 1} \qquad {}_{m x m} \quad {}_{m x 1}$$

where $\dot{R}^*$ is a vector of nominal exchange rate changes for all m countries; $\dot{R}^0$ is a vector of required trade-weighted exchange rate changes based on equation 16; I is the identity matrix; Φ is a matrix of trade weights (with the elements in row i being the shares of each column country j in the total trade turnover—exports plus imports—of country i); and the expression $[I - \Phi]^{-1}$ refers to the inverse of the $[I - \Phi]$ matrix.[36]

---

36. This formula is derived as follows. The trade-weighted exchange rate change of country i will equal its own appreciation minus the trade-weighted sum of its partners' appreciations. Thus,

$$dR_i^0 = dR_i^* - \sum_j \Phi_{ij} \, dR_j^*,$$

Data and Elasticities

This section identifies the basic data that are used in this study and the sources of the empirical estimates of the various elasticities that are applied.

Trade and Tariff Data

The basic data set used in this study is the same as that made available by the GATT to participants in the Tokyo Round of trade negotiations. The data base contains import values in dollars for 1971 by tariff-line item for each of ten industrial countries—the United States, Canada, Japan, Austria, Finland, Norway, Sweden, Switzerland, Australia, New Zealand —and for the nine-member EEC as a single importing area. The tariff-line data are grouped under appropriate four-digit BTN categories, providing the basis for classifications of common commodities across countries at that level. The import data distinguish among approximately 200 supplier countries (or regions and territories).

For each tariff line, the tariff as of January 1973 is given in the data set. The tariffs are thus those resulting after the final cuts of the Kennedy Round of negotiations. For EEC or EFTA tariff-line categories in which variable levies apply, the fact is indicated in the data base (and, accordingly, the tariff-liberalization model of this study omits the category from the calculations, leaving protection of the item for separate treatment as a nontariff barrier).

The basic data set is large. For the eleven importing areas altogether, there are on the order of 50,000 tariff-line categories, each having data on imports from up to 200 suppliers. Nevertheless, all of the basic calculations discussed above, except for the expansion from 1971 data to 1974 data, are conducted at the individual tariff-line level. This feature of the model is a fundamental strength of the analysis for proper evaluation of

---

where dR_i^0 is the trade-weighted exchange rate change for country i, dR_j^* is the nominal exchange rate change for country j, and Φ_{ij} is the weight of country j in the total trade turnover of country i. In matrix notation,

$$\dot{R}^0 = \dot{R}^* - \Phi\dot{R}^*.$$

Factoring out, and solving for $\dot{R}^*$, we have:

$$\dot{R}^* = [I - \Phi]^{-1}\dot{R}^0.$$

alternative tariff-cutting formulas, because tariff averages at more aggregate levels would predict inaccurately the impact of certain types of tariff-cutting formulas, especially harmonization formulas in which higher tariffs are cut by a larger proportion than lower tariffs.

It should be noted that for Canada, Australia, and the United States, the import data and the tariff data on the GATT data tapes had to be converted from an f.o.b. to a c.i.f. basis.[37] This conversion is particularly important for tariff "harmonization" formulas, which reduce high tariffs by larger proportions than low tariffs. This is because tariffs charged on an f.o.b. basis (as in the United States) are actually lower than tariffs appearing to be identical in rate but charged on a c.i.f. basis.

With respect to the OECD data used for the 1971 to 1974 "updating," details are discussed above and in appendix B below.

Finally, it should be noted that the definition of "bloc" suppliers includes EEC and EFTA in a single free-trade bloc for industrial goods (BTN 2501 and higher) but excludes EFTA suppliers from the EEC free-trade bloc for agricultural goods.

Price Elasticities of Imports

Empirical estimates of import elasticities are essential statistical building blocks for any calculations of the trade effects of tariff liberalization. In the past, the whole field of empirical estimation of trade elasticities has suffered from pervasive doubts about the reliability of any such estimates. The single most damning critique of elasticity estimates was the classic article by Guy H. Orcutt published in 1950.[38] Orcutt's work criticized many postwar empirical studies that had found trade elasticities too low (that is, imports and exports too unresponsive to price) for devaluation to be effective in correcting trade balance deficits. Citing strong theoretical reasons for the elasticities to be much higher, Orcutt presented several arguments that all pointed to the same conclusion: statistical biases had caused the estimated elasticities to be too low. Orcutt's most important

---

37. The abbreviations f.o.b. and c.i.f. mean "free on board" and "including cost, insurance, and freight to the point of destination," respectively. Thus, if the ratio of c.i.f. to f.o.b. value is 1.1 for a category, the adjusted import values are all 1.1 times original import values, and the adjusted tariff is 1/1.1 times the original tariff.

38. Guy H. Orcutt, "Measurement of Price Elasticities in International Trade," *Review of Economics and Statistics,* vol. 32 (May 1950), pp. 117–32.

argument was that simultaneous shifts of the supply and demand curves would cause estimated import price elasticities to be downward biased.

Orcutt's critique appears to have cast a persistent shadow of doubt over empirical estimates of the elasticities. More recent work, however, has tended to refute Orcutt's critique.[39] The argument has even been made that a generation of subsequent researchers, seeking to avoid downward-biased estimates, had "mined" their data and experimented with estimating forms in order to obtain higher elasticities. Thus, according to this argument, import elasticity estimates are now likely to be biased upward rather than downward.[40]

More recently, analysts have emphasized the difficulties of obtaining the proper price data for estimating trade elasticities. Irving B. Kravis and Robert E. Lipsey, after a careful examination of specially constructed international price series, have concluded that the price series usually used for estimation are not very reliable. Of the two types of price series typically used, wholesale prices are found to be preferable to unit-value prices (which are particularly erratic because of changing import composition), although neither type of price series inspires much confidence for estimating elasticities.[41]

Murray C. Kemp has shown that, when import values are deflated by import price indexes containing random errors to obtain real imports as the dependent variable (a common estimating technique), the result will be to bias elasticity estimates toward unity rather than toward zero.[42] Therefore, the typical use of price series containing errors in observation probably tends to bias downward the estimates of elasticities for finished

39. With respect to the fundamental critique of simultaneous shifts in supply and demand, Magee has cited recent empirical results of his own and of J. David Richardson. These results show very high elasticity of export supply and therefore reduce to inconsequential proportions the bias because of simultaneity. Magee, "Prices, Incomes, and Foreign Trade," p. 204. Concerning Orcutt's various critiques taken as a whole, Leamer and Stern concluded in their 1970 textbook: "It is now believed that Orcutt's arguments were not so conclusive and general as they first appeared to be. In addition, as more data points became available for the post-World War II period, a number of studies using least squares regression were made of import and export demand functions with results that seemed quite plausible in view of a priori theoretical considerations concerning price elasticities." Edward E. Leamer and Robert M. Stern, *Quantitative International Economics* (Allyn and Bacon, 1970), pp. 1–2.

40. Magee, "Prices, Incomes, and Foreign Trade," p. 218.

41. Kravis and Lipsey, *Price Competitiveness in World Trade*, pp. 169–96.

42. Murray C. Kemp, "Errors of Measurement and Bias in Estimates of Import Demand Parameters," *Economic Record*, vol. 38 (September 1962), pp. 369–72.

manufactures, which tend to be greater than unity, and to bias upward estimates of elasticities for raw materials, which tend to be less than unity.

On balance, these considerations suggest that existing empirical estimates may tend to understate actual price elasticities, but that, insofar as this problem remains at all in the current body of estimates, it is far less serious than in the early estimates so roundly condemned by Orcutt. For policy purposes, the implication is that our estimates of trade effects of tariff liberalization are more likely to underestimate than to overestimate trade changes. Accordingly, our estimates of the welfare gains from liberalization are likely to be conservative rather than overly optimistic. At the same time, our calculations may somewhat understate possible dislocations from liberalization, with respect to trade balance reductions for some countries and in terms of job losses resulting from increased imports. Nevertheless, as will be shown below, our estimates indicate that these dislocative effects are extremely small, so that there exists ample room for margin of error with no change in the basic policy conclusion that prospective dislocation would be too small to warrant the imposition of impediments to liberalization.

In the light of these general considerations on elasticity estimates, we may now turn to the specific elasticities used in this study.

In all cases, this study applies the best available empirical estimate of the relevant import elasticity, including those available for Japan estimated in the course of the study (see appendix C). Elasticity estimates are not available at the level of disaggregation of the individual tariff-line item (typically some 5,000 categories for a country). Therefore, the following procedure is adopted: for any tariff line falling within a broader trade category to which the most detailed, empirically estimated elasticity applies, the calculations apply that elasticity—that is, the one for the "parent group" of the more detailed line item.

The use of elasticities for broader levels of aggregation than the tariff-line categories to which they are applied raises the question of why the calculations could not be carried out at more aggregated levels, consistent with the elasticities, in the first place. As mentioned above and shown in appendix G, trade liberalization effects that are calculated using aggregated data and broad tariff averages would be biased, especially for harmonization tariff-cutting formulas that reduce high tariffs by a greater proportion than low tariffs. This fact alone requires that, in order to avoid introducing a known bias by throwing away vital information at detailed levels, the available detailed data on trade and tariffs should be applied in the calculations, even though these detailed data must be combined with import elasticities for broader categories.

A related question is whether the application of elasticities for broader categories to individual tariff-line items introduces other biases into the results (even though such application removes possible aggregation biases). In all probability, there are biases introduced into the estimates for any given tariff-line item, and therefore our results for individual items should be viewed with caution. There is, however, no reason to expect these biases to be other than randomly distributed above and below "true" values. Thus, there is every reason to expect the final aggregated results to be unbiased estimates of the "average" impact of tariff liberalization.[43]

In collecting the elasticities and, where necessary, selecting between alternative estimates, the following principles were used. We required that there be elasticities for all commodities. For some countries, this principle required the use of elasticities estimated at highly aggregated levels. However, once all commodities were covered by an aggregate elasticity, we next proceeded to override these broad elasticities with the most disaggregated elasticity estimate available. The final principle was that zero elasticities were not accepted, since complete lack of response of imports to price is unacceptable conceptually and zero estimates almost unequivocally would represent downward bias in the estimate of the elasticity.

43. At first glance, it might appear that the true detailed product elasticities should be higher than the broader category elasticities. For example, price elasticity of the demand (both total and import) for beef might be higher than that for meat, which would be higher than that for food, and so forth. Following this reasoning, liberalization estimates based on more aggregative elasticities might understate total trade effects. A closer analysis, however, would suggest that higher elasticities for more detailed categories would basically reflect substitution among alternative goods within those categories. This substitution effect would be absent if tariffs were reduced by similar amounts for all products within a given category, and the relevant detailed product elasticity would be lower than the elasticity for the product when holding all other prices constant. Thus, with tariffs tending to fall by similar amounts for all products within a category, the relevant price elasticities of these products for individual trade effects would tend to be the same as the single elasticity for the group as a whole. Correspondingly, the direct use of elasticities for individual tariff-line items—if they existed—would introduce an upward bias in estimates of total trade effects unless account were taken of the offsetting effects on demand for one line item caused by the simultaneous reduction of the import price in another, affiliated line item.

The elasticity estimates of G. B. Taplin are used as the foundation estimates that cover all goods.[44] These estimates are the only ones available that are fully comprehensive in coverage, albeit at the cost of being estimated only for highly aggregated commodity groupings. The Taplin estimates are for four-product groups for each country. The categories are SITC groups 0 + 1 (food and live animals; beverages and tobacco); 2 + 4 (crude materials except fuels; animal and vegetable fats and oils); 3 (mineral fuels and lubricants); and 5–9 (manufactured products).

Taplin's estimates are based on linear regression of the logarithm of real import value on the logarithms of (1) an activity variable, and (2) domestic price relative to import price. Real imports are obtained by deflating import values by a unit-value index of import prices (the case examined by Kemp, giving an expected bias toward unity). The activity term consists of government expenditure, investment, and exports, all in constant prices. For the relative price term, domestic price indexes are deflated by the index of import unit values. The statistical results overall are less than fully satisfactory; fewer than one-third of the commodity-group price elasticity estimates for the countries examined in this study are statistically significant at the 5 percent level. Results for the activity coefficient are much more successful: 92 percent of the estimates are statistically significant at the 5 percent level.

In using the Taplin estimates, we have rejected those elasticities reported as zero. Because theory strongly opposes complete absence of response of imports to price, it is highly likely that zero estimates represent unsuccessful statistical measurement rather than economic reality. For these cases of zero estimates, we substituted relevant alternative estimates.[45]

44. G. B. Taplin, "A Model of World Trade," in Robert J. Ball, ed., *The International Linkage of National Economic Models* (Amsterdam: North-Holland, 1973), pp. 177–223.

45. For cases with zero estimated elasticities, an elasticity value estimated for the same commodity group in a neighboring country was selected as the alternative. The most serious case was that of Australia, for which three of four Taplin estimates were zero. Estimates for New Zealand were substituted for the three zero commodity groups as well as for the fourth on the assumption that for Australia the estimates as a whole were unreliable. For Finland, we used the Swedish estimate for the category "mineral fuels and lubricants" rather than zero. In the above cases, we merely substituted one Taplin estimate for another. In the case of Austria, the zero estimates covered "food and live animals," "beverages and tobacco," and "mineral fuels and lubricants." In this case, German estimates were used. However, in this case, we

Once the foundation elasticities were given, the next step was to supersede them where possible with more detailed estimates. In the following importing countries, however, the estimates provided by Taplin were the only ones used: Australia, Belgium and Luxembourg, Canada, Denmark, Finland, Ireland, Italy, the Netherlands, New Zealand, and Switzerland.

The sources used for the preferred, more disaggregated elasticities vary by country. For the United States, two recent estimates of detailed import elasticities are provided in a study by Mordechai Kreinin[46] and in another study by Clopper Almon, Jr., and others.[47] Kreinin's estimates are based on regressions of the logarithm of import volume on the logarithm of import price divided by domestic wholesale price for the category, and the logarithm of real GNP. Kreinin prepared special indexes of import unit value to obtain greater detail than that available in official indexes. His index of import volume is based on import value deflated by the index of import unit value. Kreinin carried out estimates for a total of fifty-six product sectors (for which only twenty-eight sectors with the "best" statistical results were reported), using quarterly data from 1964 through the first quarter of 1970. Although he experimented with lags, Kreinin obtained better results using unlagged variables. The statistical results were generally good. Out of twenty-eight sectoral estimates, twenty-three showed R^{-2} (fraction of variation "explained") of two-thirds or higher, and twenty showed "t-ratios" (coefficient divided by standard error) of 2 or better for the price coefficient (indicating statistical significance at the 5 percent level). Most of the price elasticity estimates were in the range from -0.5 to -1.5; the activity income elasticities estimated tended to be high.

The estimates reported by Kreinin appear to be the best available for the United States. Their principal limitation is that they do not cover all product categories. SITC categories 1 through 4 are especially underrepresented in the reported results.

---

were not restricted in our choice of estimates to Taplin's since more disaggregated estimates were used for Germany. The rule then was to use a nonzero Taplin estimate as our first choice for a commodity; next in precedence was a disaggregated German elasticity; and our backup was a Taplin estimate for Germany.

46. Mordechai E. Kreinin, "Disaggregated Import Demand Functions—Further Results," *Southern Economic Journal,* vol. 40 (July 1973), pp. 19–25.

47. Clopper Almon, Jr., and others, *1985: Interindustry Forecasts of the American Economy* (Lexington Books, 1974).

The alternative source for detailed U.S. elasticities is the study by Almon and others. This study estimates fifty sectoral import functions of the form:

$$M_t = (a + bD_t) \, P^\eta,$$

where M is "imports in domestic port prices," D is domestic demand for the product (output minus exports plus imports), P is the ratio of foreign price to domestic price, and η is the price elasticity. The form chosen avoids high income elasticities, which would cause serious problems when forecasting over a decade, as is done in that study.

For several reasons the estimates by Almon and others appear less satisfactory than those by Kreinin. First, it is unclear whether the dependent variable is in current or real terms. Generally, it is undesirable to use current value of imports as the dependent variable.[48] Second, the import prices used are less satisfactory than those developed by Kreinin. In some sectors, Almon and others applied German and Japanese export price indexes as proxies for U.S. prices of imports from all sources. In other sectors, the study applied unit-value indexes (the official indexes, for five broad commodity groups, much broader categories than those prepared by Kreinin). Third, Almon and his colleagues have forced their estimates, when possible, to comply with a priori values assigned on the basis of previous estimates for very broad categories.[49] Therefore, in practice, many of the sectoral estimates are merely the broad aggregate import elasticities obtained by other researchers in earlier studies. Fourth, the demand term used contains import value, thereby placing imports on the right side of the estimating equation as well as the left, and raising questions of simultaneity bias.

The principal merit of the estimates by Almon and others is that they are exhaustive; they provide fifty detailed sectoral parameters covering all commodities. Because the estimates by Kreinin appear to be more reliable, we have used them in preference to the estimates by Almon and

---

48. Leamer and Stern, *Quantitative International Economics*, p. 9. Moreover, if the dependent variable is in current value terms, the elasticity η is an expenditure elasticity, smaller (in absolute value) than the import demand elasticity by unity.

49. Rather than using normal regression measuring $\bar{R}^2$, the authors maximized $\bar{R}^2 - 0.5 \, \dfrac{\eta - \bar{\eta}}{\eta}$, where $\bar{\eta}$ was an a priori value for the elasticity; Almon and others, *1985: Interindustry Forecasts of the American Economy*, p. 126.

others for those sectors in which Kreinin has reported results. For other sectors, we apply the elasticities by Almon and others as the backup set of estimates.

For Japan, Noboru Kawanabe has prepared new estimates of detailed import elasticities at the level of seventy-seven commodity categories, as reported in appendix C. These estimates are from regressions of the logarithm of import value, deflated by import price, on the logarithm of import price relative to domestic price and the logarithm of domestic expenditure in the relevant category. In addition, the explanatory variables are changed for imports of intermediate inputs to take account of relevant influences such as production level in the user industry and inventory level for the input. The models incorporate distributed lags. The import price indexes used are notable in that, for most products, they are derived from actual contract prices of well-specified commodities. Therefore, the typical problem of measurement error when using unit-value indexes is avoided. Kawanabe has obtained extremely good empirical results in terms of statistical significance of the price elasticity and overall degree of explanation ($\bar{R}^2$).

Detailed import price elasticities are also available for Germany and for the United Kingdom. Glismann has prepared estimates at the level of thirty comprehensive product categories for German imports.[50] His estimating form relates real imports to import price relative to domestic price, and to real GNP. The equations are linear in logarithms for most sectors, and either semilogarithmic or linear in the others. The estimates are for short-run elasticities, indicating import response to price changes within one year. Unfortunately, the study does not discuss the nature of the data series used for the estimates. High degrees of explanation are achieved ($\bar{R}^2$ is less than two-thirds in only one sector, and it is greater than 85 percent in twenty-nine of the thirty sectors). However, the price elasticity estimate is significant at the 10 percent level or higher in only thirteen of the thirty sectors.

For Britain, Terence Barker has estimated import demand functions at the level of about eighty categories, although fewer than half of the sectoral functions include a relative import price term.[51] The basic estimating

50. Hans H. Glismann, *Die Gesamtwirtschaftlichen Kosten der Protektion,* Kiel Discussion Paper 35 (Kiel: Institut für Weltwirtschaft, October 1974).
51. Terence Barker, *The Determinants of Britain's Visible Imports, 1949–1966: A Programme for Growth,* no. 10 (Cambridge: Chapman and Hall for the Department of Applied Economics, Cambridge University, 1970), pp. 36–39.

form relates the logarithm of imports (at constant prices) to the logarithm of demand (equal to import value, including tariff, plus domestic output) and the logarithm of import price relative to domestic output prices (with unit-value indexes for both price series). Estimates were made using annual data for the period 1949–66. For the most part, statistical results obtained in the study were favorable (in terms of degree of explanation and significance of the import price term).

The various studies just described complete our sources for estimates of import elasticities.[52] For the EEC, because the GATT data base contained import data for the EEC as a whole but not for individual members, it was necessary to obtain aggregate EEC import elasticities based on existing estimates at the country level. In obtaining these aggregate elasticities, our procedure was to adopt a weighted average of the member country elasticities described above. Ideally, the weight would vary by commodity. However, if information on weights by commodity and country had been readily available, it would not have been necessary to use a weighted-average EEC elasticity; instead, all results could have been calculated at the member country level. Only one weighting pattern was applied to all commodities: the weights were proportional to each country's total imports from nonbloc suppliers. The weights were: Belgium-Luxembourg, 0.061; Denmark, 0.034; France, 0.148; Germany, 0.260; the Netherlands, 0.093; Ireland, 0.001; Italy, 0.132; United Kingdom, 0.263.

With respect to the final degree of disaggregation used, our most detailed sectoral import elasticities are for Japan (seventy-seven categories; see appendix C); the United States (twenty-eight sectors, Kreinin; forty-nine sectors, Almon and others); Germany (thirty sectors); and Great Britain (thirty-six sectors). Estimates by Kreinin provided selected, noncomprehensive sectoral estimates, as follows: Norway, nine sectors; France, ten sectors; Belgium, four sectors; Sweden, five sectors; the Netherlands, four sectors. For all other countries, we relied on the Taplin estimates at the level of four broad category groups covering all trade.[53]

Table 2-2 summarizes the data sources used for the elasticities applied in the model of tariff negotiations. For countries with multiple listings,

---

52. Kreinin, "Disaggregated Import Demand Functions," pp. 22–23, provides elasticity estimates for selected commodity groups for Norway, Sweden, and France in addition to the estimates for the United States. Where available, these estimates are used in preference to the Taplin estimates.

53. Further details are reported in Thomas Williams, "Data Survey for Elasticities for Use in Trade Negotiations Simulations" (Washington, D.C., 1975; processed).

Table 2-2. *Sources for Estimates of Import Elasticities*

Country	Source (by order of preference)
United States	Kreinin; Almon and others; Taplin
Canada	Taplin
Japan	Appendix C; Taplin
EEC	
United Kingdom	Barker; Taplin
France	Kreinin; Taplin
Germany	Glismann; Taplin
Others	Taplin
Austria	Taplin (nonzero); Germany/Glismann; Germany/Taplin
Finland	Taplin; Sweden/Taplin
Norway	Kreinin; Taplin
Sweden	Kreinin; Taplin
Switzerland	Taplin
Australia	New Zealand/Taplin
New Zealand	Taplin

Sources: Clopper Almon, Jr., and others, *1985: Interindustry Forecasts of the American Economy* (Lexington Books, 1974). Terence Barker, *The Determinants of Britain's Visible Imports, 1949–1966: A Programme for Growth,* no. 10 (Cambridge: Chapman and Hall for the Department of Applied Economics, Cambridge University, 1970). Hans H. Glismann, *Die Gesamtwirtschaftlichen Kosten der Protektion,* Kiel Discussion Paper 35 (Kiel: Institut für Weltwirtschaft, October 1974). Mordechai E. Kreinin, "Disaggregated Import Demand Functions—Further Results," *Southern Economic Journal,* vol. 40 (July 1973), pp. 19–25. G. B. Taplin, "A Model of World Trade," in Robert J. Ball, ed., *The International Linkage of National Economic Models* (Amsterdam: North-Holland, 1973), pp. 177–223.

those listed first override the sources listed subsequently, wherever commodity groups overlap.

Finally, it is important to know the overall pattern of elasticities resulting from the procedure described here, even though no alternative procedure would yield "better" elasticities and still be based on empirical estimates. In particular, if the empirical estimates systematically show much higher elasticities for one country than for most others, there may be reason to expect that the import increases (and trade balance reductions) calculated for that country are biased upwards. To throw light on this question, table 2-3 presents weighted-average import elasticities used in the model for each of the eleven importing areas and by major commodity groups, or BTN "sections" (see table B-1 in appendix B for a fuller description of these product groupings).

The final row in table 2-3 reports an aggregated weighted-average price elasticity of imports for each importing area, with weights based on the share of each commodity group in the value of dutiable imports. As may be seen, this weighted-average elasticity is similar for the United States and Canada (-1.85 and -1.94, respectively); it is somewhat lower for Japan (-1.39). Some of the individual European countries, and Australia and New Zealand, also show relatively low elasticities.

For the EEC, the aggregate elasticity shown in table 2-3 does not represent an import elasticity for the community as a whole with respect to imports from outsiders. Instead, it is the weighted average of each member country's import elasticity for purchases from all suppliers, including partners in the community. In order to arrive at the elasticity for imports of the EEC as a unit from outsiders, it is necessary to incorporate the effect of substitution away from partner supply toward outside supply when outsiders' prices fall relative to partner and domestic prices for an EEC country.[54]

In order to obtain a more precise view of the relationship of the weighted average of individual member import elasticities, on the one hand, and the combined influences of that weighted elasticity and the substitution elasticity on bloc imports from nonbloc suppliers, on the other hand, table 2-4 reports three alternative weighted-average elasticities for the EEC. The first alternative is the average import elasticity for individual member countries (repeated from table 2-3). The second and third alternatives incorporate the influence of the substitution effect into a weighted-average elasticity for imports from nonbloc suppliers. The final column represents this hybrid elasticity as actually used in the calculations of this study (with a substitution elasticity of -2.5, as discussed below). To provide information on the sensitivity of the results to this

54. An analogy between the United States and the EEC helps clarify this fact. The United States may be conceived of as a large free-trade area. Each state in this area has some unobserved import elasticity for supplies from all sources, including other U.S. states. When a single import elasticity for the United States is measured for goods from abroad, it captures the joint effects of the individual states' total import elasticities and their substitution away from purchases from each other toward outside suppliers as the relative outside price falls. Similarly, each EEC member state has an import elasticity for goods from all sources—the individual country elasticities actually measured. By incorporating the additional effect of substitution away from EEC partner suppliers when outside prices fall relative to EEC prices, we may construct the composite price elasticity of EEC imports from outsiders. The difference between the two cases is that for the United States we observe (measure) only the final external elasticity, whereas for the EEC we observe only the intermediate "individual state" elasticities and we construct the final external elasticity by adding the substitution effect.

Table 2-3. Weighted-Average Price Elasticity of Imports, by Product and Importing Area[a]

BTN section	United States	Canada	Japan	EEC	Austria	Finland	Norway	Sweden	Switzerland	Australia	New Zealand
01 Animals, products	-0.53	-0.84	-1.13	-0.50	-0.55	-0.09	-0.56	-0.47	-0.15	-1.12	-1.62
02 Vegetable products	-0.90	-0.85	-0.47	-0.52	-0.58	-0.20	-0.70	-0.45	-0.16	-1.15	-1.13
03 Fats, oils	-0.43	-2.30	-0.62	-0.57	-0.41	-0.95	-1.00	-0.70	-0.69	-1.65	-1.51
04 Food, beverages, tobacco	-1.13	-0.76	-0.58	-0.56	-0.60	-0.09	-0.82	-0.41	-0.17	-1.12	-1.12
05 Mineral products	-0.22	-1.81	-1.59	-0.96	-0.56	-0.99	-1.27	-0.26	-1.41	-1.44	-1.68
06 Chemicals	-0.97	-2.07	-1.37	-0.96	-0.72	-0.98	-0.50	-0.90	-1.05	-1.22	-1.23
07 Plastics, rubber	-3.57	-2.13	-2.96	-1.32	-0.74	-0.99	-0.72	-1.11	-0.90	-1.24	-1.23
08 Hides, leather goods	-2.46	-2.07	-1.32	-1.09	-0.74	-0.99	-2.61	-4.38	-0.97	-1.23	-1.23
09 Wood, cork articles	-0.96	-2.14	-1.33	-0.83	-0.57	-0.99	-2.47	-1.53	-0.61	-1.62	-1.64
10 Paper, products	-1.44	-2.07	-1.74	-0.79	-0.70	-0.99	-2.80	-1.29	-0.85	-1.27	-1.23
11 Textiles	-2.43	-2.09	-1.56	-1.07	-0.74	-0.99	-1.99	-2.09	-0.95	-1.24	-1.23
12 Footwear, headgear	-1.23	-2.07	-1.42	-1.27	-0.74	-0.99	-2.53	-5.73	-1.05	-1.23	-1.23
13 Stone, ceramics, glass	-1.37	-2.07	-1.42	-1.20	-0.74	-0.99	-0.89	-1.60	-1.05	-1.23	-1.23
14 Jewelry	-3.77	-2.07	-0.99	-1.21	-0.74	-0.99	-2.80	-1.31	-0.57	-1.24	-1.48
15 Base metals	-1.99	-2.07	-2.36	-1.47	-0.74	-0.99	-1.85	-1.31	-1.05	-1.23	-1.23
16 Machinery, electrical equipment	-0.87	-2.07	-1.78	-0.92	-0.74	-0.99	-3.51	-1.27	-1.05	-1.23	-1.23
17 Transportation equipment	-2.53	-2.07	-1.87	-1.15	-0.74	-0.99	-1.03	-1.27	-1.05	-1.23	-1.23
18 Precision instruments	-1.70	-2.07	-2.22	-1.26	-0.74	-0.99	-1.89	-4.72	-1.05	-1.23	-1.23
19 Arms	-3.02	-2.07	-1.42	-1.75	-0.74	-0.99	-2.80	-4.50	-1.05	-1.23	-1.23
20 Miscellaneous manufactures	-4.44	-2.07	-1.42	-1.38	-0.74	-0.99	-2.80	-5.80	-1.05	-1.23	-1.23
21 Art	-3.02	-2.07	-1.42	-2.45	-0.74	-0.99	-0.50	-5.80	-1.05	-1.23	-1.23
Total	-1.85	-1.94	-1.39	-0.92	-0.65	-0.61	-1.72	-1.50	-0.69	-1.24	-1.23

Source: Derived from sources listed in table 2-2.
a. Weighted by value of imports (from suppliers outside bloc, for EEC and EFTA) by four-digit BTN sector.

Table 2-4. *Composite and Simple Import Elasticities for the EEC*

BTN section	Simple import elasticity[a]	Composite elasticity,[b] $\sigma = -1.5$	Composite elasticity,[b] $\sigma = -2.5$
1	−0.50	−0.86	−1.09
2	−0.52	−0.74	−0.89
3	−0.57	−0.98	−1.26
4	−0.56	−0.84	−1.02
5	−0.96	−1.62	−2.07
6	−0.96	−1.89	−2.50
7	−1.32	−2.48	−3.25
8	−1.09	−1.84	−2.33
9	−0.83	−1.59	−2.09
10	−0.79	−1.87	−2.60
11	−1.07	−1.99	−2.61
12	−1.27	−2.17	−2.77
13	−1.20	−2.38	−3.17
14	−1.21	−2.06	−2.64
15	−1.47	−2.54	−3.25
16	−0.92	−1.95	−2.63
17	−1.15	−1.92	−2.43
18	−1.26	−2.18	−2.79
19	−1.75	−2.84	−3.56
20	−1.38	−2.35	−3.00
21	−2.45	−3.84	−4.77
Total weighted average	−0.92	−1.67	−2.17

a. Weighted average of import elasticities of all member countries individually.
b. With respect to imports from nonbloc suppliers.

particular value of the substitution elasticity, the middle column reports the composite elasticity using a substitution elasticity of −1.5 instead of −2.5.

As may be seen in the table in the final row, the incorporation of the substitution effect raises the composite price elasticity of the EEC for imports from nonbloc suppliers to −2.17, a level moderately higher than the import elasticities used for the United States and Canada. A slightly higher external import elasticity for the EEC than for the United States might be explained by a greater sensitivity of European firms to import possibilities than is true in the United States (to the extent that U.S. firms are more accustomed to traditional domestic suppliers), or to taste differences making European consumers more sensitive to import price changes.[55]

Finally, our empirical estimates apply sensitivity analysis that varies the elasticity estimates in order to examine the extent to which alternative sets of elasticities would yield different results and policy implications. For this purpose, we have relied upon a survey of existing elasticity estimates, prepared by Stern and others.[56] Stern's survey reviews more than 100 empirical studies, of which the vast majority present import elasticity estimates at quite aggregate levels.[57] Stern has synthesized the large body of empirical estimates into a central set of "best" elasticity estimates for each of the same eighteen industrial countries examined in our own study. Those estimates are at the level of four broad, aggregated commodity categories. In chapter 3 below, we use the central estimates supplied by Stern to provide a sensitivity check on our own estimates of trade effects of tariff liberalization.

Elasticity of Substitution

The elasticity of substitution in import demand among alternative suppliers is a parameter for which very few empirical estimates exist, far fewer than estimates of the price elasticity of import demand. As a result, it is not possible to distinguish differing substitution elasticities by importer and product. Instead, the available empirical estimates are all considered in arriving at a single substitution elasticity to be used for all countries and products. The value chosen for this elasticity is -2.5, on the basis of the following considerations.

Several authors in the past have used the single estimate of -3.0 for the elasticity of substitution.[58] However, these studies assume this value.

55. The major case in the other direction, that of Japan, is consistent with the notion that complexities of the Japanese marketing system (for example, numerous and fragmented wholesalers, the presence of trading companies, language and cultural barriers) make Japanese imports relatively insensitive to prices.

56. Robert M. Stern, with the assistance of Jonathan H. Francis and Bruce Schumacher, "Price Elasticities in International Trade: A Compilation and Annotated Bibliography of Recent Research" (University of Michigan, 1975; processed).

57. Stern's review does not include the following crucial studies: Almon and others for the United States; Glismann for Germany; and Kawanabe for Japan.

58. See in particular William H. Branson, "The Trade Effects of the 1971 Currency Realignments," *Brookings Papers on Economic Activity*, 1:1972, pp. 15–69; and Paul S. Armington, "The Geographic Pattern of Trade and the Effects of Price

In contrast, actual empirical estimates have tended to be somewhat lower. Kravis and Lipsey obtained estimates in the range of -3.0 when using aggregate data for U.S. exports compared with those from the United Kingdom, Germany, and Japan. When using data at the three- and four-digit SITC level, however, they obtained estimates ranging from -1.04 to -1.47 for their most recent data period (1961–64).[59] Hickman and Lau estimated substitution elasticities for the four LINK categories, and all estimates were substantially smaller in absolute value than -3.0. The estimates ranged from -1.13 for SITC groups 2 and 4 to -1.73 for SITC groups 5 through 9.[60]

The general spirit of the calculations of this study is to employ actual empirical estimates of elasticities wherever possible. Following this rule would lead to the application of the Hickman-Lau estimates, the most detailed and complete available. There is a strong argument, however, for considering these estimates to be downward biased, for the purposes of our calculations. The estimates refer to broad categories. These categories contain many dissimilar goods, as well as supplier specialization in some goods but not in others. As a result, for a single, well-defined good (such as is involved at the individual tariff-line level, at which our data are available), the broader aggregate substitution elasticity is very likely to understate the degree of substitutability among suppliers. This consideration alone is sufficient reason to depart from the empirical estimates made by Hickman and Lau, accepting a somewhat higher range of the substitution elasticity. A reasonable compromise would seem to be somewhat below the traditional -3.0 frequently assumed but well above the Hickman-Lau range. Hence, we obtain the estimate of -2.5.

Another important question is whether the substitution elasticity should vary by product. To answer this question we may consider the Hickman-Lau estimates by SITC group.[61] The estimates are: for SITC groups 0 and 1, an elasticity of -1.506; for groups 2 and 4, an elasticity of -1.129; for group 3, an elasticity of -1.647; and for aggregate group 5 through 9, an

Changes," *International Monetary Fund Staff Papers*, vol. 16 (July 1969), pp. 179–201.

59. Kravis and Lipsey, *Price Competitiveness in World Trade*, pp. 133–34, 139.

60. Bert G. Hickman and Lawrence J. Lau, "Estimates of Elasticities of Substitution for Commodity Imports Disaggregated According to Project LINK Classification" (Stanford University, August 1974; processed), p. 27.

61. Ibid.

elasticity of -1.732. The lowest estimate is for categories 2 and 4: crude materials excluding fuels, and animal and vegetable oils and fats. It is strange that this group should have the lowest elasticity of substitution and that the group of 5 through 9, which is manufactures, should have the highest. One would expect exactly the opposite: iron ore is iron ore regardless of the source, but an American automobile is differentiated from a Japanese automobile. Undoubtedly, the problem lies in the broad coverage of the group. Suppliers providing very different products are included in the single group, and it is not surprising that their relative shares of the group fail to vary much in response to changes in relative prices. For example, consider just one of the several categories within SITC 2 and 4: ores. Iron ore imports from Brazil will not vary much relative to copper ore imports from Chile, even though some relative price index of ore for the two countries changes. Yet, at the relevant level of disaggregation—the tariff-line level—one would expect very sensitive changes in the source of supply for the product iron ore alone, for example, in response to a change in relative supplier price. In short, the only evidence of difference among product categories for the elasticity of substitution goes in the wrong direction, showing a low elasticity for crude materials and a high elasticity for manufactures, when one should expect the opposite because of the greater homogeneity of the former if the product is sufficiently narrowly defined (as it must be for tariff-line application). For this reason, it seems reasonable to reject the available empirical evidence on the relative magnitude of substitution elasticity by product group, and to remain with a single estimate to be applied to all commodities.

The other relevant question on variation of the estimate concerns country specificity. Is there any reason to believe that one importing country would have a higher elasticity of substitution among suppliers of its imports than would another importing country? There is no particular a priori reason to expect such a difference. Empirically, the Hickman-Lau estimates show a relatively narrow range for the bloc-member countries considered.[62] This fact lends support to our procedure of utilizing the same substitution elasticity regardless of the importing country.

62. For these countries, absolute values of the substitution elasticity are: Belgium, 1.829; France, 1.241; Germany, 1.825; Italy, 0.890; Netherlands, 2.194; Austria, 1.196; Sweden, 1.660; United Kingdom, 0.690; Finland, 1.451. The unweighted average of these estimates is 1.442. Excluding the two extreme cases, the remaining estimates range from 27 percent above the unweighted mean to 38 percent

Employment Data

Given the estimates of trade changes from tariff liberalization, the only data required to obtain corresponding estimates of employment effects are "job coefficients." For the United States, input-output job coefficients for 1970, for direct and total labor, are used. They are assigned to corresponding BTN categories.[63] The coefficients are adjusted for price inflation from their 1963 price base to 1971 using the wholesale price index. For Japan, labor coefficients available from the input table are applied.[64]

For the EEC, a weighted-average direct job coefficient for each sector is obtained on the basis of data contained in the 1973 edition of the United Nations' publication *The Growth of World Industry*.[65] Unfortunately, estimates of indirect job coefficients by sector are not available for the EEC.

For Canada, it is assumed that the job coefficients for the United States (both direct and indirect) represent a reasonable estimate of those that characterize Canada, and the U.S. coefficients are applied to obtain the Canadian employment estimates.

---

below it. It should be noted that the corresponding substitution elasticities estimated for nonbloc members are: United States, 0.860; Canada, 2.680; Japan, 1.374; Australia, 1.359. Ibid., p. 28.

63. See U.S. Department of Labor, Bureau of Labor Statistics, *The Structure of the U.S. Economy in 1980 and 1985*, BLS Bulletin 1831 (1975). The job coefficients are available at the level of ninety-two nonservice sectors.

64. "Employment Table," and "Output Table," in *1970 Input-Output Tables* (Government of Japan, 1974). The correspondence used to relate input-output to trade classifications is that given in the same source. The job coefficients for Japan are available at the level of 160 input-output categories.

65. United Nations, *The Growth of World Industry 1973 Edition*, vol. 1, *General Industrial Statistics*, ST/ESA/STAT/SER.P/11 (vol. 1), 1975. For the United Kingdom, Germany, Italy, and Denmark, this publication reports production and employment for each of approximately thirty industrial categories (three-digit International Standard Industrial Classification groupings). Because data reported for the other five EEC members were at more aggregate levels, it was necessary to apply the percentage composition among industrial subsectors based on the data for the initial core group of four countries, in order to extend the disaggregated estimates to the remaining five members and to obtain detailed data for the EEC as a whole. Mid-1971 exchange rates were used to convert national currency output values to dollar values. (For Belgium it was necessary to convert value-added data to gross output data, using sectoral ratios between the two based on data for Luxembourg and, when necessary, the Netherlands.) Employment and output data for the agricultural sector were drawn from *Basic Statistics of the Community, 1973–74* (Luxembourg, 1975).

Conclusion

The above discussion completes the description of the methodology underlying this study's model of tariff liberalization and of the data applied to obtain estimates using the model. The following chapter reports the results of estimations made for twelve specific tariff-cutting formulas. To recapitulate, the model represents a comprehensive system for evaluating the effects of a hypothesized tariff-cutting formula on exports, imports, welfare, exchange rates, and employment for the major industrial countries. The central element in the model is the calculation of the increase in imports of a given product (into a given country and from a specific supplier) on the basis of the percentage reduction in consumer price caused by tariff reduction, combined with the price elasticity of importation and operating on the base level of imports. In calculating increased imports, special account is taken of imports into free-trade areas (the EEC and the EFTA) from suppliers outside these areas, because these trade changes will include a "substitution effect" in addition to the normal "trade creation" effect from reducing tariffs. The reason for this substitution effect is that, as the tariff wall around the free-trade bloc declines, outside suppliers will tend to substitute bloc members in the provision of import supply. Once detailed import estimates are calculated, the trade changes across all importing areas may be summed up for a single supplier to determine the impact of liberalization on that country's exports. An additional impact on exports is calculated to take account of the respending of new foreign exchange earnings by developing countries and other countries not reducing their own tariffs in the negotiations but benefiting from the expansion of their own exports as the industrial countries reduce tariffs.

The model applies the most disaggregated empirically estimated elasticities available. It applies completely detailed trade and tariff data (with data at the individual tariff item level). These exceedingly detailed results for 1971 are "expanded" by still quite detailed expansion factors to obtain results for 1974. This is a necessary step in view of the serious disequilibrium of trade in 1971, a year with a large U.S. trade deficit (and thus a year that, if used as the basis for analysis, will bias estimates toward a trade balance deterioration for the United States, since the import base was abnormally large and the export base abnormally small).

In addition to these trade effects, the model calculates detailed estimates of static welfare gains from liberalization. The relationship of total welfare gains to these static effects, based on studies of European integration, is used to obtain an approximate estimate of total welfare benefits. Possible exchange rate effects are examined by calculating the change in exchange rates that would be required to offset the initial trade balance effects of liberalization.

Finally, the model computes the impact of liberalization on employment: the displacement of jobs by increased imports and the increase in jobs because of extra exports. These calculations incorporate both direct effects and indirect job effects (working through input-output relationships for intermediate inputs). Because of data limitations, employment effects are calculated for only the four major parties in the negotiations.

On the basis of the results obtained for the twelve formulas for cutting tariffs, examined in the following chapter, it is possible to draw conclusions on the overall gains to be obtained through tariff liberalization, and on the extent to which alternative formulas succeed in providing for "reciprocity" in the negotiations—that is, an equitable balance among all participants in the outcome of liberalization.

CHAPTER THREE

Trade, Welfare, and Employment Effects of Tariff Liberalization: Empirical Results

THIS CHAPTER presents the empirical results of the model of tariff negotiations set forth in chapter 2. The estimates refer to twelve different "tariff-cutting formulas" for which calculations have been made using the model. These formulas cover the principal types of formulas under active consideration in the negotiations of the Tokyo Round in 1975 and 1976.

We first consider the estimates of trade and welfare effects of the alternative liberalization formulas. The aggregate results for all eleven importing areas are examined, followed by a more detailed analysis of the separate results for the four major participants in the negotiations: the United States, Canada, Japan, and the EEC. The results are examined with regard to overall patterns for each area from liberalization generally, and also with respect to the relative advantages and disadvantages of the various formulas for each of the four major participants. The discussion then turns to the issue of reciprocity. The relative rankings of alternative tariff-cutting formulas are evaluated, taking into account the separate rankings of the formulas for the individual importing areas, on the grounds of welfare effects, on the one hand, and of the effects on exports relative to those on imports, on the other hand. The estimates of exchange rate effects, employment effects, and labor adjustment costs are then presented.

The traditional analytical approach to reciprocity in tariff negotiations is to compute a weighted-average "depth of cut" for tariffs resulting from any tariff-cutting formula, to ensure that the various participants have comparable cuts.[1] Because of its serious theoretical drawbacks, that approach is not included in this chapter, although estimates using the approach are presented in appendix A.

Tariff-Cutting Formulas

One of the important issues in the Tokyo Round of trade negotiations is the precise nature of the tariff cuts to be negotiated. In negotiations before the Kennedy Round it was conventional to negotiate reductions on an item-by-item basis. In the Kennedy Round a much more powerful device for general liberalization was adopted: the application of a single "tariff-cutting formula" for all tariff reductions, with any exceptions specifically negotiated on an exceptions list. Although other formulas were considered, the negotiators adopted the simple yet quite liberalizing "formula" of a 50 percent cut in existing tariffs.

In the Tokyo Round there has been general agreement that an overall tariff-cutting formula should be used once again, rather than returning to the earlier practice of item-by-item negotiation. There has been disagreement, however, on precisely what tariff-cutting formula should be used. As this study goes to press, the issue of the precise tariff-cutting formula to be adopted in the Tokyo Round remains unresolved. Earlier in the negotiations, it appeared that a formula might be agreed upon fairly soon, serving as tangible evidence of progress in the negotiations that then might lead to agreements in other, more difficult areas (such as the liberali-

1. The average depth of cut refers to the weighted-average percentage cut in tariffs. For example, if tariffs begin at an average of 10 percent and are cut to an average of 5 percent, the depth of cut is 50 percent. For a discussion of the theoretical limitations of the concept (especially its failure to capture the proportionate price effect of a tariff cut, the most relevant phenomenon for assessing probable import changes), see appendix A.

zation of agricultural nontariff barriers). The subsequent delay in reaching agreement on a tariff-cutting formula reflected the general change in the negotiating climate in a protectionist direction, as well as the difficulties posed by agriculture in particular. In July of 1977, however, a compromise between the United States and the EEC set the stage for more rapid progress. The United States accepted a separation of agricultural negotiations from negotiations on other products. Earlier U.S. strategy had been to insist on joint discussion of agricultural and non-agricultural liberalization. Under the new timetable agreed upon in the compromise, offers for liberalization of both tariff and nontariff barriers would be submitted by January 15, 1978.[2] Moreover, in September of 1977 the United States and the EEC reached a compromise on a "joint working hypothesis" for a tariff-cutting formula that seemed likely to emerge as the general formula agreed upon in the Tokyo Round.[3] That formula is extremely close to one considered in the estimates of this chapter, as discussed below. Regardless of that agreement and ensuing interim deadlines, however, it may prove difficult to reach formal agreement on a definitive tariff-cutting formula, and firm commitment to tariff cuts offered under the formula, before the completion of negotiations concerning nontariff barriers as well. Participants may want to reserve final commitments on their tariff cuts until they can judge the entire set of negotiation agreements as a package.

There have been essentially two elements in the dispute over the alternative possible tariff-cutting formulas. First, should the cuts be "linear," an equal percentage cut in tariff regardless of the original height of the tariff; or should they be "harmonization" cuts, with the percentage tariff cut higher, the higher the original tariff. Second, should the resulting overall cut be deep or modest?

The European Economic Community has advocated "harmonization," in the belief that the United States has many very high tariffs, while the EEC has a much more uniform set of intermediate-level tariffs, primarily as the result of its integration process in which tariff rates of the various members were forced to converge to an average-level, common, external tariff. Moreover, the particular form of the harmonization approach fa-

2. "Compromise Speeds Tokyo Round," *Business Week* (July 25, 1977), p. 53.
3. European Community Information Service, "EC-U.S. Agree on Principles for Cutting Tariffs," Background Note No. 25/1977 (ECIS, September 23, 1977; processed).

vored by the EEC tends to cut tariffs overall by small amounts because, in the most important range where most tariffs are clustered (say, from 5 percent to 12 percent), the formula generates small cuts. By contrast, the United States has tended to favor relatively large "linear" tariff cuts. The initial approach set forth by the United States for purposes of discussion in the early stages of the Tokyo Round was a flat 60 percent cut for all tariffs.[4] This cut would be the maximum possible for the United States under the authority of the Trade Act of 1974, except for tariffs of 5 percent or lower, which could be completely eliminated under the authority of the act.

The calculations for the tariff-liberalization model of this chapter are applied for twelve different tariff-cutting formulas. Analysis of the results of the calculations therefore permits a detailed examination of the relative economic effects of the alternative formulas, both for the negotiating parties overall and for the individual countries. The formulas considered are designed to span the range of principal "families" of tariff-cutting formulas. These families are the following: (1) strictly linear cuts; (2) linear cuts with special treatment of tariffs below 5 percent; (3) harmonization cuts based on formulas "iterating" cuts equal to the tariff itself; (4) harmonization formulas applying a combination of linear and harmonization cuts; and (5) the "sector harmonization" approach in which tariffs are reduced to the minimum among the major negotiating parties for the product in question.

The first three formulas are especially important because they represent formulas actually submitted for purposes of discussion in the Tokyo Round, particularly in 1975. In addition, formula 12 has special significance because it is extremely close to the compromise working hypothesis agreed upon between the United States and the EEC in September 1977.

The first formula considered is a linear cut of 60 percent in all tariffs. As noted above, this cut is the maximum provided for in the United States trade legislation for tariffs above 5 percent. Although the legislation per-

4. In March 1976 the United States tabled a formal proposal that provided for a small degree of harmonization but that was essentially similar to a 60 percent cut. According to press reports, all tariffs above 7 percent would be reduced by 60 percent. Lower tariffs would be cut by smaller proportions, but in no case by less than 50 percent. See "Quest for Worldwide Formula to Cut Tariffs Resumes Soon," *Journal of Commerce*, July 2, 1976. Note that from the example cited in this source the U.S. formula would appear to be: $y = 1.5x + 50$, where y is percentage cut, and x is the original tariff expressed as a percentage.

mits total elimination of tariffs below 5 percent, current resistance to the elimination of these low tariffs within the United States suggests that a straight 60 percent cut is a more realistic variant than a 60 percent cut combined with complete elimination of tariffs below 5 percent.

The second alternative formula draws on the principle that the percentage cut in a tariff is equal to the tariff itself. This type of cut, proposed by the EEC in the negotiations, is a harmonization cut since it reduces high tariffs by a larger proportion than low tariffs. The particular version of the principle used in the calculations is "three iterations" of the rule. For example, consider a tariff of 30 percent. On the first iteration it would be cut by 30 percent, falling to 21 percent. On the second iteration the 21 percent tariff is cut by 21 percent, leaving a tariff of 16.59 percent. On the third iteration this 16.59 percent tariff is cut by 16.59 percent, leaving a final tariff of 13.84 percent. The specific choice of three iterations resulted from the fact that this particular proposal was current in the multilateral trade negotiations (MTN) discussions in the first half of 1975.[5] It should be noted that the formula applies strictly only to tariffs below 50 percent. For tariffs over 50 percent, the formula would generate very low tariffs, lower than those resulting from cuts in other tariffs that initially were below these tariffs over 50 percent. (To see this problem, consider a tariff of 100 percent. It would immediately fall to zero in a single iteration.) Therefore, in the calculations presented here, for all tariffs initially exceeding 50 percent, the "iterative" formula generates a final tariff equal to that which would result from strict application of the formula to an initial tariff of only 50 percent. (This resulting tariff floor for tariffs initially over 50 percent is 15.23 percent.)

---

5. Throughout this study, the "three-iterative" formula is referred to as the EEC formula. However, this version was only an illustrative formula submitted early in the negotiations for purposes of discussion. The formal EEC proposal, tabled in July 1976, provided for the same form of tariff cut but with four iterations instead of three. See, for example, "Common Market Proposes Tariff Cuts," *Wall Street Journal,* July 8, 1976. The difference between the two variants is small. Specifically, for a tariff of 10 percent, trade-liberalization effects estimated using the three-iteration variant would rise by about 23 percent if recalculated using the four-iteration version (or by less if a 60 percent cut ceiling were observed). Although somewhat more liberal, the four iteration variant would still be quite restrictive compared with a 60 percent cut and with several other major formulas under consideration. Furthermore, the conclusions of this chapter regarding the three-iterative formula relative to all other formulas would remain generally valid with respect to the four-iteration proposal.

Figure 3-1. *Tariff-Cutting Formulas 1 through 3*

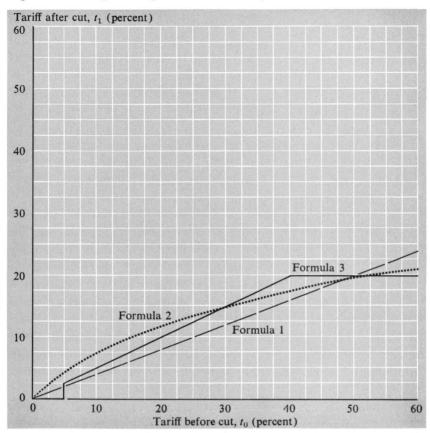

Tariff after cut, t_1 (percent)

Tariff before cut, t_0 (percent)

The third formula resembles another harmonization formula under consideration within the MTN during 1975 which was proposed by Canada. In this formula, tariffs below 5 percent initially are eliminated; tariffs above 40 percent are cut to 20 percent; and tariffs between 5 percent and 40 percent are cut to one-half their original level.

Figure 3-1 shows the profile of tariff cuts under these three formulas, with the initial tariff shown on the horizontal axis and the resulting tariff on the vertical axis.

The fourth tariff-cutting formula considered is a 100 percent cut, or complete liberalization. Although free trade is not being considered as an option in the Tokyo Round, calculations for this "formula" nonetheless provide the useful function of indicating the maximum extent of tariff-liberalization effects as a benchmark against which the results for other formulas may be compared.[6]

Formula 5 is a harmonization formula that incorporates a linear element as well. It sets the percentage cut of the tariff equal to 30 percent plus the tariff itself. For very low tariffs, the result is essentially a linear cut of 30 percent. This guarantees that some cutting occurs even for low tariffs (by contrast to the "iterative" formula 3, which makes almost negligible cuts for very low tariffs). Again it is necessary to avoid a "leap-frogging" problem in this formula (whereby some higher tariffs would be so severely cut that they would wind up even lower than some of the intermediate tariffs). Thus, for tariffs of 35 percent or higher (the turning point where the paradoxical leapfrog effect begins), a floor of 12.25 percent is placed on the resulting tariff.

Formula 6 is another type of harmonization approach. It cuts tariffs by 60 percent, then adds a flat tariff rate of 3 percent on top of the resulting schedule of tariffs. For tariffs of 5 percent and below, there is no change in tariffs at all, because the 3 percent add-on would otherwise boost the tariff above the original level. The effect of formula 6 is to maintain low tariffs relatively untouched and to move to essentially a linear cut somewhat below 60 percent for high tariffs.

Formula 6 is of special interest because it is close to the tariff-cutting formula proposed by Japan in October 1976. According to press reports, the Japanese formula calls for a 70 percent tariff cut plus a tariff shelf of 3.5 percent.[7]

Formulas 7, 8, and 9 are variations on linear cuts. Formula 7 is a flat 43.4 percent tariff cut. This particular figure is chosen because it gives approximately the same "average depth of cut" of tariffs for the United States as formula 5, a harmonization formula. (See appendix A.) Therefore, examination of the results for formulas 5 and 7 permits inferences on

6. Note that the results are not, strictly speaking, merely 1.667 times as large as the 60 percent cut. Referring to equations 5 and 6 of chapter 2, the term involving T in the denominator prevents the results for one formula from being a simple multiple of results for another formula, even if both are linear cut formulas. In practice, however, the results are very close to a simple multiple relationship, as may be seen from the estimates reported below for three linear formulas (numbers 1, 4, and 7).

7. Chamber of Commerce of the United States, International Group, *Trade Negotiation Information Service,* Bulletin No. 5 (Washington, D.C., November 29, 1976), p. 1. Also see "Le Projet Japonais de Réductions Tarifaires," *Journal de Genève,* no. 241 (October 15, 1976), p. 5.

the effects of harmonization versus linear cuts for a generally equal overall degree of liberalization (at least as conventionally viewed under the depth-of-cut concept). As will be shown, however, it is basically meaningless to generalize on the results of harmonization versus linear cuts without specifying the precise type of harmonization as well as the overall degree of liberalization.

Formula 8 is the most liberalizing "practical" formula. It is the full authority of liberalization under the U.S. Trade Act of 1974—namely, a 60 percent cut in all tariffs above 5 percent and the elimination of tariffs of 5 percent and below. Formula 9 is again a 60 percent cut in tariffs above 5 percent, but tariffs below 5 percent are left untouched, and a floor of 5 percent is set for the result of cutting other tariffs. This yields a cut by less than 60 percent for tariffs between 5 percent and 12.5 percent. This formula captures the political reality of substantial resistance by business to the reduction of tariffs below 5 percent. For the special case of the United States, this resistance reflects the fact that much of U.S. trade enters at tariffs below 5 percent.[8] By the same token, formula 9 represents the opposite of the spirit of the Canadian proposal (similar to formula 3 here), which calls for the elimination of tariffs below 5 percent—a range applying to a large portion of Canada's exports to the United States.

Formula 10 is unique in that it is not based on a universally applied relationship of the tariff before and after liberalization. Instead, it represents the "sector harmonization" approach. The Trade Act of 1974 contains language suggesting this approach, arguing for "equal access" to markets within product categories. The argument sometimes made in favor of the approach is that most of the industrial countries now have similar characteristics in terms of the abundance of labor and capital and in terms of levels of technology. As a result, according to the argument, no country needs more protection than any other country for any particular type of product.

Although the economic logic for an identical tariff structure by product among the industrial countries is open to serious question, there are without doubt cases where the "equal access" argument is persuasive. For example, the U.S. tariff on automobiles is only 3.3 percent, while

8. Of the total nonagricultural MFN imports subject to tariffs, 50 percent enter the United States at duties of 5 percent or lower. Contracting Parties to the General Agreement on Tariffs and Trade, *Basic Documentation for the Tariff Study, Summary by Industrial Product Categories* (Geneva, March 1974), p. 1.

Japan's tariff is 10 percent and the EEC tariff is 11 percent.[9] It makes little sense for Japan and Europe, both strong exporters of automobiles to the U.S. market, to retain tariffs higher than those of the United States.

The particular form of "sector harmonization" used in formula 10 is the following. For each four-digit BTN category, the lowest tariff among the four major importing areas (United States, Canada, Japan, EEC) is first identified.[10] Then, for a detailed tariff-line item, if the tariff exceeds the "four-area minimum average," the formula reduces the tariff to this minimum, subject to the limitation of a maximum cut by 60 percent. If the tariff is below the four-area minimum average, the tariff is left unchanged.

Formula 11 is another harmonization variant: percentage tariff cut equals 20 percent plus three times the original tariff. The formula thus has a milder linear element and a stronger harmonization component than the corresponding harmonization formula, number 5, with the same algebraic form. Finally, formula 12 applies the "iterative" harmonization approach once again, this time with six operations of a tariff cut equal to the preceding tariff, rather than the less liberalizing three-iteration variant (formula 2). Like formula 10, the final two formulas place a ceiling of 60 percent on the amount of the tariff cut (a restriction absent in harmonization formulas 2, 3, and 5), in order to remain within the realistic bounds imposed by the U.S. negotiating authority under the Trade Act of 1974.[11]

Formula 12 takes on major policy significance because it is very close to the compromise working hypothesis agreed upon by the United States and the EEC, which is based on the Swiss formula. That formula calls for cutting tariffs as follows: $z = (ax)/(a + x)$, where z is the final tariff and x is the original tariff, both in percentage terms, and a is a parameter (set at 14 in the Swiss proposal).[12] U.S. Special Trade Representative Robert Strauss specifically cited the Swiss formula in his public announcement concerning the U.S.-EEC working hypothesis. EEC sources, however, pointed out that the EEC had adopted the principle of the general form of

9. Computed on a trade-weighted basis from the trade and tariff data described in chapter 2.

10. From Contracting Parties to the General Agreement on Tariffs and Trade, *Basic Documentation for the Tariff Study: Summary by Industrial Product Categories.* The average tariff used is the trade-weighted tariff on dutiable imports.

11. Note that in the Kennedy Round the final agreement did not exceed the full authority initially allowed under the U.S. legislation. It is unlikely that cuts beyond U.S. authority will be agreed on in the Tokyo Round either.

12. Chamber of Commerce of the United States, International Group, *Trade Negotiation Information Service,* p. 1.

the Swiss formula but not necessarily its particular values.[13] The Swiss formula itself is almost identical to our tariff formula 12.[14]

Figure 3-2 depicts the relationship of the tariff after liberalization (vertical axis) to the tariff before reform for formulas 5, 6, 7, 11, and 12. Formula 10 cannot be shown in this manner because it varies depending on the individual BTN category and the importing country. Formula 4 is merely complete tariff elimination. Formulas 8 and 9 are 60 percent cuts with different treatment of the zone below 5 percent. As may be seen from the graph, some of the harmonization formulas focus on cutting higher tariffs while others make relatively deeper cuts in the lower ranges as well. Generally, the 60 percent linear cut (figure 3-1) is more liberalizing than all of the harmonization formulas in the lower range of tariffs (for example, up to the range of 5 percent to 10 percent).

Table 3-1 summarizes the details of the twelve tariff-cutting formulas considered in this study.

Estimates of Trade and Welfare Effects

This section examines the principal empirical estimates of trade and welfare effects using the model of tariff liberalization set forth in chapter 2. It is only possible to report our estimates at relatively high levels of aggregation, given the immensity of the full set of detailed results at the tariff-line level.[15]

The estimates exclude crude and refined petroleum (BTN 2709 and 2710) from all results on the grounds that, in the special case of petroleum, tariffs and trade will be determined by factors wholly outside any general tariff-cutting formulas agreed upon in the Tokyo Round. Furthermore, the central estimates of this study omit textiles as well (BTN section 11). Almost all trade in textiles is controlled by the regime of

13. European Community Information Service, "EC-U.S. Agree on Principles for Cutting Tariffs." As the parameter *a* in the general formula rises, the depth of tariff cut declines, and a restrictive version of the formula could be devised.

14. The Swiss formula is relatively liberal, providing an average tariff cut of 44 percent; see ibid. Formula 12 in this study provides an average tariff cut of 42 percent (appendix A, table A-5). The difference between the post-reform tariffs resulting from the two alternative formulas is less than 0.25 percentage point, over the full range of tariffs (assuming a 60 percent ceiling on tariff cuts under the Swiss formula). Evaluated at a 10 percent initial tariff, the Swiss formula would cause only about 5.6 percent larger increases in trade than would formula 12 here.

15. The full details are, however, available for consultation by interested readers.

Figure 3-2. *Tariff-Cutting Formulas 5, 6, 7, 11, and 12*

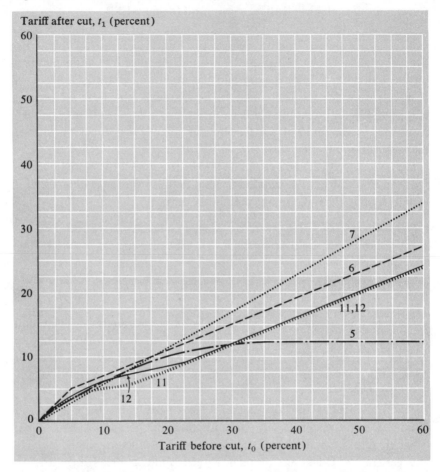

voluntary export quotas provided for by the "multifibers agreement." Therefore, even if tariffs on textiles were reduced in accordance with a general tariff-cutting formula, imports would not increase above their levels already set by quotas. Because it is highly unlikely that the regime of voluntary export quotas will be abolished by the Tokyo Round, it is essential to exclude the textiles sector in order to obtain meaningful estimates of the effects of tariff liberalization.[16]

16. In addition, all calculations exclude four cases of preferential entry not likely to be affected in the negotiations: Canadian preferential supply to the United States

Table 3-1. *Tariff-Cutting Formulas*

Formula number	Verbal statement	Mathematical statement[a]
1	60% linear cut	$y = 0.60$
2	Three-iteration harmonization (EEC variant)	$t_1 = t_0(1 - t_0)$ 3 times
3	Canadian-type formula	If $t_0 < 5\%$, $t_1 = 0$; if $t_0 > 40\%$, $t_1 = 20\%$; otherwise, $t_1 = 0.5\,t_0$
4	100% linear cut	$y = 1.0$
5	Harmonization, 30% + tariff	$y = 0.3 + t_0$
6	60% cut plus absolute 3% tariff	$t_1 = 0.03 + 0.4\,t_0$
7	43.4% linear cut	$y = 0.434$
8	Full U.S. authority	$y = 0.60$; if $t_0 < 0.05$, $t_1 = 0$
9	60% cut with 5% floor	$y = 0.60$ except: if $t_0 < 0.05$, $t_1 = t_0$; if $t_0 < 0.125$, $t_1 = 0.05$
10[b]	Sector harmonization	$t_1 = \mathrm{Min} \begin{cases} t^* \\ t_0 \end{cases}$
11[b]	Harmonization, 20% + 3 times tariff	$y - 0.2 + 3t_0$
12[b]	Six-iteration harmonization	$t_1 = t_0(1 - t_0)$ 6 times

a. Abbreviations: y = proportionate tariff cut; t_0 = original tariff; t_1 = tariff after cut; t^* = four-area BTN minimum tariff.
b. Subject to maximum cut of 60 percent.

The first and most important policy question to be examined is: What are the potential economic benefits from tariff liberalization in the negotiations? Table 3-2 reports the estimates of total increase in imports and static welfare for the eleven industrial country importing areas considered, for each of the tariff formulas examined. As shown in the table, except for the case of complete tariff elimination, the greatest increase in trade and welfare would occur under the full U.S. authority to cut tariffs (formula 8). It is therefore useful to consider the economic benefits attainable under this formula. As shown in the table, the flow of static welfare gains would be approximately $1.7 billion annually. However, total welfare gains would be far in excess of this figure.[17] Several important wel-

---

(mainly automobiles); and preferential supplies to trading partners from Australia, New Zealand, and South Africa.

17. These gains would occur even though there could also be offsetting welfare costs of adjustment for dislocated labor. Labor adjustment costs are examined later in this chapter.

Table 3-2. *Total Import and Welfare Effects of Alternative Tariff-Cutting Formulas for Eleven Industrial Importing Areas,*[a] *1974 Base*
Millions of dollars; excluding textiles and petroleum

Formula[b]	Imports[c]		Static welfare effect		Welfare as a percent of imports	Average depth of cut for four areas[d]	
	Value	Rank	Value	Rank		Percent	Rank
1	10,158	3	1,681	3	16.5	60.0	3
2	5,738	11	1,397	9	24.3	32.5	10
3	9,780	4	1,601	6	16.4	59.1	4
4	16,930	1	1,991	1	11.8	100.0	1
5	7,989	6	1,603	5	20.1	46.4	6
6	5,411	12	1,330	11	24.6	29.9	11
7	7,449	8	1,374	10	18.4	43.4	7
8	10,976	2	1,686	2	15.4	65.2	2
9	7,566	7	1,568	7	20.7	42.0	8
10	5,769	10	1,098	12	19.0	23.2	12
11	8,670	5	1,622	4	18.7	49.9	5
12	7,403	9	1,530	8	20.7	42.0	9

a. The importing areas are the United States, Canada, Japan, the EEC, Austria, Finland, Norway, Sweden, Switzerland, Australia, and New Zealand.
b. For a description of the formulas, see table 3-1.
c. Imports do not include trade in textiles or in crude and refined petroleum. These figures are net of reduced imports by EEC member countries from each other.
d. Calculated from appendix A, table A-12.

fare effects are excluded from the traditional static welfare measure: gains from increased economies of scale; increased growth rates caused by the stimulus to investment provided by new market opportunities; increased efficiency resulting from the incentive for greater technological change provided by greater import competition; and the output-saving effect made possible through the downward pressure exerted on domestic inflation through greater competition from imports (and therefore the greater room for continued output expansion through macroeconomic policies seeking to balance the objective of full employment on the one hand and price stability on the other).[18]

Because of the importance of these nontraditional welfare effects it is

18. In principle, the anti-inflationary effect would be a one-time gain as prices fell by the amount of tariff reduction (or less, if foreign supply were less than infinitely elastic). Nevertheless, given the existence of mechanisms propagating even one-time effects into still further inflation in the future (such as wage escalator clauses), the anti-inflationary influence could also have an ongoing effect.

important to attempt to quantify them, even if the resulting estimate is less solidly based on empirical data than the static welfare effects. In a recent study on economic integration in Europe, Bela Balassa provides estimates of some of the nontraditional welfare gains from trade liberalization within the European Common Market.[19] His estimates indicate that the gains from greater economies of scale achieved through increased intra-EEC trade amounted to 0.5 percent of gross national product for the bloc. In addition, the new investment induced by greater market opportunities added perhaps another 0.2 percent to GNP (accelerating the growth rate). By contrast, the static welfare gains from trade creation in the Common Market amounted to only 0.15 percent of GNP (before deducting the static costs of trade diversion and those of the common agricultural policy).[20] Therefore, it appears that, on the basis of the experience of the European Common Market, the total welfare gains from trade liberalization are several times as large as the static welfare effects alone.

As an approximation of total welfare gains, we would suggest a figure five times as large as static welfare gains—a multiple more conservative than that implied by Balassa's findings.[21] On the basis of this multiple, the welfare benefits of tariff cuts under full U.S. authority would reach approximately $8.5 billion annually. Moreover, these gains would repeat year after year, and they could be expected to grow along with the base level of trade. Assuming an annual growth rate of trade of 5 percent in real terms, and using a time discount rate of 10 percent a year to evaluate the future stream of welfare gains, a reasonable estimate of the present discounted value of these welfare effects would be twenty times the initial annual rate—or a total of $170 billion. In other words, the once-for-all value of a decision by negotiators at Geneva to cut tariffs by the full U.S. authority would be approximately $170 billion in welfare benefits. The economic stakes in the Tokyo Round are therefore large.

19. Bela Balassa, "Trade Creation and Diversion in the European Common Market: An Appraisal of the Evidence," in Bela Balassa, ed., *European Economic Integration* (Amsterdam: North-Holland, 1975), pp. 79–118.

20. Ibid., pp. 113–15.

21. The results found by Balassa indicate a multiple of 5.7 to 1. Moreover, his welfare estimates do not include the effect of stimulus to technological change, nor the output effect of a reduced inflation rate. On the other hand, other researchers have estimated somewhat smaller welfare gains for the effects measured by Balassa. See Lawrence B. Krause, *European Economic Integration and the United States* (Brookings Institution, 1968), p. 44.

A qualification on our estimate of the present value of total welfare gain is that the dynamic effects from tariff liberalization at present could well differ from those experienced during European integration. It might be argued, for example, that for European countries the critical gains in economies of scale were achieved when these countries moved to their own free-trade area, leaving little room for further gains from scale economies. In this viewpoint, the extra gains from economies of scale through further export expansion for Europe might be smaller, in relation to trade creation, than those calculated on the basis of integration experience. The same line of reasoning would suggest that extra economies of scale for the United States, a country with an extremely large market already, might be smaller, in relation to the value of increased exports, than would be expected on the basis of experience in European integration. Therefore, total annual welfare gains for the United States and Europe might be smaller than our estimate of five times the static welfare gains. By contrast, for Canada the gains from economies of scale could be much larger, relatively, than would be expected on the basis of European experience. Indeed, recent studies on Canada have arrived at truly enormous estimates of dynamic welfare gains from trade liberalization.[22]

Therefore, within our global estimate of dynamic welfare gains there may be a tendency to overstate gains for some countries (United States, EEC) and to understate them for others (Canada). Nevertheless, considering that our estimate excludes additional dynamic welfare gains from

22. For example, Wonnacott has estimated that a free-trade area between Canada and the United States alone would provide welfare gains equal to 2.3 percent of Canadian GNP through specialization even without returns to scale, and additional gains of 5.9 percent of GNP from increased economies of scale. Total gains, 8.2 percent of Canadian GNP, would amount to $11.5 billion (on a 1974 base). By contrast, our estimate of Canadian welfare gains from a 100 percent tariff cut (including textiles) is $292 million in static gains (see table 3-8 below) and therefore approximately $1.5 billion in total welfare gains. Wonnacott's estimates appear to be exaggerated, however. They assume that, through increased economies of scale, the entire Canadian manufacturing sector suddenly would reach the real productivity levels found in the United States as the result of free trade between the United States and Canada. The real productivity levels in the United States are now 27 percent above those in Canada. This procedure would appear to have much less justification than the approach used by Balassa, in which only a proportion of the value of increased exports is measured as welfare gain from increased economies of scale. See Ronald J. Wonnacott, *Canada's Trade Options* (Ottawa: Economic Council of Canada, 1975), pp. 176–78.

stimulus to technical change and from macroeconomic output gains associated with the avoidance of inflation, it would appear that our estimate of total welfare gain is not overstated, despite these qualifications on the component for economies of scale.[23]

It is important to consider the welfare gains from the anti-inflationary impact of reducing protection, although we have no formal estimates for this influence. For the United States, full authority tariff cuts would reduce weighted import prices by 4.33 percent for dutiable goods (appendix A, table A-4). Dutiable imports represented 5.3 percent of gross national product in 1974, so that the corresponding direct impact on the overall consumer price index would be a reduction by approximately 0.23 percentage point.[24] A downward shift in inflation by this amount could permit authorities to reduce unemployment by approximately 0.31 percentage point without raising inflation above its original level.[25] Under "Okun's law," a reduction of unemployment by this amount would trans-

23. Two additional considerations reinforce this conclusion. First, Balassa's parameter for gains from economies of scale in relationship to trade creation is a generalized one; it is not limited specifically to the case of European integration. Elsewhere, Balassa has argued that gains from increased economies of scale through trade liberalization are likely to be relatively important even in countries already possessing large internal markets. Bela Balassa, *Trade Liberalization among Industrial Countries: Objectives and Alternatives* (McGraw-Hill for Council on Foreign Relations, 1967), pp. 96–97. Second, because tariffs were higher in preintegration Europe than in most industrial countries at present, the ratio of static welfare gain to trade creation would have been higher during integration than would be expected from current liberalization. This is because static welfare gain rises with the square of the tariff, whereas trade creation rises less than proportionately with the height of the tariff. By relating our estimates of total welfare gains to static welfare gains and by applying the relationship from European integration experience, we therefore will have understated total welfare gains, insofar as they relate more to magnitudes of trade change than to size of static welfare gains.

24. Dutiable imports account for 76 percent of U.S. imports (calculated from the GATT trade and tariff data base). The text figures are based on the application of this fraction to U.S. merchandise imports, and on gross national product, for 1974 as reported in International Monetary Fund, *International Financial Statistics*, vol. 30 (June 1977), pp. 39 and 378.

25. Based on the Phillips curve recently estimated by Michael L. Wachter, "The Changing Cyclical Responsiveness of Wage Inflation," *Brookings Papers on Economic Activity, 1:1976*, p. 144. The trade-off between inflation and unemployment is measured at the 1974 unemployment rate of 5.6 percent; Organisation for Economic Co-operation and Development, *Economic Outlook*, vol. 19 (July 1976), p. 31.

late into an increase in gross national product of about 1 percent,[26] or approximately $14 billion for 1974. This magnitude would represent an addition of about one-third to the total present discounted value of welfare gains found in our basic estimates discussed above (which would be approximately $50 billion for the United States). Therefore, the anti-inflationary impact could contribute significantly to total welfare benefits and, as a result, our main estimates of total welfare gains from trade liberalization are likely to be understated.

These calculations of anti-inflationary effects are sensitive to particular assumptions, and we include them for the United States for illustrative purposes only. The effects would be smaller if domestic and international export supply were less than infinitely elastic, causing import prices to fall by less than the reduction in tariff and causing some new inflation in export sectors. The effects would be larger, however, if the Phillips curve used included a large carry-over term so that reduced inflation this year would help reduce inflation for several years to come.[27] Because of these and other uncertainties, we omit the anti-inflationary impact from our basic estimates of total welfare gain from trade liberalization.

As for the choice among tariff-cutting formulas, it is clear from table 3-2 that the greatest possible welfare gain would occur under the full U.S. authority cut (formula 8), omitting the case of complete elimination of tariffs (formula 4). If instead the restrictive EEC or Japanese approaches were adopted (formulas 2 and 6, respectively), static annual welfare gains would be about 19 percent lower. If the Swiss formula (discussed above) were adopted, static welfare gains would be about 9 percent below those attainable under full U.S. tariff-cutting authority (based on formula 12, table 3-2). Total welfare gains under these alternative approaches would fall proportionately further below the gains achievable under full U.S. authority, because some dynamic benefits depend on the magnitude of trade change rather than on the size of static welfare gains. Compared with results under full U.S. authority tariff cuts, trade created would be about 50 percent lower for the EEC and Japanese approaches, and about

26. Arthur M. Okun, "Potential GNP: Its Measurement and Significance," American Statistical Association, Business and Economic Statistics Section, *Proceedings: 1962* (Washington, D.C.: ASA, 1962), pp. 98–104.

27. See, for example, Franco Modigliani and Lucas Papademos, "Targets for Monetary Policy in the Coming Year," *Brookings Papers on Economic Activity, 1:1975*, pp. 141–63.

33 percent lower for the Swiss formula (based on our results for formula 12).

With respect to the magnitude of trade effects, table 3-2 indicates that the complete elimination of tariffs would increase imports into the eleven industrial areas by approximately $17 billion (excluding the textile and petroleum sectors). This magnitude represents 3 percent of total imports for these countries in 1974 ($570 billion).[28] This maximum potential impact on trade is a reasonable level when the relevant trade base of dutiable imports is considered. The exclusion of petroleum and textiles reduces the 1974 import base by approximately $111 billion and $38 billion, respectively. The removal of intra-EEC/EFTA trade reduces the base by approximately another $175 billion. The elimination of items that are either duty free or controlled by variable levies reduces the base by perhaps another $82 billion and $10 billion, respectively.[29] As a result, the 1974 trade base relevant for liberalization (in net terms, ignoring substitution effects for free-trade blocs) is only approximately $154 billion. Finally, the $17-billion import increase from total tariff liberalization represents a figure net of reduced trade within the EEC and EFTA blocs. The corresponding gross figure for increased world imports (that is, not netting out reduced imports of bloc partners from each other) is approximately $22 billion, or 14 percent of the relevant world import base just discussed. Considering that the average tariff is on the order of 10.7 percent (table 2-1), this result is consistent with an overall weighted import-price elasticity of approximately -1.48. This implied elasticity reflects the range of elasticities used in the calculations as discussed in chapter 2.

With these aggregate welfare and trade effects in mind, we may turn to the following areas of more detailed analysis: comparisons among the tariff formulas examined; the special case of the textiles sector; the pattern of trade flow changes among countries; and detailed trade effects by tariff formula for the major participants in the negotiations.

The aggregate results shown in table 3-2 indicate essentially three clusters of trade creation effects. The first, or benchmark, level is the

28. Calculated from International Monetary Fund, *International Financial Statistics,* vol. 29 (February 1976), p. 39.

29. These estimates are all quite approximate. They draw on Organisation for Economic Co-operation and Development, *Trade by Commodities: Country Summaries,* Series B (OECD, January–December 1974), and on the detailed GATT data base for 1971 trade and 1973 tariffs.

amount of trade created by complete elimination of tariffs. A second level represents a cluster of formulas that go only about two-thirds of the way toward the free-trade result: the full U.S. authority (formula 8), a 60 percent tariff cut (formula 1), and the formula similar to suggestions by Canada (formula 3). This second tier of formulas represents trade creation of approximately $10 billion, compared with $17 billion created by the complete elimination of tariffs. The third and lowest tier of formulas goes only about one-third of the way to the trade effect of complete tariff elimination. This lowest cluster of formulas creates only about $5.5 billion in new trade. This grouping of formulas includes the three-iteration harmonization cut (formula 2), the sector harmonization approach (formula 10), and the 60 percent cut with a 3 percent tariff shelf added to all resulting tariffs (formula 6). Other formulas lie in between these three tiers.

The most important alternatives in view of the actual negotiations are in the two clusters that may be called liberal and restrictive formulas, respectively. The early U.S. suggestion of a 60 percent tariff cut, as well as the Canadian-type formula, are in the liberal tier; the EEC-type cut (three-iteration harmonization) and the Japanese-type formula (number 6) are in the restrictive tier. The U.S. and Canadian approaches would create approximately twice as much trade as the EEC and Japanese approaches ($10.2 billion and $9.8 billion, versus $5.7 billion and $5.4 billion, respectively).[30]

Table 3-2 shows the average depth of tariff cut for the United States, Canada, Japan, and the EEC. As would be expected, the ordering of formulas by amount of trade created closely parallels their ordering on the basis of average depth of cut.

Finally, as shown in the table the level of static welfare gain associated with each formula has a ranking almost identical to that for the level of trade creation. However, the amount of welfare gain relative to trade creation is the highest for the harmonization formulas (2, 5, 11, 12). This pattern reflects the fact that the welfare gain rises geometrically with the level of tariff, so that harmonization formulas—which cut higher tariffs by greater proportions than lower tariffs—produce greater welfare gains per unit of trade change than do linear formulas.[31]

30. As noted above, the precise proposals by the United States, the EEC, and Japan are all slightly different from the three corresponding formulations reported here. However, the differences are insufficient to affect these conclusions significantly.

31. The welfare measure involves multiplying the tariff by the trade change. But

The results in table 3-2 refer to liberalization excluding textiles. It is important to recognize, however, that increased textile imports could be extremely large if liberalization extended to this politically sensitive sector. This study assumes that textiles will not be liberalized, but the calculations consider the impact that liberalization in the sector would have. The inclusion of the sector in liberalization would raise total import creation by approximately 30 percent.[32]

The key role of textiles may be seen in greater detail in table 3-3, which refers to the four major negotiating partners and is limited to the first two tariff-cutting formulas. The table shows that the most dramatic effect of excluding textiles occurs in the United States, where textiles would amount to fully one-third of the increase in total imports if included in liberalization. With textiles in the negotiations, a 60 percent linear cut would give the United States a negative impact of $1.4 billion on its direct trade effects (that is, excluding exports induced by rest-of-world respending). In the absence of liberalization of textiles, the corresponding trade balance effect would be positive ($211 million). A similar comparison holds for the three-iteration harmonization formula.

Although excluding textiles radically improves the impact of liberalization on U.S. trade balance, it is very costly in terms of welfare gains sacrificed. As shown in table 3-3, maintaining protection on textiles would cut in half the $1 billion in annual static welfare gains that would otherwise be gained by the United States from liberalization (under the 60 percent cut).

For Canada and, to a more limited degree, the EEC, the same general

---

the trade change itself depends on the tariff (and the trade base). Thus, the measure involves a product of two terms involving the tariff, and the result rises geometrically with the tariff.

32. In the 60 percent linear cut, the import effect would rise from $10 billion to $13 billion; in the three-iteration formula (number 2), it would rise from $5.7 billion to $8.1 billion. For detailed information on trade effects of the 60 percent tariff cuts when textiles are included, see table E-4 in appendix E.

Note that in our estimates including textiles it is assumed that quotas would be removed along with the reduction in tariffs in order to permit the tariff reduction to have its liberalizing effect. Note also that the estimates for textiles will be biased downwards unless the voluntary export quotas by textile suppliers are precisely at levels that provide an amount of supply that would be demanded given the textile tariff alone. If quotas are lower than this amount, then the excess of domestic price over foreign price exceeds the tariff, and the joint removal of quotas and reduction of tariffs would raise textile imports by amounts greater than estimated here.

Table 3-3. *Trade and Welfare Effects of Tariff Liberalization, Including and Excluding Textiles,*[a] *for Four Major Negotiating Areas, 1974 Base*

Millions of dollars

Effect	60 percent cut				3-iteration cut			
	United States	Canada	Japan	EEC	United States	Canada	Japan	EEC
Including textiles								
Increased imports	5,461	2,061	1,872	2,483	3,525	1,219	1,135	1,201
Increased direct exports	4,095	605	2,800	−114	2,055	276	1,602	511
Balance	−1,366	−1,455	928	−2,597	−1,470	−942	467	−690
Static welfare	990	245	304	536	917	183	278	363
Excluding textiles								
Increased imports	3,611	1,680	1,737	2,102	1,924	922	1,067	987
Increased direct exports	3,821	565	2,237	−100	1,875	249	1,157	432
Balance	211	−1,116	501	−2,202	−49	−673	90	−555
Static welfare	490	178	289	451	438	124	268	304

a. Textiles include all products within BTN section 11.

effects of excluding textiles would apply: that is, there would be a reduction in both the import and the welfare effects of liberalization. For Japan, by contrast, the principal effect of excluding textiles from the negotiations would be to reduce severely the increased exports for the country. As will be shown below, however, Japan systematically shows a strong trade balance increase from tariff liberalization, so that including textiles in the negotiations would mean widening still further the trade balance gap from liberalization between Japan and the other major participants.

In sum, the exclusion of textiles from liberalization means a major sacrifice in welfare gains combined with a substantial increase in the trade balance, especially for the United States but also for Canada and the EEC. For Japan, the exclusion of textiles from liberalization means a lost opportunity to expand its exports still further beyond a trade balance outcome that is already positive excluding textiles.[33]

We turn now to the country trading patterns contained in our results. Tables 3-4 and 3-5 present the estimates for total "direct" trade effects of tariff-cutting formula 1 (60 percent tariff cut) and formula 2 (three-iteration harmonization cut), respectively. These tables refer to 1974 values (in millions of dollars) for nonpetroleum and nontextile trade. The vertical columns refer to importing areas and the horizontal rows to supplying countries. Thus, for example, in table 3-4 the third-row, second-column entry shows that Canada's imports from Belgium-Luxembourg would rise by $17 million under a 60 percent tariff cut. The total increase in imports for each area is shown in the fifth-from-bottom row (TOT). Since each country's direct exports—that is, excluding indirect exports induced by the respending of "free-rider" earnings—equal the sum of

---

33. A further technical note on textiles warrants attention. In the debate between advocates of "linear" and "harmonization" formulas, it is often ignored that much of the upper tier of tariffs in the United States is concentrated in textiles. As a result, if textiles are excluded from liberalization, the supposed advantages to the EEC of a harmonization formula, and to the United States of a linear formula, collapse to minor dimensions. This point is evident in table 3-3. When textiles are excluded, the three-iteration formula generates 0.53 times as much extra imports in the United States as the 60 percent linear cut; the corresponding ratio is 0.47 in the EEC. These two ratios are relatively similar, indicating little advantage for the EEC from a harmonization formula without textile liberation. By contrast, when textiles are included, the three-iteration formula generates 0.65 times as much extra imports as the 60 percent cut for the United States, whereas the corresponding ratio for the EEC is only 0.48. Here the discrepancy is clearly significant and a harmonization formula does show substantially better trade results for the EEC than the linear formula.

Table 3-4. *Matrix of Trade Effects of Tariff Formula 1, 1974 Base*[a]

Millions of dollars; excluding textiles and petroleum

Exporting country	Importing country											Total exports
	USA	CND	JPN	EEC	ATA	FIN	NOR	SWD	SWZ	ALA	NWZ	
ALA	30	19	90	51	0	0	0	0	0	0	49	240
ATA	40	5	6	−37	0	−1	−1	−2	−3	2	1	11
BLX	86	17	10	−259	−1	−1	−1	−3	−2	6	1	−146
CND	283	0	64	187	1	1	2	4	1	17	4	565
DEN	21	7	10	−45	−1	−1	3	−4	0	5	1	−4
FIN	1	5	2	−55	−1	0	0	−5	0	2	0	−45
FRA	337	34	41	−406	−2	−1	−1	−5	−2	11	6	12
GFR	380	71	136	−708	−24	−6	−7	−24	−14	66	19	−112
IRE	19	3	1	−35	0	0	0	0	0	1	0	−11
ITL	349	36	25	−292	−3	−1	−1	−2	−3	30	6	143
JPN	949	192	0	758	21	9	18	38	20	193	40	2,237
NLD	68	13	19	−410	−1	0	−1	−1	−1	6	3	−306
NWZ	5	2	12	24	0	0	0	0	0	18	0	61
NOR	10	2	9	−15	0	−1	0	−4	0	1	0	3
SWD	47	20	24	−122	−2	−6	−2	0	−2	14	2	−28
SWZ	54	12	72	−72	−3	−1	0	−2	0	6	5	70
UK	228	109	60	−238	−3	−4	−3	−12	−3	111	77	323
USA	0	1,056	587	1,844	18	13	52	61	24	114	53	3,821
EEC	1,487	290	302	−2,393	−34	−13	−12	−51	−25	235	114	−100
SBT	2,912	1,602	1,169	171	−1	1	58	41	15	601	266	6,835
ROW	698	78	567	1,931	33	20	1	53	15	−50	−24	3,323
TOT	3,611	1,680	1,737	2,102	33	21	58	94	30	551	242	10,158
BST	909	−1,038	1,068	−271	11	−46	−55	−69	55	−362	−204	0
BTW	211	−1,116	501	−2,202	−22	−66	−55	−122	40	−311	−181	−3,323
TL2	3,835	1,717	1,705	2,275	41	22	74	103	39	638	269	10,718
RW2	924	115	432	2,098	41	21	17	63	24	37	4	3,776

a. ALA, Australia; ATA, Austria; BLX, Belgium-Luxembourg; CND, Canada; DEN, Denmark; FIN, Finland; FRA, France; GFR, Germany; IRE, Ireland; ITL, Italy; JPN, Japan; NLD, Netherlands; NWZ, New Zealand; NOR, Norway; SWD, Sweden; SWZ, Switzerland; UK, United Kingdom; USA, United States; EEC, European Economic Community; SBT, subtotal; ROW, rest of world; TOT, total; BST, balance of trade with subtotal; BTW, balance of trade with world. For TL2 and RW2, see text. Figures are rounded.

increased imports from them by other participants in the negotiations, the increase in exports for each country is shown in the final column, which is the sum of the other columns in the table. Then, the corresponding direct trade balance effect—that is, increased exports less increased imports—is shown in the third-from-bottom row of the table (BTW). In addition, the row immediately above shows the trade balance effect restricting attention to the eleven industrial importing areas and omitting the rest of the world (BST).

The final two rows of table 3-4 indicate alternative estimates for total increased imports and increased imports from the rest of world, generated by a different option in the 1971–74 expansion procedure. These additional estimates are of only secondary interest, as the central estimates for these two categories are the entries in the rows TOT (total) and ROW (rest of world).[34]

Appendix E presents similar tables for other tariff-cutting formulas of special interest (the Canadian-type and Japanese-type formulas, and a compromise formula discussed below, number 11). In addition, the appendix reports similar trade flow results for a 60 percent tariff cut when textiles are included in liberalization.

A number of important features of the results emerge from tables 3-4 and 3-5. First, these tables (and those in appendix E) show the negative influence of the "trade substitution" effect on the exports of free-trade bloc members to their partners. In table 3-4, for example, exports from West Germany (row GFR) to the EEC (fourth column) are shown to decline by $708 million. Indeed, the negative substitution effect on bloc trade often swamps the positive effect of liberalization on their exports to the United States, Japan, Canada, Australia, and New Zealand. Thus, in table 3-4 the total effect of liberalization on exports both to partners and to other countries is shown to be negative for all of the EEC countries except France, Italy, and the United Kingdom (see the entries in the final column). By contrast, table 3-5 shows negative total export effects for

34. Specifically, every importing area has a 1971 to 1974 expansion factor for total imports in each BTN section, as well as a number of individual country expansion factors specific to suppliers within that BTN section. We consider expansion of total import increase based on a "total" expansion factor to be more reliable as an estimate of the 1974 total import increase (TOT) than the alternative total estimate (TL2) obtained by summing up the individual country expansions. This is especially because for non-OECD suppliers the country-specific expansion factor is a single rest-of-world factor based on the residual supply both in 1971 and in 1974.

Table 3-5. *Matrix of Trade Effects of Tariff Formula 2, 1974 Base*[a]
Millions of dollars; excluding textiles and petroleum

Exporting country	Importing country											Total exports
	USA	CND	JPN	EEC	ATA	FIN	NOR	SWD	SWZ	ALA	NWZ	
ALA	17	15	78	20	0	0	0	0	0	0	48	179
ATA	21	3	3	-11	0	0	0	-1	-1	2	1	16
BLX	23	9	5	-121	-1	0	-1	-1	0	4	1	-81
CND	119	0	32	79	0	0	1	1	0	12	3	249
DEN	7	4	7	-21	-1	0	3	-1	0	5	1	5
FIN	2	3	1	-24	-1	0	0	-2	0	1	0	-19
FRA	293	19	23	-205	-1	0	0	-2	1	9	7	144
GFR	171	38	63	-309	-15	-2	-3	-8	-3	58	19	8
IRE	16	2	0	-19	0	0	0	0	0	1	0	1
ITL	307	23	13	-153	-2	0	-1	-1	0	27	6	219
JPN	445	107	0	342	15	4	9	12	5	183	35	1,157
NLD	42	8	10	-209	-1	1	0	0	0	5	3	-142
NWZ	1	1	8	16	0	0	0	0	0	15	0	41
NOR	3	1	6	-2	0	-1	0	-1	0	1	0	8
SWD	16	11	11	-46	-1	-3	1	0	0	12	1	2
SWZ	29	7	40	-22	-2	0	0	0	0	5	5	61
UK	123	62	36	-106	-2	-2	-1	-4	0	95	78	278
USA	0	558	292	808	11	5	24	19	5	103	50	1,875
EEC	983	164	157	-1,143	-21	-5	-2	-16	-3	205	114	432
SBT	1,637	870	627	18	1	1	32	13	5	540	257	4,001
ROW	287	51	440	969	22	12	1	19	6	-49	-20	1,737
TOT	1,924	922	1,067	987	22	13	32	32	11	491	237	5,738
BST	238	-622	530	413	15	-20	-23	-11	57	-361	-216	0
BTW	-49	-673	90	-555	-7	-31	-24	-30	50	-311	-196	-1,737
TL2	2,104	945	1,031	1,049	28	13	41	36	14	575	260	6,095
RW2	467	75	353	1,029	27	12	9	23	9	35	4	2,043

a. For abbreviations, see table 3-4. Figures are rounded.

only two of the eight EEC suppliers shown. The difference between the two tables indicates that the three-iteration formula would reduce EEC country exports to partners and to EFTA by relatively less than would the 60 percent tariff cut. This result stems from the fact that the three-iteration formula does very little tariff cutting for moderate tariffs, say, in the range of 5 percent to 12 percent. Since most of the EEC tariffs are in this range, the community's tariff wall declines by little in this formula. Thus, there is little scope for trade substitution by outside suppliers to reduce exports of EEC countries to each other.

Second, the matrix of trade effects may be used to examine specific bilateral balance effects. For example, in table 3-4 it is evident that liberalization may raise difficulties for the bilateral trade balance between Canada and the United States. In a 60 percent linear tariff cut, Canada would increase imports from the United States by $1.06 billion while exporting only an additional $283 million to the United States. By contrast, under the "Canadian" proposal (formula 3; see table E-1 in appendix E), Canada's imports from the United States would rise by only $898 million while her exports to the United States would rise by $333 million. The improved, though still negative, bilateral balance result for Canada in formula 3 represents the effect of completely eliminating tariffs below 5 percent in that formula.

Third, tables 3-4 and 3-5 indicate the large share of the rest-of-world suppliers in increased imports (the row labeled ROW). In the 60 percent tariff cut (table 3-4), the rest of world supplies one-third of the total increase in industrial country imports, or $3.3 billion (final column entry). As will be shown in chapter 7 below, the bulk of these increased exports would come from the developing countries.

Finally, it is useful to examine in depth the import, export, and trade balance effects for each of the four major negotiating areas: the United States, Canada, Japan, and the EEC. In order to complete the estimates of increased exports resulting from liberalization, we must first add in the induced exports to rest-of-world countries resulting from the "respending" of those countries' earnings of foreign exchange, obtained from their increased exports to the liberalizing industrial countries. Table 3-6 presents these "respending effect" exports by industrial country, for each tariff-cutting formula.[35]

35. Note that the estimates of respending effects contains an adjustment to make them comparable with the estimates of direct export effects. The respending estimates

Table 3-6. *Impact of Rest-of-World Respending on Exports of Industrial Countries Using Alternative Tariff-Cutting Formulas, 1974 Base*

Millions of dollars; excluding textiles and petroleum

Exporting country[a]	Formula[b]											
	1	2	3	4	5	6	7	8	9	10	11	12
ALA	36.7	20.3	31.4	60.5	28.2	19.8	27.0	38.7	28.1	12.3	31.6	27.2
ATA	37.9	16.9	34.1	62.3	26.5	16.8	28.0	41.2	25.3	13.8	30.6	24.9
BLX	45.1	23.1	41.2	74.6	33.6	22.1	33.3	48.8	31.9	14.8	37.5	31.6
CND	51.2	34.1	50.9	84.6	44.6	28.8	37.7	55.6	37.9	12.5	43.8	38.3
DEN	27.4	20.5	27.8	45.1	25.7	16.1	20.1	29.1	21.4	6.2	23.9	21.3
FIN	17.0	7.4	16.8	27.9	11.8	6.9	12.6	19.5	10.2	5.9	13.4	10.7
FRA	152.9	80.3	139.2	251.3	115.4	76.6	112.8	164.2	109.9	40.9	128.4	107.6
GFR	273.9	135.6	248.7	451.2	200.8	150.8	201.7	295.9	191.1	85.7	225.6	188.1
IRE	2.6	1.4	2.4	4.2	2.0	1.3	1.8	2.7	1.8	0.9	2.1	1.8
ITL	115.1	62.1	107.3	189.8	88.7	57.3	85.0	124.5	80.7	40.4	95.6	80.8
JPN	325.8	192.6	287.4	538.8	259.5	185.9	239.6	340.1	258.7	105.4	286.9	249.7
NDL	58.4	31.1	53.4	96.1	44.5	29.4	43.0	62.6	41.7	17.9	48.7	41.1
NWZ	5.9	3.2	5.6	9.9	4.5	3.0	4.4	6.6	4.3	2.1	5.0	4.1
NOR	14.5	1.5	13.1	23.7	10.4	6.5	10.6	15.7	9.8	5.0	11.6	9.6
SWD	46.7	23.8	43.3	77.0	34.8	22.5	34.3	50.9	30.6	16.3	38.5	32.1
SWZ	52.7	27.2	47.5	87.0	39.3	26.3	38.8	56.7	37.8	17.5	44.1	37.1
UK	206.8	115.8	193.0	340.7	162.4	106.7	152.3	223.7	148.5	62.1	173.9	148.3
USA	420.8	223.8	386.6	708.5	322.3	215.5	315.3	459.7	307.3	119.2	358.8	303.3

a. For abbreviations, see table 3-4.
b. For a description of the formulas, see table 3-1.

Our estimates of respending effects involve considerable leakage of foreign exchange earnings by free-rider countries. Out of a total of $3.32 billion earned by these outside areas under a 60 percent tariff cut (table 3-4, line ROW), only $1.89 billion, or 57 percent, returns to the liberalizing industrial areas through induced exports. The leakage is attributable to the fact that, at least on the first round of respending, the outside areas do not purchase all extra imports from the industrial areas. As a result, an overall trade balance deficit for the industrial liberalizing areas is built into the analysis, despite our incorporation of the respending effect into the analysis. This fact should be kept in mind in assessing the estimates discussed below.

Given the estimates of induced exports attributable to the respending effect, an overview of all trade effects may be obtained by examining the impact of alternative tariff-cutting formulas on imports, direct exports, induced exports, and trade balances. Table 3-7 presents this overview for the four major parties in the trade negotiations. The trade results for the EEC refer to changes in trade with countries outside the community, because the EEC negotiates as a single unit. However, detail on direct export effects by individual member countries of the EEC may be found in tables 3-4, 3-5, and E-1, E-2, and E-3.

A broad pattern of the results immediately evident in table 3-7 is that the United States and Japan tend to experience trade balance increases from liberalization, while Canada and the EEC experience trade balance

---

are initially obtained by applying import coefficients (for purchases from the industrial countries) to the estimates of increased exports from liberalization for individual rest-of-world countries. However, the individual rest-of-world export estimates for 1974 tend to be overstated by the expansion procedure updating 1971 to 1974 results. A more reliable estimate of total extra rest-of-world exports is obtained by subtracting industrial area supply from the total increase in imports for 1974 (based on expansion of totals across all suppliers for the importing country and for the product sector in question). The discrepancy between these two alternative estimates of rest-of-world exports may be seen by comparing entries RW2 and ROW, respectively, in the trade balance matrices (tables 3-4, 3-5, and E-1, E-2, and E-3). Because it is the ROW estimates that are compatible with direct export and import estimates for the industrial countries, all of the estimates of respending effects for each formula are reduced by multiplying the initial estimates (described in chapter 2) by the ratio ROW/RW2 for total eleven-area imports from the rest of world, for the formula in question.

If there is any direction of bias introduced by this adjustment, it is toward an understatement of the respending effect on industrial area exports (because the RW2 estimate of free-riders export earnings exceeds the ROW estimate).

Table 3-7. *Trade Effects of Alternative Tariff-Cutting Formulas
for Four Major Negotiating Areas, 1974 Base*
Millions of dollars; excluding textiles and petroleum

Area and formula[a]	Imports	Exports (direct)	Trade balance (direct)	Exports (respending effect)	Total exports	Trade balance (total)
United States						
1	3,611	3,821	211	421	4,242	632
2	1,924	1,875	−49	224	2,099	175
3	3,773	3,460	−313	387	3,847	74
4	6,018	6,321	303	708	7,029	1,011
5	2,820	2,756	−63	322	3,078	259
6	1,639	1,966	327	216	2,182	543
7	2,648	2,811	163	315	3,126	478
8	4,130	4,019	−112	460	4,479	348
9	2,225	2,941	716	307	3,248	1,023
10	1,736	2,514	778	119	2,633	897
11	2,858	3,294	437	359	3,653	796
12	2,391	2,732	340	303	3,035	643
Canada						
1	1,680	565	−1,116	51	616	−1,065
2	922	249	−673	34	283	−639
3	1,431	603	−828	51	654	−777
4	2,801	936	−1,864	85	1,021	−1,779
5	1,255	400	−855	45	445	−810
6	1,023	221	−802	29	250	−773
7	1,232	415	−817	38	453	−779
8	1,705	664	−1,041	56	720	−985
9	1,500	326	−1,174	38	364	−1,136
10	1,314	313	−1,002	12	325	−990
11	1,561	436	−1,125	44	480	−1,081
12	1,342	349	−993	38	387	−955
Japan						
1	1,736	2,237	501	326	2,563	827
2	1,067	1,157	90	193	1,350	283
3	1,683	2,176	493	287	2,463	780
4	2,894	3,709	815	539	4,248	1,354
5	1,424	1,687	263	260	1,947	523
6	994	1,106	112	186	1,292	298
7	1,273	1,644	371	240	1,884	611
8	1,834	2,458	624	340	2,798	964
9	1,385	1,586	201	259	1,845	460
10	927	1,318	392	105	1,423	497
11	1,521	1,866	346	287	2,153	633
12	1,312	1,556	243	250	1,806	493

Table 3-7 (*continued*)

Area and formula[a]	Imports	Exports (direct)	Trade balance (direct)	Exports (responding effect)	Total exports	Trade balance (total)
EEC[b]						
1	4,495	2,293	−2,202	882	3,175	−1,320
2	2,130	1,575	−555	470	2,045	−85
3	4,105	2,244	−1,861	813	3,057	−1,048
4	7,376	3,827	−3,549	1,453	5,280	−2,096
5	3,201	2,046	−1,165	673	2,719	−492
6	2,215	1,370	−845	460	1,830	−385
7	3,318	1,681	−1,637	650	2,331	−987
8	4,746	2,466	−2,280	952	3,418	−1,328
9	3,339	1,768	−1,571	627	2,395	−944
10	2,214	1,540	−674	269	1,809	−405
11	3,793	1,985	−1,808	736	2,721	−1,072
12	3,125	1,775	−1,350	621	2,396	−729

a. For a description of the formulas, see table 3-1.
b. Refers to trade of EEC with nonmember countries and therefore excludes changes in trade among countries within the EEC.

declines, regardless of the formula chosen. The magnitudes of the changes depend on the formula.[36] Systematic trade balance reductions for Canada and the EEC hold whether or not induced respending exports are included in the analysis. Similarly, for Japan, the positive trade balance effects hold with or without the respending effect. For the United States, all formulas yield positive trade balance results when the respending effect is included, although for four out of the twelve formulas the narrower measure excluding respending exports shows a trade balance reduction.

These overall country patterns may be explained as follows. For Japan, a strong competitive position and favorable trade balance in the 1974 base year (at least for items included in the analysis, which omits pe-

36. This general pattern would still hold true even if all foreign exchange earnings by free-rider countries were forced to be respent on imports from the liberalizing industrial areas. For example, under the 60 percent tariff cut, the United States and Japan experience trade balance increases of $632 million and $827 million, respectively; Canada and the EEC show trade balance reductions of $1,065 million and $1,320 million, respectively. If the "leakage" in respending-effect estimates were eliminated, allocating the extra exports in the same proportions as the initial respending estimates, the pattern of increased and decreased trade balances would not change qualitatively, although the specific estimates would change (to increases of $951 million and $1,074 million for the United States and Japan, respectively; and to decreases of $1,026 million and $652 million for Canada and the EEC, respectively).

troleum) dominate the results and yield favorable trade balances generally from liberalization. Another factor affecting the results for Japan is that the weighted-average import elasticity for the country (-1.39) is on the order of 30 percent below the average import elasticities of the three other major areas.[37]

For the United States, the driving forces behind the results appear to be the significant opening of Canadian and EEC markets through liberalization—the first because of high Canadian tariffs, and the second because of the partial replacement of EEC suppliers as the tariff wall around the free-trade bloc declines. The importance of Canada and the EEC to U.S. export increases may be seen in table 3-4, for example, which shows 76 percent of U.S. direct export increases concentrated in these two markets alone.

An important feature of the Canadian case, which helps explain Canada's trade balance reductions under liberalization, is that the country has high tariffs on those products which are subject to duty but allows a high share of imports to enter duty free. Thus, Canada's overall tariff average for nonagricultural products is 14.2 percent on dutiable goods, compared with 10.7 percent for the eleven industrial reporting areas altogether.[38] However, Canada permits 50.5 percent of her imports to enter duty free, compared with 24.0 percent in the United States and 29.7 percent in the EEC (excluding goods from bloc partners). Only Japan has a comparably high portion of duty-free entry, at 49.4 percent.[39]

The other source of Canada's trade balance reductions from liberalization is probably the nature of her exports, which tend to be raw materials already facing low tariffs (or else nontariff barriers) abroad.[40] By con-

37. Note, however, that even if the import elasticities for Japan were raised to a weighted average of -2.0, the level at which the average elasticities cluster for the United States, Canada, and the EEC (for external imports), Japan would still show a trade balance increase from deep tariff cuts. For example, under full U.S. authority cuts (formula 8), Japan would have a trade balance increase of approximately $160 million (rather than the $964 million estimated with the elasticities actually used), even ignoring extra exports from the responding effect given higher import increases for Japan.

38. See chapter 2, table 2-1.

39. Calculated from the detailed GATT data base for 1971 trade and 1973 tariffs.

40. The import results for Canada would not appear to be biased upward by the elasticities used in the calculations. The weighted-average import elasticity for Canada is close to that for the United States, slightly lower than the elasticity for EEC imports from outside suppliers and somewhat higher than the average import elasticity for Japan.

trast, Japan's exports are concentrated in industrial products facing relatively high protection.

In the case of the EEC, one reason for the pattern of negative trade balance effects is the substitution effect through which supplies from bloc partners are replaced by imports from outside areas. This effect is probably of relatively limited importance, however, in view of the fact that, even taking the substitution into account, the import elasticity of the EEC for purchases from outside areas is not dramatically higher than the import elasticity of other major countries. (The elasticity is -2.17 for the EEC, -1.85 for the United States, -1.39 for Japan, and -1.94 for Canada; see tables 2-3 and 2-4.) An important additional factor appears to be that in the estimated trade effects the community experiences a relatively high increase in imports from the rest of world, making the free-rider problem somewhat greater for the EEC than for other areas. Rest-of-world suppliers account for 43 percent of the increase of EEC imports from nonmembers, whereas the corresponding figures are 33 percent for Japan, 4.6 percent for Canada, and 19 percent for the United States. (See, for example, table 3-4.) Accordingly, the EEC experiences a sizable deterioration in trade balance with respect to the rest of world; responding exports to the outside areas are approximately $1 billion less than increased imports from them in the 60 percent cut, for example.[41]

Despite these patterns, the salient feature of the trade balance effects is that they are all extremely small. Under the 60 percent tariff cut, for example, the trade balance increase for the United States would amount to only 0.6 percent of 1974 exports; that for Japan, 1.5 percent. Similarly, the trade balance decline for Canada would represent 3.1 percent of 1974 exports; that for the EEC would be 1.0 percent of 1974 exports to nonmember countries.[42] It must be kept in mind that even these small changes would be staged over a phasing-in period of five or more years. Thus, the

41. The figures are $882 million in responding exports (table 3-7) and $1,931 million in imports (table 3-4). Note that the concentration of rest-of-world suppliers in increased imports for the EEC reflects a similar concentration in its base level of imports. These suppliers accounted for only 15.4 percent of Canadian imports and 42 percent of U.S. imports in 1974; by contrast, they represented 60 percent of EEC imports. Their share in Japan's imports was also 60 percent, but it appears that much of their supply to Japan entered free or at low duties, in view of the smaller share of these suppliers in Japan's increased imports resulting from liberalization. Supply shares for 1974 are calculated from OECD, *Trade by Commodities: Country Summaries,* Series B.

42. See table 3-13 below for data on 1974 exports.

principal conclusion must be that, under any of the tariff formulas, any trade balance declines would be too inconsequential to constitute a legitimate basis for opposing liberalization.

Before we turn to the issue of preferred rankings of tariff formulas, we must emphasize that the trade effect estimates should not be considered to be highly precise. They are the estimates that result from applying the best empirical information available. Nevertheless, there is unavoidably a degree of uncertainty associated with the empirical base, especially in the elasticities used. Therefore, the estimates should be interpreted as "best" or "central" estimates, but they should not be taken rigidly as exact measurements. However, any likely range of error in the estimates would not reverse the main policy conclusion that all trade balance effects would be extremely small. Subsequently in this chapter, we examine the reliability of our specific estimates through the use of "sensitivity analysis" that varies the import elasticities used in the calculations.

Tariff Formula Rankings and Reciprocity

The estimates for export, import, and welfare effects of alternative tariff-cutting formulas provide the basis for examining each negotiating country's presumed ranking of the various formulas. Those rankings in turn constitute the grounds for determining which formulas would be the most desirable for all negotiating countries considered jointly. The following discussion of these questions concentrates on the results for the four major negotiating areas: the United States, Canada, Japan, and the EEC.[43]

There are two broad criteria for ranking the tariff formulas for each country: welfare effects and trade effects. As was discussed in chapter 2, the rankings of formulas by total welfare gains (including effects on investment, economies of scale, technical change, and anti-inflationary effects) should correspond to the rankings based on estimated static welfare

43. The smaller European countries (Austria, Finland, Norway, Sweden, and Switzerland) have much smaller trade effects at stake, even considered as a group, than any one of the big four negotiating areas. (See, for example, table 3-4.) The trade effects are larger for Australia and New Zealand, but there appears to be some doubt that these countries will adopt the general tariff-cutting formula agreed upon in any event.

Table 3-8. *Static Welfare Gains from Alternative Tariff-Cutting*
Formulas for Four Major Negotiating Areas, Including
and Excluding Textiles, 1974 Base
Millions of dollars; excluding petroleum

For-mula[a]	United States		Canada		Japan		EEC	
	Value	Rank	Value	Rank	Value	Rank	Value	Rank
Excluding textiles								
1	490.3	4	178.2	3	289.3	5	451.2	3
2	437.8	9	124.5	12	268.5	9	304.4	11
3	470.3	6	159.4	7	296.2	2	415.5	5
4	583.7	1	212.1	1	344.4	1	527.7	1
5	491.0	3	151.5	8	293.7	3	384.6	7
6	395.2	12	134.4	11	244.4	10	317.8	10
7	400.6	10	145.6	10	236.4	11	374.3	9
8	491.1	2	178.4	2	289.9	4	453.0	2
9	448.9	8	171.5	5	276.8	7	409.4	6
10	395.4	11	150.2	9	83.7	12	235.1	12
11	470.8	5	174.0	4	281.7	6	426.9	4
12	451.1	7	160.4	6	270.5	8	384.5	8
Including textiles								
1	990.5	4	245.3	3	303.8	5	536.0	3
2	917.2	8	182.7	12	278.2	9	362.5	11
3	917.2	9	219.3	7	309.2	2	491.6	6
4	1,179.1	1	292.0	1	361.7	1	626.7	1
5	1,004.4	2	215.3	8	305.8	3	455.9	8
6	842.8	10	192.3	11	254.8	10	382.0	10
7	809.4	12	200.4	10	248.3	11	441.1	9
8	991.3	3	245.4	2	304.5	4	537.8	2
9	948.0	6	238.4	5	290.4	7	492.2	5
10	827.8	11	208.1	9	89.6	12	264.1	12
11	970.3	5	240.9	4	295.7	6	510.0	4
12	947.2	7	226.8	6	283.2	8	460.5	7

a. For a description of the formulas, see table 3-1.

effects. Table 3-8 reports these welfare estimates for the four major negotiating areas, both excluding and including textiles from liberalization.
The difference between the two cases shows the importance of textiles in
the potential welfare gains of each area.

For a practical assessment of liberalization, the more relevant welfare
gains are those excluding textiles. Not surprisingly, under the welfare

criterion the most favorable formula for all participants is complete elimination of tariffs (formula 4). For all areas except Japan, the next most favorable formula is the full U.S. authority case (formula 8). For Japan, formulas 3 and 5 create slightly higher welfare gains than the U.S. authority cut because both formulas cause cuts of greater than 60 percent for high tariffs.

The rankings of the formulas generally parallel the degree of liberalization associated with each formula. The lowest ranked formulas are: formula 10, the sector harmonization formula (except for Canada, which apparently must make more frequent and deeper cuts than the other areas to reach the four-area sectoral minimum tariff); formula 6, which adds a 3 percent shelf onto all tariffs after a 60 percent cut; and formula 2, the three-iteration cut, which creates relatively little trade.

The second basis for evaluating alternative tariff-cutting formulas from the standpoint of each country is that of their effects on exports relative to imports. These trade effects of liberalization represent the concept of reciprocity. Under the objective of reciprocity, other things being equal, each country seeks to obtain from negotiations the maximum possible increase in export opportunities in exchange for the increase in trade opportunities it confers on others by liberalizing its own import market.

Economists have criticized negotiators as being irrational for pursuing reciprocity or trade balance objectives in view of the welfare gains from import liberalization by itself; or, as a minimum, negotiators have been viewed as seeking objectives, such as a preference for industrial output and employment, outside the realm of traditional welfare gains.[44]

For various reasons, however, it is reasonable for negotiators to consider export effects relative to import effects. As was discussed in chapter 2, a number of reasons exist for paying attention to increased export opportunities in a trade negotiation. Negotiations represent a bargaining situation. The bargaining objective, as distinct from an objective that could be pursued by each country in isolation, is to obtain the maximum possible liberalization of export markets in exchange for the liberalization of the home country's own import market. If import liberalization alone were the objective, each country could reduce tariffs unilaterally. Moreover, some of the dynamic welfare gains from liberalization are associated

44. Harry G. Johnson, "An Economic Theory of Protectionism, Tariff Bargaining, and the Formation of Customs Unions," *Journal of Political Economy,* vol. 73 (June 1965), pp. 256–83.

more with increased exports than with increased imports (namely, economies of scale and stimulus to investment). Another reason for attention to trade effects is that, if a country's imports will increase far more than its exports from a particular proposal, the country will face adjustment costs necessary to offset the reduction in trade balance.[45] Finally, on strictly political grounds, the domestic support necessary to the success of negotiations is less likely to be forthcoming if legislative, business, and labor circles believe that a serious reduction in trade balance will result from the negotiations.[46]

We propose two measures for ranking tariff formulas under the reciprocity objective: change in trade balance and percentage increase in exports relative to percentage increase in imports. Other things being equal, a negotiating country will prefer a formula that produces a larger trade balance increase over one that gives the country a smaller increase or a decrease. The trade balance effect of liberalization may be a misleading indicator of the reciprocity objective, however. If a country's tariffs and trade base are such that any liberalization is likely to cause a reduction in trade balance, it does not follow that the country should prefer that no liberalization occur. A country in this situation may desire to liberalize its trade to obtain the welfare benefits of liberalization. If so, the country may profitably participate in negotiations in order to obtain the maximum possible reduction in the protection of the other countries.

Some relative measure of export change compared with import change will be a more accurate gauge of success in this endeavor than will the trade balance change itself. The relative measure we have chosen is the ratio of percentage increase in exports to percentage increase in imports.

45. Under flexible exchange rates, the adjustment costs will involve a depreciation in the country's exchange rate and probably a decline in its terms of trade. For countries usually in a condition of a surplus of payments, this cost will be negligible (because otherwise these countries would appreciate). Countries facing chronic payments deficits would have a higher cost associated with additional depreciation induced by changes in protective structure domestically and abroad.

46. Whatever the actual objectives of U.S. negotiators during the Kennedy Round, it is clear that, at the level of public presentation, an increase in the U.S. trade balance through the reduction in the tariff wall around the European Common Market was an objective. According to Ernest H. Preeg, this public objective was articulated in "the eloquence with which the American administration had linked passage of the Trade Expansion Act with an improved balance of payments." Ernest H. Preeg, *Traders and Diplomats: An Analysis of the Kennedy Round of Negotiations under the General Agreement on Tariffs and Trade* (Brookings Institution, 1970), p. 5.

Table 3-9. *Ranks of Tariff Formulas According to Trade Effects
in the Four Major Negotiating Areas, 1974 Base*
Excluding textiles and petroleum

Area and formula[a]	Trade balance change		Percentage increase		Ratio of percentage changes[b]	
	Dollars (millions)	Rank	Imports	Exports	Exports/ imports	Rank
United States						
1	632	6	3.34	4.31	1.29	7
2	175	11	1.78	2.13	1.20	9
3	74	12	3.49	3.90	1.12	12
4	1,011	2	5.57	7.14	1.28	8
5	259	10	2.61	3.12	1.20	10
6	543	7	1.52	2.22	1.46	3
7	478	8	2.45	3.17	1.29	6
8	348	9	3.82	4.55	1.19	11
9	1,023	1	2.06	3.30	1.60	2
10	897	3	1.61	2.67	1.66	1
11	796	4	2.65	3.71	1.40	4
12	643	5	2.21	3.08	1.39	5
Canada						
1	−1,065	9	4.86	1.80	0.37	4
2	−639	1	2.67	0.83	0.31	7
3	−777	3	4.14	1.91	0.46	1
4	−1,779	12	8.10	2.98	0.37	5
5	−810	5	3.63	1.30	0.36	6
6	−773	2	2.96	0.73	0.25	11
7	−779	4	3.56	1.32	0.37	3
8	−985	7	4.93	2.10	0.42	2
9	−1,136	11	4.34	1.06	0.24	12
10	−990	8	3.80	0.95	0.25	10
11	−1,081	10	4.52	1.40	0.31	8
12	−955	6	3.88	1.13	0.29	9
Japan						
1	827	3	2.80	4.61	1.65	4
2	283	12	1.72	2.43	1.41	12
3	780	4	2.71	4.43	1.63	6
4	1,354	1	4.66	7.65	1.64	5
5	523	7	2.29	3.50	1.53	9
6	298	11	1.60	2.32	1.45	11
7	611	6	2.05	3.39	1.65	3
8	964	2	2.95	5.04	1.71	2
9	460	10	2.23	3.32	1.49	10
10	497	8	1.49	2.56	1.72	1
11	633	5	2.45	3.88	1.58	7
12	493	9	2.11	3.25	1.54	8

Table 3-9 (*continued*)

Area and formula[a]	Trade balance change		Percentage increase		Ratio of percentage changes[b]	
	Dollars (millions)	Rank	Imports	Exports	Exports/ imports	Rank
EEC						
1	−1,320	10	2.98	2.37	0.80	11
2	−85	1	1.41	1.53	1.08	1
3	−1,048	8	2.72	2.28	0.84	6
4	−2,096	12	4.88	3.94	0.81	10
5	−492	4	2.12	2.03	0.96	2
6	−385	2	1.47	1.37	0.93	3
7	−987	7	2.20	1.74	0.79	12
8	−1,328	11	3.14	2.55	0.81	7
9	−944	6	2.21	1.79	0.81	8
10	−405	3	1.47	1.35	0.92	4
11	−1,072	9	2.51	2.03	0.81	9
12	−729	5	2.07	1.79	0.86	5

Sources: For trade balance changes, see table 3-7. Increases in imports and exports calculated from table 3-7 and International Monetary Fund, *International Financial Statistics*, vol. 29 (February 1976), pp. 38–39, for the United States, Canada, and Japan; import and export figures for the EEC are based on Organisation for Economic Co-operation and Development, *Trade by Commodities: Country Summaries*, Series B (OECD, January–December 1974).

a. For a description of the formulas, see table 3-1.

b. Because import base is c.i.f. and export base is f.o.b., the ratio is higher (by perhaps up to 10 percent) than if both trade bases were in f.o.b. terms.

Under this measure the most favorable tariff formula may produce a negative trade balance effect and yet still accomplish the objective of obtaining the maximum opening of export markets relative to liberalization of the import market. This relative measure has another advantage: it should reduce the sensitivity of formula rankings to the particular year chosen for the trade data base. When the trade balance change itself is examined, deep tariff cuts will tend to be preferred by a country with a strong trade surplus in the base year, but the same country could prefer no liberalization at all (on this criterion) if the base were another year in which it had a large trade deficit. A measure of relative percentage increase in exports and imports abstracts from this problem of trade balance in the base year.

Table 3-9 reports the rankings of tariff-cutting formulas under the two criteria of trade effects, for the four major negotiating areas. The rankings of formulas under the criterion of trade balance and under the criterion of relative percentage increase of exports and imports show a close correspondence between the two standards for the United States, Japan, and the EEC but a substantial divergence for Canada.

For the United States, the most favorable formula from the standpoint of trade effects would be formula 9, a 60 percent tariff cut with a floor of 5 percent below which tariffs would not be cut. The formula ranks first on the trade balance criterion and second on the relative change criterion. The formula causes sizable tariff cuts relevant for U.S. exports, while it exempts from reduction the significant portion of U.S. imports entering at tariffs already at 5 percent or below. Based on the two trade effect criteria, the second-ranked formula is the sector harmonization formula (number 10), indicating that the United States frequently already has the lowest tariff among the four major areas.[47] As discussed below, however, the sector harmonization formula is unattractive in that it severely restricts trade creation. Furthermore, the formula is impractical in that it does not include countries other than the four largest areas in the computation of the lowest existing sectoral tariff. This raises the question of whether those other countries would adhere to the formula and therefore whether the estimated trade balance increases for the United States and the other major areas would in fact be realized.

The third-ranked formula for the United States, based on the two trade criteria jointly, is formula 11, a particular variant of harmonization (tariff cut equals 20 percent plus three times the tariff, with a 60 percent maximum cut). As will be seen, this particular formula could be an attractive candidate for a compromise solution.

The least favorable formula for the United States under both trade effect criteria is formula 3, which resembles suggestions submitted by Canada. This formula eliminates tariffs below five percent. Similarly, the "full U.S. authority" formula (number 8) ranks low, again presumably because it eliminates tariffs of five percent and below, affecting a large portion of U.S. imports. The formula closest to the EEC proposal (formula 2) also ranks low for the United States.[48]

47. Note that, under the trade balance criterion, formula 4, the complete elimination of tariffs, ranks second for the United States, although that ranking depends on the important effect of induced exports caused by responding (see table 3-7). This result indicates that for the United States larger trade balance increases are associated with greater liberalization, at least when abstracting from the structural question of the importance of imports entering at tariffs below 5 percent or the alternative structural question of sector harmonization.

48. Note, however, that the calculations do not limit cuts to 60 percent under the

One of the issues facing American negotiators has been whether harmonization formulas would be seriously less favorable than linear formulas with respect to trade balance effects. The results of table 3-9 indicate that no one answer exists to this question; an answer depends on the specification of the harmonization or linear formula. A quite favorable trade balance outcome is obtained with a 100 percent linear cut, but the next linear formula (60 percent) ranks lower than several harmonization formulas. The main points in this regard are twofold. First, once textiles are excluded, the "teeth" of harmonization are largely missing for the U.S. case (as noted above). Second, because of the large portion of imports at tariffs below 5 percent in the United States, a harmonization formula that tends to omit them from liberalization, while making substantial cuts in higher tariffs and therefore opening up foreign markets, tends to produce the highest trade balance increases for the United States. Hence, formula 9, a harmonization formula in the sense that it cuts high tariffs by more than low ones, is the preferred case.[49]

A final point, best illustrated with the case of the United States, is that the use of 1974 trade values as the basis for the analysis makes a crucial difference to the overall trade balance results estimated, but very little difference in the ranking of formulas for each participant. As shown in table E-5 in appendix E, there is virtually no variation between the two years in the formula rankings (based on trade balance) for the United States and for the other major importers. However, the 1974 trade balance results are substantially improved over those of 1971 for the United States (confirming the importance of using 1974 rather than 1971, the year of serious deficit, as the base year). For example, the 100 percent and the 60 percent linear cuts show trade balance reductions in 1971 but trade balance increases in 1974. The fact that the formula rankings are generally consistent between the two years, for all four major participants in the negotiations, provides a degree of assurance that the procedure for

---

three-iteration harmonization formula (number 2). In practice, the United States probably would apply its 60 percent maximum cut limit, so that results under the formula might yield a larger trade balance increase than shown here. However, exemption from the formula to impose this maximum cut limit might warrant offsetting, additional concessions by the United States.

49. Note that one specific test of the harmonization issue may be made by comparing formulas 5 and 7, which have almost identical depth of tariff cuts but are harmonization and linear formulas, respectively. Their results are quite similar, but the linear formula is slightly preferable on grounds of trade effects.

expanding 1971 results to 1974 does not jeopardize the reliability of the results.[50]

In the case of Canada, the tariff formula rankings are sensitive to the trade effect criterion chosen. Under the trade balance criterion, formulas involving greater liberalization tend to rank lower than more restrictive formulas, because liberalization in general tends to create reductions in trade balance for Canada, for the reasons discussed above. However, under the criterion of percentage export increase relative to percentage import increase, certain formulas involving deep tariff cutting rank high. In particular, under the relative percentage trade change criterion (table 3-9), the most favorable formula for Canada is formula 3—the country's own variant, or the closest version to it among those considered here— which is a very liberal formula (as is shown by table 3-2 and table A-2 in appendix A). The second-ranked formula is the most liberalizing practical formula, full U.S. tariff-cutting authority (formula 8). By contrast, the highly restrictive formula 2 (three-iteration harmonization) and formula 6 (60 percent cut plus a shelf of 3 percent tariff) rank highest under the criterion of trade balance effect but rank low under the relative percentage trade change criterion. Both criteria clearly show the importance of the structural characteristic of Canada's large exports (primarily to the United States) in items facing tariffs of 5 percent and below. Under both criteria, the formula eliminating these tariffs (formula 3) ranks high for Canada and the formula setting 5 percent as a tariff floor (formula 9) ranks extremely low.

Of the four major negotiating parties examined here, Canada is the country for which the calculations of trade balance effects are perhaps the most misleading. As an exporter of raw materials, Canada confronts limitations to exports of processed goods because of "tariff escalation" in other countries (much higher "effective" protection—or protection on "value added"—for processed goods than for raw materials). Because the methodology used for these estimates does not take into account tariff escalation or considerations of effective protection, but deals instead with nominal tariffs, it is likely that these estimates tend to underestimate the

---

50. The emergence of a large U.S. trade balance deficit in 1977 should not alter the basic pattern of our results using the 1974 base. The 1977 deficit was primarily attributable to the high import bill for petroleum and to the different stages of economic recovery in the United States and abroad. Neither factor is germane for our calculations, which refer to nonoil trade and longer term effects.

export increases in processing activities that could be anticipated from multilateral tariff liberalization. Moreover, Canada could well be the country in which dynamic welfare gains from trade liberalization would be the greatest in proportionate terms, because of the strong impetus to increased efficiency through the resulting reorganization of industry that could be expected.[51]

Finally, in the case of Canada there may be an important linkage between tariff and nontariff liberalization. Past experiences with nontariff barriers imposed by the United States appear to have made Canada especially concerned about nontariff restrictions. Moreover, the U.S. Trade Act of 1974, with its increased flexibility for the application of trade-restricting measures for safeguard purposes, appears to have heightened this concern. Thus, to the extent that the Tokyo Round could achieve an overall package providing for codes of conduct in the nontariff area as well as sizable cuts of tariffs, the special gains for Canada in the field of nontariff barriers might more than offset any reductions in trade balance from tariff liberalization.[52]

For Japan, the more liberal tariff-cutting formulas are generally the higher ranked on both trade effect criteria, and the relationship is especially close under the trade balance criterion. Full U.S. tariff-cutting authority ranks second under both measures. The trade balance criterion shows complete elimination of tariffs (formula 4) as highest ranked.

---

51. The Economic Council of Canada has recently published a study emphasizing this benefit of trade liberalization for Canada. The study states that it would require very deep tariff cuts, ideally an elimination of tariffs, to accomplish the required stimulus to industry, and accordingly it rejects the more gradual tariff-cutting approaches. The study also points out that adjustment to liberalization would not be difficult, for two reasons. First, much of the change in trade would occur in "intra-industry" trade specialization, in which firms would drop some products and lengthen production runs for others, but entire firms and industries would be unlikely to drop out of production (in contrast to possible results of interindustry specialization). Second, detailed industry studies of the early 1960s and more recently suggest that there are many industrial sectors in which Canadian firms have a favorable competitive position relative to firms located in the United States for sales to the North American market. See Economic Council of Canada, *Looking Outward: A New Trade Strategy for Canada* (Ottawa: Information Canada, 1975), pp. 62–83.

52. In this regard, one reason Canadian negotiators appear strongly committed to the complete elimination of tariffs of 5 percent and below is that they consider a zero tariff to be qualitatively different from a "low" tariff in that the complete absence of a tariff may represent a firmer commitment to nonprotectionist policy in the product sector in question.

When the relative percentage trade change criterion is used, the structural characteristics of the sector harmonization formula (number 10) give it the highest rank. The lowest rankings under both criteria are for the most restrictive formulas—formula 2 (three-iteration harmonization) and formula 6 (60 percent cut with 3 percent tariff shelf added). The three-iteration proposal ranks lowest of all, for two reasons. First, it creates little trade, limiting the scope for trade balance increase. Second, the harmonization aspects of the formula appear to have a strong effect on the relatively high Japanese tariff structure (see appendix A on average-depth-of-tariff cuts).

In the light of these results for Japan, the Japanese proposal submitted in October 1976, which was discussed above, is paradoxical. That proposal most closely resembles the restrictive formula 6, among the formulas examined here. Yet, that formula ranks next to last for Japan on criteria of trade effects (table 3-9). The formula also ranks very low on welfare grounds for Japan (table 3-8) because it is restrictive. It appears, then, that Japanese policy on the tariff negotiations is determined on the basis of either analytical work greatly different from that of this study, or else qualitative political considerations favoring restriction.

Finally, the case of the EEC is unambiguous. Its most favorable formula under both trade effect criteria is the tariff cut most similar to its own proposal, formula 2. Under this formula, the EEC experiences almost a zero trade balance change. Other formulas show larger trade balance reductions. The essential advantage of the formula is that the bulk of EEC tariffs lie in a range (5 percent to 10 percent) in which the formula does little cutting.

Two separate features of formula 2 give it the preferred ranking for the EEC (on trade effect grounds, though not on welfare grounds): its harmonization nature and its restrictiveness. Harmonization favors the moderate and uniform EEC tariff structure; restrictiveness limits the magnitude of trade balance reductions. To obtain a clearer picture of the role of harmonization itself, it is useful to compare results for the EEC under the harmonization formula 5 (cut equals 30 percent plus tariff) and linear formula 7 (43.4 percent cut), both of which have approximately the same average depth of tariff cut for the EEC (see appendix A, table A-2). Of these two formulas the harmonization cut is preferable for the EEC, and the difference is especially marked when using the criterion of relative percentage change in trade.

The position of the EEC on the issue of harmonization itself, as opposed to the degree of liberalization, is crucial to the outcome of the negotiations. To the extent that the EEC opposes deep tariff cuts in principle —because, for example, the result would be a serious weakening in the "cement" in the wall around the community—the prospects for substantial tariff liberalization are bleak. With tariffs already relatively low, however, it is doubtful that a cut in tariffs from, say, 10 percent to 7 percent would be much different from a cut to 4 percent in terms of preserving the symbolic function of the common external tariff. If, instead, the EEC position is that harmonization is desirable and that deep liberalization is also desirable, or at least acceptable, then prospects for major liberalization are much brighter, because there do exist harmonization formulas that achieve deep liberalization. Of the formulas considered in this study, formulas 5, 11, and 12 are all harmonization tariff cuts that achieve much greater liberalization than the three-iteration variant closest to the EEC proposal (formula 2).

Analysis of Sensitivity

Before turning to the question of overall reciprocity and the best formula for all participants considered jointly, it is important to examine the degree of sensitivity of our results to the particular elasticity estimates used. At the broadest policy level, our results indicate that the welfare gains of trade liberalization may be achieved with very little difficulty of adjustment from the standpoint of declines in trade balance for individual negotiating countries. At this level, our results are supported by those found by Baldwin and by Deardorff, Stern, and Baum.[53] These two independent studies of the Tokyo Round of trade negotiations apply methodologies and elasticities different from ours (see appendix F); nevertheless, they reach the same important policy conclusion as we do concerning the absence of any major trade balance deficits resulting from liberalization.

53. Robert E. Baldwin, "Trade and Employment Effects in the United States of Multilateral Tariff Restrictions" (Washington, D.C., 1975; processed); and Alan V. Deardorff, Robert M. Stern, and Christopher F. Baum, "A Multi-Country Simulation of the Employment and Exchange-Rate Effects of Post-Kennedy Round Tariff Reductions" (University of Michigan, June 1976; processed).

The estimates of trade effects of tariff liberalization reported above provide detail on broad patterns as well as on the effects of individual tariff formulas for the negotiating countries. In order to determine whether these results are sensitive to the elasticities used, we have conducted two basic sensitivity analyses. The first recalculates our results by adjusting for alternative sets of elasticities. The second explores a wide variety of results stemming from different combinations of "high" elasticities for some participating countries and "low" elasticities for others.

The first sensitivity exercise applies the "best" estimates of elasticities in the survey by Robert Stern discussed in chapter 2.[54] For the four major importing areas—the United States, Canada, Japan, and the EEC—we recompute all import (and therefore export) effects using these "Stern" elasticities. This test also includes a case in which we assume that import elasticities are *identical* for all four areas, set equal to a single elasticity of -2.0 for all products for the four major importing areas. Within each of these two cases, we apply two alternative assumptions about the elasticity of substitution (σ), relevant for the EEC substitution effect. One assumption is that the substitution elasticity is 2.5, as in our central estimates. The other assumption is that the substitution elasticity is only 1.5, lying within the range of some of the lower estimates discussed in chapter 2, especially those by Bert G. Hickman and Lawrence J. Lau.

The methodology for this first sensitivity test is as follows. For each country, we compute a single, weighted, aggregate import elasticity based on the Stern estimates. For this purpose we apply the BTN-SITC correspondence shown in appendix B (because Stern's estimates are for broad SITC categories, whereas our trade data are classified by BTN categories), weighted by the fraction of dutiable imports within each category for the country in question (according to the GATT data base). Table 3-10 reports the resulting aggregate import elasticities based on Stern's "best" elasticities and compares them with the aggregate weighted elasticities of our own study. The weighted elasticities exclude the textile and petroleum sectors, because we intend to apply them to estimates of trade changes excluding these sectors.

It is clear from table 3-10 that the weighted-average Stern elasticities are very close to those used in this study. This result is to be expected for

54. Robert M. Stern, with the assistance of Jonathan H. Francis and Bruce Schumacher, "Price Elasticities in International Trade: A Compilation and Annotated Bibliography of Recent Research" (University of Michigan, 1975; processed).

Table 3-10. *Alternative Aggregate Import Elasticities, Weighted by Sectoral Dutiable Imports*
Excluding textiles and petroleum

Country	Stern	This study
United States	1.60	1.80
Canada	1.88	1.92
Japan	1.16	1.38
EEC[a]		
Simple	1.36	0.91
Composite ($\sigma = 2.5$)	2.58	2.13
Composite ($\sigma = 1.5$)	2.09	1.64

Sources: For the Stern elasticities, see Robert M. Stern, with the assistance of Jonathan H. Francis and Bruce Schumacher, "Price Elasticities in International Trade: A Compilation and Annotated Bibliography of Recent Research" (University of Michigan, 1975; processed). For the elasticities used in this study, see chapter 2.
a. See the text for an explanation of "simple" and "composite."

Canada, because the Stern survey relies heavily on the Taplin estimates for Canada, also our source. The similarity is more impressive for the United States, however, considering that we incorporate estimates by Clopper Almon, Jr., and others that are not reviewed by Stern. The similarity is even more striking for Japan, for which we have prepared totally new estimates. In short, for all three countries our elasticity estimates when aggregated are very close to the central range derived from the extensive body of empirical estimates surveyed by Stern.

The elasticities shown in table 3-10 for the EEC include (a) the "simple" import elasticity for imports from all sources, and (b) the "composite" import elasticity for imports from nonbloc suppliers. The composite elasticity (for which two alternative values are given, depending on the substitution elasticity assumed) incorporates the combined influence of total trade creation and trade substitution in evaluating the responsiveness of imports from outsiders when tariffs decline (as discussed in chapter 2). For the EEC, the Stern estimate of the simple import elasticity is almost 50 percent higher than our estimate.[55]

An alternative set of elasticity assumptions is that all import elasticities are equal across countries and commodities. In the absence of any empirical estimates whatsoever (or in case one completely distrusted such

55. The corresponding "Stern" composite elasticities are not supplied by Stern but are calculated in this study by the formula $\rho = \eta + \phi_B \sigma$, where ρ is the composite elasticity, η is the simple elasticity, σ is the substitution elasticity, and ϕ_B is the weighted share of bloc suppliers in imports.

estimates), equal import elasticities might be a meaningful working hypothesis.[56] For the equal elasticity case, we have chosen a value of -2.0. In this case, we define the composite EEC import elasticity as equal to -2.0, following the reasoning suggested in chapter 2, whereby we identify the composite EEC external elasticity, rather than the simple import elasticity, as the appropriate counterpart of the import elasticity for, say, the United States.

Given the alternative estimates of weighted aggregate elasticities, we multiply the appropriate trade effect estimates of our basic results by the relevant ratios of the "sensitivity" elasticity to our original elasticity, in order to compute results for trade effects under the alternative elasticity set. For example, estimated U.S. import increases from each supplier are reduced by the ratio 1.6/1.8 (see table 3-10). In the case of the EEC, the adjustment factor depends on whether the supplier is a bloc or a non-bloc supplier.[57]

Table 3-11 shows the results of the first sensitivity exercise, for each of the twelve tariff-cutting formulas. These results refer to direct export and import effects only (that is, excluding exports due to the responding effect). For comparison, the table also shows our basic estimate of trade effects.

The results of the four sensitivity tests shown in table 3-11 indicate almost no significant changes in policy implications from our basic estimates. Total trade creation for the four main areas varies little, ranging from a decline of 6 percent to an increase of 10 percent compared with our base estimates. There are few changes in relative attractiveness of

56. Although one could also argue that a priori elasticities should be inversely related to the shares of trade in GNP, because with smaller trade shares a given import change as a fraction of demand would represent a larger percentage increase in imports.

57. More completely, consider a matrix of trade changes such as table 3-4. For the United States, Canada, and Japan each column entry is multiplied by the ratio η^s/η^o, where η^s is the Stern elasticity and η^o is our original aggregate elasticity. For the column pertaining to the EEC, all entries for nonbloc suppliers (that is, nonbloc rows) are multiplied by the ratio ρ^s/ρ^o, where ρ^s is the Stern composite elasticity and ρ^o is our original composite elasticity. The entries in the EEC column referring to bloc suppliers (both EEC and EFTA) are all multiplied by the ratio σ^s/σ^o, where σ^s is the "sensitivity" value of the substitution elasticity (2.5 or 1.5) and σ^o is our original value (2.5). All other elements in the trade change matrix—increased imports by countries other than the four main participants—remain unchanged, because the sensitivity analysis varies the elasticities for only the four main areas.

each tariff formula for each country on the basis of trade effects.[58] As for the broad pattern of trade balance changes, our base estimates showed general increases from liberalization for the United States and Japan, and decreases for Canada and the EEC. The Stern elasticities make this pattern even more pronounced, while the "equal elasticity" case substantially moderates it. (For a full assessment of the trade balance effect it would be necessary to add in extra exports from the responding effect.) The reasons for this result are the following: first, the main surplus country is Japan, and Stern's import elasticity for Japan is even lower than ours, whereas it requires almost a 50 percent increase in the Japanese elasticity to raise it to the "equal elasticity" of 2.0 (thereby greatly increasing Japanese imports); and, second, the Stern-based estimates aggravate the EEC deficits (because they involve higher EEC simple and composite import elasticities), while the equal elasticity case moderates the EEC deficit by reducing the composite import elasticity.

Although greater detail by country and by tariff formula is available from table 3-11, the salient findings for our purposes are that these sensitivity tests suggest that our basic estimates are robust. All of the sensitivity tests show patterns by tariff formula similar to our basic results. Furthermore, insofar as broad country results are concerned, the two alternative sensitivity tests yield results lying on either side of our basic results (that is, the Stern case increases the sizes of surpluses for the United States and Japan and of deficits for Canada and the EEC, while the equal elasticity case reduces these sizes). This suggests that our estimates represent a central set of estimates rather than results with pronounced bias in one direction or another.

In addition to the above tests, we have conducted a second type of

58. This conclusion holds even in the case most likely to reverse the relative attractiveness of formulas, that of Japan when using equal import elasticities of 2.0 for all areas and products. This variant raises Japan's import effect by approximately one-half, in comparison with our base estimates. One might expect that in this variant, formulas giving freer trade would have lower rankings than in our basic case for Japan. In fact, although complete elimination of tariffs (formula 4) no longer ranks high on trade balance grounds in this variant, the most liberal practical formula (full U.S. authority, formula 8) is the most favorable among the various formulas. Moreover, the EEC-type formula (number 2) and the formula closest to Japan's own proposal (number 6) continue to rank very low on grounds of trade balance effects even in this sensitivity case with a much higher average import elasticity for Japan than those based on empirical estimates.

Table 3-11. Results of Sensitivity Analysis: Trade Effects for Four Major Negotiating Areas, Excluding Respending Effect, 1974 Base

Millions of dollars

	Basic estimates		Sensitivity cases							
			Stern elasticities				Elasticities = 2.0[b]			
			σ = 2.5		σ = 1.5		σ = 2.5		σ = 1.5	
Area and formula[a]	Export increase	Import increase	Export increase	Import increase	Export increase	Import increase	Export increase	Import increase	Export increase	Import increase
United States										
1	3,821	3,611	4,102	3,206	3,678	3,206	4,018	4,011	4,018	4,011
2	1,875	1,924	1,990	1,708	1,804	1,708	1,981	2,138	1,981	2,138
3	3,460	3,773	3,725	3,351	3,333	3,351	3,626	4,192	3,626	4,192
4	6,321	6,018	6,779	5,344	6,083	5,344	6,652	6,686	6,652	6,686
5	2,756	2,820	2,946	2,504	2,654	2,504	2,902	3,133	2,902	3,133
6	1,966	1,639	2,082	1,455	1,890	1,455	2,084	1,821	2,084	1,821
7	2,811	2,648	3,019	2,351	2,706	2,351	2,955	2,942	2,955	2,942
8	4,019	4,130	4,322	3,668	3,870	3,668	4,218	4,589	4,218	4,589
9	2,941	2,225	3,125	1,976	2,826	1,976	3,115	2,472	3,115	2,472
10	2,514	1,736	2,670	1,542	2,421	1,542	2,652	1,929	2,652	1,929
11	3,294	2,858	3,521	2,538	3,169	2,538	3,474	3,175	3,474	3,175
12	2,732	2,391	2,909	2,124	2,628	2,124	2,887	2,657	2,887	2,657
Canada										
1	565	1,680	563	1,648	520	1,648	614	1,751	614	1,751
2	249	922	247	904	229	904	271	961	271	961
3	603	1,431	594	1,404	553	1,404	659	1,491	659	1,491
4	936	2,801	932	2,747	861	2,747	1,018	2,918	1,018	2,918
5	400	1,255	397	1,231	368	1,231	436	1,308	436	1,308
6	221	1,023	224	1,003	205	1,003	241	1,066	241	1,066
7	415	1,232	414	1,209	382	1,209	451	1,284	451	1,284
8	664	1,705	656	1,673	609	1,673	724	1,777	724	1,777

9	326	1,500	332	1,472	302	1,472	353	1,563	353	1,563
10	313	1,314	319	1,289	291	1,289	333	1,370	333	1,370
11	436	1,561	437	1,531	402	1,531	474	1,627	474	1,627
12	349	1,342	349	1,316	321	1,316	380	1,398	380	1,398
Japan										
1	2,237	1,736	2,290	1,459	2,115	1,459	2,305	2,516	2,305	2,516
2	1,157	1,067	1,179	896	1,100	896	1,191	1,546	1,191	1,546
3	2,176	1,683	2,195	1,414	2,045	1,414	2,259	2,439	2,259	2,439
4	3,709	2,894	3,792	2,431	3,506	2,431	3,823	4,194	3,823	4,194
5	1,687	1,424	1,718	1,196	1,598	1,196	1,739	2,063	1,739	2,063
6	1,106	994	1,144	835	1,056	835	1,129	1,440	1,129	1,440
7	1,644	1,273	1,683	1,070	1,555	1,070	1,694	1,845	1,694	1,845
8	2,458	1,834	2,492	1,540	2,315	1,540	2,546	2,657	2,546	2,657
9	1,586	1,385	1,654	1,164	1,515	1,164	1,615	2,007	1,615	2,007
10	1,318	927	1,376	778	1,264	778	1,340	1,343	1,340	1,343
11	1,866	1,521	1,922	1,277	1,772	1,277	1,915	2,203	1,915	2,203
12	1,556	1,312	1,600	1,102	1,479	1,102	1,596	1,902	1,596	1,902
EEC (external trade)										
1	2,293	4,495	2,073	5,521	2,073	4,538	2,606	4,207	2,606	4,327
2	1,575	2,130	1,436	2,608	1,436	2,136	1,761	1,996	1,761	2,038
3	2,244	4,105	2,021	5,044	2,021	4,147	2,545	3,842	2,545	3,954
4	3,827	7,376	3,460	9,059	3,460	7,446	4,348	6,904	4,348	7,100
5	2,046	3,201	1,849	3,927	1,849	3,223	2,292	2,998	2,292	3,074
6	1,370	2,215	1,252	2,713	1,252	2,222	1,541	2,076	1,541	2,120
7	1,681	3,318	1,519	4,076	1,519	3,350	1,910	3,106	1,910	3,195
8	2,466	4,746	2,223	5,832	2,223	4,795	2,802	4,442	2,802	4,572
9	1,768	3,339	1,612	4,094	1,612	3,358	2,002	3,128	2,002	3,203
10	1,540	2,214	1,406	2,736	1,406	2,264	1,736	2,068	1,736	2,157
11	1,985	3,793	1,808	4,663	1,808	3,828	2,257	3,558	2,257	3,651
12	1,775	3,125	1,615	3,731	1,615	3,142	2,003	2,927	2,003	2,997

a. For a description of the formulas, see table 3-1.
b. Note that for the United States, Canada, and Japan, where the elasticities = 2.0, the increases are the same for both $\sigma = 2.5$ and $\sigma = 1.5$. The reason is that in this variant the EEC composite elasticity, ρ, remains constant at 2.0, regardless of the substitution elasticity, σ.

sensitivity experiment. In the second exercise, we have varied all elasticities by plus and minus 50 percent for each of the four major areas. We have then examined the resulting combinations of high elasticities for some countries and low elasticities for others. When the original estimates are included, there is a total of eighty-one possible combinations of this sort.[59]

In statistical terms, a band of 50 percent around a statistically significant parameter (with a ratio of standard deviation to parameter estimate of one-half or less) should include the true parameter value with a probability of at least 68 percent, for a normally distributed random variable.

The results of this second sensitivity exercise confirm the base estimates as most likely central values (as expected, given the construction of the test—using base elasticities flanked by higher and lower values). However, the results indicate that there could be a considerable range of uncertainty in the trade balance estimates. For example, under a 60 percent tariff cut, out of the eighty-one cases explored the trade balance effect for the EEC turns positive (rather than negative as in the base case) one-third of the time; similarly, in 47 percent of the cases the trade balance effect could be negative for the United States rather than positive as in our central estimate. Both statements refer to effects including "respending exports."

Overall, the two sensitivity exercises provide a considerable degree of assurance that our base results represent reliable central estimates of the trade results of tariff liberalization. The second set of tests does indicate, however, that a relatively wide range of conclusions may be drawn if one is prepared to assert that elasticities of one set of countries should be set at an upper extreme and that those of the other countries should be set at lower extremes.

Overall Reciprocity

To return to our basic estimates, by using the formula rankings based on static welfare effects (table 3-8) and trade effects (table 3-9), it is possible to examine the overall reciprocity and desirability of tariff formulas for the major negotiating areas considered jointly. Under the concept of reciprocity, all parties should be relatively pleased with the outcome of

59. That is, with three alternative elasticity sets (original, high, and low) for each of four importing areas, there is a total of $3^4 = 81$ possible combinations.

the negotiations, even if this condition means that no party manages to achieve the adoption of its own favorite option. In order to examine the overall reciprocity of the alternative formulas, we apply weights for each of the four major parties in the negotiations to their individual rankings of formulas to obtain overall weighted-average rankings of the formulas.

The concept of weighted voting is firmly established in international economic endeavors, such as the International Monetary Fund. Voting shares in such groups typically correspond approximately to the economic size of individual members. The logic behind this type of weighting is that a neutral, mutual economic cooperation involves the distribution of both economic burdens and benefits in proportion to what each participant has at stake in economic terms. In the case of tariff negotiations, the most appropriate basis for assigning voting weights would be the value of each country's dutiable imports. That is, in a negotiation on tariffs the value of what each participant has to "offer" the others will depend on the size of the country's dutiable import base. A country with large but duty-free imports would be making no new contribution to liberalization and therefore could not expect to have a large voice in the liberalization to be undertaken by the other parties.[60]

The weights applied to each area's preferences are based on the value of dutiable imports in 1971, calculated from the GATT trade and tariff data base. These weights give somewhat higher weight to the United States (45 percent) than to the EEC (33 percent), and lower but approximately equal weights to Canada (9.7 percent) and Japan (11.5 percent).[61] Table 3-12 presents the weighted-average rankings of formulas based on these weights. The table excludes the formula completely eliminating tariffs (formula 4), adjusting rankings accordingly.

Table 3-12 presents two separate weighted-average rankings. The first set of rankings is for trade effects and represents the combined rankings based on the two alternative criteria (trade balance and relative percentage export and import increase). The second set of rankings is for welfare effects. Finally, the table reports the combined effect of the two

60. There does exist the principle in GATT negotiations that credit is given for the continuation of low or zero tariffs. Implicitly, we are assuming that any such credit is distributed across participants in the same proportion as the distribution of their dutiable imports.

61. The exclusion of intra-EEC trade, industrial imports from EFTA, and agricultural trade entering under nontariff barriers accounts for the fact that the weight for the EEC is lower than might be expected on the basis of total import figures.

Table 3-12. *Consolidated Rankings of Alternative Tariff-Cutting Formulas, 1974 Base*
Excluding textiles and petroleum

For-mula[a]	Trade effect rankings[b]						Welfare rankings						Sum of rankings	
	United States	Canada	Japan	EEC	Four areas[c]		United States	Canada	Japan	EEC	Four areas[c]			
					Weighted average	Rank					Weighted average	Rank	Weighted average	Rank
1	6	7	2	11	7.3	9	3	2	4	2	2.7	2	10.0	3
2	9	2.5	11	1	5.9	5	8	11	8	10	9.0	9	14.9	10
3	11	1	4	6.5	7.7	11	5	6	1	4	4.3	5	12.0	7
5	9	5	7	3	6.4	7	2	7	2	6	3.8	4	10.2	4
6	4.5	6	10	2	4.4	2	11	10	9	9	10.0	10	14.4	9
7	7	2.5	4	9	6.9	8	9	9	10	8	8.8	8	15.7	11
8	9	4	1	9	7.6	10	1	1	3	1	1.2	1	8.8	1
9	1.5	11	9	6.5	5.0	3	7	4	6	5	5.9	6	10.9	5
10	1.5	9.5	4	4	3.4	1	10	8	11	11	10.3	11	13.7	8
11	3	9.5	6	9	6.0	6	4	3	5	3	3.7	3	9.7	2
12	4.5	8	8	5	5.4	4	6	5	7	7	6.4	7	11.8	6

a. For a description of the formulas, see table 3-1. Original formula 4 (100 percent tariff cut) is omitted; rankings are adjusted accordingly.
b. Trade effect rankings are based on case including exports due to rest of world responding.
c. Applies the following weights to country rankings: United States, 0.454; Canada, 0.097; Japan, 0.115; EEC, 0.334.

sets, weighting trade effects and welfare effects equally, as discussed below.

If trade balance effect alone is the criterion for choosing the most preferred formula, the favored result is the sector harmonization formula (number 10).[62] The "second choice" is formula 6. Both have high rankings because they create little trade, therefore limiting the size of negative trade balances which can be generated for all parties.

The three-iteration formula (number 2) ranks at an intermediate level. It is low in the rankings of the United States and Japan, but it is ranked first by the EEC and between second and third by Canada. The most liberalizing formula (number 8, full U.S. authority) ranks low (tenth). The reason for this is that only Japan gives a high ranking to a high degree of liberalization per se on the trade effect basis (because the greatest liberalization maximizes the size of the trade balance increase for Japan).

The consolidated average rankings based on welfare effects are very different. They follow a strict ordering according to the degree of overall liberalization provided by each formula, and most of the individual country rankings are consistent with the consolidated rankings.

In principle, it should be possible to weight the two sets of rankings to obtain an overall ranking that takes account of both the trade effect and the welfare effect. However, there is no theoretical basis on which to obtain the relevant weights of the two approaches. In practice, policymakers consider effects on the trade balance and on exports, relative to imports, to be important, but the standard body of economic theory contains no easily applicable formulation for computing a "welfare impact" of trade balance changes. If such measures existed (for example, based on a "shadow price" of foreign exchange above the market rate for countries

62. To some extent, this weighted-average preference is biased by the fact that in the identification of the "lowest tariff" for each category only the tariffs of the four major importing areas were considered. If other countries had been considered as well, the harmonization formula would have called for deeper reductions in tariffs for those sectors in which those other countries had lower tariffs than the four largest importing areas. Accordingly, the sector harmonization approach would then have tended to show larger trade balance reductions for at least some of the four major negotiating partners. The bias in the preference ranking for formula 10 becomes more apparent when its results are considered for some of the countries other than the four main importing areas. Thus, an examination of trade change tables similar to tables 3-4 and 3-5 for all formulas indicates that under the trade balance criterion Australia and New Zealand both would rank formula 10 as the least favorable formula considered (excluding the 100 percent tariff cut formula).

in deficit and below it for countries in surplus), then it would be possible to add up the welfare impact of the trade balance effect and that of the traditional welfare effect to determine an overall measure of welfare—and, thus, a unique ranking of formulas for each country.[63] Any welfare costs associated with labor adjustment difficulties could be taken into account as well in this ideal comparison.

In the absence of a more rigorous basis for weighting traditional welfare effects and the trade balance effect, it is informative to weight them equally in order to obtain an overall weighted ranking of formulas. This combination of the two criteria may be done by adding the weighted average rankings of a given formula under the two approaches. The result of this procedure is shown in table 3-12 in the final column.

In the overall consolidated rankings including both trade balance and welfare effects, it is the welfare rankings that dominate, because they tend to be unanimous among the parties, while the trade balance rankings diverge. As a result, the most favored formula is the most liberalizing: formula 8 (full authority under U.S. law; a 60 percent cut in tariffs and elimination of tariffs under 5 percent). However, perhaps the most interesting result in the set of consolidated rankings is the case of formula 11, a harmonization formula with tariff cut equal to 20 percent plus three times the tariff, with a 60 percent maximum cut. This formula ranks second on the consolidated basis, third on the welfare basis, and fifth on the trade balance basis. If negotiators give a somewhat heavier weight to trade balance effects than to welfare effects of liberalization, then this formula could well be a desirable compromise with favorable performance on both counts.[64]

The harmonization formula number 11 has another strong point in its favor: in the critical range in which most tariffs lie (say, 5 percent to 12 percent), the formula follows a path that is intermediate between a linear 60 percent cut, on the one hand, and the three-iteration harmoniza-

---

63. See C. Fred Bergsten and William R. Cline, "Increasing International Economic Interdependence: The Implications for Research," *American Economic Review,* vol. 66 (May 1976), pp. 155–61.

64. An indication of the basic reasons for the high overall ranking of formula 11 may be seen by examining table 3-2. The formula is quite liberalizing, as may be seen in the figure for increased imports under the formula. At the same time, its harmonization feature gives it a high ratio of welfare gain to trade change, as may be seen by comparing the formula with the 60 percent linear cut, which has a welfare effect that is practically identical even though its import effect is approximately 17 percent higher than that for formula 11.

tion formula, on the other hand. Therefore, the formula represents a compromise between the positions of the two major participants in the negotiations, the United States and the EEC, respectively.[65] This fact should enhance the political practicality of this particular formula.

The compromise solution more likely to emerge from the negotiations is the Swiss formula, as discussed above. The Swiss proposal is almost identical to our formula number 12. As shown in table 3-12, that formula ranks sixth among those we have examined in terms of overall reciprocity. Compared with our own second-ranked formula (number 11), the Swiss formula achieves a less favorable ranking on welfare criteria but a more favorable ranking under criteria of trade effects (because, being somewhat more restrictive, it reduces the sizes of possible trade deficits).

In sum, the principle of reciprocity suggests two formulas as the most desirable, considering a "balanced" result of the negotiations for all four major participants: first, full U.S. authority (60 percent cut, with elimination of tariffs below 5 percent); second, a harmonization formula, of the particular form in which tariff cut equals 20 percent plus three times the tariff (with a maximum cut of 60 percent). Although individual countries would tend to achieve more favorable results under alternative formulas considered (especially if judged on the trade effects criteria), these formulas, in this order, achieve the greatest degree of overall reciprocity for the major participants, taking into account the two objectives of joint welfare gains and relative balance in trade effects for each country. The Swiss formula, a likely compromise solution, is less successful in achieving overall reciprocity, because it is somewhat more restrictive. The Swiss formula does achieve a greater degree of overall reciprocity than the EEC, Canadian, and Japanese approaches, however (formula 12 compared with formulas 2, 3, and 6 in table 3-12).

Exchange Rate Impact

The estimates of trade balance effects of tariff liberalization may be translated into corresponding estimates in exchange rate changes, follow-

65. As noted above, the formula tabled by the United States in March 1976 is close to a 60 percent linear cut, even though at low tariffs the cut can fall to only 50 percent. Similarly, the formal EEC proposal in July 1976 called for four iterations of tariff cut equal to tariff, but that proposal differs little from the three-iteration variant examined here.

Table 3-13. *Changes in Exchange Rates Required to Offset Trade Balance Effects of a 60 Percent Tariff Cut*
Excluding textiles and petroleum

Country	Trade balance effect (millions of dollars) (1)	Base level, imports (billions of dollars) (2)	Base level, exports (billions of dollars) (3)	Import elasticity (4)	Export elasticity (5)	Trade-weighted exchange rate change (percent) (6)	Nominal exchange rate change (percent) (7)
United States	632	108.0	98.5	-1.82	-2.0	0.16	-0.28
Canada	-1,065	34.6	34.2	-1.94	-2.0	-0.79	-1.13
Japan	827	62.1	55.6	-1.39	-2.0	0.42	0.16
EEC[a]	-1,320	151.0	133.9	-2.17	-2.0	-0.22	-0.79
Austria	16	9.0	7.2	-0.65	-2.0	0.08	-0.64
Finland	-49	6.8	5.5	-0.61	-2.0	-0.32	-1.08
Norway	-41	8.4	6.3	-1.72	-2.0	-0.15	-0.89
Sweden	-75	15.8	15.9	-1.50	-2.0	-0.14	-0.90
Switzerland	93	14.4	11.9	-0.69	-2.0	0.28	-0.44
Australia	-275	12.4	11.0	-1.24	-2.0	-0.73	-1.17
New Zealand	-175	3.7	2.4	-1.23	-2.0	-1.87	-2.48

Sources: Column 1: tables 3-4, 3-6, 3-7. Columns 2 and 3: International Monetary Fund, *International Financial Statistics*, vol. 29 (February 1976), pp. 38–39; and OECD, *Trade by Commodities: Country Summaries*, series B (1974). Column 4: tables 2-3 and 2-4. Column 5: assumed values. Columns 6 and 7: calculated from columns 1 through 5; trade shares used in the calculation of column 7 are based on OECD, *Trade by Commodities: Country Summaries*, Series B.
a. EEC entries refer to trade external to the EEC.

ing the method set forth in chapter 2. In order to consider the magnitude of exchange rate changes necessary to offset initial trade balance changes, we examine the case of a 60 percent tariff cut. Table 3-13 sets forth the elements of this calculation and the corresponding estimates of exchange rate changes. As shown in the table, the calculations apply the estimated aggregate import elasticities reported in chapter 2; and, in the absence of corresponding export demand elasticities, it is assumed that this elasticity is −2.0 for each country or area.[66]

It is obvious from table 3-13 that any exchange rate changes associated with a 60 percent tariff cut would be inconsequential. This result corresponds to the finding that the initial trade balance changes from liberalization would be of negligible size relative to trade volumes. Even for the countries with the largest exchange rate changes (New Zealand, with a depreciation of 1.87 percent in the trade-weighted exchange rate; Australia, with a depreciation of 0.73 percent; and Canada, with a depreciation of 0.79 percent), the changes would be small, and even these changes would be gradually phased in over the five years or more required for implementation of tariff cuts.

The final column of table 3-13 indicates the change in the nominal exchange rate with respect to a constant outside standard. This change is less meaningful than the change in the trade-weighted exchange rate. The nominal changes are all somewhat larger depreciations (or smaller appreciations) than the trade-weighted changes. The reason for this result is that as a group the eleven negotiating areas would need to depreciate slightly with respect to the rest of the world, in order to offset the trade balance leakage to nonparticipants in the negotiations. Under the 60 percent tariff cut, for example, out of a total increase in imports by the eleven areas of $12.6 billion—including $4.5 billion increased EEC imports from non-EEC countries—nonparticipant rest-of-world countries would supply $3.3 billion. However, induced exports to these nonparticipants through the respending effect would amount to only $1.9 billion. This would leave a trade deficit of $1.4 billion to be corrected by depre-

66. This value would be consistent with the finding by H. S. Houthakker and Stephen P. Magee that for the United States, and for all other industrial countries on the average, the export elasticity is somewhat larger than the import elasticity. H. S. Houthakker and Stephen P. Magee, "Income and Price Elasticities in World Trade," *Review of Economics and Statistics,* vol. 51 (May 1969), p. 114. We do not apply the Houthakker-Magee estimates themselves because for import elasticities the estimates presented in chapter 2 of this study should be more reliable.

ciation of the participants as a group with respect to nonparticipants. To achieve a given trade-weighted depreciation, a country would have to depreciate its nominal exchange rate (stated in terms of an outside standard) by a still greater amount because most of its trading partners would also be depreciating. However, even the nominal exchange rate changes listed in the table are extremely small, and they have little meaning in economic terms because it is the trade-weighted exchange rate changes that affect the real cost of imports.[67]

As may be seen in table 3-7, the trade balance effects for the full U.S. authority tariff cut would differ little from those for a 60 percent tariff cut, so that even under the most liberalizing formula exchange rate changes would be practically imperceptible. We may therefore proceed to the analysis of employment and sectoral effects without going into a detailed examination of exchange rate results by formula.

Estimates of Employment Effects

Table 3-14 reports the estimates of the aggregate changes in 1974 employment calculated for each of the twelve alternative tariff-cutting formulas. The detailed calculations underlying these results are based on employment effects estimated at the four-digit BTN level for the base year 1971, with total export and import labor effects expanded from 1971 to 1974 by aggregate expansion factors for the physical volume of exports and imports, respectively.[68] The estimates are available only for the United States, Canada, Japan, and the EEC; and the calculations for the EEC omit the "indirect" effect on employment in intermediate products, because of the absence of data on "job coefficients" for these intermediate effects in the EEC. All of the estimates understate the gains in new export jobs, because they exclude employment associated with extra exports resulting from the respending effect. Because the increased exports attributable to respending are estimated at the aggregate level, employment cal-

67. Furthermore, the general depreciation reflected in the nominal exchange rate changes probably overstates any depreciation that in fact would be required. This is because the estimated respending by nonparticipant countries is understated by failing to capture that portion of nonparticipants' increased export earnings that they would spend on each others' goods in the first round but on goods from the participating countries in subsequent spending rounds.

68. See chapter 2 for a discussion of our procedure for updating estimates of employment effects.

Table 3-14. *Changes in Employment from Tariff Liberalization for Four Major Importing Areas, Excluding Responding Effect, 1974 Base*
Thousands of jobs; excluding petroleum and textiles

Area and formula[a]	Job loss from increased imports		Job gain from increased exports		Net balance (gain minus loss)	
	Direct	Total	Direct	Total	Direct	Total
United States						
1	65.2	140.7	84.0	169.6	18.8	28.9
2	29.8	67.5	40.3	81.6	10.5	14.1
3	66.6	146.2	76.4	154.2	9.8	8.0
4	108.7	234.4	139.0	280.6	30.3	46.2
5	46.8	103.8	60.1	121.5	13.3	17.7
6	27.2	59.6	41.8	85.1	14.6	25.5
7	47.8	103.1	61.8	124.8	14.0	21.7
8	74.4	161.7	88.7	179.0	14.3	17.3
9	39.3	84.1	62.6	127.4	23.3	43.3
10	26.5	58.6	52.9	108.4	26.4	49.8
11	51.1	109.9	71.5	144.8	20.4	34.9
12	41.7	90.2	59.1	119.8	17.4	29.6
Canada						
1	37.4	76.2	11.7	25.6	−25.7	−50.6
2	20.7	42.2	4.8	10.8	−15.9	−31.4
3	31.6	64.7	12.2	26.9	−19.4	−37.8
4	62.3	127.0	19.4	42.4	−42.9	−84.6
5	28.0	57.2	8.0	17.7	−20.0	−39.5
6	22.8	46.6	4.4	9.8	−18.4	−36.8
7	27.4	55.9	8.6	18.8	−18.8	−37.1
8	37.8	77.1	13.6	29.9	−24.2	−47.2
9	33.2	67.8	6.7	14.7	−26.5	−53.1
10	29.5	59.4	5.6	12.6	−23.9	−46.8
11	34.6	70.7	9.0	19.7	−25.6	−51.0
12	30.1	61.1	7.1	15.7	−23.0	−45.4
Japan						
1	98.4	239.9	101.0	263.8	2.7	23.9
2	57.7	223.9	57.7	142.8	−0.1	−81.2
3	86.6	222.0	95.1	254.4	8.5	32.4
4	163.9	399.9	167.5	437.7	3.6	37.8
5	76.9	200.2	79.3	202.6	2.5	2.4
6	59.1	147.4	56.1	138.0	−3.0	−9.4
7	72.0	174.8	74.2	193.9	2.2	19.1
8	101.1	246.1	108.3	287.9	7.2	41.8
9	82.8	200.4	78.5	193.7	−4.3	−6.7
10	29.6	87.9	61.8	152.1	32.2	64.7
11	88.8	218.7	88.2	224.5	−0.6	5.8
12	79.0	224.3	75.8	190.1	−3.2	−34.2

Table 3-14 (*continued*)

Area and formula[a]	Job loss from increased imports		Job gain from increased exports		Net balance (gain minus loss)	
	Direct	*Total*	*Direct*	*Total*	*Direct*	*Total*
EEC						
1	91.8	n.a.	−20.4	n.a.	−112.2	n.a.
2	44.2	n.a.	4.4	n.a.	−39.8	n.a.
3	83.4	n.a.	−11.5	n.a.	−94.9	n.a.
4	153.1	n.a.	−27.8	n.a.	−180.8	n.a.
5	65.4	n.a.	−2.2	n.a.	−67.6	n.a.
6	46.5	n.a.	−4.8	n.a.	−51.3	n.a.
7	71.8	n.a.	−13.5	n.a.	−85.3	n.a.
8	102.5	n.a.	−13.6	n.a.	−116.1	n.a.
9	75.8	n.a.	−15.2	n.a.	−91.0	n.a.
10	35.8	n.a.	15.0	n.a.	−20.8	n.a.
11	84.5	n.a.	−16.0	n.a.	−100.5	n.a.
12	70.8	n.a.	−9.0	n.a.	−79.8	n.a.

n.a. Not available.
a. For a description of the formulas, see table 3-1.

culations are not possible; the employment estimates require information by detailed four-digit BTN sectors.

The results shown in table 3-14 are for the case excluding textiles, our central case. As shown below in the discussion of sectoral results, the exclusion of textiles makes an extraordinarily large proportionate difference in overall estimates of employment effects of liberalization.

Among the various formulas, the employment results for the four major areas parallel very closely those for trade balance effects (with respect to imports and direct exports, excluding the respending effect). Using the net balance between export jobs gained and import jobs lost, for the United States the most favorable formulas are number 10 (sector harmonization), number 4 (free trade), and number 9 (60 percent cut with 5 percent floor); the least favorable formula is number 3 (Canadian-type). These results resemble those for the rankings based on direct trade balance effects (excluding respending effects; table 3-7) except for the substantially higher ranking of the formula eliminating tariffs.

For Canada, with a systematic loss of jobs regardless of the formula, employment losses are minimized under the formulas that liberalize trade the least (number 2, the EEC iterative proposal, and number 6, the 60 percent cut with a 3 percent add-on). Employment reductions are the largest under the most liberalizing formula (number 4, the elimination of tariffs). Once again, however, for Canada the relative attractiveness of alternative formulas depends on whether an absolute or a relative measure is used. Under a relative measure—that is, the increase in export jobs divided by the decrease in import-competing jobs—liberal tariff-cutting formulas are much more attractive, and the most favorable formula for Canada is its own (formula 3). The next three highest ranked formulas for relative employment effects would be (in order): full U.S. authority (formula 8), 60 percent cut (formula 1), and the elimination of tariffs (formula 4).

For Japan, the employment results imply a conclusion about the most favorable formula that is different from that based on trade effects. The largest net gain in jobs occurs under the sector harmonization formula (number 10), rather than under the most liberalizing formulas (numbers 4 and 8) which, by contrast, maximize direct trade balance gains for Japan (see table 3-7). Moreover, the large net gain is associated with relatively small changes in trade, even though the difference between increased export jobs and decreased import jobs is large. This anomaly appears to stem from the fact that under sector harmonization the other industrial countries would tend to reduce tariffs primarily in labor-intensive industries, whereas Japan would do little reduction of tariffs for labor-intensive sectors. This would cause a sizable gain for Japan's employment in labor-intensive exports but little loss in jobs from extra imports. The most unfavorable formula for Japan, however, is the same on the basis of both employment effects and trade balance effects: the three-iteration harmonization formula (number 2).

The employment estimates for the EEC include effects of changes in trade among partner countries inside the bloc. For this reason, job gains in exports are negative for most formulas, indicating that the increase in exports to outside countries falls short of the reduction in exports to partner countries within the EEC.[69]

69. By contrast, our trade effects for the EEC reported in table 3-7 above refer to changes in external imports and exports of the EEC considered as a bloc. Because intra-EEC import changes must equal intra-EEC export changes, either approach yields the same trade balance effect for the EEC for a given formula, although the focus on external trade alone yields higher absolute figures for increased imports and, correspondingly, for increased exports. Estimates of employment effects associated with external trade effects alone would similarly show higher absolute job losses from increased imports and positive, instead of negative, job gains from extra ex-

For the EEC the results with respect to employment again parallel those for trade balances, in terms of the relative attractiveness of the alternative tariff-cutting formulas. However, the first-ranked formula on the trade balance basis, the EEC's own proposal (formula 2), moves to second place when judged on the basis of employment, exchanging places with the sector harmonization formula (number 10). This result suggests that, like Japan, the EEC tends to have low tariffs already in relatively labor-intensive sectors.

The overall results of the employment estimates resemble those of the trade balance estimates with respect to country rankings of individual tariff-cutting formulas. The only exception is somewhat greater preference for the sector harmonization formula (for Japan and the EEC). Even this difference would, however, tend to be reduced if respending export jobs were included in the employment analysis, because this formula creates little trade overall and therefore generates little respending by free-rider countries.

By far the most important implication of the results in table 3-14, however, is that under all formulas the employment effects are very small indeed.[70] Considering the most liberalizing formula other than free trade —that is, full U.S. tariff-cutting authority, formula 8—the number of jobs lost to increased imports would amount to 0.19 percent of total employment for the United States, 0.87 percent for Canada, and 0.47 percent for Japan. The decrease in direct jobs from import expansion would amount to 0.10 percent of the EEC labor force and, even if indirect jobs raised this amount to a level twice as high, it would still be extremely small.[71] And these percentages overstate by far the dislocation to employment resulting from liberalization, because they do not "net out" export jobs

---

ports. The balance of job gains minus job losses would tend to be the same as shown in table 3-14 if computed solely with respect to external trade, although there would be some difference in the results. Whereas the inclusion of intra-EEC effects changes the import and export estimates by identical amounts and leaves the trade balance unaltered, because export job coefficients may differ from those for imports, the inclusion of job effects of intra-EEC trade changes (as done in table 3-14) should cause differences, probably minor, from estimates based on job effects of external trade changes alone in terms of the final net balance of job changes.

70. Baldwin reaches this same conclusion in "Trade Employment Effects in the United States of Multilateral Tariff Restrictions," p. 45. See appendix F below.

71. Total employment figures are from Organisation for Economic Co-operation and Development, *Labour Force Statistics: 1962–1973* (Paris: OECD, 1975).

gained. If instead the net job balance between export-related and import-related employment changes are considered, then under the most unfavorable formula for each area (excluding free trade) the job changes as a proportion of total employment would be: +0.01 percent for the United States, −0.57 percent for Canada, −0.16 percent for Japan; and (direct jobs only) −0.11 percent for the EEC.

It is possible to translate our estimates of employment effects of tariff liberalization into corresponding estimates of labor adjustment costs. These costs then may be compared to the welfare gains from liberalization in order to determine the net gains from liberalization.[72] This procedure attributes no social cost to the obsolescence of fixed capital caused by change in trade policy. We agree with Jan Tumlir that no social cost should be assigned to such capital equipment because, upon the change in international trade conditions, its social value is zero.[73]

The standard approach in assessing labor adjustment cost per worker is to multiply the average weekly wage per worker by the number of weeks of unemployment anticipated as the worker seeks a new job. For the United States, the available estimates indicate that workers who lose their jobs because of increased imports remain unemployed for approximately thirty weeks before obtaining new work.[74] Charles R. Frank, Jr., applies the average U.S. manufacturing wage to this labor duration of unemployment to obtain an estimate of adjustment cost per worker for 1974.[75] Corresponding estimates for other countries are not available; however, in order to obtain an approximate magnitude for labor adjustment costs in other countries, we have multiplied the U.S. cost by the ratio, for each country in question, of the country's average manufactur-

---

72. For an earlier analysis along these lines, see Robert E. Baldwin and John H. Mutti, "Policy Issues in Adjustment Assistance: The United States," in Helen Hughes, ed., *Prospects for Partnership: Industrialization and Trade Policies in the 1970s* (Johns Hopkins University Press, 1973), pp. 149–77.

73. Jan Tumlir, "Adjustment Cost and Policies to Reduce It" (paper presented at Massachusetts Institute of Technology Workshop on Specific Proposals and Desirable DC Response to LDC Demands Regarding the New International Economic Order, May 17–20, 1976; processed).

74. Charles R. Frank, Jr., with the assistance of Stephanie Levinson, *Foreign Trade and Domestic Aid* (Brookings Institution, 1977), p. 169. See also Malcolm D. Bale, "Estimates of Trade-Displacement Costs for U.S. Workers," *Journal of International Economics*, vol. 6 (August 1976), p. 247.

75. Frank, *Foreign Trade and Domestic Aid*, p. 169.

Table 3-15. *Labor Adjustment Costs Compared to Welfare Gains for Full U.S. Tariff-Cutting Authority, 1974 Base*
Excluding textiles

Area	Labor adjust- ment cost per job displaced (dollars) (1)	Jobs displaced by imports (2)	Total labor cost of adjustment (col. 1 × col. 2) (millions of dollars) (3)	Total static and dynamic welfare gains, present value (millions of dollars) (4)	Welfare gains ÷ adjustment cost (col. 4 ÷ col. 3) (5)
United States	3,780	161,700	611.2	49,110	80.4
Canada	3,720	77,100	286.8	17,840	62.2
Japan	2,420	246,100	595.6	28,990	48.7
EEC	2,310	205,000ᵃ	473.6	45,300	95.7

Sources: Column 1: United States, Charles R. Frank, Jr., with the assistance of Stephanie Levinson, *Foreign Trade and Domestic Aid* (Brookings Institution, 1977), p. 169; Canada, Japan, and EEC based on U.S. cost as adjusted by relationship of average manufacturing wage rate to U.S. wage rate, as calculated from International Labor Office, *Yearbook of Labor Statistics: 1976* (Geneva, 1976), table 19. Column 2: table 3-14. Column 4: table 3-8; static gains are multiplied by 5 to obtain "total" welfare gains, and multiplied again by 20 to obtain present discounted value of future streams of benefits.

a. Direct job estimate multiplied by 2.0 to obtain approximate number of direct plus indirect jobs displaced by increased imports.

ing wage to the corresponding U.S. wage. This procedure assumes that the duration of unemployment from import-displaced jobs is the same in other countries as in the United States.

Given the labor adjustment cost per job, multiplication by the total number of jobs displaced by imports yields the estimate of total labor adjustment cost. This final result totally ignores the facilitation of labor absorption through increased export job opportunities resulting from liberalization. In addition, it is a high estimate of the labor adjustment cost, because our basic estimate of jobs lost to increased imports is a high estimate. It assumes all increased imports represent reduced domestic production rather than increased domestic consumption; and it makes no allowance for the gradual phasing in of liberalization over time (and, thus, for labor adjustment through the normal process of attrition as workers retire or seek new jobs voluntarily).

Table 3-15 reports the results of labor adjustment costs estimated for the most liberalizing tariff-cutting formula, full U.S. authority (for the case excluding textiles). The labor adjustment costs range up to $611 million for the United States. The table also reports the present discounted value of total welfare gains from tariff liberalization, based on our earlier discussion of welfare effects. It is evident that these total welfare gains dwarf the labor adjustment costs. For the United States, for example, the present value of welfare gains is nearly $50 billion (in 1974 values), or 80 times the size of labor adjustment costs. Therefore, there is strong evidence that the welfare benefits of trade liberalization far exceed the social costs of labor adjustment. Much more refined estimates of adjustment costs would be desirable, with separate costs per worker by industrial sector, and perhaps with detailed time profiles related to the phasing in of liberalization. There is virtually no likelihood, however, that refinements of this type would change the policy conclusion that the welfare gains of liberalization greatly exceed labor adjustment costs, at least at the aggregate level.

Results by Major Product Sector

The results of calculations using the model of tariff negotiations are available at several levels of aggregation: individual tariff-line items for imports; and, for both imports and exports, four-digit BTN categories and broad BTN "sections" (twenty-one categories). Although it is beyond the scope of this volume to report detailed results, it is important to examine at least the major patterns of the results by broad product categories. For this purpose, table 3-16 reports the trade and direct employment effects of a 60 percent tariff cut, at the level of BTN sections for the four major parties in the negotiations.[76] Indirect employment effects are not available by the sector in which the job is created or displaced.[77] The figures exclude exports attributable to the responding effect, because these exports are computed at the aggregate rather than the sectoral level.

The table reports results for 1971. The aggregate labor estimates for 1974 above (table 3-14) apply single overall expansion factors to the total labor effects for 1971. At the sectoral level, the only available employment estimates are for 1971. Nevertheless, the patterns of differences among product sectors from the 1971 results should be a good guide to

76. For the United States, more detailed sectoral results comparing employment effects of liberalization to sectoral employment levels are provided in Baldwin, "Trade and Employment Effects in the United States of Multilateral Tariff Restrictions."

77. Because the total job coefficient for each sector refers to direct labor in that sector but includes indirect labor from all sectors that supply intermediate inputs to it.

Table 3-16. *Trade and Employment Effects by Product Groups for the 60 Percent Tariff Cut Case, 1971 Base*
Millions of dollars; thousands of jobs

Area and BTN section	Trade			Direct jobs			Net jobs as percent of sectoral employment
	Imports	*Exports*	*Balance*	*Imports*	*Exports*	*Balance*	
United States							
1 Animals, products	18.3	8.6	−9.7	0.5	0.2	−0.3	n.a.
2 Vegetable products	21.3	33.5	12.2	1.1	1.7	0.6	n.a.
3 Fats, oils	2.8	8.1	5.3	0.1	0.2	0.1	n.a.
4 Food, beverages, tobacco	152.5	50.0	−102.5	3.8	2.1	−1.7	−0.10
5 Mineral products[a]	2.1	19.0	17.0	0.1	0.6	0.5	0.14
6 Chemicals	45.1	215.6	170.5	0.9	4.2	3.3	0.31
7 Plastics, rubber	324.5	147.1	−177.4	3.9	3.3	−0.5	−0.09
8 Hides, leather goods	54.9	5.8	−49.2	3.9	0.4	−3.5	n.a.
9 Wood, cork articles	25.6	10.0	−15.6	1.1	0.5	−0.7	−0.15
10 Paper, products	7.8	78.9	71.1	0.3	2.5	2.2	0.35
11 Textiles	831.4	113.0	−718.4	41.6	4.6	−37.0	−1.65
12 Footwear, headgear	73.0	2.6	−70.4	4.1	0.2	−3.9	n.a.
13 Stone, ceramics, glass	37.8	27.4	−10.4	1.5	1.1	−0.4	−0.07
14 Jewelry	45.5	3.2	−42.3	1.8	0.1	−1.7	n.a.
15 Base metals	319.6	143.8	−175.8	8.9	4.5	−4.4	−0.18
16 Machinery, electrical equipment	160.8	657.6	496.8	5.8	22.7	16.9	0.49
17 Transportation equipment	251.2	190.4	−60.8	5.9	5.9	0.0	0.00
18 Precision instruments	99.9	146.6	46.7	3.8	5.4	1.6	n.a.
19 Arms	7.8	2.2	−5.6	0.2	0.1	−0.2	n.a.
20 Miscellaneous manufactures	176.9	37.4	−139.5	8.0	1.6	−6.4	n.a.
21 Art	0.1	0.0	−0.1	0.0	0.0	0.0	n.a.
Total excluding oil	2,658.8	1,900.8	−758.0	97.3	61.8	−35.6	
Total excluding oil and textiles	1,827.4	1,787.8	−39.6	55.7	57.2	1.4	
Manufacturing excluding textiles[b]	1,630.4	1,668.6	38.2	50.1	52.4	2.3	

Canada

1	Animals, products	3.6	6.1	2.6	0.1	0.2	0.1	n.a.
2	Vegetable products	7.7	13.4	5.7	0.4	0.7	0.3	n.a.
3	Fats, oils	4.4	1.7	−2.7	0.1	0.0	−0.1	n.a.
4	Food, beverages, tobacco	25.7	29.0	3.3	0.6	0.8	0.2	0.09
5	Mineral products[a]	1.2	1.5	0.3	0.0	0.0	0.0	0.00
6	Chemicals	60.0	12.7	−47.3	1.2	0.3	−0.9	−1.15
7	Plastics, rubber	57.9	33.7	−24.2	1.2	0.5	−0.7	−1.56
8	Hides, leather goods	11.5	3.8	−7.8	0.8	0.3	−0.6	n.a.
9	Wood, cork articles	10.6	13.6	3.0	0.5	0.7	0.2	0.22
10	Paper, products	28.8	32.7	3.9	1.1	1.0	−0.1	−0.08
11	Textiles	163.2	24.7	−138.5	7.0	1.2	−5.8	−2.93
12	Footwear, headgear	22.9	1.7	−21.2	1.5	0.1	−1.4	n.a.
13	Stone, ceramics, glass	26.2	3.7	−22.5	1.1	0.2	−0.9	−1.73
14	Jewelry	3.1	0.5	−2.6	0.1	0.0	−0.1	n.a.
15	Base metals	106.5	72.3	−34.2	3.5	1.5	−2.1	−0.88
16	Machinery, electrical equipment	271.9	40.9	−231.0	9.7	1.5	−8.2	−3.90
17	Transportation equipment	117.5	33.3	−84.2	3.0	1.1	−1.9	−1.27
18	Precision instruments	40.3	9.9	−30.3	1.5	0.4	−1.1	n.a.
19	Arms	1.8	1.3	−0.5	0.1	0.0	−0.0	n.a.
20	Miscellaneous manufactures	28.0	13.5	−14.5	1.3	0.7	−0.6	n.a.
21	Art	0.0	0.0	−0.0	0.0	0.0	−0.0	n.a.
	Total excluding oil	992.7	349.9	−642.8	34.7	11.0	−23.6	
	Total excluding oil and textiles	829.4	325.2	−504.2	27.7	9.8	−17.9	
	Manufacturing excluding textiles[b]	787.0	273.5	−513.4	26.5	8.1	−18.4	

Table 3-16 (*continued*)

Area and BTN section	Trade			Direct jobs			Net jobs as percent of sectoral employment
	Imports	Exports	Balance	Imports	Exports	Balance	
Japan							
1 Animals, products	36.6	2.5	−34.1	3.8	0.5	−3.3	n.a.
2 Vegetable products	54.5	0.8	−53.7	33.9	0.1	−33.8	n.a.
3 Fats, oils	1.7	0.4	−1.3	0.0	0.0	−0.0	n.a.
4 Food, beverages, tobacco	92.8	10.6	−82.2	2.3	1.3	−1.0	−0.09
5 Mineral products[a]	13.7	0.0	−13.7	0.0	0.0	−0.0	0.00
6 Chemicals	61.6	28.4	−33.2	2.8	1.4	−1.4	−0.28
7 Plastics, rubber	18.0	95.5	77.5	1.5	9.9	8.3	1.92
8 Hides, leather goods	3.3	17.4	14.0	0.5	4.2	3.7	n.a.
9 Wood, cork articles	4.0	10.0	6.0	0.4	1.2	0.8	0.13
10 Paper, products	9.7	7.8	−1.9	0.4	0.6	0.2	0.06
11 Textiles	45.8	249.7	203.9	6.8	47.5	40.7	2.44
12 Footwear, headgear	4.4	22.2	17.8	0.6	4.4	3.8	n.a.
13 Stone, ceramics, glass	2.8	28.6	25.8	0.3	5.5	5.2	0.93
14 Jewelry	5.6	5.1	−0.4	0.5	0.6	0.1	n.a.
15 Base metals	70.2	191.7	121.5	3.4	7.9	4.5	0.28
16 Machinery, electrical equipment	170.4	172.3	1.9	10.5	12.0	1.5	0.06
17 Transportation equipment	46.5	201.1	154.6	2.3	9.5	7.2	0.83
18 Precision instruments	38.8	93.0	54.3	4.0	8.8	4.8	n.a.
19 Arms	4.5	1.5	1.0	0.1	0.2	0.1	n.a.
20 Miscellaneous manufactures	18.9	77.4	58.4	2.1	8.7	6.6	n.a.
21 Art	0.0	0.0	0.0	0.0	0.0	0.0	n.a.
Total excluding oil	699.8	1,215.8	516.0	76.4	124.4	48.0	
Total excluding oil and textiles	654.0	966.3	312.2	69.6	76.9	7.3	
Manufacturing excluding textiles[b]	454.7	951.8	497.1	29.6	75.0	45.4	

EEC

1	Animals, products	32.8	-26.1	-58.9	3.5	-4.6	-8.1	n.a.
2	Vegetable products	114.5	-71.1	-185.6	20.9	-17.7	-38.6	n.a.
3	Fats, oils	16.8	-19.0	-35.8	0.5	-0.6	-1.1	n.a.
4	Food, beverages, tobacco	115.9	-31.4	-147.3	3.2	-0.7	-3.8	-0.16
5	Mineral products[a]	13.5	-14.5	-28.0	1.4	-1.5	-2.9	-0.31
6	Chemicals	99.6	-60.2	-159.8	4.0	-2.4	-6.4	-0.34
7	Plastics, rubber	63.9	123.9	60.0	3.0	10.6	7.5	0.78
8	Hides, leather goods	13.3	2.6	-10.7	1.1	0.2	-0.9	n.a.
9	Wood, cork articles	20.4	-9.1	-29.5	1.4	-0.6	-2.0	-0.28
10	Paper, products	31.8	-16.4	-48.2	1.9	-0.9	-2.8	-0.38
11	Textiles	171.0	-5.8	-176.9	15.8	-1.2	-17.1	-0.49
12	Footwear, headgear	20.5	7.6	-12.9	2.1	0.9	-1.2	n.a.
13	Stone, ceramics, glass	16.5	5.0	-11.5	1.1	0.3	-0.8	-0.06
14	Jewelry	2.6	20.5	17.9	0.2	1.4	1.3	n.a.
15	Base metals	107.3	34.2	-73.1	5.7	2.0	-3.7	-0.09
16	Machinery, electrical equipment	180.5	-92.7	-273.2	11.9	-6.2	-18.0	-0.28
17	Transportation equipment	79.9	87.1	7.1	4.7	5.1	0.4	0.01
18	Precision instruments	77.8	-23.0	-100.8	6.6	-1.9	-8.5	n.a.
19	Arms	1.2	3.5	2.3	0.1	0.2	0.2	n.a.
20	Miscellaneous manufactures	30.9	12.9	-18.0	2.1	0.9	-1.2	n.a.
21	Art	0.0	0.1	0.1	0.0	0.0	0.0	n.a.
	Total excluding oil	1,210.8	-72.2	-1,283.1	91.1	-16.6	-107.8	
	Total excluding oil and textiles	1,039.7	-66.4	-1,106.1	75.3	-15.4	-90.7	
	Manufacturing excluding textiles[b]	746.2	125.7	-620.5	45.8	9.7	-36.1	

n.a. Not available.
a. Excludes oil.
b. Excludes sections 1–5 and 11.

the sectoral differences that would be observed for 1974 data, even though the results presented above for 1974 are more meaningful for questions concerning aggregate trade balance and employment effects.

For the United States, Canada, and the EEC it is clear that the textiles sector (BTN section 11) is of primary importance to overall results for imports and, even more importantly, employment effects. Japan shows the mirror image of this fact: including textiles in liberalization would raise Japan's export increases from liberalization by approximately 25 percent and raise her increased employment in export activities by approximately 62 percent. For the United States, the inclusion of textiles in liberalization would raise the total number of jobs lost to increased imports by approximately 75 percent. This proportion for jobs exceeds the corresponding proportion for import value (approximately 40 percent), reflecting the relative labor intensity of U.S. textile imports compared with its imports in other sectors. In short, the sectoral employment figures reinforce our earlier conclusion that the liberalization of textiles would constitute the single largest sectoral impact from negotiations.

Even in the textiles sector, however, liberalization effects would appear to be limited in relative terms. For the United States, the 41,600 direct jobs in textiles that would be displaced from a 60 percent tariff cut (table 3-16) represent only approximately 2 percent of total employment in the textiles sector.[78] Considering the fact that liberalization would be phased in over a period of years, it would appear that labor adjustment problems would be limited even in the textiles sector, if the sector were included in liberalization.

For the United States, other important sectors in which import increases would substantially outweigh export increases include basic metals (15), plastics and rubber (7), miscellaneous manufactures (20), footwear (12), transportation equipment (17), and leather goods (8). Employment would decline on balance in the same sectors (although by very little in plastics, rubber, and transportation equipment). Sectors in which export gains would significantly exceed import increases include machinery and electrical appliances (16), chemicals (6), paper products

---

78. In 1971 the United States had approximately 2.2 million workers in the textile and wearing apparel sectors (SIC 321 and 322). United Nations, Statistical Office, *The Growth of World Industry: 1973 Edition,* vol. 1: *General Industrial Statistics* (New York, 1975), p. 575.

(10), and precision instruments (18). Net increases in employment would also be the most important in these sectors.[79]

When the employment effects are expressed in relative terms (final column, table 3-16), it appears that individual sectoral effects all would be small in the United States except for the case of textiles. The change in net jobs expressed as a percentage of existing sectoral employment would range from +0.49 percent in machinery and electrical equipment to −0.18 percent in basic metals.[80]

For Canada, sizable trade balance reductions occur in machinery and electrical equipment (16) and in transportation equipment (17). Net declines in employment are focused in these sections, as well as in basic metals (15) and footwear (12). Canada's net trade (and employment) gains, though small, occur in the agricultural sectors (1, 2, and 4) and in the wood (9) and paper (10) sectors. In relative terms, net job reductions for Canada would be most pronounced in machinery and electrical equipment (−3.9 percent of sectoral employment) and textiles (−2.93 percent). In addition, reductions of more than 1 percent of sectoral employment would occur in chemicals, plastics, nonmetallic minerals, and transportation equipment.

Aside from textiles, the sectors with the largest trade balance increases for Japan are transportation equipment (17), basic metals (15), and plastics and rubber (7). Net employment increases are most significant

79. For the United States and the other areas shown in table 3-16, employment effects generally correspond to trade effects in terms of size and direction of the balance between export and import effects. However, the correspondence is far from rigid. The variations appear to represent the fact that labor intensity differs between exports and imports in a given BTN section, probably because the sections are fairly broad groupings, and increased imports within a given section may be very different goods from increased exports in the same section. In addition, labor intensities vary across sections.

80. However, the sectoral employment effect as a percentage of existing employment may be estimated for only eleven out of the twenty-one BTN sections (table 3-16) because of difficulties in arriving at category correspondences between BTN and International Standard Industrial Classification (ISIC) groupings at this level of aggregation. Note that for the sectors with results reported, the following correspondence was used (BTN/ISIC): 4/311, 312, 313, 314; 5/210, 230, 290; 6/351, 352; 7/355, 356; 9/331; 10/341; 11/321, 322; 13/361, 362, 369; 15/371, 372, 381; 16/382, 383; 17/384. Sectoral employment data used in calculating the relative employment effect (final column, table 3-16) are from United Nations, *The Growth of World Industry: 1973 Edition.*

in these same sectors and, in addition, in nonmetallic mineral products (13) and miscellaneous manufactures (20). The only significant trade balance reductions occur in agricultural products (sectors 1, 2, and 4) and, of these, only one sector (vegetable raw materials, sector 2) represents a sizable net employment decline. Relative to existing sectoral employment, net job increases would be most important in plastics (close to 2 percent), nonmetallic minerals, and transportation equipment (both close to 1 percent), and, if liberalized, textiles (2.4 percent).

For the EEC the sectoral results are striking. They indicate systematic declines in trade balances and employment, with only two significant exceptions. In plastics and rubber products (7) and jewelry and precious stones (14) there are important trade balance and employment increases. The most notable sectoral trade balance reductions occur in the agricultural sectors (1–4), machinery and electrical equipment (16), chemicals (6), and precision instruments (18). Reductions in employment also are focused in these sectors. The strong tendency toward declines in trade balances and employment for the EEC reflects the fact that in most sectors exports decline, rather than rise, because the negative impact of the substitution of outsider supply for goods previously imported from bloc partners swamps the positive impact of increased exports to the outsider countries. Despite the general pattern of negative trade balance and employment effects, any net job losses for the EEC would be extremely small relative to existing sectoral employment. The largest net job loss measured for a sector is a decline of one-half of one percent of employment in the textiles sector, which is unlikely to be liberalized; otherwise, even the largest relative job reductions are only approximately one-third of one percent of sectoral employment (mineral products, chemicals, paper).

Finally, for all four importing areas two major patterns are evident in table 3-16. First, both imports and exports generally rise within a given sector from liberalization. This result reflects the well-known phenomenon of two-way trade even within industry groups, that is, intra-industry specialization in trade rather than interindustry specialization. The presence of both increased exports and imports in individual sectors also reflects the very broad inclusion of the twenty-one BTN sections. Second, manufacturing industries are, by far, more important than agriculture or raw materials in the increases in trade resulting from liberalization. Even excluding textiles, manufactured goods (BTN sections 6–21 excluding 11) account for 89 percent of increased imports for the United States, 95 percent for Canada, 70 percent for Japan, and 72 percent for the EEC. The corresponding shares of manufactures in increased exports are 93 percent for the United States, 84 percent for Canada, and 98 percent for Japan. The predominance of manufactured goods in trade creation, even for areas that depend heavily on imported agricultural and raw materials (Japan and EEC), reflects the fact that tariff protection is already low for raw materials, and that for agricultural products, in which protection is high, nontariff barriers rather than tariffs are the chief limitations to trade.

The preeminence of the manufacturing sector holds true for employment effects as well as trade effects for the United States and Canada. In the case of Japan, however, manufacturing accounts for only 42.5 percent of the employment displaced by extra imports, and in the EEC the corresponding figure is only 60.8 percent. Thus, the high labor intensity of agriculture in these two importing areas means that agriculture represents a much larger share in total employment effects from tariff liberalization than in increased import values to be expected from liberalization.

Conclusion

The central conclusion of the empirical estimates presented in this chapter is that tariff liberalization in the Tokyo Round of Multilateral Trade Negotiations can achieve significant welfare gains through freer trade with virtually no serious threat of either trade balance losses or employment dislocation. For the industrial countries as a whole, the once-for-all value of total welfare gains could amount to $170 billion (in 1974 values) under the more liberalizing tariff cuts being considered, and could rise even higher in view of dynamic effects omitted in our calculations (the anti-inflationary impact and the stimulus to technological change).[81] Welfare gains would be much higher if, in addition, textiles were liberalized (for example, static welfare gains measured for the United States double when textiles are included), but the regime of voluntary export

81. The corresponding estimate for traditional static efficiency gains is $1.7 billion annually. On the basis of experience in European integration, total welfare effects—including induced investment, economies of scale, and technical change, as well as anti-inflationary effects—could be more than five times the amount for static effects. Growing at the same rate as the trade base—perhaps 5 percent annually in real terms—these total gains would have a present discounted value of at least $170 billion, discounting at 10 percent a year.

quotas controlling trade in the sector is unlikely to be changed in the Tokyo Round.

Despite a considerable total welfare gain from liberalization, the magnitudes of the underlying trade increases would be relatively small. The most liberalizing tariff cut under consideration would increase total imports of the industrial countries by only about 2 percent ($11 billion in 1974), and the complete elimination of tariffs would raise the figure to only 3 percent. This small impact is explained by the already low level of tariffs (averaging slightly more than 10 percent) and, more importantly, by the fact that virtually three-quarters of total imports are in categories not subject to tariff liberalization by virtue of the nature of trade (duty-free imports of EEC and EFTA from member countries) or because political considerations make liberalization irrelevant (petroleum) or unlikely (textiles).

Among the four major parties in the negotiations, liberalization would tend to increase the trade balance for Japan and the United States and reduce it for Canada and the EEC. The trade balance effects include those from extra "induced" exports to free-rider countries not liberalizing their own tariffs but gaining increased foreign exchange from additional exports to the liberalizing countries (the responding effect). Trade balance effects must be examined on the basis of recent years (1974) rather than on the basis of 1971 (the year of the complete trade data base) because of the serious disequilibrium in 1971 (and, in particular, the deficit of the United States in that year).

For the United States liberalization increases the trade balance primarily by opening markets in Canada and the EEC, tending to replace "partner supply" behind the tariff wall of the EEC. Japan's trade balance increases appear to come from the country's strong competitive position generally, and the increases tend to be greater for the more liberalizing tariff-cutting formulas. Canada tends to experience a trade balance reduction from liberalization, because the country has relatively high tariffs on dutiable trade, and because foreign markets opened by tariff reduction tend to be for manufactured goods, whereas Canada's exports are concentrated in agricultural goods and raw materials. For the EEC, the sources of trade balance deterioration from liberalization are the "substitution effect" through which supply from partners is replaced by supply from countries outside the free-trade bloc as the external tariff wall declines, and the relatively high incidence of EEC import increases from rest-of-world countries not reducing their own tariffs.

Despite these general patterns, the principal finding is that all trade balance effects would be extremely small. Under a 60 percent tariff cut the trade balance would rise by 0.6 percent of 1974 exports for the United States and by 1.5 percent for Japan; it would decline by 3.1 percent of exports for Canada and by 1 percent of external exports for the EEC. Considering that gradual phasing in of tariff cuts would delay even these small effects, the policy conclusion must be that any difficulties caused by trade balance reductions would be too small to warrant opposition to tariff liberalization.[82]

Detailed examination of tariff-cutting formulas yields the following results. First, on welfare grounds, the four major areas (United States, Canada, Japan, and the EEC) systematically show the highest welfare gains from the most liberalizing formulas (especially cuts by full U.S. authority, that is, a 60 percent tariff cut and the elimination of tariffs of 5 percent and below). Among the major proposals considered, those by the EEC and Japan rank low on welfare criteria, because they do little tariff cutting in the range relevant for most tariffs.

Second, on the basis of trade effects, both the EEC and Canada would do "best" under their own formulas, respectively (though for Canada this finding holds only when comparing percentage export increases relative to percentage import increases). For the United States the most favorable formula is a 60 percent tariff cut but with a floor of 5 percent, below which tariffs are not cut. This formula increases U.S. exports by opening up foreign markets, while leaving unchanged the relatively large portion of U.S. imports entering at duties of 5 percent and below. For Japan the most favorable formula is the most liberalizing: full U.S. tariff-cutting authority. Ironically, Japan's own proposal is restrictive; according to our analysis, it would rank lower for Japan on both trade effect and welfare grounds than almost all other formulas (including those closest to the proposals by the United States and Canada).

82. Moreover, for Canada even the modest trade balance reductions estimated are probably overstated, because new output and exports could be expected from structural transformation away from raw materials and toward processing activities, in view of the important reduction in effective rates of protection on processing activities abroad. Our model makes no special evaluation of this phenomenon.

Third, on the question of linear versus harmonization cuts the results show that, if textiles are excluded, linear cuts do not have a more positive effect on the U.S. trade balance than harmonization cuts. In fact, the largest trade balance increase for the United States occurs under a particular type of harmonization formula: a 60 percent cut with a 5 percent floor on tariffs. Another result concerning harmonization is that the EEC-type harmonization cut creates little trade. Alternative harmonization approaches create much more trade and, if the EEC commitment is to the concept of harmonization per se rather than to restrictive tariff cuts, then it should be possible to identify harmonization formulas that are much more favorable to overall trade creation and welfare gains than the three- (or four-) iteration cut suggested by the EEC.[83]

Fourth, an analysis of overall "reciprocity" that calculates joint weighted rankings among tariff-cutting formulas, with weights proportional to dutiable imports of the four major parties in the negotiations, indicates that on the combined (equally weighted) bases of trade and welfare effects the "best" formula for all major parties is the most liberalizing: full U.S. tariff-cutting authority (60 percent tariff cut with the elimination of tariffs below 5 percent). The second-ranked formula in this analysis deserves special attention. It is a specific harmonization formula: percent cut in tariff equals 20 percent plus three times the tariff (with a limit of 60 percent cut). This formula is quite liberalizing, so that its welfare gains are sizable. If negotiators are not prepared to adopt the more liberalizing full U.S. authority tariff cut, then this alternative formula would be an attractive compromise giving a high degree of "reciprocity," as judged by rankings taking into account both trade balance and welfare effects. In addition, this formula has the pragmatic advantage that it lies between the EEC and the U.S. positions in the negotiations to date. The Swiss formula is a more likely compromise solution, however, in view of discussions between the United States and the EEC in September 1977. This formula ranks lower in overall reciprocity be-

83. Moreover, there is little substance in the notion that the EEC could maintain the "cement in the tariff wall" more effectively through restrictive rather than generous liberalization in the Tokyo Round. With the common external tariff already as low as 10 percent on the average, remaining tariffs after further liberalization will play primarily a symbolic role in supporting unity of the EEC. This symbolic role can be as easily performed by a 4 percent external tariff as by a 7 percent tariff (the resulting levels after a 60 percent cut and a 30 percent cut—implied by the three-iteration formula—respectively).

cause it is somewhat more restrictive, but it does appear to be a more favorable formula for overall reciprocity than either the more restrictive EEC and Japanese approaches or the more liberal Canadian approach.

The exchange rate effects of tariff liberalization, like the trade balance effects, would be extremely small. Estimates applying our empirically based import demand elasticities and an assumed export demand elasticity indicate that trade balance changes resulting from a 60 percent tariff cut could be fully offset by an appreciation in the trade-weighted exchange rate by 0.16 percent for the United States and 0.42 percent for Japan, and a depreciation in the trade-weighted exchange rate by 0.79 percent for Canada and 0.22 percent for the EEC.

Estimates of the employment effects of tariff liberalization systematically show that any dislocation from a loss of jobs to increased imports would be extremely small. Under the most liberalizing practical formula (full U.S. authority), the net job balance between export employment gains and losses of jobs to imports would be only +0.02 percent for the United States, −0.53 percent for Canada, +0.08 percent for Japan, and (direct jobs only) −0.11 percent for the EEC. The gross dislocation of jobs in import-competing activities also would be small, even without counting new export jobs. For the United States, tariff cuts by full U.S. authority would displace a maximum of 162,000 import-competing jobs (or 0.19 percent of the labor force) Employment effects of tariff liberalization would appear to be limited at the more detailed sectoral levels as well. The most sensitive sector for the United States is textiles. If liberalization took place in this sector, it would reduce employment by less than 2 percent of the sector's work force, and this effect would be spread out over a gradual phasing-in period.

With respect to trade effects at the level of individual product sectors, the single dominant finding is that the liberalization of textiles (both tariff and nontariff barriers) by itself would represent an enormous achievement for freeing trade. For example, under the full U.S. authority tariff cut, total imports of the industrial countries would rise by $11 billion without textiles but by $14 billion if textiles were included in liberalization (1974 base). The proportionate contribution of textiles to welfare gains would be even higher, because of the high tariffs in the sector.

The other sectoral patterns evident in more detailed analysis of tariff liberalization effects are the following. U.S. trade balance and employment gains would be focused in machinery and electrical appliances, chemicals, paper, and precision instruments. The absence of agriculture from the list reflects the fact that nontariff barriers rather than tariffs constitute the impediment to U.S. agricultural exports. Trade balance and employment reductions would be concentrated in basic metals, plastics and rubber, miscellaneous manufactures, footwear, transportation equipment, and leather goods.

For Canada, trade balance reductions would be concentrated in machinery and electrical equipment and in transportation equipment; limited increases would take place in the agricultural, wood, and paper sectors. Japan's trade balance increases would be primarily in transportation equipment, basic metals, and plastics and rubber. Only in agricultural sectors would Japan experience trade and employment reductions from tariff liberalization.

For the EEC, net trade and employment reductions would generally characterize all sectors, especially agriculture, machinery and electrical equipment, chemicals, and precision instruments. Only two sectors— plastics and rubber, and jewelry and precious stones—show significant trade balance and employment increases from tariff liberalization.

Beyond these conclusions there are a myriad of more detailed implications of the results presented in this study and in the unpublished, disaggregated results. For example, bilateral trade balance effects may be examined (using tables 3-4 and 3-5 above and the tables in appendix E). The salient conclusion of the results, however, is that significant welfare gains through freer trade can be achieved through tariff liberalization negotiated in the Tokyo Round with virtually negligible negative side effects in terms of possible trade balance deterioration, on the one hand, or job losses to increased imports, on the other hand. Moreover, the detailed analysis of alternative tariff-cutting formulas in this study permits the identification of individual formulas that would be the most desirable in terms of reciprocity, taking into account both the trade balance and welfare effects for all of the major parties in the negotiations.

CHAPTER FOUR

Agricultural Nontariff Barriers in Europe

WORLD TRADE in agricultural products faces much more severe restrictions than industrial trade, with the exception of some commodity groups such as textiles. Whereas average tariffs on industrial goods in the developed countries generally range from 10 percent to 15 percent, on agricultural goods the nontariff barriers restricting trade frequently correspond to tariff equivalents of well over 100 percent.

The most significant agricultural protection is in Europe, in the form of "variable levies," and Japan, in the form of quotas. The United States has a limited number of significant quotas on agricultural goods as well. The purpose of this chapter and the next is to estimate the magnitude of trade, welfare, and employment changes that would be likely to follow alternative degrees of liberalization of these nontariff barriers.

Background

The variable levy is the foreign trade counterpart of the farm income policies of the principal European countries. The instrument exists in the European Community in addition to EFTA countries. Within the EEC, the Common Agricultural Policy establishes target prices for certain agricultural goods, principally grains, as part of the program of maintaining

farm income. In order to enforce these prices, import levies are established that are equal to the difference between the world price and the
domestic price. These levies are "variable"; they rise as the world price
falls and fall as the world price rises, leaving domestic prices insulated
from changes in the world market.

The European viewpoint is that variable levies are not "nontariff barriers" subject to trade negotiation but that, instead, they are merely deriva-
tive measures established not for the purpose of protection per se but as
necessary consequences of the social policy of farm income maintenance.[1]
Defenders of the levies point out that, since their imposition in the early
1960s, overall imports of agricultural goods from the United States and
other world suppliers have grown quite rapidly, even though imports of
the particular commodities under levies (especially grains) have been
generally stagnant (with very rapid growth in uncontrolled items, notably
soybeans, taking up the slack). Furthermore, in 1973–74, a period of
extremely high world grain prices, variable levies fell virtually to zero
because world grain prices were as high as domestic European prices, or
higher.

Regardless of the social policies giving rise to variable levies, however,
they are clearly restrictions on trade and as such they are reasonable
candidates for reduction through trade negotiations. There exist alternative farm income policies that would avoid penalizing imports, such as
direct subsidies for income maintenance. The argument that overall farm
imports have been buoyant ignores the fact that they could have been
expected to grow even more rapidly under free entry. The disappearance

1. Under GATT rules, although quantitative restrictions on imports generally
are illegal, article XI:2(c) excepts "import restrictions on any agricultural or fisher-
ies product" when the exemption is "necessary to the enforcement of governmental
measures." General Agreement on Tariffs and Trade, *Basic Instruments and Selected
Documents,* vol. 1 (Geneva, May 1952), p. 28. This large loophole in GATT legislation permits import quotas in support of domestic programs that raise farm prices
and incomes.

The variable levy acts in its economic effect as a severe nontariff barrier similar
to a quota; see, for example, Robert E. Baldwin, *Nontariff Distortions of International Trade* (Brookings Institution, 1970), p. 33. The semantic and legal question
of whether it is a tariff or a nontariff barrier does not concern us here. If it is considered to be a tariff, however, then under GATT rules it may be legally "reserved"
from liberalization in negotiations, just like any other tariff. If it is considered to be
a nontariff barrier similar to a quota, then it would be exempt from necessary liberalization under GATT article XI:2(c).

of levies in the 1973–74 period was a temporary phenomenon and, as discussed below, variable levies of quite substantial magnitudes reappeared in 1975 and 1976. Furthermore, some of the features of the levies make them particularly onerous as trade-distorting measures. In particular, receipts from the levies within the EEC are available for subsidizing exports of agricultural products in excess supply. Outside suppliers are therefore doubly damaged: they face high levies on sales to the EEC and, at the same time, face competition from subsidized EEC exports in third-country markets.

European agricultural protection is surely one of the most difficult areas in the Tokyo Round of negotiations. The Kennedy Round of negotiations was widely perceived as a failure for agricultural exporting countries because it did not succeed in heading off the growing program of European agricultural protectionism. Therefore, in the current Tokyo Round of negotiations, these exporting countries are especially determined to obtain European agricultural concessions. Yet, it would appear that the Europeans are equally determined to exclude these protective instruments completely from the negotiations. As of mid-1977, there did appear to be a growing possibility that the United States and the EEC would reach agreement in the related area of establishing grain reserves and seeking to limit price fluctuations to prescribed corridors. If such agreements were reached, they would facilitate parallel agreements providing for some form of reduction in agricultural nontariff barriers.

The negotiations are further complicated by the extraordinary conditions of agricultural trade during the period since 1973. Not only was there a radical increase in world grain prices, but in addition there were complete physical interruptions in supply, most importantly in the case of U.S. export restrictions on soybeans and, although more informally, grains. In the light of this experience with "shocks" from the world market, the case for European agricultural self-sufficiency can only have been enhanced as a natural form of insurance of supply of vital commodities. Correspondingly, the bargaining position of the United States in particular has been reduced; it is difficult to plead the case of an aggrieved supplier to customers only recently told to look elsewhere for supplies. This experience makes it likely that agreements assuring noninterruption of supply would be a necessary condition for European agricultural liberalization.

Estimation Method

Various methods may be used to estimate the impact that the liberalization of variable levies would have on agricultural trade. The method chosen in this study is to obtain the tariff equivalents of the levies, and then to compute the impact of reduction of these "tariff-equivalents" in precisely the same manner as if they were simple tariffs, using the same formulations presented in chapter 2.

The first step in the estimation procedure is to identify tariff-equivalents of variable levies. Fortunately, an extensive study of GATT presents highly detailed estimates of these tariff-equivalents for the EEC and other European countries for the year 1969.[2] These tariff-equivalents were estimated by the importing countries themselves and therefore reflect official estimates for the year in question. Estimates from official sources are not available for later years, but the highly atypical experience of the years 1973 and 1974 would make tariff-equivalents for those years unrepresentative in any case. The current and future relevance of estimates based on tariff-equivalents from 1969 are discussed in more detail below.

The second step in estimation is to apply appropriate base-level import values by tariff-line category. These import data are available from the GATT trade data base for 1971, the same basic data source used in the estimations of chapter 3. Matching the trade data with the tariff-equivalent estimates is unambiguous because the tariff category nomenclatures for the EEC (and the other European countries considered) correspond directly with those in the data base. There is the complicating fact that the 1971 import data for the EEC include the United Kingdom, Denmark, and Ireland whereas the 1969 tariff-equivalent data refer only to the original EEC of six member nations. However, under the assumption that the general levels of agricultural protection of the EEC of six will prevail in determining protection of the expanded community, it is reasonable to apply the estimates to the imports of the EEC of nine.[3]

2. General Agreement on Tariffs and Trade, Agriculture Committee, *Import Measures: Annex 3: Variable Levies and Other Special Charges,* Com. AG/W/68/ Add. 3, April 28, 1971.

3. This procedure probably biases upward the estimates of increased EEC imports which would result from reduction of variable levies. By including in the import base the three countries not imposing high levels of protection, the procedure overstates the base level of imports that would be expected for the EEC of nine under common agricultural protection. As discussed below, however, there are

A third step in the estimation procedure involves the assignment of appropriate price elasticities of import demand, following the basic model set forth in chapter 2. Here the problem is that, in principle, empirically estimated price elasticities could not be expected to be a reliable guide to liberalization effects if during the period there existed variable levies that distorted normal import response to price changes. In practice, this problem is partially circumvented by the fact that the elasticities used for the EEC involve weighted averaging of the elasticities for individual member countries,[4] including the important case of the United Kingdom, which did have quite free importation of agricultural goods during the estimation period. Nevertheless, the elasticities probably give a downward bias to the estimates of trade changes because, for the EEC of six, the sectoral elasticities do refer to estimates during a period of variable-levy control and, therefore, they probably record artificially small import response to price.[5]

In practice, the import price elasticities applied for the most important cases of EEC variable levies (butter, wheat, barley, maize, sugar) all lie within the range −0.52 to −0.59. This range is not particularly low, in absolute terms, when it is recognized that the price elasticities of both the underlying consumer demand and the domestic supply are likely to be low for foodstuffs. The price elasticities will probably be low also for feedgrains as intermediate inputs into meat, at least when all feedgrains are considered jointly as a class.[6]

---

alternative reasons to expect the estimates of the trade impact of liberalization to be biased downward.

4. With weights proportional to total imports from non-EEC suppliers, across all products.

5. It should also be noted that, except for the United Kingdom and West Germany, the country elasticities going into the EEC average are for the very broad category of aggregate SITC groups 0 plus 1 (food and live animals; beverages and tobacco).

6. Note the equation

$$\eta_m = \eta_D \frac{D}{M} - \epsilon_s \frac{S}{M},$$

where

η_m = price elasticity of import demand (derived demand);
η_D = price elasticity of total domestic demand;
ϵ_s = price elasticity of domestic supply;
D = total domestic demand;
S = total domestic supply;
M = imports.

Finally, the method of this study includes a "substitution effect," whereby imports from outside suppliers partially replace those from member countries in the common market. This effect raises the estimate of the outsiders' increase in exports as a result of liberalization by a large amount over the increase that would be predicted on the basis of the import price elasticity alone.[7]

In sum, from the standpoint of the elasticities approach used in the method, there may be a downward bias in the estimates of trade effects that are obtained, but this bias is not likely to be large.

Before turning to the estimates obtained, it is necessary to consider the special problems of agricultural protection that complicate trade-liberalization estimates. First, unlike most industrial sectors, agriculture in many countries is subject to market interventions for domestic social objectives. Therefore, a comprehensive analysis of liberalization ideally would evaluate the alternative trade responses likely under alternative changes in domestic policies—such as price supports, income payments, export subsidies, and stockpiling programs—that would take place in the face of import liberalization. An investigation of this nature is beyond the scope of this study. However, our analysis does assume that existing domestic policies would have to change to be consistent with the postulated reduction in import barriers. For example, farm target or support prices at levels far above the world market price would have to decline to the level of world price plus the postliberalization variable levy.

A second complication is that cross-product and input-output relationships are probably more important than in the case of industrial tariff liberalization.[8] As a major example, the liberalization of EEC variable

---

Applying the reasonable share of one-fourth for imports as a fraction of EEC demand for variable-levy items, and assuming low domestic supply and demand elasticities of 0.1 and −0.1, respectively, this relationship would yield a hypothetical import demand elasticity of −0.7—that is, $(-0.1 \times 4) - (0.1 \times 3)$—a figure close to the range of the empirical estimates cited above.

7. In the case of the estimates here for the EEC, agricultural export gains from the main outside suppliers, such as the United States and Canada, are approximately evenly divided between increases because of the substitution effect and those because of the trade creation effect. If there is any direction of bias in these substitution estimates, which are already large relative to trade creation, it is probably downward. The general substitution elasticity of 2.5 used in chapter 2 is applied here as well, even though substitutability among suppliers for a given agricultural good is probably higher than that for a class of manufactured goods.

8. See chapter 2 for a more general discussion of these effects.

levies on wheat, corn, and other feedstuffs for livestock would tend to reduce EEC imports of soybeans, a major alternative feedstuff not covered by variable-levy protection. Similarly, the liberalization of grain imports into the EEC would tend to improve the EEC's comparative advantage in livestock production, leading to higher exports and lower imports of meat.

These effects could be examined through a detailed sectoral model of agricultural trade liberalization. In the absence of reliable existing estimates from such a model,[9] it would appear that, as a first approximation, our approach using tariff-equivalents and elasticities should shed light on agricultural liberalization.

Empirical Estimates

Table 4-1 reports the estimates of increased EEC imports of agricultural products, by supplier, which would be expected from reductions in the tariff-equivalent levels of variable levies. The estimates are for three alternative tariff-cutting formulas, the first three explored in the study of tariff liberalization in chapter 3. The calculations refer to values in 1971 dollars based on imports of the EEC of nine, and they employ the 1969 tariff-equivalent rates computed by the EEC of six and reported to GATT.

The aggregate results indicate EEC import increases of approximately $500 million annually as the result of liberalization of variable levies. Because the levies include some extremely high tariff-equivalents, the two harmonization formulas yield substantially higher estimates of increased imports than does the 60 percent linear cut formula.

Much more striking than the estimated aggregate import increases are the corresponding welfare gains. For the three tariff-cutting formulas, welfare gains are $850 million, $920 million, and $914 million annually (compared with net import increases of $425 million, $570 million, and $538 million, respectively). The relationship of welfare gain to import increase is radically higher than in the case of the general tariff-liberalization estimates of the previous chapter. For the bulk of industrial goods, tariffs

9. The principal existing comprehensive modeling effort is in *Agricultural Trade and the Proposed Round of Multilateral Negotiations,* prepared by the U.S. Foreign Agricultural Service for the Senate Agriculture and Forestry Committee (GPO, 1973). As discussed in chapter 5, the estimates of that study appear to overstate the trade effects of agricultural nontariff barrier liberalization in an extreme degree.

Table 4-1. *Increase in EEC Imports Resulting from Alternative Cuts in Tariff-Equivalents, by Supplier, 1971 Base*
Thousands of dollars

Supplier	Formula 1 (60% cut)	Formula 2 (3-iteration harmonization)	Formula 3 (5%–20% harmonization)
United States	228,013	285,584	265,561
Canada	123,284	159,193	150,294
Japan	1,916	1,659	1,634
Belgium-Luxembourg	−34,194	−41,555	−39,636
Denmark	−36,344	−46,025	−45,061
France	−274,141	−335,601	−320,192
Germany	−28,649	−34,352	−32,957
Ireland	−21,478	−27,208	−26,246
Italy	−3,190	−3,230	−3,125
Netherlands	−88,900	−109,729	−106,401
United Kingdom	−6,210	−7,360	−7,263
Austria	5,441	7,149	6,956
Finland	14,422	19,534	19,061
Norway	1,547	1,926	1,851
Sweden	18,199	23,194	21,873
Switzerland	1,862	2,345	2,237
Australia	101,564	136,405	130,494
New Zealand	108,300	153,155	150,879
Rest of world[a]	313,096	385,104	367,948
Total	424,538	570,188	537,907

a. Includes less developed countries.

average approximately 10 percent to 15 percent, so that the welfare gain is only a modest fraction of the import increase (for example, approximately one-sixth for the case of a 60 percent tariff cut). But the EEC variable levies are extremely high, so that almost two dollars in welfare is gained for each dollar of increased imports.

The aggregate estimates reported in table 4-1 should understate the total of increased imports for 1971 to some extent, because they do not include all variable-levy items. The EEC estimates submitted to GATT specifically excluded a list of items for which no estimate of the tariff-equivalent could be obtained. On the basis of the GATT trade data base for the EEC of nine, imports of goods controlled by the EEC variable levy amounted to a total of $8 billion in 1971. Of this total, only $5.75 billion correspond to items included in the liberalization estimates presented here. If the excluded items had tariff-equivalent protection equal to the average of those items directly included in the analysis here, then estimates of the impact of liberalization of all variable-levy items would be on the order of 40 percent higher than the figures reported in table 4-1. That is, the total increase of EEC imports would be in the vicinity of $700 million annually rather than the approximate level of $500 million shown for the three alternative tariff-cutting formulas in table 4-1.

With respect to supplier detail, the results indicate export increases ranging from $228 million to $286 million for the United States, and from $102 million to $159 million for Canada, Australia, and New Zealand. The less developed countries as a group would gain exports in the neighborhood of $300 million annually. France and the Netherlands experience the largest export reductions as the result of substitution by outside suppliers to the EEC. Their annual exports decline by $300 million and $100 million, respectively.

Table 4-2 presents the estimates of net increases in EEC imports (that is, increased imports from outsiders minus decreased imports from partners) by major product under the three alternative tariff-cutting formulas, as well as the estimated tariff-equivalent for each product. The table shows exceedingly high tariff-equivalents, with rates ranging from 100 percent to more than 300 percent for sugar, butter, and cheese, and ranging from 64 percent to 98 percent for corn (or maize), oats, barley, and wheat.

Corn is by far the single most important product in terms of magnitude of increased imports expected from liberalization, followed by wheat, barley, butter, and sugar. The high concentration of increased imports in the feedgrains sector suggests that a major consequence of the liberalization of variable levies would be a strong stimulus to the growth of the livestock-producing sector, based on cheaper imported feedstuffs.

Austria, Finland, Sweden, and Switzerland also use variable levies to implement their agricultural policies, and they have reported to GATT their estimates of the tariff-equivalents of these levies. Accordingly, for these countries estimates of the trade effects of liberalization under the three alternative tariff-cutting formulas are reported in table 4-3. Although the absolute magnitudes involved are quite small, they are appreciable relative to the increased imports of industrial goods that these countries would experience under tariff liberalization. For example, for the 60 percent tariff cut, additional variable-levy imports would amount to approximately one-third the value of additional imports of goods covered

Table 4-2. *Major Trade Changes in EEC Imports, by Product,*
from Alternative Cuts in Tariff-Equivalents, 1971 Base
Increases in millions of dollars

BTN 4-digit	EEC sub-category	Product	Tariff-equivalent (percent)	Increase in imports		
				Formula 1	Formula 2	Formula 3
201	11	Meat[a]	47	4.9	5.5	4.7
201	15	Meat[b]	52	5.5	6.7	5.9
403	10	Butter[c]	342	34.4	54.8	54.0
403	90	Butter[d]	313	23.0	36.5	35.9
404	60	Cheese	121	5.1	7.5	7.1
1001	10	Wheat	76	53.9	71.8	66.2
1001	50	Durum wheat	69	22.2	28.9	26.4
1003	00	Barley	98	41.9	59.1	55.7
1004	00	Oats	84	9.0	12.2	11.4
1005	92	Maize	64	109.8	139.5	125.9
1007	95	Sorghum	48	8.5	9.6	8.2
1701	10	Sugar[e]	192	5.2	8.0	7.8
1701	30	Sugar[f]	95	11.6	16.2	15.2
1701	50	Sugar[g]	219	7.6	11.8	11.5
1701	71	Sugar[h]	212	28.5	44.1	43.0
1701	79	Sugar[i]	164	12.6	19.1	18.5

Source: Authors' estimates based on information in General Agreement on Tariffs and Trade, Agricultural Committee, *Import Measures, Annex 3: Variable Levies and Other Special Charges,* COM.AG/W/ 68/Add. 3, April 28, 1971.
a. Beef hindquarters, fresh or frozen.
b. Bone pieces from cattle, fresh or frozen.
c. Butter with 84 percent fat content or less.
d. Butter with more than 84 percent fat content.
e. White, denatured sugar.
f. Crude, denatured sugar.
g. White, nondenatured sugar.
h. Crude, nondenatured sugar, for refining.
i. Crude, nondenatured sugar, other than for refining.

by tariffs in Austria, Sweden, and Switzerland, based on 1971 results (see chapter 3).

Updating the Estimates

The estimates presented above are based on 1971 trade values and 1969 variable-levy tariff-equivalents. It is important to consider the likely changes in the estimated trade effects when taking account of changes in protection and trade base levels in later years. A question that immedi-

Table 4-3. *Trade Effects of Alternative Reductions in Variable Levies on Agricultural Imports in Austria, Finland, Sweden, and Switzerland, 1971 Base*

Thousands of dollars

	Importer			
Exporter and formula	*Austria*	*Finland*	*Sweden*	*Switzerland*
Formula 1 (60% cut)				
United States	433	5	1,112	363
Canada	98	3	446	189
Belgium-Luxembourg	32	2	22	22
Denmark	80	14	5,488	162
France	38	2	618	1,137
Germany	431	2	583	555
Netherlands	155	4	467	383
Italy	173	4	76	176
United Kingdom	257	3	157	21
Australia	2	0	454	45
New Zealand	1	0	58	4
Rest of world	1,359	18	6,887	1,896
Total	3,059	57	16,368	4,953
Formula 2 (3-iteration cut)				
United States	497	6	1,406	283
Canada	71	3	485	135
Belgium-Luxembourg	31	2	19	24
Denmark	68	19	6,562	158
France	23	2	861	1,002
Germany	404	2	744	687
Netherlands	156	5	582	492
Italy	160	4	81	71
United Kingdom	253	4	150	18
Australia	2	0	601	26
New Zealand	1	0	74	0
Rest of world	1,105	29	9,153	1,989
Total	2,771	76	20,718	4,885
Formula 3 (5%–20% cut)				
United States	427	5	1,294	337
Canada	84	3	450	200
Belgium-Luxembourg	26	2	22	25
Denmark	67	18	6,089	222
France	32	2	822	1,025
Germany	362	2	713	658
Netherlands	135	5	545	483
Italy	145	3	73	173

Table 4-3 *(continued)*

| | Importer | | | |
Exporter and formula	Austria	Finland	Sweden	Switzerland
United Kingdom	217	3	151	21
Australia	2	0	565	48
New Zealand	1	0	68	7
Rest of world	1,145	27	8,685	2,055
Total	2,643	70	19,477	5,254

ately arises is whether the 1969 tariff-equivalent rates are valid even for the period of the trade base year (1971) and, more generally, for the longer term future. Official estimates of these tariff-equivalent rates were not completed subsequent to the 1969 GATT study. However, data are available that permit an estimation of tariff-equivalents in later years.

The EEC *Bulletin* publishes data on variable levies collected per unit of agricultural product. The same source reports the "threshold price" for each good in the variable-levy scheme. Since the levy equals the difference between the world price and the threshold price, these data provide information for estimating the tariff-equivalent of the levy.[10]

The most recent year for which variable levies stood at a "typical" or longer run level was 1972. Thereafter, unusually high world grain prices drove the levies to unusually low levels. Therefore, it is useful to investigate the levels at which the tariff-equivalents for 1972 stood in relation to the levels for 1969, which were used to estimate the import changes expected from liberalization. Table 4-4 presents the comparison for selected variable-levy import items, including the most important products on the basis of value of imports covered.

The table shows that for most products, including the important cases of maize and wheat, the tariff-equivalent of the variable levy was even higher in 1972 than in 1969. Therefore, it is likely that, if any bias is introduced by using 1969 tariff-equivalent estimates applied to 1971 trade levels, it is a downward bias in the estimated trade effects of liberalization.[11]

10. With $P_t =$ threshold price and $L =$ levy collected, the tariff-equivalent (t) is the levy as a fraction of the c.i.f. world price, or: $t = \dfrac{L}{P_t - L}$.

11. Note that alternative estimates of the trade effects of variable-levy liberalization have been prepared using the 1972 tariff-equivalents for those items in which they are available, combined with the 1969 tariff-equivalents for remaining items.

Table 4-4. *Tariff-Equivalents of EEC Variable Levies on Selected Agricultural Products, 1969 and 1972*

Percent

Tariff	Category	Product	1969	1972[a]
0202	82	Turkey drumsticks	n.a.	51.9
0405	12	Hatching eggs	7.0	24.5
1001	10	Wheat	76.0	109.5
1001	50	Durum wheat	69.0	99.0
1002	00	Rye	75.0	108.6
1003	00	Barley	98.0	84.6
1004	00	Oats	84.0	109.1
1005	92	Maize	64.0	75.9
1006	10	Paddy rice, round	n.a.	96.1
1006	30	Paddy rice, long	n.a.	107.3
1006	25	Rice, husked, long	n.a.	107.3
1006	27	Rice, husked, round	n.a.	96.1
1006	43	Rice, semimilled, long	n.a.	154.3
1006	45	Rice, bleached, round	n.a.	104.6
1006	47	Rice, bleached, long	n.a.	186.4
1007	91	Millet	71.0	41.8
1007	95	Sorghum	48.0	72.5
1101	20	Wheat and maslin flow	76.0	99.7
1501	11	Lard	55.0	93.4
1501	19	Lard	n.a.	93.4
1602	22	Prepared meat, minimum of 57% poultry	n.a.	27.9
1602	23	Prepared meat, minimum of 25% to 57% poultry	n.a.	28.1

Source: For 1969, GATT, *Import Measures, Annex 3.* For 1972, estimates prepared by Larry Wipf from information in European Economic Community, *Marches Agricoles: Produits Vegetaux* (EEC, 1972) and *Marches Agricoles: Produits Animaux* (EEC, 1972).

n.a. Not available.

a. Crop year for grains, calendar year for other products.

A second and more fundamental question of the date of the estimates concerns the behavior of variable levies after 1972. In most of the period 1973–75, the levies dropped to zero or very low levels because of exceptionally high world prices for grain. Nevertheless, it would be inappropriate to consider the low levels of the levies during this period as "typical" and therefore representative for purposes of trade negotiations.

The resulting total increases in 1971 imports for the EEC of nine are estimated at $495 million for the 60 percent tariff cut formula, $680 million for the three-iteration formula, and $643 million for the 5 percent to 20 percent harmonization formula. These results are all higher than the corresponding estimates using 1969 tariff-equivalents (table 4-1). However, the original results have the advantage that they rely on tariff-equivalent rates officially estimated by the EEC.

Indeed, by 1976 world grain prices had retreated, and EEC threshold prices advanced sufficiently to produce sizable variable levies once again. Thus, by April 1976, the variable levy as a fraction of c.i.f. import price (Rotterdam) was back up to 23.2 percent for wheat, 38.6 percent for corn, and 42.6 percent for sorghum,[12] compared to the rates of 76 percent, 64 percent, and 48 percent, respectively, used in the analysis above (see table 4-2).

Over the longer term it is highly likely that, in the absence of nego-tiated reductions, variable levies will return to their high levels typified by the 1969 tariff-equivalent estimates reported by GATT and used in the analysis above. World grain prices are likely to fall to longer run levels in the neighborhood of 1972 prices plus the subsequent increase in production costs, while at the same time EEC domestic prices are likely to continue advancing. One group of experts have projected the probable level of the tariff-equivalent of variable levies, once world prices fall back to their equilibrium levels, at 120 percent for wheat, 96 percent for corn, and 120 percent for cheese.[13] These levels are even higher than the 1969 rates applied in the analysis above. In short, it appears that the calcula-tions based on 1969 tariff-equivalents do not overstate the impact of liberalization of EEC variable levies, even though in recent years those levies were extremely low. Over the longer term, levels of protection are likely to be at least as high as those in 1969, unless reductions of variable-levy protection are negotiated in the Tokyo Round.

The third element affecting an updating of the estimates of variable-levy liberalization concerns product prices and magnitudes of physical trade. To the extent that more recent trade values are higher than the 1971 levels, the results above will be understated. Unlike the case of industrial trade, it is inappropriate to bring the results up to date by applying expan-sion factors based on the most recent available data on detailed trade values (1974). The reason is that agricultural prices, especially those for grains, were atypically high in 1974. Table 4-5 reports world grain prices for important variable-levy grains in 1971, 1974, and 1975. As shown in the table, the use of 1974 world grain prices to update 1971 estimates of trade impacts would involve a quadrupling of rice prices, almost a

12. Calculated from *U.S. Department of Agriculture News,* USDA 991-76 (April 1976).

13. Atlantic Council of the United States, *GATT Plus: A Proposal for Trade Reform* (Washington, D.C.: Atlantic Council, 1975), p. 96.

Table 4-5. *Selected World Prices of Wheat, Corn, and Rice, 1971, 1974, and 1975*

Dollars per metric ton

Product	1971	1974	1975	Inflation expansion factor	
				1974/1971	1975/1971
Wheat[a]	73.97	203.00	154.00	2.74	2.08
Corn[b]	67.91	145.00	134.00	2.14	1.97
Rice[c]	129.31	505.00	362.00	3.91	2.80

Source: U.S. Department of Agriculture, *Foreign Agricultural Trade of the United States*, February 1976, February 1975, August 1972.

a. U.S. #2 hard winter, c.i.f. United Kingdom/Rotterdam.
b. U.S. #3 yellow, c.i.f. United Kingdom/Rotterdam.
c. Thailand white.

tripling of wheat prices, and a doubling of corn prices. The table also indicates that by 1975 these prices were already declining from their high 1974 levels.

Probably the most reasonable assumption is that in the longer run prices of grains will return to levels consistent with the rate of inflation of farmers' costs of production. Assuming that 1971 prices were reasonably "typical" of long-run equilibrium, an appropriate price inflator to apply in order to update 1971 values to 1974 long-run values would be the index of prices paid by farmers for production costs. Such an index is maintained by the U.S. Department of Agriculture; the index stood at 115 in 1971 and 172 in 1974,[14] giving an inflation expansion factor of 1.50. Therefore, a meaningful updating of estimates of 1971 values for agricultural trade liberalization may be obtained by applying this cost-inflation expansion factor of 50 percent.

Finally, updating the 1971 results might involve changes in physical quantities. Unlike the case of industrial trade, however, the trend in physical quantities of EEC imports of items under agricultural levies has been stagnant or even declining. Therefore, there is no need to introduce an expansion factor for physical trade.

To recapitulate, in order to obtain estimates of the trade effects of European agricultural trade liberalization for 1974 dollar values (but at 1974 "long-run" prices rather than the abnormally high actual 1974 prices), the values estimated for 1971 may simply be expanded by 50 per-

14. U.S. Department of Agriculture, *The Farm Index*, monthly issues.

Table 4-6. *Increases in Imports in Response to Liberalization of Agricultural Variable Levies in Europe, 1974*
Long-Term Values
Millions of dollars

Supplier	Formula 1 (60% cut)			Formula 2 (3-iteration)			Formula 3 (5%–20%)		
	EEC	EFTA-4[a]	Total	EEC	EFTA-4[a]	Total	EEC	EFTA-4[a]	Total
United States	478.8	2.9	481.7	599.8	3.3	603.1	557.8	3.1	560.9
Canada	258.9	1.1	260.0	334.3	1.0	335.3	315.6	1.1	316.7
Denmark	−76.2	8.6	−67.6	−96.6	10.2	−86.4	−94.7	9.6	−85.1
France	−575.6	2.7	−572.9	−704.8	2.8	−702.0	−672.4	2.8	−669.6
Germany	−60.1	2.4	−57.7	−72.2	2.8	−69.4	−69.3	2.6	−66.7
Netherlands	−186.7	1.5	−185.2	−229.5	1.8	−227.7	−223.4	1.8	−221.6
Australia	213.4	0.8	214.2	286.4	0.9	287.3	274.0	0.9	274.9
New Zealand	227.4	0.1	227.5	321.7	0.1	321.8	316.9	0.1	317.0
All suppliers	891.5	36.7	928.2	1,198.3	42.7	1,241.0	1,129.6	41.2	1,170.8

Sources: For EEC, table 4-1, expanded by 40 percent to include omitted variable-levy items, and by an additional 50 percent to obtain 1974 long-run prices. For EFTA, table 4-3, expanded by 50 percent to 1974 long-run prices.
a. Austria, Finland, Sweden, Switzerland.

cent, which was the increase in agricultural production costs in the United States.

Table 4-6 presents a summary of the trade-liberalization estimates for these adjusted 1974 values, for alternative tariff-cutting formulas applied to variable levies in the EEC and four EFTA countries. In order to provide a more accurate global estimate of the impact of variable-levy liberalization, for the EEC the table includes an additional expansion of 40 percent above the original estimates. This expansion will take into account variable-levy items for which no calculations were made because of the absence of tariff-equivalent estimation in the 1969 GATT study, as discussed above.

The final results of table 4-6 indicate that reduction in variable-levy protection by any of the three basic tariff-cutting formulas would increase European agricultural imports by approximately $1 billion in 1974 dollars. For EEC member countries, the net increase in imports of about $900 million would comprise a gross rise in imports from outsiders by approximately $1.9 billion, partially offset by a reduction in imports from partners by about $1 billion (60 percent tariff-equivalent cut; see table 5-12 below). Accordingly, the trade balance change for the EEC would be a reduction of approximately $1.9 billion for a 60 percent cut (see table 5-12) and comparable levels for the two alternative formulas examined here. The United States would experience approximately $500 million in additional exports to the EEC; Canada, Australia, and New Zealand each would have export increases of approximately $300 million. France's agricultural exports to EEC partners would decline by approximately $600 million. The only other major export reduction would be that for the Netherlands, in an amount of approximately $200 million annually.

Comparing these results to those for tariff reductions (chapter 3, 1974 estimates), the following features emerge. First, agricultural liberalization would add approximately 40 percent to the amount of import increases that the EEC could expect from tariff liberalization alone ($2.1 billion net increase in imports by EEC member countries for the 60 percent tariff cut). Second, U.S. export increases from general tariff liberalization (approximately $4 billion for the 60 percent cut) would be augmented by approximately one-eighth by the inclusion of European variable levies in tariff reduction. Third, for Canada, the export gains from European variable-levy liberalization would equal approximately 50 percent of the export increases from tariff liberalization alone; for Australia, the corresponding figure would be more than 80 percent; and for New Zealand, close to 300 percent (60 percent tariff cut case; see tables 3-4 and 4-5). These comparisons contradict the notion, that new U.S. export opportunities from trade negotiations hinge primarily on European agricultural liberalization. Instead, U.S. export increases from traditional tariff cuts, primarily on industrial items, far outweigh those calculated for agricultural products facing European variable levies. However, a more complete assessment of the relative importance of the liberalization of agricultural nontariff barriers to U.S. exports is possible only after taking into account estimates for the case of Japan, the other major importing area with serious barriers (see chapter 5).

For Canada, Australia, and especially New Zealand, it does appear that the liberalization of European variable levies on agricultural goods represents a more important source of increased net exports than does generalized tariff liberalization.

Employment Effects

For the EEC and EFTA, we have no rigorous estimates of employment effects of liberalizing agricultural nontariff barriers. As discussed above, however, a 60 percent cut in the tariff-equivalent of variable levies on agricultural imports would cause an expected net decline of approximately $1.9 billion in the trade balances of the EEC member countries. If we apply to this figure the ratio of employment change to trade balance change, for the principal agricultural sector (BTN section 2) examined in our analysis of tariffs in chapter 3 (table 3-16), the result is an approximate estimate of 395,000 jobs that would be displaced by a 60 percent cut in variable-levy protection in the EEC. If these orders of magnitude are correct, the liberalization of agricultural nontariff barriers in the EEC would cause more than four times the total job loss that would occur from tariff liberalization (excluding textiles; see table 3-16). Even so, the effect of liberalizing agricultural nontariff barriers would still amount to only about one-third of 1 percent of the EEC labor force, an extremely small impact.

Conclusion

By applying three of the general tariff-cutting formulas considered in this study to the tariff-equivalents of European variable levies, it has been possible to estimate the trade impact of a reduction of European agricultural protection. After expansion to take account of excluded items, and updating to 1974 values (but at "long-run" prices rather than exceedingly high actual prices of 1974), the results show that a net increase of approximately $1 billion in European imports would result from variable-levy cuts comparable to the principal tariff cuts under consideration in the Tokyo Round.[15] In absolute terms, the largest increase in exports would be from the United States, but Canada, Australia, and especially New Zealand would experience large export increases in proportionate terms. For the United States, the export increases would be relatively limited compared with those from general tariff reduction on all products, particularly manufactures. Especially France and the Netherlands, but also Germany and Denmark, would experience a decline in exports to their EEC partners from agricultural liberalization. These basic outcomes, as well as the fundamental policy questions relating to alternative agricultural incomes policies in the absence of the variable levy, are important to keep in mind in evaluating overall reciprocity in the multilateral trade negotiations.

With respect to employment, approximate estimates suggest that net job losses would be considerably higher for the liberalization of agricultural variable levies than for tariff liberalization. Nevertheless, these estimates suggest that job losses would be extremely small relative to the labor force for both types of liberalization. Labor adjustment, therefore, presumably could be accommodated without great difficulty, especially given the gradual staging of liberalization over a period of years.

Alternative estimates of the impact of liberalizing agricultural nontariff barriers have been prepared by other sources; these are considered in chapter 5, following the discussion of this study's estimates for the cases of Japan and the United States.

15. This figure refers to increased imports from outsiders less the decrease in imports from EEC partners. The corresponding figure for the gross increase in imports from outsiders alone is approximately $1.9 billion (see table 5-12). Considering that there would be virtually no increase in EEC agricultural exports to EFTA, the corresponding trade balance effect of liberalizing European variable levies would also be a reduction by approximately $1.9 billion.

CHAPTER FIVE

Agricultural Nontariff Barriers in Japan and the United States

THIS CHAPTER presents estimates of the trade effects of liberalizing agricultural quotas in Japan and in the United States. These results are then combined with those in the previous chapter for Europe to obtain an overall assessment of the impact of liberalizing nontariff barriers to agricultural trade. Alternative quantitative estimates of these effects, by the U.S. Department of Agriculture (USDA) and by the UN Food and Agriculture Organization (FAO), are taken into account in the final evaluation of these results.

Japan

Quotas on agricultural imports constitute a serious barrier to trade in Japan. This study attempts to estimate the import effect of removal of these quotas, using the tariff-equivalent method. Because in many cases the available data for this estimation are not the most desirable in concept or measurement, the resulting estimates must necessarily be considered to be approximate.

Method of Calculation

The imposition of an import quota causes a wedge between the import price and the domestic price of the imported commodity. Conversely, the removal of a quota reduces the domestic price to the level of the import price. Under the assumption of perfectly elastic foreign supply, the removal of the import quota will increase imports of a given commodity by an amount that depends on the initial level of imports, the percentage reduction in price, and the price elasticity of the import. That is,

$$\Delta M = \eta M_0 \frac{P_d - P_m}{P_d},$$

where ΔM is the increase in imports, η is the import price elasticity for the product in question, P_m is the import price, P_d is the domestic price, and M_0 is the initial import level of the commodity.

The tariff-equivalent of the quota is equal to the percentage by which the domestic price exceeds the price of the imported good, or $(P_d/P_m) - 1$. This percentage tariff-equivalent is applied in the same way as the percentage tariff for normal tariff protection in the methodology for estimating trade liberalization discussed in chapter 2. The final term in the equation above translates this tariff-equivalent into a percentage change in product price resulting from elimination of the quota.[1]

Most of the agricultural commodities controlled by import quotas are also subject to tariffs. The calculations here therefore assume that the removal of the import quota is accompanied by complete elimination of the tariff as well.

Data

The effect of eliminating quotas and tariffs was calculated for all of the "residual" agricultural import quota items, and for four of the government trade items—butter, wheat, barley, and rice. At the level of four-

1. Specifically, with a tariff-equivalent of $(P_d/P_m) - 1$, the percentage change in domestic price after elimination of the quota will be the entire tariff-equivalent divided by unity plus the tariff-equivalent (just as the percentage price change following the elimination of a tariff equals the full tariff divided by unity plus the tariff; see chapter 2). Thus, the percentage price change will be:

$$\frac{(P_d/P_m) - 1}{1 + [(P_d/P_m) - 1]} = 1 - \frac{P_m}{P_d} = \frac{P_d - P_m}{P_d}.$$

The final expression here is the percentage price change shown in the final component of the text equation above.

Table 5-1. *List of Japanese Commodities: All "Residual" Agricultural Import Quota Items and Four Government Trade Items*
Japanese Trade Classification (JTC) in parentheses

BTN code	Commodity
Agricultural "residual" items	
02.01	Beef (011-100, 610)
03.01	Herring, cod, cod roe, yellowtail, sardine, mackerel, jack mackerel, and saury, live, fresh, chilled, or frozen (031-131, 142, 143, 152, 161, 192)
03.02	Herring, cod, cod roe, yellowtail, sardine, mackerel, jack mackerel, and saury, salted or dried and smoked herring (031-212, 221, 229, 230)
03.03	Squid and cuttlefish and scallop (031-314, 315, 323)
04.01	Milk and cream, fresh (022-300)
04.02	Milk and cream, evaporated, condensed, or dried (022-111, 112, 121, 122, 190, 210, 222, 223, 224, 230, 240, 299)
04.04	Cheese and curd, except natural cheese (024-010, 020)
07.05	Beans and peas, dried (054-210, 220, 230, 240, 250, 260, 290)
08.02	Oranges and tangerines, fresh (051-110, 120)
08.11	Oranges and tangerines, temporarily preserved (053-632)
11.01	Cereal flour (046-011, 012, 020; 047-011, 019)
11.02	Cereal meals and groats (046-030, 040; 047-023, 029; 048-112, 119)
11.07	Malt (048-200)
11.08	Starches and inulin (599-511, 512, 513, 514, 519, 520)
12.01	Peanuts (221-100)
12.08	Laver and other seaweeds and konjak (054-871, 872, 879, 880)
16.02	Prepared or preserved meat, except bacon, ham, and sausages (013-811, 819, 820, 891, 893, 899)
17.02	Sugars and syrups, except those of beet and cane (061-911, 912, 920, 931, 941, 942, 949, 950, 960, 970, 981)
20.05	Fruit purees and pastes (053-330, 340)
20.06	Fruit pulp and prepared pineapple (053-911, 919, 962)
20.07	Tomato juice and fruit juices (053-511, 513, 514, 521, 529, 530, 541, 542, 543, 545, 549, 550)
21.04	Tomato sauce and ketchup and seasonings mainly containing sodium glutamate (099-041, 042)
21.07	Food preparations containing sugar and prepared milk, seaweeds, and cereals (099-084, 091, 093, 094, 098, 099)
Government trade items	
04.03	Butter (023-000)
10.01	Wheat and maslin (041-000)
10.03	Barley (043-000)
10.06	Rice (042-110, 120, 210, 220, 290)

Source: *Genko Yunyu Seido Ichiran* [The List of Current Import System] (Japan: Agency for Research on Industry and Trade, 1974). Four-digit numbers are BTN codes; six-digit numbers in parentheses are corresponding JTC codes.

Table 5-2. *Import Price, Domestic Price, and Tariff-Equivalent of Twenty-four Japanese Commodities, 1970*
Prices in yen per kilogram

BTN code	JTC code	Commodity	Import price[a]	Domestic price[a]	Tariff-equivalent
02.01	011-100	Beef	345.5	794.5	1.2996
03.01	031-142	Yellowtail	286.0	460.1	0.6087
	-143	Herring	78.8	90.6	0.1497
03.03	031-314	Squid and cuttlefish	259.3	317.4	0.2241
04.02	022-111	Evaporated milk, sugared	121.3	234.9	0.9365
	-112	Skimmed milk, sugared	141.2	150.8	0.0680
	-121, 122	Evaporated milk, not sugared	99.6	277.1	1.7821
	-210	Powdered milk	176.9	423.5	1.3940
	-221	Powdered skimmed milk	78.5	327.0	3.1656
04.03	023-000	Butter	221.5	591.5	1.6704
04.04	024-010, 020	Cheese	276.8	608.9	1.1998
07.05	054-210	Small red beans	116.0	180.2	0.5534
	-220	Broad beans	51.8	53.7	0.0367
	-230	Peas	46.2	112.1	1.4264
	-240	Green beans	61.2	142.9	1.3350
	-250	French beans	54.7	105.1	0.9214
	-260	Pegrin beans	51.4	139.4	1.7121
08.02	051-110	Oranges	104.5	252.0	1.4115
10.01	041-000	Wheat	24.5	60.2	1.4571
10.03	043-000	Barley	19.5	58.5	2.0000
10.06	042-210	Rice, polished	50.3	149.6	1.9742
11.08	599-51	Starch	27.7	62.8	1.2671
12.01	221-100	Groundnuts (peanuts)	120.9	286.7	1.3714
21.04	099-041	Tomato ketchup	187.0	273.0	0.4599

Sources: The import price is calculated from the import quantity and value in Ministry of Finance, *Nihon Boeki Geppyo* [Japan Exports and Imports]. The domestic price is taken from: for beef, yellowtails, herring, squid and cuttlefish, wheat, barley, rice, and peanuts, *Norin Suisan Tokei Geppo* [Monthly Statistics of Agriculture, Forestry, and Fisheries] (Japan: Ministry of Agriculture and Forestry); for oranges, *Mainichi Shinbun* [The Daily Mainichi], February 14, 1975; for others, *1970 Input-Output Table of Japan* (Government of Japan, 1974).
a. The import and domestic prices are 1970 figures except for oranges, for which 1972 figures were used.

digit BTN categories, a total of twenty-seven items are considered in the analysis. Table 5-1 lists these commodities. Because not all of the commodities contained within each four-digit BTN category are under import quotas, the measurement is performed using data at the level of six-digit Japanese Trade Classification (JTC) categories.[2]

The tariff-equivalents were calculated for twenty-four JTC six-digit items from import and domestic prices of 1970, as shown in table 5-2. In

2. The code numbers of the Japanese Trade Classification (JTC) coincide with Standard International Trade Classification (SITC Revised) at the four-digit level.

Table 5-3. *Assignment of Tariff-Equivalents to Japanese Commodities*

BTN code	JTC code[a]	Tariff-equivalent	Remark on tariff-equivalent[b]
02.01		1.2996	011-100
03.01	031-142	0.6087	
	-143	0.1497	
	-131, 152, 161, 191	0.3792	031-142, 143
03.02		0.3792	031-142, 143
03.03		0.2241	031-314
04.01		1.4692	022-111, 112, 121, 122, 210, 221
04.02	022-111	0.9365	
	-112	0.0680	
	-122, 122	1.7821	
	-210	1.3940	
	-221, 222, 223	3.1656	022-221
	-190, 230, 299	1.4692	022-111, 112, 121, 122, 210, 221
04.03		1.6704	
04.04		1.1998	
07.05	054-210	0.5534	
	-220	0.0367	
	-230	1.4264	
	-240	1.3350	
	-250	0.9214	
	-260	1.7121	
	-290	0.9975	054-210, 220, 230, 240, 250, 260
08.02		1.4115	051-110
08.11		1.4115	051-110
10.01		1.4571	
10.03		2.0000	
10.06		1.9742	042-210
11.01		1.6746	041-000; 043-000; 042-210; 599-51
11.02		1.6746	041-000; 043-000; 042-210; 599-51
11.07		1.6746	041-000; 043-000; 042-210; 599-51
11.08		1.2671	599-51
12.01		1.3714	
12.08		1.1844	All
16.02		1.2996	011-100
17.02		1.1844	All
20.05		1.4115	051-110
20.06		1.4115	051-110
20.07	053-511, 513, 514	0.4599	099-041
	-521, 529, 530, 541	1.4114	051-110
	-542, 543, 545, 549,		
	-550		
21.04		0.4599	099-041
21.07		1.1844	All

a. This column is left vacant for those BTN items all of whose JTC components are assigned with the same tariff-equivalent.

b. This column shows which tariff-equivalent is assigned. For example, "011-100" means the tariff-equivalent calculated for the JTC item 011-100 is assigned for all the components of BTN item 02.01; and "031-142, 143" means the arithmetic average of the tariff-equivalents for JTC items 031-142 and 031-143.

this table, the import prices are unit values at six-digit JTC, that is, weighted averages of c.i.f. prices of products contained within each six-digit category. The domestic prices represent a variety of concepts. The domestic price of beef is the wholesale price of domestically produced beef. The domestic price of yellowtails is the wholesale price of fresh yellowtails, including both domestic and imported. For herring, squid, and cuttlefish, the domestic prices are the wholesale prices of frozen goods that are principally imported. The domestic price of oranges is the wholesale price of the imported product. All the wholesale prices cited above are those of the Tokyo wholesale market. For all the other items, the domestic prices are the producer's prices.

For those commodities for which tariff-equivalents were not obtained directly, the tariff-equivalent is based on that estimated for a similar commodity or on the average of the tariff-equivalents for a number of similar commodities. The details for this procedure are reported in table 5-3.

The import price elasticities used are shown in table 5-4. These elasticities are taken from the more comprehensive set of estimates presented in appendix C of this study and used in the calculations of trade effects of alternative tariff-cutting formulas (chapter 3).

Results

The potential increases in imports resulting from the removal of quotas, in 1971 values, is summarized for four-digit BTN items in table 5-5. In 1971, the total import value of food items under import quotas was $686 million, or 24.1 percent of total food imports. The sum of the potential increments from quota removal is $311 million, or 45.3 percent of the initial import value. The total welfare gain, calculated by traditional "triangle" method,[3] is $230 million. If wheat imports (item 10.01) are excluded, considering possible problems on the supply side for that commodity, the

---

See the UN Department of Economic and Social Affairs, Statistical Office, *Standard International Trade Classification, Revised,* UN Statistical Papers, Series M, no. 34 (New York, 1961).

3. Note the equation:

$$W = 0.5 \Delta M \left(\frac{P_d}{P_m} - 1 \right),$$

where $W =$ welfare gain, $\Delta M =$ increase in imports, $P_d =$ domestic price, $P_m =$ import price. This measure corresponds to the welfare measure in equation 12 of chapter 2 when the postliberalization tariff (t_1) is zero and the domestic price equals import price plus the original tariff (t_0).

Table 5-4. *Import Price Elasticities of Japanese Commodities*

Commodity (SITC code)	Elasticity	Applied to commodity (BTN code)
Food (0)	0.4716	08.02, 08.11, 12.08, 20.05, 20.06, 20.07, 21.04, 21.07
Beef (011-1)	0.9819	02.01, 16.02
Milk and cream (022)	0.5217	04.01, 04.02
Cheese and curd (024)	1.9400	04.03, 04.04
Fish and fish preparation (03)	1.2920	03.01, 03.02, 03.03
Wheat and maslin (041)	0.7628	10.01, 10.03, 10.06, 11.01, 11.02, 11.07, 11.08
Beans and peas (054-2)	0.8225	07.05
Sugar and milk preparations (06)	0.7623	17.02
Oil and seeds (22)	0.2419	12.01

total initial import value is $342 million and the import increment becomes 45.3 percent of that value, or $155 million. The welfare gain is $116 million. As expected, the welfare gain is considerably higher, relative to import value, than that brought about by cutting tariffs on industrial goods (chapter 3).

Table 5-6 shows Japan's import increases by exporting countries. The high rates of the increase of Norway, Sweden, Finland, Austria, Switzerland, and Denmark are because of the commodity composition of imports from these countries, especially the high shares of dairy products (butter and cheese) that have high import price elasticities.

Contrary to the case of tariff liberalization, removal of agricultural quotas would cause relatively small increases of imports from the rest of world in comparison with import increases from the industrial countries. Another important feature of the results is that, when wheat imports are excluded, the increase of imports from the United States becomes strikingly small.

Table 5-7 shows actual rates of import increases of food items under quota in the three years 1971 through 1973. Comparing these figures with the estimated increase of imports because of quota removal (table 5-5), it appears that, in more than half of the items, estimated import increases from liberalization are in fact less than the actual import increases, because of successive increases in quota ceilings during the period from 1970 to 1973. However, the 1973 values reflect large price increases, whereas the liberalization estimates refer to 1971 prices, so that the actual increases in import values for quota items are much smaller in physi-

Table 5-5. *Import Increase and Welfare Gain, by Commodity,*
for Selected Japanese Commodities, 1971 Base
Thousands of dollars

BTN code	Original imports (M_0)	Increase in imports (ΔM)	Percentage change ($[\Delta M/M_0]100$)	Welfare gain
02.01	49,962	27,724	55.5	18,015
03.01	3,510	1,043	29.7	200
03.02	983	349	35.5	66
03.03	17,799	4,209	23.7	472
04.01	0	0	0.0	0
04.02	19,952	7,698	38.6	11,528
04.03	780	947	121.4	791
04.04	22,740	24,061	105.8	14,434
07.05	40,881	14,799	36.2	7,613
08.02	2,498	690	27.6	487
08.11	0	0	0.0	0
10.01	344,781	155,979	45.2	113,639
10.03	59,087	30,046	50.9	30,046
10.06	1,137	576	50.6	568
11.01	38	18	47.4	15
11.02	548	262	47.8	219
11.07	44,447	21,228	47.8	17,774
11.08	5,768	2,459	42.6	1,558
12.01	19,220	2,689	14.0	1,844
12.08	6,670	1,705	25.6	1,010
16.02	1,210	671	55.5	436
17.02	13,585	5,615	41.3	3,325
20.05	97	27	27.9	19
20.06	20,937	5,778	27.6	4,078
20.07	2,226	572	25.7	380
21.04	13	2	15.4	1
21.07	7,626	1,950	25.6	1,155
Total	686,495	311,097	45.3	229,673

cal terms. Nevertheless, the data in table 5-7 suggest that, especially for individual products (such as beef), the estimates of the effect of liberalization are sensitive to the base year that is chosen.[4]

4. To the extent that import increases between 1970 and 1973 are because of price movements alone, however, the choice of the base year would not affect the estimates expressed as proportions of imports. By contrast, if the large import increases in this period reflected rapid liberalization of physical quotas, then the use

Table 5-6. *Japan's Import Increases by Supplying Countries,*
Including and Excluding Wheat, 1971 Base
Thousands of dollars

Exporter	Original imports (M_0)	Increase in imports (ΔM)	Percentage change $([\Delta M/M_0]100)$
Including wheat			
Iceland	35	12	34.3
Norway	4,999	5,151	103.0
Sweden	475	429	90.3
Finland	125	133	106.4
Austria	29	28	96.6
Switzerland	105	102	97.1
Denmark	3,213	2,448	76.2
United Kingdom	3,666	1,559	42.5
Ireland	199	100	50.3
Netherlands	6,110	3,824	62.6
France	7,906	3,234	40.9
Belgium	3,724	1,816	48.8
West Germany	4,919	2,277	46.3
Italy	595	182	30.6
EEC	30,332	15,440	80.9
Canada	146,682	68,280	46.5
United States	201,667	89,322	44.3
Australia	169,974	87,581	51.5
New Zealand	15,101	9,587	63.5
Rest of world	116,978	35,034	29.9
Excluding wheat			
Canada	52,585	25,819	48.9
United States	20,733	7,468	36.0
Australia	99,983	55,917	55.9

Finally, table 5-8 presents 1974 "long-term value" estimates of the import effects of removing quotas. As discussed in chapter 4, although product prices rose to exceptionally high levels between 1971 and 1974, "long-run" prices in 1974 values can best be approximated by inflating 1971 values, using the index of agricultural production costs. This index for the United States, the chief agricultural exporting country, rose by 50

---

of a later base year would give liberalization estimates that would be lower proportions of imports than those based on the earlier year.

Table 5-7. *Rate of Increase in Japan's Import of Commodities under Agricultural Quotas, 1970–73*
Import values in thousands of dollars

BTN code	1970 import value	1973 import value	Rate of increase (percent)
02.01	24,323	314,585	1,193.4
03.01	3,526	17,113	385.3
03.02	1,228	3,142	155.9
03.03	14,032	32,738	133.3
04.01	0	0	0.0
04.02	14,150	40,565	186.7
04.03	667	18,988	2,746.8
04.04	20,559	38,969	89.5
07.05	31,743	45,471	43.2
08.02	1,422	6,829	380.2
08.11	0	0	0.0
10.01	318,364	662,559	108.1
10.03	41,628	143,395	244.5
10.06	2,397	5,292	120.8
11.01	48	49	2.1
11.02	521	673	29.2
11.07	22,297	79,082	254.7
11.08	5,487	11,164	103.5
12.01	19,816	39,596	99.8
12.08	10,172	16,262	59.9
16.02	2,224	5,407	143.1
17.02	17,291	5,183	−70.0
20.05	109	464	325.7
20.06	18,830	8,948	−52.5
20.07	1,631	2,339	43.4
21.04	12	383	3,091.7
21.07	4,042	13,576	235.9

percent in the period. Accordingly, table 5-8 presents the 1971 results increased by 50 percent to arrive at 1974 values in long-term prices. The table includes both the estimates for full quota removal and a figure corresponding to only a 60 percent cut in the tariff-equivalent of the quotas. This latter figure can be compared with the 60 percent tariff cut formula investigated in chapter 3 (all tariff items) and chapter 4 (European variable levies on agricultural imports).

Table 5-8. *Effect on Japan's Imports of Total Removal of Agricultural Quotas and 60 Percent Cut in Tariff-Equivalents, 1974 Base at "Long-Term" Agricultural Prices*
Millions of dollars

Supplier	Total removal	60 percent tariff-equivalent cut
United States	134.0	80.4
Canada	102.4	61.5
Belgium	2.7	1.6
Denmark	3.7	2.2
France	4.8	2.9
Germany	3.4	2.0
Ireland	0.2	0.1
Italy	0.3	0.2
Netherlands	5.7	3.4
United Kingdom	2.3	1.4
Austria	0.0	0.0
Finland	0.2	0.1
Norway	7.7	4.6
Sweden	0.6	0.4
Switzerland	0.2	0.1
Australia	131.4	78.8
New Zealand	14.4	8.6
Rest of world	52.6	31.5
Total	466.6	280.0

Source: See table 5-6, second column.

Qualifications

There are three major sources of possible bias in our measurements: tariff-equivalents, import price elasticities, and the assumptions regarding foreign supply. However, no definite conclusions may be drawn about the direction and magnitude of any final bias.

TARIFF-EQUIVALENT. In most of the items, the wholesale or producer's price of the domestic product is substituted for the domestic price of the imported commodity. As a consequence, the difference in quality between the imported commodity and the domestically produced product is not taken into account. For instance, in the case of beef, imported beef is regarded as of lower quality than beef produced domestically in Japan. In this case, the tariff-equivalent is overestimated. There may, however, be opposite cases, and it is impossible to generalize about the direction of bias in the calculated tariff-equivalents.

Second, because the import prices are on a c.i.f. basis, they do not include the normal costs on the way to the wholesale market, such as costs of storage and transportation. Consequently, when the import prices are compared with wholesale prices, the tariff-equivalents are overestimated. When the import prices are compared with producer's prices, the direction of bias cannot be determined in the absence of information on differences in systems of distribution.

Finally, the import prices of commodities facing quotas might be higher than the normal international prices. That is, foreign suppliers may raise their price to Japan in order to appropriate part of the excess price associated with the restrictive effect of the quota. If this is the case, the tariff-equivalents are underestimated.

IMPORT PRICE ELASTICITY. One problem concerning price elasticity of imports is that, although free-trade elasticities are desirable for this kind of measurement, the only available estimates of elasticities are those estimated using data on imports entering under quotas. This fact may cause an underestimation of the effect of quota liberalization on imports. There is no evidence, however, that the estimated import elasticities of commodities under quota are significantly lower than those of similar nonquota commodities.[5]

Another and more serious problem is that the estimated elasticities are based on relatively small changes in prices. By contrast, in general, the removal of import quotas would cause price reductions on the order of 50 percent. When the domestic price of a commodity is reduced and approaches a certain critical level, below which producers find it necessary to go out of business, the price elasticity of domestic supply of the commodity would become much larger; consequently, the import price elasticity would become larger. For Japan, it is quite possible that the removal of agricultural quotas would reduce domestic prices to or below these critical levels. In this respect, therefore, our estimates of the increase in imports following liberalization may be seriously underestimated.[6]

5. See appendix C.

6. On the other hand, for the single most important product, wheat, other studies suggest import elasticities lower than that used here. Therefore, on the basis of available elasticity estimates, our calculations do not appear to be biased downward. Greenshields has estimated the price elasticity of internal demand for wheat in Japan

Table 5-9. *Japan's Imports before and after Removal of Agricultural Quotas, 1969–73*
Millions of yen

Commodity	1969	1970	1971	1972	1973
Pork	18,624	17,534	11,220[a]	30,506	63,835
Ham and bacon	84	80	73	459[a]	2,225
Grapefruit	229	296	1,599[a]	10,279	9,779
Biscuit	556	760	732[a]	724	1,092

Source: *Gaikoku Boeki Gaikyo* [Summary Report of Trade of Japan] (Japan: Ministry of Finance, monthly reports).
a. Year of liberalization.

ASSUMPTION ON FOREIGN SUPPLY. In the calculations of trade effects of liberalizing quotas, it is assumed that foreign supply is perfectly elastic. However, in view of of the large price change resulting from liberalization and considering the fact that Japan's food imports represent more than a marginal share of world trade in these commodities, the validity of this assumption is questionable. Therefore, this assumption may cause overestimation of import increases resulting from the removal of quotas.

As another basis for examining possible biases in our measurement, table 5-9 presents the actual increases of imports for some commodities for which import quotas were removed in the past. For example, grapefruit imports were liberalized in 1971, and the import value increased more than fivefold the following year. Because there is no evidence of any dramatic increase in the import price of grapefruit,[7] and since the growth of income in one year would cause only a small import increase,[8] most of the large observed increase may be attributed to liberalization. Considering this experience, it would appear that our estimate of the increase in

---

to be −0.54. Bruce L. Greenshields, *Impact of a Resale Price Increase on Japan's Wheat Imports,* U.S. Department of Agriculture, Economic Research Service, Foreign Agricultural Economic Report No. 128 (1977), p. 9. Considering that domestic wheat production is almost negligible, the corresponding import price elasticity (if imports were not restricted by quotas) would also be approximately −0.5. Our estimate applies a higher import elasticity (−0.76; see table 5-4), suggesting that our results for increased wheat imports are not biased downward.

7. The average import price of grapefruit increased by 7.8 percent from 1971 to 1972. *Norin Suisan Tokei Geppo* [Monthly Statistics of Agriculture, Forestry, and Fisheries] (Japan: Ministry of Agriculture and Forestry).

8. An estimate of the income elasticity of demand of fruit is 0.837. *Shokuryo Jukyu Hyo* [Tables of Demand and Supply of Food] (Japan: Agricultural Statistics Association).

imports of oranges (a 26.7 percent rise over initial import levels) may be substantially understated.

To recapitulate, biases may exist in both directions in our estimates, and there is no firm basis for determining whether our results are likely to be overstated or understated. The reliability of these estimates is examined further in the discussion below comparing our estimates with those of other studies.

Employment Effects

Appendix D of this study presents an analysis of the employment effects of liberalizing agricultural nontariff barriers. The results shown in the appendix indicate that total removal of Japanese quotas on agricultural imports would reduce employment by between 492,000 and 1.4 million jobs (for 1971 or 1974 base years, respectively). This represents from 0.94 percent to 2.7 percent of the total labor force, and from 4 percent to 12 percent of total employment in agriculture, fishing, forestry, and food manufacturing. Thus, for the case of Japan, the employment effects of removing agricultural nontariff barriers would dwarf the employment effects of tariff liberalization, which were discussed in chapter 3. Even so, as pointed out in appendix D, these employment effects could still be viewed as moderate when compared with the annual rates of decrease of agricultural employment already taking place in Japan. Therefore, even the much more appreciable job losses from liberalizing quotas on agricultural imports could be accommodated without serious dislocation, especially if quotas were liberalized gradually over a period of years.

United States

Agricultural nontariff barriers in the United States are very limited and involve significant distortions to trade in only two sectors: meat and dairy products. Legislation in 1964 amending the Tariff Act of 1930 called for voluntary export quotas to be applied by foreign suppliers of meat to the U.S. market, with provision for import quotas in the event that foreign voluntary restrictions were inadequate to moderate U.S. imports.[9]

9. 78 Stat. 594.

On the basis of a comparison of U.S. meat prices with world meat prices, Harry H. Bell estimated that the tariff-equivalent of this restriction amounted to 20 percent.[10]

Quotas on agricultural imports into the United States apply to only four commodity groups: wheat for human consumption, specific types of cotton, peanuts, and dairy products.[11] Of these, the import magnitudes of wheat, cotton, and peanuts are negligible so that, even under extremely high assumptions about import price elasticities, and despite high tariff-equivalents of quotas, their increased imports from liberalization would be inconsequential.

Quotas existed on sugar imports until 1975, and in the early 1970s the welfare costs of these restrictions were very high.[12] In 1974 and 1975, however, world sugar prices tripled from their levels of 1970 to 1972,[13] and in 1975 U.S. quotas on sugar imports expired.

By contrast, quotas on dairy products remain serious barriers to imports. Table 5-10 presents estimates of the tariff-equivalent and the estimated increases in imports from both complete and 60 percent liberalization of dairy products and meat. The calculations use the 1970 tariff-equivalent estimates by Bell because there is no evidence of a major increase or decrease in the levels of protection in these two commodities since then. The estimates apply actual 1974 import values as the trade base. Unlike the cases of EEC and Japanese agricultural nontariff barriers, the U.S. barriers exclude feedgrains and, therefore, avoid the prob-

10. Harry H. Bell, "Some Domestic Price Implications of U.S. Protective Measures," in U.S. Commission on International Trade and Investment Policy, *United States International Economic Policy in an Interdependent World,* vol. 1: *Compendium of Papers* (July 1971), p. 465.

11. *Agricultural Trade and the Proposed Round of Multilateral Negotiations,* prepared by the U.S. Foreign Agricultural Service for the Senate Agriculture and Forestry Committee (GPO, 1973), p. 40 (hereinafter referred to as *Agricultural Trade Report*). With respect to sugar quotas, see discussion below.

12. Stephen P. Magee estimated the welfare costs of sugar quotas to be $403 million annually in 1971, or approximately half the value of sugar imports in that year. Stephen P. Magee, "The Welfare Effects of Restrictions on U.S. Trade," *Brookings Papers on Economic Activity, 3:1972,* p. 673. Bell estimated the 1970 tariff-equivalent of the sugar quota at 100 percent. Bell, "Some Domestic Price Implications of U.S. Protective Measures," p. 480). Assuming an import price elasticity of −0.5, the 1971 imports of sugar would have been $1.02 billion instead of $813 million if imports had been wholly liberalized.

13. International Monetary Fund, *International Financial Statistics,* vol. 29 (February 1976), p. 31. However, world prices of sugar declined dramatically during 1976, creating new pressures for protection of the U.S. market.

Table 5-10. *Effect on U.S. Imports of Removal of Major Agricultural Nontariff Barriers, 1974 Base*
Imports in millions of dollars

Product	SITC	1974 imports	Tariff-equivalent of quotas and tariffs (percent)	Import price elasticity	Increased imports, complete liberalization	Increased imports, 60 percent cut in tariff-equivalent
Meat	01	1,343.6	20	−0.44	98.5	59.1[a]
Dairy products (milk, butter, cheese)	022, 023, 024	322.1	90	−0.5	76.3	45.8[b]

Sources: For 1974 imports, Organisation for Economic Co-operation and Development, *Trade by Commodities: Country Summaries*, Series B (OECD, January-December, 1974). For tariff-equivalents, Harry H. Bell, "Some Domestic Price Implications of U.S. Protective Measures," in U.S. Commission on International Trade and Investment Policy, *United States International Economic Policy in an Interdependent World*, vol. 1: *Compendium of Papers* (July 1971), p. 479. For import price elasticity of meat, Mordechai E. Kreinin, "Disaggregated Import Demand Functions—Further Results," *Southern Economic Journal*, vol. 40 (July 1973), p. 20; of dairy products, assumed value.
a. Breakdown by principal supplier: Canada, 2.9; Australia, 16.0; New Zealand, 8.2; EEC, 12.9 (all others, 19.1).
b. Breakdown by principal supplier: Canada, 3.3; Australia, 2.2; New Zealand, 7.4; EEC, 23.5 (all others, 9.4).

lem of 1974 prices far in excess of longer term prices. For the case of meat, an estimated import price elasticity is available from Mordechai E. Kreinin;[14] for dairy products, it is assumed that the price elasticity of imports is −0.5.

The resulting estimates indicate increases in meat imports by approximately $100 million and in dairy imports by $76 million (in 1974 prices) as the result of complete removal of the nontariff barriers. The corresponding effects for a 60 percent cut in the tariff-equivalent are also shown in table 5-10.

Alternative Estimates

In 1973, the U.S. Department of Agriculture prepared estimates of the trade effects of liberalizing agricultural nontariff barriers in Europe, Ja-

14. Mordechai E. Kreinin, "Disaggregated Import Demand Function—Further Results," *Southern Economic Journal*, vol. 40 (July 1973), p. 20. Because the nontariff barriers are voluntary export quotas rather than import quotas, the estimated import demand price elasticity should not be distorted by the presence of protection.

pan, and the United States.[15] Because of the comprehensive nature of that study, and considering its official source, it is important to compare the findings of that study with those reported here and in chapter 4.

The methodology of the *Agricultural Trade Report* was radically different from the approach of this study. Rather than applying import elasticities and tariff-equivalent estimates to actual base-year import data (as is done here), the study made projections of domestic production, consumption, and foreign trade by 1980 under alternative assumptions. The "base" projection assumed no change in trade policies; the "liberalization" case assumed complete liberalization. The trade effects of eliminating protection were determined from the difference between the projections.

In broad terms, the *Agricultural Trade Report* forecast complete elimination of EEC grain imports by 1980 in the absence of liberalization. By contrast, it projected extremely large increases in Japanese imports of beef and dairy products if liberalization occurred, and a shift of European agriculture toward specialization in the production of beef and dairy products. This shift for Europe was projected to require much higher grain imports for feed purposes, on the one hand, and it assumed high levels of European beef and dairy exports to Japan, on the other hand. The central estimates of the study were that full liberalization of the feed-grains and livestock sector would cause a net increase in the U.S. trade balance by $8 billion, a deterioration in the trade balance of Japan by $14 billion, and a deterioration in the trade balance of the EEC by $0.5 billion.[16] Although these figures were for nominal values of 1980, they were based on 1970 values expanded by annual price increases of 4 percent, yielding a 50 percent price increase by the end of the decade. As discussed above, the increase in long-term grains prices (as opposed to higher actual prices) between 1971 and 1974 amounted to 50 percent, so that in very approximate terms the estimates of the *Agricultural Trade Report* should be comparable in dollar values to the estimates in this study.

Table 5-11 compares specific components of the estimates by the U.S. Department of Agriculture with the corresponding estimates of this study. The estimates prepared here are much smaller than those of the U.S. Department of Agriculture.

Table 5-11 also reports estimates based on a study by the Food and

15. See *Agricultural Trade Report.*
16. Ibid., pp. 21–22.

Table 5-11. *Alternative Estimates of Increased Imports Resulting from Complete Removal of Agricultural Nontariff Barriers*
Millions of dollars

Importing area and products	USDA	FAO	This study
EEC of nine			
Beef	1,022	n.a.	135
Wheat	646	1,275	411
Feedgrains	1,935	1,322	843
Soybeans	1,005	n.a.	0
Total, four products	4,608	n.a.	1,389
Japan			
Beef	6,199	n.a.	42
Milk, dairy products	5,109	169	50
Wheat	90	80	234
Feedgrains	1,623	n.a.	45
Soybeans	889	n.a.	0
Total, five products	13,910	n.a.	371
United States			
Beef	−189	n.a.	98
Dairy products	929	1,420	76
Total, two products	740	n.a.	174
Total, three importing areas	19,258	n.a.	1,934

Sources: For USDA, calculated from U.S. Department of Agriculture, Foreign Agricultural Service, *Agricultural Trade and the Proposed Round of Multilateral Negotiations* (April 30, 1973), pp. 153–54, 158–59. For FAO, calculated from Food and Agricultural Organization, *Agricultural Protection and Stabilization Policies: A Framework of Measurement in the Context of Agricultural Adjustment*, C75/Lim/2 (Rome: FAO, October 1975), table 3-6. Physical quantity trade changes for 1971 are converted to value changes by using 1971 unit import values as reported in FAO, *Trade Yearbook 1974*, and, for dairy products, the producer price net of subsidy as shown in FAO, *Agricultural Protection and Stabilization Policies*, appendix A. These values are converted to 1974 long-term prices by a uniform 50 percent increase above the 1971 value levels. For this study, project calculations (referring to imports from nonbloc suppliers for the EEC); table 5-5 (expanded by 50 percent to arrive at 1974 long-term prices); table 5-10; "beef" includes other meats.
n.a. Not available.

Agriculture Organization.[17] That study consolidates all tariff, nontariff, and other measures of government intervention into a single measure of producer subsidy (or tax) and consumer tax (or subsidy) for each major product. Using assumed elasticities of domestic supply and demand, the study then calculates the change in consumption, production, and net exports (exports minus imports) that would be expected from the elimination of government intervention for each product. We have converted

17. Food and Agriculture Organization, *Agricultural Production and Stabilization Policies: A Framework of Measurement in the Context of Agricultural Adjustment*, C75/Lim/2 (Rome: FAO, October 1975).

the study's estimates of changes in physical volumes of trade for the base year 1971 into corresponding value estimates for trade changes.[18] After a further conversion (increasing values by 50 percent to obtain long-run 1974 values), these estimates of trade impact are presented in table 5-11.

As shown in table 5-11, for the EEC the estimated import effect of eliminating nontariff barriers on wheat and feedgrains is about twice as high in the USDA and FAO studies as the estimates in this study. For Japan, however, the FAO results are close to those of this study (for the products with available estimates), while the USDA estimates are much higher.[19] By contrast, the FAO estimate for the impact of U.S. dairy liberalization is even higher than the USDA estimate, and both are far greater than our estimate.

These alternative estimates suggest two basic patterns: first, the USDA estimates are grossly overstated for the case of Japan; second, for the EEC and the United States, our own estimates of increased imports may be understated. As for the second pattern, one explanation may be the difference between our approach, which uses import elasticities, and the alternative approach, which derives imports residually from changes in domestic supply and demand. In particular, the import elasticity method must apply percentage changes to an import base and, if quotas are completely successful in eliminating imports, the import base will be zero—and there will be no base upon which even large percentage increases can operate. In addition, to the extent that measured import elasticities reflect trade insensitivity to price caused by nontariff barriers, the import elasticity approach will tend to understate trade changes from liberalization.

If our own estimates are biased downward because of the import elasticity approach, it should nevertheless be recalled that for the EEC in particular the estimates involve an offsetting upward bias if the levels of nontariff barriers as of 1969 (our base year for rates of protection) are considered to be higher than long-term levels, in the view of much lower

18. Based on unit values of imports in 1971 for wheat, barley, and maize; and on the producer price minus government subsidy-equivalent, as reported in the FAO study, for milk.

19. Note, however, that the FAO study does show significantly larger estimates than this study for rice in the case of Japan. Our estimate indicates only $0.6 million for increased rice imports under complete elimination of nontariff barriers: the FAO estimate is $512 million in increased imports. Both figures are for 1971 volumes and prices. This case probably reflects a tendency of our method toward underestimation in the case of products with an extremely low import base.

protection during recent years of agricultural scarcity. Moreover, some of the estimates of the USDA's *Agricultural Trade Report* appear to be exaggerated in the extreme. A main feature of the study is its high estimate of increased Japanese consumption and imports of beef and dairy products after liberalization. In particular, the study projects an increase of Japanese beef consumption in 1980 from 1.0 billion pounds without liberalization to 9.46 billion pounds with liberalization. The corresponding impact of liberalization on the consumption of dairy products is a rise from 18.1 billion pounds of milk-equivalent to 85.4 billion pounds.[20] Almost surely, these projections are completely beyond any reasonable bounds.

The excess of Japanese price over world price (shown in table 5-3 above) is 130 percent for beef and a weighted average of 196 percent for dairy products. The corresponding percentage price reduction to Japanese consumers from elimination of quotas would be 56.5 percent and 66.2 percent, respectively. Thus, in order for beef consumption to multiply 9.5 times, the price elasticity of consumer demand (not imports) would have to be −15.0; for dairy consumption to multiply by 4.7 times from liberalization, the price elasticity of consumer demand would have to be −5.6.[21] These implicit price elasticities of consumer demand are, to put it mildly, excessive. More realistic price elasticities would not exceed unity. Based on unitary consumer demand elasticity, 1980 consumption would rise by 57 percent for beef and 66 percent for dairy goods, or from 1 million pounds to 1.56 billion pounds of beef and from 18.1 billion pounds to 30 billion pounds of milk, from liberalization in 1980. Correspondingly, liberalization would increase imports by only 0.56/9.46 or 6.6 percent of the amount estimated by the USDA for beef, and by 11.9/67.3 or 18 percent of the amount estimated for dairy products.[22] If

20. *Agricultural Trade Report,* p. 149.

21. Calculated as follows: percentage increase in demand (850 percent, beef; 370 percent, dairy products) equals percentage decrease in price (56.7 percent and 66.2 percent, respectively) multiplied by demand elasticity required.

22. The increased imports probably would not exceed the increased consumption by much because domestic production in Japan may be expected to be quite insensitive to price. Therefore, domestic Japanese production may be expected to decline little in the face of lowered prices. In any event, domestic Japanese production is projected by the USDA to be small even without liberalization (0.75 billion pounds of beef and 13.0 billion pounds of milk); see *Agricultural Trade Report,* p. 155. This leaves little scope for extra imports on the side of reduction in domestic output as opposed to increase in consumption.

these fractions are applied to the *Agricultural Trade Report* estimates shown in table 5-11, then Japan's increased beef and dairy imports from liberalization would be $409 million and $920 million (rather than $6.2 billion and $5.1 billion), respectively.

Once the estimates of trade liberalization of the *Agricultural Trade Report* are recognized to be vastly overstated for Japan, particularly for beef and dairy products, the remaining estimates begin to appear exaggerated as well. Specifically, the report projects increased EEC exports of dairy products of $5.3 billion—of which most are premised on the high estimate of increased Japanese dairy imports. In order to produce the extra dairy exports, the EEC is presumed to import more feedgrains and soybeans— mainly from the United States. As a result, the exaggerated dairy import estimates for Japan lead to overstated projections of EEC dairy exports and excessive estimates of increased EEC imports of feedgrains and soybeans. Indeed, soybeans are not covered by variable-levy protection, so that this study estimates no impact at all of liberalization on EEC imports of soybeans. By contrast, the *Agricultural Trade Report* estimates an increase from liberalization of $1 billion in these imports. This increase is because of indirect effects of expansion in the livestock sector—mostly due, it would appear, to unacceptably high estimates of increased Japanese dairy imports furnished by the EEC.

In short, the estimates of the *Agricultural Trade Report* must be regarded as extremely overstated. The much lower estimates of this study are given support by comparable FAO estimates for Japan in selected products. Nevertheless, our estimates may be somewhat understated for the reasons given above.

The policy implications of the results for agricultural nontariff barriers are extremely important. Some U.S. policymakers appear to have viewed agricultural liberalization as an absolutely essential condition of the Tokyo Round of negotiations, whereas the EEC is perceived to regard agricultural liberalization as anathema. It is quite likely that the emphatic positions taken on both sides reflect exaggerated official notions of the impact on trade of agricultural liberalization, perhaps based on studies such as that of the USDA. Yet, if the estimates of the present study are correct, and even if there is an allowance for some downward bias in our estimates, then the overriding emphasis on agricultural nontariff barriers has been exaggerated out of proportion to their relative importance in liberalizing trade. This fact may be more fully appreciated by an overall evaluation of the impact on trade of liberalizing agricultural nontariff barriers relative to that of liberalizing tariffs on all products.

Overall Assessment

Table 5-12 consolidates the results of chapters 3, 4, and 5 for the trade impact of a 60 percent cut in tariffs on all products and in the tariff-

Table 5-12. *Relative Importance of Tariff Liberalization and Agricultural Nontariff Barrier Liberalization under a 60 Percent Tariff Cut,*
1974 Base
Millions of dollars

| | | | | EEC | |
| | United | | | *Including* | *External* |
Description	*States*	*Canada*	*Japan*	*intra-EEC*	*trade*
Increased imports					
1. Tariff items[a]	3,611	1,680	1,737	2,102	4,495
2. Agricultural nontariff barriers	105	0	280	892	1,927
3. Total	3,716	1,680	2,017	2,994	6,422
4. Line 2 as percent of total	2.8	0	13.9	29.8	30.0
Increased exports[b]					
1. Tariff items[a]	3,821	565	2,237	−100	2,293
2. Agricultural nontariff barriers	562	328	0	−968	67
3. Total	4,383	893	2,237	−1,068	2,360
4. Line 2 as percent of total	12.8	36.7	0	n.a.	2.9
Trade balance					
1. Tariff items[a]	211	−1,116	501	−2,202	−2,202
2. Agricultural nontariff barriers	457	328	−280	−1,860	−1,860
3. Total	668	−788	221	−4,062	−4,062
4. Respending effect, tariff items	421	51	326	882	882
5. Line 1 + line 4	632	−1,065	827	−1,320	−1,320
6. Line 5 + line 2	1,089	−737	547	−3,180	−3,180

Sources: Tables 3-4, 3-7, 4-6, 5-8, 5-10, and project calculations.
n.a. Not applicable.
a. Excludes oil and textiles.
b. Excludes effect of respending by rest of world.

equivalent of agricultural imports facing nontariff barriers. The results show that, although agricultural nontariff barriers are indeed important, they by no means dominate the effects of trade liberalization. They account for only 13 percent of the direct U.S. export increase from 60 percent liberalization. Even if our estimates for agricultural nontariff barriers were doubled to allow for possible underestimation, still less than one-fourth of U.S. export expansion from liberalization would be derived from the liberalization of agricultural nontariff barriers. Moreover, even when considering the net trade balance, the extra agricultural exports would represent only two-fifths of the increase in the U.S. trade balance (when induced U.S. exports attributable to rest-of-world respending are included).

For Canada, liberalization of agricultural nontariff barriers constitutes a more important source of export increase, amounting to 36.7 percent of direct export gains and reducing the trade deficit caused by liberalization from $1.1 billion to $737 million (including the respending effect). For Japan, the inclusion of agricultural quota liberalization would account for 14 percent of total import increases and would reduce the overall trade balance gain from liberalization from $827 million to $547 million (including the respending effect).

The most important relative impact of including agricultural nontariff barriers is in the EEC. The inclusion not only provides 30 percent of the area's total import increase from liberalization, but it also causes a major decline in exports (mainly because of the decrease of French and Dutch agricultural exports to EEC partners). The net result of including agricultural variable levies in the 60 percent liberalization scheme is to raise the EEC trade deficit from $1.3 billion to $3.2 billion (including the respending effect).

In short, the liberalization of agricultural nontariff barriers would figure importantly into overall trade liberalization results, especially for Canada and for the EEC. (For Australia and New Zealand, the reduction of agricultural barriers would also be very important to exports of grains.) However, the major impact of trade results would come from tariff reductions on all products, not from the reduction of agricultural nontariff barriers. Needless to say, this conclusion could be radically reversed if one adopted the U.S. Department of Agriculture's projections in the *Agricultural Trade Report,* which would indicate that liberalization of nontariff barriers

Table 5-13. *Annual Static Welfare Gain from a 60 Percent Cut in Tariff or Tariff-Equivalent Protection, 1974 Base*
Millions of dollars

Area	Tariff items (1)	Agricultural nontariff barriers (2)	Total (3)	Column 2 as percent of column 3 (4)
United States	490	37[a]	527	7.0
Canada	178	0	178	0
Japan	289	207[b]	496	41.7
EEC	451	1,785[c]	2,236	79.8

Sources: Table 3-3; chapters 4 and 5.
  a. Meat: $8.3 million; dairy, $28.9 million.
  b. See text for results of removal of quotas for Japan: $230 million welfare gain for 1971 complete removal. This figure is expanded by 50 percent to 1974 long-run prices, then multiplied by 0.6 to obtain corresponding 60 percent cut welfare gain.
  c. Table 4-1 and chapter 4 text indicate $424.5 million increase in 1971 import value and $850 million welfare gain. The ratio of these figures is applied to expanded 1974 results of table 4-5.

would cause trade changes as large as those to be expected from the liberalization of tariff protection on all goods.[23]

Finally, it is important to consider the relative weight of welfare benefits from the liberalization of agricultural nontariff barriers relative to welfare gains from the liberalization of tariffs. Table 5-13 presents these estimates for the four major participants in the negotiations, for the case of a 60 percent cut in tariffs. The notes to the table provide details regarding the estimates for agricultural nontariff barriers.

As shown in the table, the static welfare gains from liberalizing agricultural nontariff barriers are quite important in Japan, where they are two-thirds the size of the corresponding welfare gains from tariff liberalization alone. In the EEC agricultural liberalization provides still more important welfare gains, approximately four times as large as those from tariff liberalization alone. By contrast, liberalizing U.S. agricultural nontariff barriers would provide only modest additional welfare gains over those from tariff liberalization. Corresponding estimates of total welfare benefits including dynamic effects are difficult to obtain for agricultural liberalization. Because economies of scale are not prominent in agricul-

23. That is, the USDA figure of $18 billion in increased world trade from the elimination of agricultural nontariff barriers is approximately equal to our estimate of a $17 billion increase in world trade from the complete elimination of tariffs on all products excluding textiles and petroleum (table 3-2).

ture,[24] it is possible that the share of agricultural liberalization would be smaller for total welfare benefits than for static welfare benefits.

In sum, judged from the typical negotiating viewpoint of trade balance effects, the liberalization of agricultural nontariff barriers would appear to raise difficulties for the EEC and present opportunities for the United States, Canada, and other agricultural exporting countries. But judged from the consumer-oriented consideration of welfare gains through lower prices, as well as from the standpoint of overall economic savings from reducing inefficient production, the conclusion is the reverse. Among the major participants in the negotiations, the EEC would receive by far the largest gains from negotiations liberalizing agricultural trade. Moreover, these gains probably would far outweigh those that the EEC could expect from liberalization on tariff items alone.

24. See, for example, Earl O. Heady and John L. Dillon, *Agricultural Production Functions* (Iowa State University Press, 1961), pp. 629–30.

CHAPTER SIX

Other Nontariff Barriers

THE CENTRAL empirical estimates of this study refer to the effects of liberalizing tariffs and agricultural nontariff barriers. However, nontariff barriers other than those in agriculture also are important in the negotiations of the Tokyo Round. This chapter considers the principal categories of nontariff barriers, reporting previous quantitative estimates of the likely effects of removing discrimination in government procurement and discussing in qualitative terms the principal issues involved regarding other nontariff barriers.

Government Procurement

Discrimination against imports in the procurement of merchandise is explicit under U.S. law and implicit in administrative practices in other industrial countries. Under the "Buy America" Act, a part of U.S. legislation since 1933, U.S. government agencies give preference to purchases of domestic goods. Since 1954 the preference has been a 6 percent price differential, which may be increased to 12 percent if the low-bidding U.S. firm is a small business or is located in an area of unemployment. Procurement by the U.S. Defense Department is even more discriminatory. Since 1959, under the justification of balance-of-payments reasons, Defense Department procurement has accorded a 50 percent price differential preference to domestic over foreign suppliers.[1]

1. See Robert E. Baldwin, *Nontariff Distortions of International Trade* (Brookings Institution, 1970). See 41 U.S. Code, sections 10a–10d.

The continuation of the 50 percent preference for Defense Department purchases is especially flagrant after the movement to flexible exchange rates and the general improvement in the international trade position of the United States in the mid-1970s. It is also likely, however, that much of the most important defense procurement is of sophisticated systems only available from U.S. suppliers in any event.

By contrast to direct, legally stipulated government discrimination in the United States, discriminatory measures are tacit in other countries, but they are often present in the form of administrative practices. In the United Kingdom, the Treasury traditionally has exercised restraint on major government imports for balance-of-payments reasons. Preferences to domestic suppliers in the past have existed for products such as computers, post-office equipment, and military supplies. In France, although no formal general preference exists for domestic suppliers, favoritism exists for the development of particular sectors (such as the electronics industry) as well as for certain social groups (such as producers' cooperatives). Similarly, Japanese legislation makes no formal provision for preferences to domestic suppliers, but executive practices favor bids from domestic concerns on a range of items such as automobiles, office machines, computers, machinery, aircraft, machine tools, and measuring instruments. In Germany, by contrast, a specific 1960 government decree specified that foreign bids be treated identically to domestic bids. Moreover, Germany has practiced "bilateral balancing" by making purchases of U.S. military equipment to help offset U.S. balance-of-payments losses associated with the costs of stationing U.S. troops in Germany.[2]

In short, administrative flexibility to accept bids other than on the basis of price, combined with general or specific favoritism toward domestic firms, leads to the likelihood of at least some degree of discrimination against imports in the procurement of goods by most governments.

How significant is government discrimination as a nontariff barrier? A reasonable approach to the quantitative investigation of this question has been applied by Robert E. Baldwin[3] and by Thomas C. Lowinger.[4]

2. These descriptions are provided in Baldwin, *Nontariff Distortions of International Trade,* pp. 64–66.

3. Ibid.

4. Thomas C. Lowinger, "Discrimination in Government Procurement of Foreign Goods in the U.S. and Western Europe," *Southern Economic Journal,* vol. 42 (January 1976), pp. 451–60.

The method examines the sectoral composition of government purchases. Then it applies the economy-wide ratio of imports to total supply for each sector to the amounts of sectoral government purchases to compute the level of government imports that would exist if the government had "import propensities" similar to those of the private sector.[5] These hypothetical government imports are then compared with actual government imports, and the difference provides a measure of the magnitude of imports forgone because of discrimination in government procurement.

The approach has many limitations. It is uncertain whether the products purchased by the government are truly similar to those used by private firms, even within detailed product categories from input-output tables, which are the normal source of data for the estimates. Moreover, indirect effects are omitted, such as private-sector imports required to provide intermediate inputs into the manufacture of goods delivered to the government. Another effect that is omitted is any possible offsetting increase in private-sector purchases of imports induced by a lowering of import prices attributable to government discrimination against imports. This last effect, however, is unlikely to be significant in most cases since the government's potential purchases will be small relative to supply from the entire world market.

Against these weaknesses, the basic strength of the method is that it permits analysis of government discrimination regardless of source: overt preferences or invisible but dominant patterns of discriminatory administrative practices.

Table 6-1 reports estimates by Baldwin and by Lowinger of the magnitude of imports forgone by governments because of discriminatory practices, as measured by the method just described.[6] The estimates are pri-

---

5. Ideally, private-sector ratios of imports to supply rather than economy-wide ratios (including the government sector) would be used for the calculations.

6. Note that the only case in which results of the two studies may be compared directly is that of France in 1965 (see table 6-1). Here, the difference is due to the fact that Lowinger, who was writing at a later date, had available 1965 European input-output tables, whereas Baldwin had available only the 1959 input-output tables combined with a separate source on government import data (referring to 1966 instead of 1965). See Lowinger, "Discrimination in Government Procurement of Foreign Goods," pp. 456 and 460; and Baldwin, *Nontariff Distortions of International Trade,* p. 76. The other case in which a comparison may be made is that of the United States. Here, the ratio of hypothetical to actual government imports found by Lowinger for 1963 is almost identical to that found by Baldwin for 1958 (see table 6-1).

Table 6-1. *Estimates of Discrimination against Imports in Government Procurement*
Millions of dollars

Country	Year (1)	Study[a] (2)	Actual government imports (3)	Hypothetical government imports without discrimination (4)	Column 4 minus column 3 (5)	Column 5 in 1974 prices[b] (6)
United States	1958	B[c]	37	231	194	314
United States	1963	L[d]	160	1,131	971	1,571
France	1965	B[c]	44	325	281	446
France	1965	L	195	246	51	81
Germany	1965	L	1,238	346	−892	−1,415
Italy	1965	L	77	85	8	13
Netherlands	1965	L	104	101	−3	−5
Belgium	1965	L	100	88	−12	−19
United Kingdom	1968	L	356	534	178	282

a. **B** = Robert E. Baldwin, *Nontariff Distortions of International Trade* (Brookings Institution, 1970), pp. 72, 76.
L = Thomas C. Lowinger, "Discrimination in Government Procurement of Foreign Goods in the U.S. and Western Europe," *Southern Economic Journal*, vol. 42 (January 1976), pp. 451–60.
b. Inflating by U.S. dollar wholesale price index for industrial goods; International Monetary Fund, *International Financial Statistics*, vol. 29 (May 1976).
c. Excluding petroleum.
d. Excluding agriculture, mining, ordnance, petroleum.

marily for the mid-1960s. However, there is little reason to expect that the extent of discrimination has changed since then. As a minimum estimate of "forgone imports," we have inflated the estimates to 1974 dollar prices to provide an extremely approximate estimate of trade magnitudes comparable to those calculated in the rest of this study for tariff and agricultural nontariff barriers. This monetary "updating" makes no provision for real growth in the amount of government imports forgone (which would be expected in view of real growth in trade and government spending, unless offset by a decline in the relative degree of government discrimination).

Baldwin's estimates for 1958 show hypothetical government imports more than six times as high as actual government imports in the United States; Lowinger's U.S. estimates for 1963 indicate a seven-to-one relationship. Both studies therefore find very strong U.S. discrimination in relative terms. In absolute terms, stated in 1974 prices, the two studies indicate that, in the absence of discrimination, U.S. government imports would have been from $314 million to $1.6 billion higher than actually occurred. With a simple average (in the absence of the clear superiority of one study over the other), an approximate estimate of the discriminatory effect of U.S. government procurement procedures for 1974 would be in the neighborhood of $1 billion. If a "60 percent reduction" in the extent of government procurement "protection" were considered, then an increase of U.S. imports of $600 million might be expected.[7] This amount is approximately one-sixth as large as the increase in U.S. imports to be expected from a corresponding 60 percent cut in U.S. tariffs ($3.6 billion) and agricultural nontariff barriers ($105 million). (See table 5-12.)

For Germany, the Netherlands, and Belgium, the method applying private-sector import propensities yields negative estimates of government

---

7. A 60 percent reduction in the extent of protection by government discrimination is admittedly an ambiguous concept. To the extent that government discrimination is explicit in legal provisions for percentage price preferences allowed to domestic suppliers (as under U.S. practice, described above) a 60 percent cut in discriminatory protection would amount to a 60 percent reduction in the preferences allowed. The meaning of a 60 percent cut in discrimination obviously is more obscure where the discrimination takes the form of administrative practice. In this latter case, however, it might mean the submission to competitive bidding procedures of 60 percent of those government procurement cases that otherwise would have been subject to contract awards without fully competitive bidding.

discrimination against imports. In Germany, which is the most important case, this result probably reflects patterns of military purchases from the United States.[8] At the least, it may be said that these three countries do not show evidence of government discrimination *against* imports. Similarly, discrimination appears inconsequential for Italy.

For France and the United Kingdom, government discrimination appears to be relatively large. Averaging the Baldwin and Lowinger estimates after conversion to 1974 prices, French government discrimination would appear to curtail imports by about $260 million yearly. Combining this figure with the estimate for the United Kingdom (at 1974 prices), a total of $545 million would be a minimum estimate for the limiting effect on total EEC imports annually because of government discrimination. Once again considering a 60 percent cut in this "protection," liberalization of this nontariff barrier would appear likely to generate at least $330 million in additional annual imports. This amounts to only about 7 percent of the total increase in imports from outside the EEC for a corresponding liberalization of tariffs ($4.5 billion) and agricultural nontariff barriers ($1.9 billion).

In sum, it appears that the reduction of government discrimination would represent a more significant source of trade liberalization in the United States than in the EEC. (Estimates for Japan and other industrial countries are not available.) This conclusion is not startling considering the fact that only the United States has explicit legal provisions for discrimination.

Appropriate forms of liberalizing government procurement would include the reduction or elimination of legal national procurement preferences, as well as the elaboration of a standard set of procedures providing for open competitive bidding as well as for intercountry consultation in cases where exporters complain of discriminatory practices.[9]

---

8. Lowinger suggests that the estimate of discrimination is biased downward for Germany by the presence of military imports, for which no appropriate private sector propensity exists. Lowinger, however, explicitly removes military purchases in his calculations for France, the most important European case of discrimination included in our estimates below. Lowinger, "Discrimination in Government Procurement of Foreign Goods," p. 456.

9. For suggestions of appropriate reform measures in this area, see Baldwin, *Nontariff Distortions of International Trade,* pp. 78–80.

Other Nontariff Barriers

For the remaining nontariff barriers, we have no quantitative estimates of prospective effects of liberalization. For the purpose of providing an overview of the issues involved in the Tokyo Round of negotiations, however, this section briefly discusses each of the major remaining nontariff barriers.[10]

Border Tax Adjustments

European countries rely on indirect taxes, such as value-added taxes, much more heavily than the United States, which relies more on direct income taxes for revenue. Under GATT rules, indirect taxes may be rebated when a product is exported, but there is no corresponding provision for the rebate of direct taxes. Thus, European countries exempt firms from indirect taxes on exports, or rebate to the firms any indirect taxes paid. Moreover, foreign goods entering Europe face an indirect tax levied on the entire import value including tariff duty, with the indirect tax rate equal to that applied to the corresponding domestic product.

Are these "border tax adjustments" a nontariff barrier discriminating against imports into, and in favor of exports from, countries using indirect taxes and making these adjustments? The traditional answer of economists is no. Conventional analysis of the issue of border tax adjustment defines two alternative principles of taxation: by origin (production tax) or by destination (consumption tax).[11] Under the principle of taxation at the origin, there is no rebate of taxes on exports, nor any adjustment raising taxes on imports (because they in turn have been taxed in the originating country). Under the principle of destination, excise taxes imposed in the originating country are rebated when the product is exported, and imported goods are subject to a tax levy equal to the excise tax imposed

10. The reader interested in more thorough treatment is referred to: ibid.; U.S. Tariff Commission, *Trade Barriers,* part 2, *Nontariff Trade Barriers,* Report to the Senate Finance Committee T.C. publication 665 (1974); and U.S. Commission on International Trade and Investment Policy, *United States International Economic Policy in an Interdependent World* (GPO, 1971).

11. See, for example, Harry G. Johnson and Melvyn B. Krauss, "Border Taxes, Border Tax Adjustments, Comparative Advantage, and the Balance of Payments," *Canadian Journal of Economics,* vol. 3 (November 1970), pp. 595–602.

domestically. In this way, foreign buyers are not discouraged from purchasing a country's exports just because the country imposes a consumption tax on the product at home; nor are domestic consumers artificially
encouraged to purchase imports rather than the domestic good (although
they would be so encouraged if imports escaped the consumption tax).[12]

There are two principal policy problems with border tax adjustments
at present. The first involves a conflict between U.S. law on countervailing duties (dating from legislation in 1897 and 1930) and GATT provisions. The second involves different treatment of direct taxes and indirect taxes.

U.S. law has been interpreted in key precedent cases (especially *Downs
v. United States* in 1903) to require that foreign rebates of excise taxes on
exports be considered as bounties and therefore subject to offsetting
countervailing duties by the United States.[13] U.S. law therefore appears
to contradict the "destination" principle for border adjustment of indirect
taxes. International practice as established under article VI(4) of GATT
explicitly provides for treatment by the destination principle, however,
and rules out the imposition of countervailing duties against rebates of
excise taxes.[14] The first problem, then, is that U.S. law on countervailing
duties opens Pandora's box to legal assault on the generally accepted
practice of rebating excise taxes on exports, thereby casting in doubt the
status of virtually the entire list of exports to the United States from other
countries in general and from Europe in particular.[15]

12. Special problems arise, however, if indirect tax rates vary considerably across
products. In this case, the use of border tax adjustments will discriminate in favor of
heavily taxed items (by giving a relatively high rebate to their exportation and a
penalty to their importation).

13. Melvyn B. Krauss, "Border Tax Adjustments: A Potential Trans-Atlantic
Trade Dispute," *Journal of World Trade Law,* vol. 10 (March–April 1976), p. 147.

14. Contracting Parties to the General Agreement on Tariffs and Trade, *Basic
Instruments and Documents,* vol. 1 (Geneva, 1952), p. 22.

15. In the spring of 1977 this issue flared up in a U.S. Customs Court ruling that
countervailing duties must be applied to imports of Japanese television sets to offset
rebates of indirect taxes. Encouraged by this finding, U.S. steel producers pushed for
a summary judgment from the Customs Court in their own suit against the rebate
of indirect taxes on imported steel from Europe. As indicated by U.S. Special Trade
Representative Robert Strauss, if the U.S. government failed to reverse the ruling in
appeals (and, correspondingly, if the steel producers and other groups were to win
similar cases), then the whole outlook for trade liberalization would deteriorate
seriously. Because of the resulting contradiction between U.S. legal rulings and
GATT regulations, it would become necessary to introduce legislation changing

The second problem involves different treatment of direct and indirect taxes. GATT rules permit the rebate of indirect taxes (such as Europe's value-added taxes) for exports. However, GATT makes no allowance for rebates of direct taxes. Thus, in effect, GATT practice allows the choice of either the principle of origin (no adjustment) or the principle of destination (rebate on exports, extra tax on imports) when the tax is indirect, but gives no alternative to treatment by origin when the tax is direct. To the extent that direct taxes fall strictly on factor incomes to producers, this distinction makes sense. According to some analysts, however, because corporate income taxes are often passed on to consumers through higher prices, the direct tax becomes a consumption tax rather than a production tax, and therefore treatment under the destination (or consumption) principle should be allowed.[16] In this viewpoint, GATT rules should be revised to allow rebate of direct as well as indirect taxes on exports. More generally, U.S. businesses have claimed that GATT rules discriminate against them, because the United States relies more heavily on direct taxes (no rebate on exports) whereas European tax revenues come more heavily from indirect taxes. In fact the Trade Act of 1974 provides that U.S. negotiators should seek revision of GATT rules "to redress the disadvantage to countries relying primarily on direct rather than indirect taxes for revenue needs."[17]

There are practical and theoretical problems with the proposals to allow rebates on direct as well as indirect taxes on exports. At the practical level, it would be virtually impossible to sort out corporate profit tax charges as a fraction of price for countless goods, often manufactured by multiproduct companies unprepared to divulge profit rates by product line. Moreover, if rebates were limited to that component of profit tax successfully shifted onto consumers through higher prices, it would be

---

U.S. law. Yet, the introduction of new legislation in the trade area at a time of rising protectionism would run the risk of losing much of the mandate for trade liberalization obtained in the Trade Act of 1974. David S. Broder and James L. Rowe, Jr., "Strauss Raps U.S. Steel Suit," *Washington Post,* June 14, 1977. Subsequently, the U.S. Court of Customs and Patent Appeals ruled that countervailing duties should not be applied in the case of Japanese television sets, reversing the lower court ruling and, at least temporarily, defusing this potentially explosive issue concerning rebates of indirect taxes on exports. James L. Rowe, Jr., "Retaliatory Tax by U.S. on Imports Ruled Unneeded," *Washington Post,* July 29, 1977.

16. Krauss, "Border Tax Adjustments," pp. 148–56.

17. 88 Stat. 1986.

necessary to identify the proportion of tax shifted (an extremely elusive task). At the theoretical level, the entire exercise of allowing rebates of direct taxes would provide no change in competitive advantage to U.S. exporters, because general equilibrium effects (in particular, appreciation in the exchange rate) would offset any initial partial equilibrium change in competitive position.[18]

Looked at from the other side, eliminating foreign countries' rebates of excise taxes on exports and removing their extra import taxes equal to domestic excise taxes would not provide U.S. firms a competitive advantage either. Such a move would mean that European currencies would tend to depreciate, with the change in exchange rate offsetting the elimination of border tax adjustments.

In sum, current international practice of rebating indirect taxes on exports and imposing excise taxes on imports equal to those on domestic goods appears to be correct procedure for the purpose of avoiding tax distortions to international comparative advantage. U.S. legislation on countervailing duties should not be applied in a manner contrary to this practice. Moreover, those who argue that the system is unfair to the United States because it does not provide rebates of direct taxes ignore, first, the practical impossibilities of introducing such rebates and, second, their ineffectuality in changing competitive relationships once general equilibrium adjustments are taken into account.

Quantitative Restrictions

Quotas limiting the amount of imports are the most restrictive form of protection. Though greatly reduced in the postwar period, they remain important in agriculture and they may be reappearing in some sensitive industrial sectors. Under GATT rules, quotas are "illegal" except under articles XII and XVIII (allowing quotas for balance-of-payments reasons but ironically not permitting the more efficient form of protection, tariffs). An important form of quotas in recent years, the self-imposed

18. As Johnson and Krauss put it: "The fallacy [of ignoring general equilibrium effects] is exemplified by the long-standing belief in the United States that, since the US tax system relies primarily on corporation and personal income tax, to which the origin principle applies, while European tax systems rely more on consumption taxes to which the destination principle applies, United States producers are placed at an unfair disadvantage in international competition." Johnson and Krauss, "Border Taxes, Border Tax Adjustments, Comparative Advantage, and the Balance of Payments," pp. 598–99.

"voluntary export quota" applied to exporters in the face of pressure from importing countries does not appear at all in the GATT rules.[19]

The most important problem in the area of quantitative restrictions is the recent threat of new quotas, voluntary export quotas, "orderly marketing arrangements," and cartel-like regimes of "organized trade." Continued recession in Europe and in some industries in the United States led to growing pressure during 1977 for such measures, especially in the sectors of steel, shipbuilding, textiles, shoes, and some electronic goods. In the spring of 1977 the United States entered into voluntary quota agreements with South Korea and Taiwan on shoes and with Japan on color television sets. In steel, the U.S. administration resorted to a scheme of "reference prices" designed in principle to expedite antidumping procedures but which might lead in practice to a cartel-like form of market sharing with the government providing oligopolistic price leadership.[20] For its part, the European Economic Community turned to the old concept of controlling trade through cartels in order to deal with problems of excess capacity in the steel and shipbuilding industries, and concluded export restraint agreements with major suppliers of imported steel. Similarly, the EEC pressured suppliers of textile imports to reduce their quotas.[21] The trade impact of these new restrictions is difficult to judge, and it is unclear how permanent they will be, given their emergence in response to primarily cyclical phenomena.

Quantitative restrictions on trade can change abruptly. A 1972 study of U.S. protection identified substantial annual welfare costs from the following quantitative restrictions: petroleum, $1.5 billion; textiles, $1.25 billion; steel, $0.4 billion; and sugar, $0.4 billion.[22] Since that time, petroleum quotas have been eliminated. The broad set of voluntary export controls on steel has expired, although for specialty steel direct and voluntary quotas were imposed on Europe and Japan, respectively, in the spring of 1976. In the face of sharply higher world prices for sugar, restrictive U.S. country quotas expired in 1975 (although new tariffs and domestic support priecs were implemented in the fall of 1977). On bal-

19. U.S. Tariff Commission, *Trade Barriers,* part 2, *Nontariff Trade Barriers,* p. 146.

20. *Wall Street Journal,* May 23, 1977; *Washington Post,* June 22, 1977; *Washington Post,* November 27, 1977.

21. Jan Tumlir, "The New Protectionism: Transatlantic Similarities and Contrasts" (Geneva, 1977; processed).

22. Stephen P. Magee, "The Welfare Effects of Restrictions on U.S. Trade," *Brookings Papers on Economic Activity, 3:1972,* pp. 671–73.

ance, restrictions in petroleum, steel, and sugar were much less severe in 1977 than in 1972. The common theme behind the fluctuations in these restrictions was first the need to fight inflation in the period 1973–75 and then renewed pressures for protection as sectoral recession became a problem.

The case of coal is another illustration of the fluctuation in quantitative restrictions. Identified by Baldwin in 1970 as the most important single commodity affected by quotas and subsidies,[23] by the time of the Tokyo Round increased energy prices had raised world demand for coal and the sector did not feature importantly in discussions on nontariff barriers.

A recent study by the U.S. Tariff Commission attempts to examine the pattern of quantitative restrictions on trade. The study reports the "number" of restrictions by country. Unfortunately, the result is not very illuminating with respect to the extent to which trade is impeded by these restrictions.[24]

It is beyond the scope of this study to enumerate the major current quantitative restrictions on trade or to calculate their import-impeding effect. However, four generalizations on these nontariff barriers appear to be warranted. First, the most important single quantitative restriction is the arrangement of voluntary export quotas on textiles. Second, several major quantitative restrictions have been reduced in recent years, primarily as the result of anti-inflationary policies. Third, except for the textile sector, agriculture is the sector most affected by import quotas (particularly in Japan; see chapter 5). And fourth, the new pressures for "organized trade" in steel, shipbuilding, textiles, shoes, televisions, and perhaps other sectors pose a protectionist challenge that will require strong political leadership to resist.

Standards

The requirement that products meet certain standards for consumer protection frequently causes a technical barrier to trade.[25] Precise specifications of product standards vary from country to country. An imported product that is manufactured in accordance with norms of the exporting country may be subject to a serious barrier if the importing country re-

23. Baldwin, *Nontariff Distortions of International Trade,* pp. 34–35.
24. U.S. Tariff Commission, *Trade Barriers,* part 2, *Nontariff Trade Barriers.*
25. This section draws upon ibid., chapter 10.

quires that the production specifications be consistent with its own standards, or even that the import must be subjected to time-consuming and costly verifying tests conducted by the importing country. In a sense, standards favor domestic supply over foreign supply in a way similar to the favoritism to domestic supply provided by fluctuating exchange rates, under which domestic suppliers have the advantage of certainty about price quotations merely as a side effect of being located in the same country as the buyer.

Increased attention to safety and environmental standards in recent years has heightened the possibilities of trade conflict.[26] A general governmental trend toward requiring more completely specified product standards—with respect to sizes, packaging, labeling and marking, and performance ratings (especially in the electronics industry)—has meant a growing emergence of complaints by exporters against foreign limitations on their products. In addition, certain long-standing trade problems associated with standards, such as U.S. limitations on meat imports from countries with foot-and-mouth disease (as well as from countries whose inspection programs are not approved by the U.S. Department of Agriculture), continue to be of significance.

The rational way to reduce the likelihood that legitimate national standards will restrict trade is to negotiate codes providing for: the harmonization of standards wherever possible; the maximum possible recognition by importing countries of product tests conducted by authorities in exporter countries; acceptance of the principle that standards artificially designed to screen out imports are contrary to trading rules, with provision for consultative mechanisms to adjudicate alleged violations of this principle.[27]

Although there exist no comprehensive estimates on the trade-restricting effects of standards, this particular nontariff barrier appears to be significant and growing in importance.

Subsidies and Countervailing Duties

Another area of growing confrontation among countries involves countervailing duties imposed to offset government subsidies to exports.

26. Examples include the application of safety and pollution regulations to automobiles manufactured in countries with different standards, and the issue of whether permission should be granted for the Concorde aircraft to land in the United States.

27. Substantial progress had been made early in the Tokyo Round toward a code on standards.

Even in straightforward cases of subsidy to stimulate exports, certain issues are in dispute. One question is whether importing countries have the right to impose a countervailing duty even if there is no demonstrable "injury" to domestic firms. GATT regulations provide that injury must be shown in order for countervailing duties to be applied, but U.S. legislation on the subject (the Tariff Act of 1930, which predates GATT) requires use of the measure even without demonstration of domestic injury.[28]

A second issue in export subsidies is whether less developed countries should be partially or fully exempted from countervailing duties. There are reasonable arguments for at least partial exemption, in the light of the need for export stimulus in developing country economies that otherwise discriminate against exports by their general economic structure (see chapter 7).

A third significant issue regarding subsidies and countervailing duties is whether countervailing duties should be allowed when the subsidy involved is only incidentally related to exports and is primarily a part of national development policies. In view of the proliferation of national programs for the development of selected regions or industries, special "bounties" or subsidies arise in a variety of forms: tax exemption, direct government subsidies and grants, government loans at low interest rates, and so forth. If imported goods produced by firms receiving such incentives are subject to countervailing tariffs, then the stage is set for countless confrontations among trading partners.

Still another aspect of the subsidy issue involves the loss of exports to subsidized export competitors in the markets of third countries. One of the principal issues in this area concerns the practice of the EEC, under the Common Agricultural Policy, of providing agricultural export subsidies to dispose of surpluses accumulated because of high internal support prices.[29]

The reasonable direction for negotiations on countervailing duties and subsidies is to seek agreement on principles that would: first, establish

28. See Peter B. Feller, "Mutiny Against the Bounty: An Examination of Subsidies, Border Tax Adjustments, and the Resurgence of the Countervailing Duty Law," *Law and Policy in International Business,* vol. 1 (Winter 1969), pp. 17–76.

29. U.S. criticism of the practice has only recently been freed of the embarrassment of American subsidies. Such subsidies were eliminated after the abortively subsidized sale of wheat to the Soviet Union in 1972.

that countervailing duties would be applied only in cases of demonstrated injury;[30] second, provide that domestic development policies be drawn in such a way that they do not primarily subsidize firms that will produce for export rather than for domestic consumption; and, third, restrict or eliminate the use of subsidies to exports of goods in surplus because of related government programs.

Safeguards

An especially difficult area of nontariff barriers to trade is that of safeguards. It is accepted practice under GATT rules that when the existence of a domestic industry is threatened by imports, some form of temporary protection may be extended as a "safeguard." There is ambiguity, however, about what types of situations and protective measures legitimately qualify for safeguard action. Problems in this area have been increased by changes in U.S. law under the Trade Act of 1974. These changes make it easier for an industry to qualify for safeguard action. In addition, the new law shifts the weight of decision making away from the executive branch toward the Congress.

Under the Trade Act of 1974, it is easier for an industry to be found subject to import injury by the International Trade Commission than was the case under the Trade Expansion Act of 1962. The earlier law required that increased imports be a "major" cause of injury or a threat of injury; the new law applies the more lenient criterion that increased imports need be only a "substantial" cause, defined as "important and not less than any other cause."[31] In addition, whereas the earlier law had required that injury from imports be demonstrably related to tariff reductions negotiated under international agreements in order for a firm to qualify for import relief, the new law requires no such linkage of increased imports to trade liberalization.

The shift to congressional authority arises in the implementation of recommendations by the International Trade Commission. The commission may recommend import relief in the form of higher tariffs, tariff quotas, quantitative limits, orderly marketing agreements, or adjustment assistance. Under the earlier law, the President was not bound by the

30. In the absence of dislocation among domestic firms, the entry of foreign subsidized goods should be desired as a windfall gain, not opposed.

31. 88 Stat. 2012.

commission's recommendation and, in order to force executive branch compliance, the Congress would have had to pass a special law for each case. Under the new law, if the President rejects the commission's recommendation, the Congress may override the President by a simple majority vote and enforce the measures recommended by the commission.

The new teeth in U.S. safeguard provisions have been evident in two important product areas, imports of television sets and shoes. In early 1977 the International Trade Commission recommended that a combination of tariffs and quotas be imposed on shoe imports and that tariffs on imported television sets be raised from 5 percent to 25 percent.[32] The response of the Carter administration was to negotiate voluntary export quotas with Japan for television sets and with Taiwan and Korea for shoes. The severity of these voluntary export controls was undoubtedly influenced by the administration's awareness that, in the absence of decisive measures, the Congress would be likely to enforce the International Tariff Commission's recommendations.

The trend toward protectionist moves under the safeguard provisions probably reflects the increased level of unemployment associated with the 1974–75 recession, the worst since the 1930s. It is unclear whether the changes provided under the 1974 law will cause a protectionist effect over the longer term. It does appear, however, that the law represents a move on the part of the U.S. Congress to make certain that the executive branch carries out legislative intent in the area of import relief.

For the Tokyo Round of negotiations, the challenge is to arrive at a common set of procedures considered internationally acceptable in the implementation of safeguards. One key to the negotiations in this area is the determination of generally acceptable standards for the conditions that constitute import injury.

Access to Supply

Export controls represent a new nontariff barrier that has joined the ranks of major impediments to trade. Some of the recent controls, such as U.S. restrictions on soybean exports in 1973–74, have resulted from attempts to dampen domestic inflation without regard to the corresponding inflationary impact on importing countries. The other area of export

32. James L. Rowe, Jr., "U.S. Panel Urges Higher Tariffs on Imported TV Sets," *Washington Post,* March 13, 1977.

controls has been that of producer cartel action for political or economic purposes, the most dramatic case being the Organization of Petroleum Exporting Countries (OPEC). The interruption of export supply for either the anti-inflationary or the cartel reasons represents a serious recent worsening in the conditions of world trade.

A factor complicating negotiations concerning "access to supply" is the fact that many suppliers of raw materials are developing countries anxious to duplicate the success of OPEC in other products. Nevertheless, it would seem possible that negotiations would arrive at agreements providing assurances from these countries on access to supply in return for agreement on other issues of importance to them—such as special treatment for developing countries under countervailing duties.

With respect to the industrial countries, prospects for agreements limiting supply restrictions would be greatly enhanced by the establishment of national or international grain reserves. It was the depletion of U.S. grain reserves that ushered in the skyrocketing of grain prices and the resulting imposition of export controls. Even without grain-reserve agreements, however, it should be possible for industrial countries to arrive at codes severely limiting export controls.

Conclusion

This chapter has described briefly the issues involved in negotiations on several of the nontariff barriers being considered in the Tokyo Round.[33] Other authors' estimates have been reported, and updated, for

33. Some nontariff barriers are omitted entirely in this discussion, such as issues of customs valuation (especially "American selling price" treatment of certain chemical imports) and antidumping measures (including the issue of how to evaluate dumping when floating exchange rates vary the relationship of foreign to domestic price). For discussions of these and other aspects of nontariff barriers, see Baldwin, *Nontariff Distortions of International Trade,* and U.S. Tariff Commission, *Trade Barriers,* part 2, *Nontariff Trade Barriers.*

In the case of antidumping, a new potential nontariff barrier was introduced by the U.S. Trade Act of 1974. In contradiction to accepted GATT practice (article VI), the new law provides that, when foreign suppliers are selling below their cost, antidumping measures may be taken even though the foreign firms sell at the same low price in their domestic markets. 88 Stat. 2047; and Contracting Parties to the General Agreement on Tariffs and Trade, *Basic Instruments and Documents,* vol. 1, rev. ed. (Geneva, 1955), p. 16. The new provision became a live issue when, with blessings from the Carter administration, American steel firms sought to use it

the trade-impeding effect of discriminatory practices in government expenditure. This nontariff barrier is found to be significant but of relatively modest importance compared to tariffs and agricultural nontariff barriers. It is possible that the array of other nontariff barriers, although seemingly a complex web of impediments to trade, is similarly of moderate quantitative significance compared to limitations on trade through tariffs, textile quotas, and agricultural nontariff barriers. The flurry of protectionist measures in 1977 associated with prolonged sectoral recession did raise the specter of a resurgence of nontariff restrictions, however. These protectionist trends included a disturbing recourse to cartel-like "organized trade" under government auspices, especially in steel and shipbuilding in Europe. Similarly, U.S. voluntary quotas on shoes and television sets, and the "reference price" system designed to limit steel imports, although arguably less restrictive than alternative options averted by the administration, constituted a serious protectionist drift. Therefore a crucial challenge to the Tokyo Round will be to halt the spread of ad hoc restrictions such as these, as well as to reduce the previously existing set of nontariff barriers, through the negotiation of codes of conduct and consultative mechanisms for the resolution of disputes.

---

against imports from Japan. James L. Rowe, Jr., "Steel Industry Promised Enforcement, Not Quotas," *Washington Post,* October 14, 1977.

CHAPTER SEVEN

Trade Negotiations and the Less Developed Countries

T RADE LIBERALIZATION in the markets of industrial countries constitutes a critical opportunity for the developing countries. These countries typically have a scarcity of foreign exchange needed for importing the capital equipment and intermediate inputs necessary to promote sustained economic growth. Within the current world context of pressures for a "new international economic order," the reduction of tariff and nontariff barriers facing exports of less developed countries (LDCs) represents one of the few major areas in which the rich countries could benefit the poor countries, by giving them an "opportunity" rather than a concessional transfer.

The purpose of this chapter is to quantify the probable export gains the LDCs could expect from alternative outcomes in negotiations within the Tokyo Round. The chapter examines the question of what type of trade liberalization will be in the interest of the LDCs. Special attention is directed to the question of whether substantial "most-favored-nation" liberalization would be the most beneficial for LDCs, or whether the developing countries would stand to gain more from minimal liberalization by the industrial countries on the grounds that minimum liberalization might retain maximum tariff preference margins for LDCs.

A basic premise of this chapter is that the LDCs will not offer tariff concessions of their own. Instead, the analysis focuses on induced LDC

207

exports to industrial areas as the industrial countries reduce their protection. The principle of "nonreciprocity" for LDCs is well established. In any event, any "reciprocal" liberalization by most LDCs would be illusory. Their imports typically are controlled by a complex of instruments such as quotas, licenses, and prior deposits, in addition to tariffs, and it is the availability of foreign exchange that primarily determines their levels of imports. Therefore, in practice, apparent import concessions to the industrial countries by LDCs would probably do little to increase net imports from the industrial countries. Adjustments in instruments other than tariffs would take place in order to preserve the basic balance between foreign exchange availability and import levels.

This chapter first examines the quantitative estimates for the LDCs of our basic models of liberalization of tariffs and agricultural nontariff barriers. It then considers the special issue of tariff preferences. Finally, it treats LDC interests with respect to nontariff barriers.

Quantitative Estimates of Liberalization Effects on LDC Exports

Our estimates of the impact of tariff liberalization on LDC exports are computed in the same way as the export estimates for industrial countries. A given developing country's exports of a particular good are calculated to increase in a specific industrial country market on the basis of the percentage price reduction implied by the tariff cut combined with the import elasticity for the good in the particular industrial country. If the industrial area is a free-trade area, there is an additional impact caused by the LDC's participation in substitution of partner supply by outsider supply.

Our estimates do not take into account any modification in the calculation for purposes of treating the effects of tariff preferences. The reason is that, for practical purposes, the existing system of tariff preferences may be ignored from the standpoint of calculating effects of trade liberalization. The preference systems are so fettered by restrictions that essentially they already are fully exploited, or exhausted, by the LDCs. Therefore, "at the margin," for the expansion of further exports the LDCs face the same most-favored-nation (MFN) tariff and nontariff barriers that the industrial countries confront. Thus, their export gains from liberalization may be computed in the same way as those for the industrial countries.[1]

Table 7-1 presents our estimates of total LDC export gains under the twelve alternative tariff-liberalization formulas considered in this study. The table reports the LDCs included; they represent all of the low-income countries except for certain middle-income countries sometimes classified as developing (such as Yugoslavia, Romania, Spain, Portugal, and Turkey).[2] The table refers to products excluding oil and textiles. It is evident

1. To the extent that preferences are not yet fully exploited, the calculations will overstate LDC export gains from most-favored-nation (MFN) liberalization. In these cases, the LDC already faces a zero tariff and can expand exports beyond current levels, so that MFN tariff reduction will not cause still further export gains. Because of the nature of the U.S., European, and Japanese preference systems, the major LDCs accounting for the great bulk of LDC exports almost certainly are not in this position. Thus, the calculations of this chapter should be realistic in the main part, although for some of the smaller countries or for some individual products they may be overstated. Perhaps the only case of systematic overstatement is that of the African, Caribbean, and Pacific countries having free access to the European market under the Lomé (Togo) Convention (February 28, 1975) or the Mahgreb Convention (1976; involving Algeria, Tunisia, and Morocco). In these cases duty-free entry generally is not limited by quantitative restrictions, so that application of MFN tariffs "at the margin" is inappropriate. However, these cases represent a small fraction of the total value of increased exports estimated for LDCs: a fraction of the market (Europe) as applied to a fraction of suppliers. For a description of the Lomé Convention, see "Effects of the Generalized System of Preferences on Developing Countries Sharing Their Special Tariff Advantages: The Generalized System of Preferences and The Lomé Convention," UN Doc. TD/B/C.5/36, October 15, 1975.

Finally, another impact relevant to preferences is also ignored: reverse substitution as the preference margin erodes. That is, for all products currently sold under preference, lower MFN tariffs would mean lower rest-of-world supplier price relative to LDC price and therefore a substitution away from LDCs to other suppliers, analogous to the substitution effect computed among suppliers of EEC and EFTA countries. Because preference trade is limited, however, and because trade creation rather than trade diversion is the main effect of existing preferences (as discussed below), there should be little bias in our estimates on account of the effect of reverse substitution.

2. The total increase in exports for LDCs includes all extra exports from "unspecified" sources, amounting to approximately 20 percent of the reported LDC total in the case of nontextiles and 3 percent for textiles. Inclusion of unspecified sources in the LDC total is appropriate to the extent that the GATT trade data base is precise for industrial country suppliers and imprecise only for rest-of-world suppliers. An alternative treatment would be to allocate only a fraction of "unspecified" supplier export increases to LDCs, with the fraction proportional to their share in total export increases excluding those from unspecified sources. For the 60 percent

in the table that the best formulas from the standpoint of LDC export gains are the most liberalizing formulas: first, a complete elimination of tariffs (formula 4), and second, the full U.S. authority (formula 8). The 60 percent cut (formula 1) generates almost as much export gain as full U.S. authority, indicating that the great majority of tariffs facing LDC products are higher than 5 percent (because tariffs below 5 percent are eliminated under full U.S. authority). The three-iteration harmonization formula (EEC-type, formula 2) would provide only 53 percent as much in increased LDC exports as would the full U.S. authority tariff cut.

Textiles are excluded from the basic estimates of Table 7-1, because it is politically unlikely that the system of voluntary export controls on textiles will be dismantled in the Tokyo Round. Nevertheless, for longer term policy formulation it is important to consider the significance of possible effects of textile liberalization. Table 7-2 presents estimates of increased LDC exports of textiles that could be expected from tariff liberalization in the sector. The estimates probably understate the export gains because they make no special adjustment for the fact that textile trade is currently restricted not only by tariffs, which are high, but also by voluntary quotas. Even with this probable downward bias, the estimates are enormous. They show that, in this single sector, LDC export gains would practically equal their export gains from liberalization in all other sectors combined. For 1974, textile liberalization based on full U.S. authority would increase LDC exports by $2.3 billion; in all other sectors it would increase their exports by $2.6 billion.[3] Thus, the developing countries should set the highest priority on future steps to eliminate the system of

---

tariff cut, this fraction would be approximately 21 percent (for nontextiles, but more than two-thirds for textiles). This alternative treatment would reduce the estimated total LDC export gains by approximately 15 percent for nontextiles and by 1 percent for textiles. We omit alternative estimates along these lines because it is likely that unspecified suppliers are concentrated in the LDCs and also because the export increases estimated for LDCs are probably downward biased in any event, as discussed below.

3. Note that the relative weight of textiles in possible trade gains is higher using the 1974 base than it is using the 1971 base (about 50 percent of the total rather than 40 percent). The reason for the change is that, on the basis of the OECD data used for expanding 1971 results to 1974 levels, industrial country import values of textiles from non-OECD countries tripled from 1971 to 1974, whereas the corresponding expansion for all other products, excluding oil, was approximately a doubling.

Table 7-1. *Increased Exports of Less Developed Countries under Alternative Tariff-Cutting Formulas, 1971 Base and 1974 Base*
Millions of dollars; excluding textiles and petroleum

Formula[a]	1971 base	1974 base
1	1,110.4	2,501.6
2	647.8	1,421.9
3	1,687.5	2,371.4
4	1,833.1	4,133.6
5	882.2	1,966.6
6	624.0	1,361.6
7	820.3	1,929.8
8	1,154.1	2,639.6
9	874.0	1,924.1
10	432.1	1,035.2
11	966.6	2,154.9
12	833.4	1,842.2

Source: Includes the less developed countries as classified by International Monetary Fund in *International Financial Statistics:*
1. Oil-exporting countries
   Algeria, Bahrain, Brunei, Ecuador, Gabon, Indonesia, Iran, Iraq, Kuwait, Libya, Nigeria, Oman, Qatar, Saudi Arabia, Trinidad and Tobago, United Arab Emirates, Venezuela
2. Other less developed areas
   (a) Other Latin America:
   Argentina, Bolivia, Brazil, Chile, Colombia, Costa Rica, Dominican Republic, El Salvador, Guatemala, Haiti, Honduras, Mexico, Nicaragua, Panama, Paraguay, Peru, Uruguay
   (b) Other Western Hemisphere:
   Bahamas, Barbados, Guadeloupe, Guyana, Jamaica, Martinique, Netherlands Antilles, Surinam
   (c) Other Middle East:
   Cyprus, Egypt, Israel, Jordan, Lebanon, Syria, People's Democratic Republic of Yemen
   (d) Other Asia:
   Bangladesh, Burma, Republic of China, Fiji, Hong Kong, India, Khmer Republic, Korea, Laos, Malaysia, Pakistan, Philippines, Western Samoa, Singapore, Sri Lanka, Thailand, Vietnam
   (e) Other Africa:
   Angola, Central Africa (excluding Gabon), Ethiopia, Ghana, Kenya, Liberia, Malagasy Republic, Malawi, Mauritania, Mauritius, Morocco, Mozambique, Réunion, Sierra Leone, Somalia, Sudan, Tanzania, Tunisia, Uganda, West Africa (including Ivory Coast and Senegal), Zaire, Zambia.
   a. For description of the formulas, see table 3-1.

voluntary export controls and other barriers facing their exports of textiles.

Table 7-3 presents details on the country composition of increased LDC exports from tariff liberalization under a 60 percent tariff cut.[4] The striking pattern revealed in the table is that a handful of small, export-oriented

4. The figures for 1974 must be viewed with caution because they are based on expansion factors by commodity categories, that are specific to importing areas but treat all non-OECD suppliers together as "rest of world." However, to the extent that a given LDC maintained constant the commodity composition of its exports and the pattern of its trading partners between 1971 and 1974, the 1974 estimates should be reasonable approximations.

Table 7-2. *Increased Exports of Textiles by Less Developed Countries under Alternative Tariff-Cutting Formulas, 1971 Base and 1974 Base*
Millions of dollars

Formula[a]	1971 base	1974 base
1	779.5	2,313.6
2	617.9	1,908.5
3	656.0	1,939.5
4	1,291.5	3,841.3
5	729.4	2,225.9
6	592.6	1,750.2
7	573.1	1,688.0
8	781.6	2,318.1
9	759.6	2,260.2
10	470.4	1,499.3
11	764.7	2,274.1
12	719.7	2,165.9

a. For a description of the formulas, see table 3-1.

Asian economies would account for a large share of the export gains from liberalization by industrial countries. Taiwan, Hong Kong, Korea, and the Philippines alone would gain $800 million out of the LDC total of $2.5 billion additional exports (1974 basis). Moreover, these results refer to estimates excluding textiles, a sector in which these Asian countries would dominate export gains even more (see below). The other major participants in increased exports would be major developing countries, especially those that have emphasized exports in recent years: Argentina ($48 million), Brazil ($95 million), India ($59 million), Malaysia ($26 million), Mexico ($160 million), Morocco ($34 million), Peru ($22 million), and Zambia ($27 million).

If, instead of absolute magnitudes, we consider additional exports as a percentage of the base level of total exports for each country (see table 7-3), the pattern appears less concentrated. In almost half of the countries listed in the table, a 60 percent tariff cut in industrial countries (excluding textiles) would raise exports by more than 1 percent. In percentage terms, additional developing countries that would experience relatively high increased exports include Cameroon, the Dominican Republic, Haiti, Malawi, Senegal, and Yemen (besides the countries mentioned above when considering large absolute export gains).

Two caveats on the results in table 7-3 warrant attention. First, the

Table 7-3. *Increase in Exports by Less Developed Countries*
under a 60 Percent Tariff Cut, 1971 Base and 1974 Base
Thousands of dollars; excluding textiles and petroleum

	1971 base		1974 base	
Country[a]	Increase	Percent of total exports	Increase	Percent of total exports
Afghanistan	359	0.36	773	0.34
Algeria	6,436	0.75	12,065	0.28
Argentina	23,685	1.36	47,935	1.22
Bangladesh	0	0.00	0	0.00
Bolivia	212	0.12	388	0.07
Brazil	47,880	1.65	95,148	1.20
Burma	689	0.56	1,577	0.84
Burundi	160	0.84	261	0.87
Cameroon	6,082	2.94	10,832	2.27
Chad	15	0.05	27	0.08
Chile	6,542	0.68	17,702	0.71
China (Taiwan)	100,339	5.02	259,957	4.70
Colombia	9,249	1.31	16,869	1.12
Dominican Republic	12,781	5.26	25,732	4.04
Ecuador	8,121	3.50	16,704	1.56
El Salvador	2,438	1.00	4,137	0.89
Ethiopia	957	0.76	1,789	0.67
Egypt (UAR)	4,384	0.56	8,474	0.56
Ghana	6,304	1.83	14,796	1.96
Guatemala	3,675	1.27	6,100	1.04
Guinea	1,183	2.37[b]	2,123	n.a.
Haiti	1,943	4.22	4,171	5.89
Hong Kong	143,862	5.00	360,964	6.06
India	27,439	1.35	58,558	1.49
Indonesia	8,751	0.71	18,634	0.25
Iran	3,023	0.08	2,991	0.01
Iraq	1,020	0.07	2,708	0.04
Ivory Coast	8,473	1.85	13,948	1.15
Kenya	5,228	1.68	9,958	1.65
Khmer Republic	24	0.22	46	n.a.
Korea	36,688	3.44	105,233	2.36
Malagasy Republic	2,533	1.72	4,390	1.80
Malawi	1,951	2.75	3,046	2.52
Mali	116	0.40	284	0.68
Malaysia	12,937	0.79	25,860	0.61
Mexico	68,088	4.54	160,504	4.53
Morocco	19,602	3.91	33,833	1.99

Table 7-3 (*continued*)

Country[a]	1971 base		1974 base	
	Increase	Percent of total exports	Increase	Percent of total exports
Niger	425	1.12	1,020	1.92
Nigeria	5,191	0.28	10,896	0.11
Nepal	48	0.10	118	0.38
Pakistan	6,032	0.90	13,579	1.22
Peru	9,183	1.03	22,404	1.49
Philippines	37,043	3.30	77,460	2.90
Rwanda	97	0.44	160	0.43
Saudi Arabia	3,542	0.09	6,273	0.02
Senegal	5,171	4.14	11,246	3.06
Sudan	434	0.13	1,056	0.30
Sri Lanka	4,650	1.42	8,783	1.68
Syria	424	0.20	870	0.11
Tanzania	1,992	0.71	3,390	0.84
Thailand	9,298	1.12	19,910	0.81
Tunisia	4,153	1.90	7,654	0.83
Uganda	2,249	0.86	4,077	1.29
Upper Volta	23	0.14	49	0.14
Venezuela	1,073	0.03	1,896	0.02
Vietnam	107	1.34	270	n.a.
Yemen	130	3.25	266	2.42
Zaire	5,393	0.78	11,764	0.91
Zambia	5,180	0.76	26,848	1.91

Source: for calculation of increase as percent of total exports in base year, International Monetary Fund, *International Financial Statistics*, vol. 29, May 1976 for 1971 base and November 1976 for 1974 base.
a. Less developed countries with populations of 2 million or more in 1970.
b. Based on estimated total exports.

actual export effects of liberalization might be less concentrated by country than estimated here. The underlying model assumes infinitely elastic supply of exports and therefore constant supplier shares in increased supply. However, for small LDC economies that are already characterized by a high share of manufactured exports in gross national product, supply might be less than infinitely elastic. As a result, there could be a tendency for the shares in increased LDC exports to shift away from the handful of export economies and toward new LDC suppliers, reducing the degree of concentration of export gains among countries. Second, for the African, Caribbean, and Pacific countries belonging to the Lomé or

Mahgreb Convention, the estimates in the table are overstated (because exports to the EEC market already enjoy free access). However, the size of this bias is small relative to the total increase estimated for LDC exports.[5]

Table 7-4 presents country detail on increased LDC textile exports resulting from a 60 percent tariff cut. Here the concentration in a small number of countries is even more dramatic. Taiwan, Hong Kong, Korea, and the Philippines would stand to gain $1.78 billion out of the total increase of $2.3 billion in textile exports. This concentration may explain why there has been relatively limited general pressure by the LDCs to end the textile quota regime (compared, for example, with other efforts such as the pressure for an integrated fund for commodity buffer stocks). Nevertheless, considering the fact that textiles constitute an area of natural comparative advantage for many other developing countries, it would appear strongly in the interests of all LDCs to pursue the reduction of tariff and nontariff protection in textiles, despite the apparent concentration of resulting export gains in a few LDCs in the short-run future.

To place the results of tables 7-1 through 7-4 into perspective, it is useful to consider the export gains in terms relative to current export earnings. Excluding oil, merchandise exports by LDCs amounted to a total of approximately $90 billion in 1974.[6] Thus, tariff liberalization under either full U.S. authority or a 60 percent tariff cut would raise annual nonoil export earnings by approximately 2.8 percent if textiles were excluded, and by about 5.3 percent if textiles were liberalized as well.

An important feature of these export effects is that they would be concentrated in manufactured products, a sector of special interest to the LDCs in view of their desire to achieve a heavier industrial weight within their economies. The LDCs have had unfavorable past experiences with the reliance upon raw materials exports, which are known for their sizable fluctuations and, at least until the mid-1970s, are considered to confront

5. For the countries in question, total export gains listed in table 7-3 amount to only $193 million, or 8 percent of the total for all LDCs. Even a reduction of export estimates for these African-Caribbean-Pacific (ACP) countries to as little as, say, one-fourth of the initial estimates (to account for current free entry into the EEC market) would reduce the total estimate for LDC export gains by very little (6 percent).

6. International Monetary Fund, *International Financial Statistics,* vol. 29 (April 1976), p. 38. The figure here is somewhat understated because it omits all exports, rather than merely oil exports, of the oil-exporting countries.

Table 7-4. *Increased Exports of Textiles by Principal Less Developed Countries under a 60 Percent Tariff Cut, 1971 Base and 1974 Base*
Thousands of dollars

Country	1971 base	1974 base
Brazil	4,039	11,568
China (Taiwan)	157,052	525,204
Colombia	1,523	4,514
Costa Rica	2,015	7,136
Haiti	1,257	4,448
Hong Kong	286,651	814,783
India	23,648	52,709
Israel	23,499	73,062
Jamaica	4,570	16,251
Korea	117,168	395,645
Malaysia	2,276	7,215
Mexico	21,056	73,870
Morocco	3,288	6,780
Pakistan	13,742	30,804
Philippines	13,910	49,154
Singapore	9,406	28,111
Thailand	1,268	3,793
Trinidad and Tobago	1,415	4,941
Tunisia	1,353	2,831
Egypt (UAR)	2,497	5,484
Uruguay	1,546	4,594

stagnant long-run markets. Table 7-5 indicates the sectoral composition of increased LDC exports resulting from a 60 percent tariff cut. If textiles are included, manufactured goods (BTN sections 6–21) would account for 76.7 percent of increased exports; even if textiles are excluded, the share of manufactures would be 60.2 percent of the total.

In 1974, manufactured exports by LDCs not among the oil-exporting countries represented 33.6 percent of their total exports, dramatically increased from 17.4 percent in 1965.[7] Thus, incremental exports from tariff liberalization would be sharply more concentrated in manufactures than is the current structure of LDC nonoil exports, and trade liberalization would stimulate the already rapid growth of LDC manufactured ex-

7. Donald B. Keesing, "Manufactured Exports from Developing Countries and the Effects of Further Trade Liberalization" (Washington, D.C., June 1976; processed). Manufactures are defined as SITC categories 5–8 minus category 68 (nonferrous metals).

Table 7-5. *Sectoral Composition of Increased Exports from Less Developed Countries under a 60 Percent Tariff Cut, 1971 Base*
Excluding petroleum

BTN section	Increased exports (millions of dollars)	Total increase (percent)	Total increase excluding textiles (percent)
1 Animals, animal products	31.1	1.6	2.8
2 Vegetable products	150.2	7.9	13.5
3 Animal and vegetable fats and oils	24.7	1.3	2.2
4 Prepared foodstuffs, beverages, tobacco	225.6	11.9	20.3
5 Mineral products	10.8	0.6	1.0
6 Chemicals	66.7	3.5	6.0
7 Plastics, rubber	51.2	2.7	4.6
8 Hides, leather goods	42.6	2.3	3.8
9 Wood, cork articles	43.3	2.3	3.9
10 Paper, paper products	14.0	0.7	1.3
11 Textiles	779.6	41.2	...
12 Footwear, headgear	73.4	3.9	6.6
13 Stone, plaster, cement, ceramic, glass products	11.6	0.6	1.0
14 Precious stones, jewelry	24.1	1.3	2.2
15 Basic metals, articles	87.2	4.6	7.9
16 Machinery, electrical equipment	95.6	5.1	8.6
17 Transportation equipment	39.0	2.1	3.5
18 Precision instruments	27.3	1.4	2.5
19 Arms and ammunition	0.7	0.0	0.0
20 Miscellaneous manufactures, including furniture	91.3	4.8	8.2
21 Works of art	0.1	0.0	0.0
Total increase	1,890.0	100.0	...
Total increase excluding textiles	1,110.4	...	100.0

Figures are rounded.

ports. The basic reason for concentration in manufactures is that for all countries the main trade increases resulting from tariff liberalization would be in manufactured goods (as discussed in chapter 3). The LDCs would merely participate in this overall focus on increased manufactured trade.

An important qualification of the estimates of tariff liberalization effects (tables 7-1 through 7-5) is that they make no special provision for the well-known phenomenon of "tariff escalation" as it affects LDC exports. Typically, industrial country tariffs are low on raw materials and higher on finished goods. The "effective protection" on value added is therefore much higher on manufactured goods than on raw materials. The reduction of this effective protection would tend to have more dramatic effects on imports of manufactured goods than might be predicted on the basis of price changes associated with reductions in "nominal" tariffs (as calculated in this study). For the LDCs in particular, these considerations suggest that there would be a systematic shift toward the processing of raw materials that were formerly shipped to industrial countries for processing. As a result, "tariff escalation" and "effective tariff" considerations imply that LDC export gains in manufactures would be still larger than those calculated here on the basis of nominal tariff changes. This means that any overstatement of total extra LDC exports from tariff liberalization, because of nontreatment of preference effects, is probably offset by understatement of the estimates from the standpoint of nontreatment of the phenomenon of tariff escalation.[8]

To complete our assessment of quantitative effects of the Tokyo Round on LDC exports, it is necessary to incorporate estimates for agricultural goods facing nontariff barriers. Table 7-6 reports these estimates, which are based on the analyses of agricultural nontariff barriers contained in chapters 4 and 5 above. Overall, the table indicates that a 60 percent reduction in the tariff-equivalent protection provided by variable levies in the EEC and EFTA, and by quotas in Japan, would generate an additional $500 million in exports for the developing countries (1974 base). In contrast to the case of tariff reductions, it would be the LDCs that are abundant in natural resources (for example, Argentina, Brazil, Uruguay) that would have the largest shares in these export gains, rather than the resource-scarce Asian export economies that concentrate on manufactured exports.

To recapitulate, 60 percent cuts in tariffs and agricultural nontariff

8. Estimates by the United Nations Conference on Trade and Development (UNCTAD) based on 1964 tariffs support the idea that high effective protection is especially important as a barrier to products exported by the developing countries. UNCTAD estimated that for industrial countries, the overall average nominal tariff was 12.3 percent and the average effective tariff was 21.7 percent. The corresponding estimated rates of protection on goods imported by the industrial countries from the developing countries were 17.1 percent and 33.4 percent, respectively. *The Kennedy Round: Estimated Effects on Tariff Barriers,* UN Doc. TD/6/Rev. 1, 1968, p. 205.

Table 7-6. *Increased Exports of Less Developed Countries from a 60 Percent Cut in Tariff-Equivalent of Agricultural Nontariff Barriers, 1971 Base and 1974 Base*
Millions of dollars

Importing area and supplier	1971 base	1974 base[a]
EEC (variable levies)[b]		
LDC total	291.2	436.8
Principal suppliers		
Argentina	123.9	n.a.
Brazil	18.9	n.a.
Commonwealth Africa	16.7	n.a.
Guyana	15.5	n.a.
India	1.8	n.a.
Indonesia	1.8	n.a.
Jamaica	12.3	n.a.
Morocco	2.8	n.a.
Mozambique	1.8	n.a.
Réunion	13.0	n.a.
Thailand	3.8	n.a.
Trinidad and Tobago	7.4	n.a.
Uruguay	6.4	n.a.
All others	65.1	n.a.
EFTA (variable levies)		
LDC total	3.0	4.5
Japan (quotas)		
LDC total[c]	17.8	26.7
Total	312.0	468.0

n.a. Not available.

a. 1974 values at "long-term" prices are all assumed to be 50 percent higher than the 1971 base values. See table 4-6.

b. 1971 values for EEC: direct estimates expanded by 40 percent to account for variable levies omitted from the analysis. See chapter 4.

c. Based on table 5-6. Applies 84.6 percent as fraction of LDC share in rest-of-world imports in 1971. Organisation for Economic Co-operation and Development, *Trade by Commodities: Country Summaries* (OECD, January–December, 1974). Applies 60 percent to effect measured for complete quota removal.

barriers probably would increase exports of the developing countries by $2.5 billion and $0.5 billion (in 1974 values), respectively, raising their annual nonoil export earnings by somewhat more than 3 percent. Although politically unlikely, a similar liberalization of textiles would add another $2.3 billion in export gains, raising the total gains from liberalization to approximately 6 percent of nonoil exports. These gains would represent an important contribution to economic growth, in light of the chronic shortage of foreign exchange in the developing countries. Moreover, the gains would be concentrated in manufactured goods, high in the priorities of LDC development goals. However, these results would not be achieved if substantially less liberalizing proposals under consideration in the Tokyo Round (compared to the 60 percent cut or full U.S. authority) were adopted.

Tariff Preferences

More than a decade after the original UNCTAD proposal for a Generalized System of Preferences (GSP) allowing duty-free entry for LDC exports into industrial country markets, GSP mechanisms finally exist in Europe, Japan, and the United States. Three issues are important to examine in connection with preferences: (1) How significant are existing preferences for LDC exports? (2) How seriously would LDC export prospects be eroded by the reduction of preference margins as the result of negotiated reductions in most-favored-nation tariffs? (3) What are the prospects for a substantial liberalization of the restrictions currently limiting GSP export opportunities for LDCs?

Several existing studies have carried out empirical estimates of the export increases LDCs are likely to achieve because of existing tariff-preference schemes. The almost unanimous conclusion of these studies is that the severe limitations on magnitudes of imports permitted under the GSP schemes mean that the LDC export gains will be very small.[9] One of the largest estimates concludes that unrestricted tariff preferences would increase LDC exports by $1.4 billion annually but that with the network of restrictions the annual export gain is an estimated $380 million, in 1971 dollars.[10]

9. Richard N. Cooper, "The European Community's System of Generalized Tariff Preferences: A Critique," *Journal of Development Studies,* vol. 8 (July 1972), pp. 379–94; Tracy Murray, "Preferential Tariffs for the LDCs," *Southern Economic Journal,* vol. 40 (July 1973), pp. 35–46; Zubair Iqbal, "Trade Effects of the Generalized System of Preferences" (Washington, D.C., 1975; processed).

10. Iqbal, "Trade Effects of the Generalized System of Preferences," p. 17. Note that the estimate for unrestricted effects corresponds rather closely with the estimate in the present study for the effects of a 100 percent tariff cut on LDC exports under the most-favored-nation (MFN) liberalization ($1.8 billion in 1971 values; see table 7-1, formula 4). The unrestricted preference effect should be larger than the MFN effect from the standpoint of substitution for existing industrial country ex-

In general terms, the restrictions limiting duty-free entry under GSP are as follows: First, the EEC scheme sets total quotas on entry for each BTN product category based on the total imports from beneficiaries (excluding EEC members) in the most recent year for which trade data are available. Total GSP imports may not exceed the quota. Imports from a single LDC may not exceed 50 percent of the quota; or, for sensitive items, 20 to 30 percent. Second, the Japanese scheme sets ceilings similar to the EEC ceilings. Third, the U.S. program of GSP, initiated in January 1976, sets the following limits: (a) to be eligible for preferences, an LDC may not export to the United States more than 50 percent of total U.S. purchases of a given item (defined at the tariff-line level); (b) nor may the country supply more than $25 million of U.S. imports of an article at the tariff-line level. In addition to these limitations, all three industrial areas partially or wholly exclude sensitive items such as textiles, shoes, and steel.[11]

The answer to the first question, then, is that LDC export gains under the general system of preferences are generally calculated to be quite small. Turning to the question of possible future liberalization of GSP schemes, it seems relatively clear that substantial liberalization is very unlikely over the next few years. The political difficulties in establishing even the limited current systems, after extremely long preparatory periods, indicate that it would be unrealistic to expect a significant early liberalization of what are essentially new schemes. Moreover, there is an important issue of development assistance policy involved in the question of liberalization of GSP schemes: would the resulting country distribution of benefits be consistent with donor country goals? In particular, it is the relatively more advanced developing countries that benefit most from preferences, because they have the capacity to supply industrial exports. Indeed, preference benefits appear to be focused on a handful of LDCs,[12] many of them the same countries indicated in the present study as principal participants in increased LDC manufactured exports under MFN

---

ports, but smaller than our MFN estimate from the standpoint of product coverage, which is more limited under GSP schemes.

11. These restrictions are described in the references cited above as well as in Mordechai Kreinin and J. M. Finger, "A New International Economic Order: A Critical Survey of the Issues," *Journal of World Trade Law,* vol. 10 (November–December 1976), pp. 3–22.

12. Murray, "Preferential Tariffs for the LDCs," p. 44.

tariff liberalization. Yet, in most vehicles for concessional development assistance, such as the International Development Association (IDA), these very countries are considered to be too prosperous to be eligible for scarce aid resources. To be sure, duty-free access for trade constitutes a less concessional instrument than long-term, low-interest-rate lending. Nevertheless, preferential entry represents one of the few instruments available for development assistance, and it is far from clear that limited political tolerance to the instrument should be exhausted by its further liberalization if the primary beneficiaries of that liberalization will be relatively prosperous LDCs.[13]

Regardless of the ideal normative prescription for the further liberalization of preferences, a "positive," or purely descriptive, assessment must be that further liberalization is unlikely over an intermediate time horizon. We may then turn to the remaining question: how seriously will MFN tariff reductions injure LDC exports because of the concomitant erosion of existing preference margins?[14] The most direct answer to this question may be obtained by comparing total LDC export gains under MFN liberalization with total gains under GSP. Assuming the most liberal practical tariff cut (full U.S. authority), increased LDC exports from MFN liberalization would be $1.15 billion (table 7-1), or more than three times the expected LDC export gains from existing GSP schemes (if the $380 million estimate by Iqbal is accepted, with both figures in 1971 values). Ample MFN liberalization thus appears to be an unambiguously better option for the LDCs than would be the continuation of current preference schemes with no MFN liberalization.[15]

13. Instead, the ideal policy probably would be to grant unrestricted preferential access only to a list of "poorest" LDCs, such as those eligible for IDA lending.

14. LDC statements on the Tokyo Round of negotiations typically express concern about the loss of preference margins as the result of generalized MFN tariff reductions. See, for example, descriptions of positions set forth at the Manila preparatory meeting for UNCTAD IV and other "Group of 77" statements in *MTN Project News,* Newsletter No. 9, UN Doc. UNCTAD/MTN/46 GE. 76-64/10, April 1976.

15. A more narrow question, and one that is basically irrelevant given the comparison just cited, is: how much of the current LDC exports due solely to GSP would be "lost" through the erosion of preference margins—without considering the larger export gains through further opening of markets by MFN liberalization. The answer to this narrow question would appear to be on the order of $89 million in 1971 values. Iqbal computes "trade diversion" under GSP as $148 million annually. With MFN tariff cuts averaging 60 percent under the more liberal formulas, approxi-

Robert E. Baldwin and Tracy Murray have conducted a detailed analysis of the issue of preferences versus MFN tariff cuts.[16] Their basic estimates of LDC export gains under existing GSP schemes are somewhat larger than those used in the assessment above: $479 million (in 1971 values), of which $64 million would be from trade diversion. Their corresponding estimate of annual LDC export gains from a 50 percent MFN tariff cut is $848 million.[17] Therefore, Baldwin and Murray's estimates also find that LDC export gains under MFN tariff cuts surpass those under continued GSP preference with unchanged "preference margins" (that is, no decrease in MFN tariffs). The authors further point out that the MFN cuts would be perpetual, whereas preference schemes are limited to ten years duration.[18]

In sum, from substantial MFN tariff liberalization the LDCs stand to gain twice (Baldwin-Murray) to three times (this study combined with Iqbal) as much in increased exports as they may expect to gain under the tariff-preference schemes now in force in industrial countries. Therefore, it would be counterproductive from the standpoint of their own interests

---

mately 60 percent of the LDC exports achieved through trade diversion under GSP would be eliminated ($89 million annually) as the result of MFN cuts.

16. Robert E. Baldwin and Tracy Murray, "MFN Tariff Reductions and Developing Country Trade Benefits under the GSP," *Economic Journal,* vol. 87 (March 1977), pp. 30–46.

17. This estimate is in 1971 values, composed of the following: (a) $446 million from the continuation of trade creation and of one-half of trade diversion from GSP; (b) $106 million because of the absence of value limitations, compared with GSP; (c) $27 million because of likely increase in product coverage, compared with GSP; (d) $268 million because of applicability of MFN cuts to LDCs ineligible for preferences. Ibid., pp. 37 and 44. Note that the total estimated LDC export gain for MFN tariff cuts appears too small when the corresponding estimate of the present study ($1.15 billion in 1971 values) is considered, especially in view of the extremely close results for U.S. imports estimated in this study and in a similar study by Baldwin (see chapter 3 and appendix F).

18. Going still further, Baldwin and Murray examine the issue from the standpoint of the set of countries currently eligible for GSP (that is, excluding a number of other LDCs). Even for this group of countries the authors conclude that: "In contrast to this $32 million loss in annual trade flows [from reduced trade diversion] the benefits to those developing countries which currently enjoy GSP status would be $133 [million]—$106 million from 50% tariff cuts on products impacted by the value limits and $27 million from MFN cuts on products currently excluded from the GSP schemes other than textiles, shoes and petroleum. Thus, the trade advantages to the GSP beneficiaries of MFN tariff reductions amount to some 4 times the loss of GSP advantages due to the erosion of preferential tariff margins. On net the beneficiaries gain $101 million in 1971 annual trade flows." Ibid., p. 41.

for the LDCs to oppose MFN liberalization, or to advocate minimal rather than deep tariff cuts, under the misleading notion that LDC exports would stand to suffer from MFN cuts because of the erosion of tariff-preference margins.

Finally, a negotiating aspect of the GSP "erosion" issue deserves special attention. Some industrial country participants in the negotiations appear to have advocated that MFN tariffs be cut by less than indicated by an overall formula, in items of importance to LDCs under GSP, or even that these items be excluded from cuts altogether.[19] This type of proposal, apparently in the behalf of preserving LDC preference margins, should be considered with great caution by the LDCs, because there is the possibility that the proliferation of such exceptions would essentially be a means of marshalling LDC support for minimal MFN tariff cuts. Although such support would strengthen the bargaining hand of any industrial country participants basically opposed to substantial liberalization, it would tend overall to be contrary to the interests of the LDCs themselves—as shown by the evidence above on the superiority of MFN liberalization over GSP with little or no MFN liberalization, from the standpoint of the LDCs.

Other LDC Interests

In addition to the interests of developing countries in the reduction of industrial countries' tariffs and the elimination of agricultural nontariff barriers, the LDCs' major interests in negotiations of the Tokyo Round have included the following:

—Nonreciprocity: a basic premise of the LDCs is that they not be expected to make reciprocal concessions in order to participate in those offered by the industrial countries. Past experience indicates nonreciprocity generally will be observed, despite probable pressures by some industrial countries to obtain reciprocal LDC liberalization (an illusory phenomenon, as discussed earlier in this chapter).

—GSP "bindings": an objective of the LDCs is to get industrial countries to "bind," or make perpetual, preferential treatment under existing GSP schemes, in addition to extending coverage of these schemes.

19. *MTN Project News,* Newsletter No. 9, p. 5.

—Subsidies: a key issue for LDCs is whether they can obtain exemptions from countervailing duties applied to offset subsidies granted to exports into industrial countries.

—Safeguards: the LDCs seek exemptions from any "safeguard" measures limiting imports because of injury to domestic firms.

—Nontariff-barrier codes: in several areas (for example, product "standards" and government procurement) the negotiations are likely to produce "codes of conduct" with provisions for consultative procedures when nontariff barrier violations of the code occur. The LDCs generally seek special, more lenient, treatment under such codes.

Of these areas, the issue of countervailing duties on export subsidies deserves special attention.[20] An important fact to consider is that in most LDCs high tariff protection combined with the structural characteristics of the economy put a high "social price" premium on the earning of foreign exchange while the private incentive to export is lower, giving undue incentive to produce for the domestic rather than the foreign market. In principle, then, an LDC export subsidy equal to the premium of the "shadow price of foreign exchange" (or, potential increase in GNP per unit increase in foreign exchange available) over the market exchange rate is a theoretically justifiable measure. It is an arid and unrealistic response to say that, if LDCs have protective structures that discriminate against exports, they should eliminate the protection rather than subsidize exports. In some analytical approaches, the shadow price of foreign exchange may be high relative to the market price even without high protection.[21] At the pragmatic level, it is unlikely that LDCs will dismantle import protection systems because of the threat of countervailing duties

20. The political sensitivity of this issue has already been heightened by recent cases considered for countervailing by the United States, such as that concerning imports of shoes from Brazil. Note that provisions under the Trade Act of 1974 reduced the flexibility allowed to the U.S. Treasury Department to delay action on the implementation of countervailing duties—a previous means, it would appear, of refraining from countervailing against LDC exports. 88 Stat. 2049–50.

21. See the "programming approach" described, though considered somewhat unreliable for specific estimates, by Edmar Bacha and Lance Taylor, "Foreign Exchange Shadow Prices: A Critical Review of Current Theories," *Quarterly Journal of Economics,* vol. 85 (May 1971), pp. 197–224. For an econometric-model approach see: G. Siri, "Calculation of the Shadow Price of Foreign Exchange Based on the Central American Econometric Model," in W. Cline and E. Delgado, eds., "Studies on Economic Integration in Central America" (Brookings Institution, 1976; processed).

applied by industrial countries; instead, they are more likely to respond to export losses from countervailing duties by raising their own import controls still further in order to economize on foreign exchange.

In practice, a possible means of addressing the LDC export subsidy issue would be for industrial countries to agree that some standard subsidy element (say, 30 percent), if not the entire subsidy, could be exempted on LDC exports, and that countervailing would apply only beyond this level. Such an approach would take account of the special scarcity of foreign exchange in LDCs while keeping special treatment within reasonable bounds, so as to avoid rewarding the most distorted LDC economies with the highest exemptions.

Conclusion

The analyses of this chapter suggest the following conclusions: First, the LDCs have a large stake in the most complete possible liberalization of industrial countries' tariff and nontariff barriers. A tariff cut of full U.S. authority (60 percent cut and elimination of tariffs under 5 percent) would raise LDC exports by an estimated $2.6 billion annually (1974 values) even excluding textiles; a 60 percent cut in the tariff-equivalent of agricultural nontariff barriers would add another $468 million to their annual exports. Together, these export gains would amount to an increase of more than 3 percent in total annual LDC nonoil export earnings. Second, the developing countries should push hard for eventual dismantling of voluntary export quotas on textiles. Tariff reductions (for example, a 60 percent cut) on textiles, if allowed to operate by the removal of voluntary quotas, would increase LDC exports by approximately $2.3 billion annually, or fully an additional two-thirds of the amount achievable if liberalization were limited to nontextile tariffs and agricultural nontariff barriers. Third, the export gains are concentrated in manufactured goods, a result consistent with LDC desires to increase the weight of manufacturing industry in their economies. Fourth, the export gains tend to be concentrated in a handful of LDCs at intermediate development levels, especially in the case of textile export gains. Fifth, the LDCs have far more to gain than to lose from thoroughgoing liberalization. Their gains from most-favored-nation tariff cuts would far surpass any losses of exports from the corresponding erosion of tariff-preference margins. Accordingly, it is in their interest to lend support to negotiating positions advocating deep MFN tariff cuts, and the LDCs should be especially wary of supporting advocates proposing limited cuts in the name of preserving tariff-preference margins. Sixth, among other measures, agreements providing for special treatment of LDCs in the application of countervailing duties warrant emphasis, in view of the typical urgency of earning foreign exchange in developing countries and their corresponding need to provide "second-best" incentives to exports.

CHAPTER EIGHT

Conclusion

THIS STUDY has examined the present state of protection in international trade and the economic effects of future trade liberalization. Our quantitative estimates suggest that substantial economic gains can be achieved, for both the industrial and the developing countries, through trade liberalization in the Tokyo Round of negotiations. Moreover, it should be possible to obtain these benefits without jeopardy to individual countries participating in the negotiations, in view of the relatively well-balanced effects of liberalization and considering the small sizes of estimated adjustments in employment and trade balances. This chapter sets forth the major findings of the study.

Tariff Negotiations

Chapters 2 and 3 of this study develop a model of the economic effects of alternative tariff-cutting formulas which might be agreed upon in the Tokyo Round of negotiations. In addition, appendix H below explores the question of "optimal" tariff cuts designed to maximize increased trade and welfare while limiting the size of any accompanying trade balance losses of individual negotiating countries. Before discussing the results of these analyses, it is appropriate to recapitulate the nature of the tariff negotiations model. The basic calculations of the model examine the effects of reducing tariffs, with computations at the "tariff line" which are then added up to sector or global levels.

Tariff Model: Synopsis

Increased imports in response to lowered tariffs are calculated by applying empirically estimated import elasticities (percentage change in imports per unit percentage change in import price) to the base level of imports and the percentage change in consumer price caused by a particular tariff cut. Increased exports are calculated by summing up over other countries their increased imports from the supplier in question. Welfare effects—the consumer savings from importing rather than buying more costly home goods—are computed on the basis of the import increase and the height of the tariff. These static welfare gains are expanded to an approximate estimate of total welfare gains (including effects of economies of scale, induced investment, technical change, and anti-inflationary influences) on the basis of the experience of European integration as estimated in other studies. Exchange rate effects are examined by applying import and export elasticities to determine the extent of appreciation or depreciation necessary for each country to reestablish its preliberalization trade balance. Employment effects are calculated by applying "job coefficients" (both direct and indirect to account for intermediate goods requirements) to the changes in imports (job loss) and exports (job gain).

For Europe, the model has special treatment of the "substitution effect" through which outsiders (such as the United States, Japan, and Canada) increase their share in the market as the tariff wall around the EEC and EFTA declines. The model also includes the additional exports industrial countries may expect as developing countries "respend" the extra export earnings of foreign exchange they receive from increased exports to the industrial areas reducing tariffs.

The GATT trade and tariff data files prepared for the negotiations are used for the calculations. OECD trade data are used to "update" to 1974 the results obtained using the 1971 GATT trade data.

Results

Twelve tariff-cutting formulas are applied to the model. These include formulas very close to actual proposals by the United States, Canada, Japan, and the EEC, as well as a 100 percent cut formula used as a benchmark for trade free of tariffs. The main results of the model are the following:

FORMULA RESULTS. The formulas cluster in three levels (see table 3-2). Completely eliminating tariffs would raise industrial country imports by $17 billion (14 percent of the value of relevant import items).[1] A second tier of "liberal" formulas, including the maximum U.S. tariff-reducing authority as well as a simple 60 percent tariff cut (the early U.S. proposal) and the Canadian-type formula, would go about two-thirds as far as tariff-free trade, raising imports by $10 billion to $11 billion. A third and lowest tier of "restrictive" formulas, including the EEC-type harmonization formula and a formula close to the Japanese proposal, would create only about $5.5 billion in new trade, or only about one-half the amount of trade creation under the more liberal U.S. and Canadian tariff-cutting approaches. The intermediate Swiss formula, which is close to our formula 12, would raise world trade by about $7.4 billion.

Harmonization, whereby high tariffs are cut proportionately more than low ones, is no longer a meaningful issue; if textiles are excluded, U.S. tariffs are about as uniform as those in the EEC. The essence of the EEC formula is therefore its restrictive nature, not its harmonization feature; and much more liberal harmonization formulas are available.

WELFARE GAINS. Under the most liberalizing practical formula, full U.S. authority (60 percent cut plus the elimination of tariffs of 5 percent or lower), static annual welfare gains would amount to $1.7 billion yearly. Total welfare gains would be five times as large, conservatively estimated (on the basis of European integration experience). Because these gains would grow with the trade base and would recur annually into the indefinite future, the once-for-all present discounted value of total welfare gains would reach an estimated $170 billion. Actual gains could be even higher because the calculations omit the important dynamic effects of liberalization's impact in reducing inflation and stimulating technological progress. Therefore, the economic stakes in the Tokyo Round are large even for tariff liberalization alone.

If the Swiss formula were adopted, as seemed likely after the discussions between the United States and the EEC in September 1977, total welfare gains would reach somewhere between 67 percent and 90 percent

1. For comparison to the trade base, the appropriate import expansion figure is $22 billion, the gross amount before deducting for decreases in EEC and EFTA member country imports from partners.

of the total benefits estimated for the full U.S. authority tariff cut. This outcome would be a considerable accomplishment in view of the rising protectionist pressures in 1977.

TEXTILES. A single sector—textiles—represents enormous possibilities for liberalization ($3 billion increased industrial country imports under the full U.S. authority formula). However, it is excluded from the central estimates (including those reported above) because the regime of voluntary quotas on textiles is unlikely to be changed by the Tokyo Round.

RECIPROCITY. When judged on the joint basis of welfare effects and trade effects (increased exports relative to increased imports), and considering weighted rankings of all twelve formulas from the separate viewpoints of the United States, Canada, Japan, and the EEC, the "best" reciprocal (or evenhanded) formula in the full U.S. authority cut. The second-ranked formula would be more attractive if negotiators gave greater weight to trade effects than to welfare. This formula is a particular harmonization variant explored in this study but not proposed in the negotiations (of the form: $y = 20$ percent $+ 3t$, where y is percentage cut and t is the original tariff; formula subject to a maximum cut of 60 percent). This formula would appear to represent a good compromise solution encompassing U.S. objectives of fairly substantial liberalization, EEC objectives of harmonization, and generally achieving a "balanced result" in terms of country preference rankings considering both trade balance and welfare effects. The Swiss formula would be somewhat less successful in achieving overall reciprocity because of its lower welfare benefits. See table 3-12.

TRADE BALANCE. Results from all formulas tend to show positive trade balance changes for the United States and (especially) Japan, and negative changes for Canada and the EEC. The results for Canada are explained by that country's high tariffs on dutiable trade, although the absence of treatment of "industrial transformation" in the model (the shift from raw materials exports to production and export of processed goods) may bias downward the estimates of increased Canadian exports. For the EEC, the substitution effect as well as a relatively high fraction of expanded imports from nonliberalizing free-rider countries account for the reduction in trade balance. However, all trade balance changes are small relative to exports, especially considering the gradual phasing in of liberalization over five years or more. Thus, any trade balance reductions (for either Canada or the EEC) would appear to be too trivial to constitute a legitimate basis for opposition to deep tariff cuts.

EXCHANGE RATE EFFECTS. Like trade balance changes, exchange rate changes necessary to reestablish initial balances would be extremely small, with trade-weighted exchange rate changes ranging from $+0.42$ percent for Japan to -0.79 percent for Canada (see table 3-13).

EMPLOYMENT EFFECTS. Those who fear serious employment dislocation from liberalizing imports are without empirical support. The estimates for the United States, Canada, Japan, and the EEC show that, for tariff liberalization under the full U.S. authority tariff cut, the gross loss of jobs to imports (that is, even ignoring export job gains) would be less than 0.2 percent of the labor force in the United States and the EEC, 0.5 percent in Japan, and 0.9 percent in Canada. Moreover, liberalization would be phased in over a period of years so that even these magnitudes, all "upperbound" or highest likely estimates, would be all the easier to accommodate. Even adjustment in individual product sectors would appear to pose no major problems. The most important sector for possible job losses from liberalization in the United States would be textiles, and in this sector liberalization is unlikely. Even if textiles were liberalized, however, the gross loss of jobs to increased imports in the United States would be only about 2 percent of employment in the sector. Aside from textiles, the only manufacturing sector that might represent an adjustment problem is that of machinery and equipment in Canada (see table 3-16).

ADJUSTMENT COSTS. The transitional unemployment of labor displaced by extra imports would represent a cost of adjustment to trade liberalization. On the basis of U.S. experience, workers affected by imports could remain unemployed for an average of approximately thirty weeks. By applying this duration of unemployment to the average manufacturing wage, previous authors have estimated the adjustment cost per worker displaced by increased imports. Applying this cost per worker to the total number of workers that might be displaced by liberalization according to our estimates (without netting out new job opportunities in the export sectors), we estimate labor adjustment costs on the order of $600 million for the United States for full U.S. authority tariff cuts (table 3-15). By contrast, the present discounted value of future static and dynamic welfare gains from liberalization would be almost $50 billion for the United States, or eighty times as large as the labor adjustment costs.

By assuming that adjustment costs per worker in other industrial countries bear the same relationship to U.S. adjustment cost as the ratio of foreign to U.S. manufacturing wages, it is possible to make comparable approximate estimates of adjustment costs for the other major negotiating countries. These costs range from nearly $300 million in Canada to approximately $600 million in Japan. Once again the adjustment costs are dwarfed by total welfare gains from liberalization taken at their present value of future yearly gains. These welfare gains are sixty times as large as adjustment costs for Canada, almost fifty times adjustment costs in Japan, and ninety-six times labor adjustment costs for the EEC.

SUMMARY. Delay and excessive deliberation about tariff-cutting formulas are unwarranted because no formula is likely to cause serious trade balance or employment losses. The maximum cut possible under U.S. law —60 percent cut in tariffs and elimination of tariffs under 5 percent— is the "best" if welfare gains from freer trade are considered; and a compromise formula identified in this study is a good alternative if more weight is placed on trade effects. Either choice would have generally reciprocal, evenly balanced results for all major participants. The Swiss formula would also be a relatively favorable compromise. By contrast, the EEC-type "iterative harmonization" formula and the Japanese formula do very little to create trade and should be avoided as insufficiently liberalizing.

"Optimal" Tariff Reform

In order to shed further light on the desirable features of tariff reform, appendix H presents a linear-programming optimization model of tariff cuts. The model chooses among alternative tariff formulas for each product sector (with trade divided into the twenty-one broad BTN sections) in each importing country. The analysis maximizes welfare gains from increased imports, subject to the constraint that no country may experience a trade balance deterioration greater than 0.5 percent of its annual level of export earnings.

For the major countries the "optimal" tariff reform results reinforce those of the central analysis in chapter 3: the United States and Japan tend to select as their optimal tariff cuts the most liberalizing alternative, full U.S. authority cuts. The EEC selects somewhat less liberalizing formulas, but the optimal formulas for the EEC are systematically much more liberal than the three-iteration formula favored by the EEC itself. The main thrust of the results is that the United States, Japan, and (under slightly more relaxed trade balance constraints) the EEC should choose the most liberalizing formula for optimal welfare effects. By contrast, the results suggest that a limited number of countries—Canada, Finland, Australia, and New Zealand—may have a case for adopting somewhat less liberal tariff formulas because of their relatively more serious trade balance deteriorations from liberalization. However, less liberal formulas are desirable even in these countries only if a very rigid target is set limiting the size of trade balance reduction allowed to extremely small amounts.

Agricultural Nontariff Barriers

For Europe, variable levies are treated as equivalent to tariffs and the tariff model is applied to determine effects of liberalization (chapter 4). For Japan, domestic prices are compared to international prices to estimate the tariff-equivalent of quotas, and then the elasticity approach is applied to compute the increase in imports likely to follow from quota removal (chapter 5). The estimates are converted to 1974 "long-run" agricultural prices (that is, considering cost inflation but adopting lower prices than the extremely high actual product prices in 1974).

The estimates show that a 60 percent cut in the tariff-equivalent of agricultural nontariff barriers would cause a negative trade balance effect of $1.9 billion for Europe and $280 million for Japan, and positive trade balance effects of approximately $500 million for the United States and $300 million for Canada (table 5-12). These figures are all lower than corresponding effects under tariff liberalization (primarily in manufactures), suggesting that the importance of agricultural nontariff barriers in the negotiations has been overstated. However, it does appear true that, in terms of extra welfare to consumers as well as possible job losses to increased imports, the agricultural nontariff barriers are quite important in Europe and Japan. This result stems from the fact that agricultural protection is extremely high (so that welfare gains are high per unit of increased imports) and that agriculture is labor intensive. Even in the case of agricultural nontariff barriers, however, liberalization would cause relatively small job losses: approximately 1 percent to 3 percent of total labor in Japan, where agricultural employment is declining from natural forces in any event, and 0.33 percent of the labor force in the EEC.

Other Nontariff Barriers

Chapter 6 reports estimates by other authors which, after updating, suggest that a 60 percent cut in the degree of protection provided by discrimination in government procurement would cause import increases of $600 million in the United States and $545 million in the EEC in 1974 values (or one-sixth and one-twelfth, respectively, of the estimated import increases from a 60 percent cut in tariffs and in agricultural nontariff barriers). The chapter notes that border tax adjustments for indirect taxes are neutral measures, not nontariff barriers. Quantitative estimates are not available for effects of liberalizing other major nontariff barriers: discrimination against imports by "product standards"; government subsidies and countervailing duties; quantitative restrictions, including "voluntary export quotas"; safeguards; and producer export controls. In qualitative terms, however, the most serious threat in 1977 was the emergence of a protectionist trend, with a number of important restrictions in Europe and the United States tending to "organize" trade in sectors such as steel, shipbuilding, textiles, shoes, and electronics.

It is clear that, taken together, the array of nontariff barriers constitutes a significant impediment to trade as well as an ongoing source of political-economic antagonism among the industrial countries. If these sources of irritation are allowed to grow, they could cause more serious repercussions by inducing still further protectionist measures in other areas. In order to reduce them, as well as in order to foster more liberal trade, it is important to bring to a successful outcome efforts in the Tokyo Round at negotiating "codes of behavior" on nontariff barriers, with provisions for consultation procedures to deal with disputes.

Developing Countries

The less developed countries (LDCs) stand to make major gains in exports from general tariff liberalization by industrial countries, with most of the gains coming in exports of manufactured goods. The fear of LDCs that their tariff "preference margins" would be eroded by general liberalization represents a misplaced concern. Most preferences are hemmed in by quota limits, so that at the margin it is only through "most-favored-nation" tariff cuts that further export opportunities can be expected. The calculations of chapter 7, as well as those by other analysts, strongly indicate that the LDCs have far more increased exports to gain from deep cuts in most-favored-nation protection than they have to lose from any associated loss of preference margins.

Under the most liberal practical tariff formula (full U.S. authority), the LDCs would gain $2.6 billion in extra exports yearly (table 7-1). If in addition textiles were liberalized, the LDCs could expect further gains of $2.3 billion (table 7-2). Together, these tariff cut effects would represent more than a one-third share in the supply of increased imports by industrial countries. Furthermore, LDCs would gain close to $500 million in exports from a 60 percent cut in the tariff-equivalent protection of agricultural nontariff barriers (table 7-5). Altogether, these export gains would boost total nonoil export earnings of LDCs by approximately 6 percent.

In the area of nontariff barriers, the LDCs probably have a rational economic case for partial or total exemption from the application of countervailing duties, as discussed in chapter 7.

Overview

The estimates of this study indicate that relatively deep cuts in tariffs and nontariff barriers, such as the full U.S. authority, could provide important welfare gains to consumers in industrial countries as well as important export gains to developing countries. These potential gains would be approximately cut in half if, instead, negotiators adopted the more restrictive tariff-cutting formulas under active consideration in the negotiations, and still further reduced if major areas such as agricultural nontariff barriers were omitted from liberalization. The gains would be at an intermediate level between these two extremes under the tariff-cutting approach that appeared to be emerging as the central compromise in the autumn of 1977, the Swiss formula. The achievement of that degree of liberalization, although falling short of the full potential represented by U.S. negotiating authority, still would represent a substantial achievement in the negotiations in view of the restrictive initial positions of some major participants and in light of growing protectionist pressures in many countries. However, the adoption of that compromise in the tariff area would make it all the more essential to achieve major breakthroughs in the liberalization of nontariff barriers so that the Tokyo Round could come close to realizing its potential for liberalizing world trade.

Aside from narrow interests of particularistic groups, there is little reason to oppose thoroughgoing trade liberalization. The impact of liberalization on "labor displacement" would be of inconsequential magnitudes in the areas for which calculations are made (the United States, Japan, Canada, and the EEC).[2] Furthermore, any prospective trade balance losses for individual countries from even the most liberal tariff-cutting formulas would be extremely modest and would not constitute the basis for limiting the extent of liberalization.[3]

For these reasons it would appear incumbent upon negotiators in the Tokyo Round to move quickly towards agreements that substantially reduce the remaining structure of tariff and nontariff barriers to trade. Their failure to do so would sacrifice important potential gains for consumers and for productive efficiency and progress in limiting inflation in industrial countries, as well as export hopes of developing countries. Such failure would also increase the risk of moving toward increased rather than reduced protection, a danger heightened by sectoral problems of economic recession.

The Tokyo Round of Multilateral Trade Negotiations has proved to be slow in reaching agreements. Changes in national administrations and the chill of worldwide recession have contributed to the delays. Since the beginning of the Tokyo Round, protectionist flare-ups have occurred in conspicuous cases such as those of new protective measures against television sets, shoes, and steel in the United States, and steel, textiles, and shipbuilding in Europe. The political leaders of the major industrial countries have reaffirmed their commitment to successful trade negotiations, most recently at the London summit conference in April 1977. Whether

2. With the possible exception of liberalization of agricultural nontariff barriers in Japan, for which special treatment such as more protracted phasing in might be appropriate.

3. There might be some case for liberalization that would be less than full-formula in Canada, Finland, Australia, and New Zealand if extremely stringent trade balance deterioration limits were set. Such departures would not cause significant changes in trade balance effects of the other major countries; see appendix H.

the Tokyo Round will prove to be another milestone in the process of postwar trade liberalization, like the Kennedy Round before it, or whether instead the current negotiations will fall far short of their potential, will depend in large measure upon the strength of this political commitment of the chiefs of state, and upon their respective abilities in pursuing trade policies beneficial to their general publics despite protectionist pressure from domestic special interest groups.

Appendixes

Tariff-Cutting Formulas in the Multilateral Trade Negotiations: The "Average Depth of Cut" Approach

THE CENTRAL estimates of this study calculate changes in trade flows, welfare gains, and employment effects of alternative tariff-cutting formulas in the Tokyo Round of the Multilateral Trade Negotiations. Those results provide the basis for an evaluation of "reciprocity"—that is, the sharing of the benefits and obligations in the tariff negotiations. A simpler basis, however, is more commonly used by negotiators themselves in evaluating reciprocity: the "depth of cut" of tariffs. This appendix examines twelve alternative tariff-cutting formulas on the basis of this concept, identifying the formulas most favorable to each negotiating partner under this approach.

Concept and Measurement of "Average Depth of Tariff Cut"

For a single tariff the depth of cut is the change in tariff as a percentage of the original tariff. The concept, therefore, considers not the absolute level or absolute change in tariffs, but the percentage change in the tariff. Thus, as a measure of the extent of liberalization, it tends to favor countries with low tariffs. For example, a cut of a 10 percent tariff to 5 percent is treated as identical to a cut of a 20 percent tariff to 10 percent (both are 50 percent cuts), even though the former reduces the price of the imported good by only 4.5 percent while the latter reduces import price to consumers by 8.3 percent, or almost twice as large proportionately.[1] Because imports respond to the percentage change in price to consumer rather than the percentage change in tariff, the result is that import increases are likely to be proportionately larger for countries with high tariffs than for those with low tariffs when the two groups reduce tariffs by the same depth of cut.

The exception to this direction of favoring low-tariff countries is for the case of free entry. Typically, the average depth of cut is calculated for dutiable trade only. Therefore, countries with a large portion of trade entering free receive no "credit" for this fact, and their average depth of cut is computed only on the basis of the remaining imports entering under tariffs.

The basic case for examining the depth of cut of tariffs is twofold. First, it provides a useful bargaining technique. Countries may agree to a general formula of cutting tariffs by a given percentage, as participants did in the general agreement to a 50 percent tariff cut in the Kennedy Round. Second, the approach essentially gives liberalization "credit" to countries that have already established low tariffs in the past (excepting the zero tariff case) because, as noted above, they will experience a smaller proportionate "import price reduction" effect than will countries with higher tariffs, for a given depth of cut.[2]

The depth-of-cut concept is clear for a single tariff, but the average depth of cut over the whole schedule of tariffs is ambiguous because it requires some system of weighting each tariff-line item to obtain an overall weighted average depth of cut. One question is whether import values

1. The price to the consumer equals unity plus the tariff. The first cut is therefore $0.05/1.1 = 0.045$, while the second cut is $0.1/1.2 = 0.083$.

2. In this connection it is worth noting that there is already an element of "harmonization" built into a "linear" tariff cut—that is, a simple percentage cut of all tariffs by a flat rate such as 50 percent. "Harmonization" means that there is greater tariff cutting for higher tariffs and, as discussed here, even a flat percentage rate cut causes a greater proportionate cut in the import price to consumers for higher than for lower tariffs.

should be considered for these weights. It is frequently argued that weights based on import value bias average tariff estimates downward, because items with prohibitively high tariffs will receive virtually no weight since almost no imports will enter under such tariffs. In the simplest case of a flat rate cut applied to all tariffs, this problem—and the entire problem of weighting—disappears because all tariffs fall by the same flat percentage rate and the average depth of cut is that rate regardless of the weights assigned to individual tariffs. However, "harmonization" tariff-cutting formulas typically reduce high tariffs by larger *percentages* than low tariffs. Therefore, to the extent that import-value weighting understates the real weight of high-tariff items, an import-value weighted average-depth-of-cut measure would tend to *understate* the depth of cut in a harmonization tariff cut, and to *understate* the depth of cut for high-tariff countries relative to low-tariff countries in harmonization tariff-cutting formulas.

The alternative of applying no import-value weights at all, however, is far inferior to import-value weighting, because the "simple average" alternative leaves the analyst at the mercy of relatively arbitrary tariff-line categories. Thus, imports of toothbrushes will receive equal weight with imports of automobiles if each of the two commodities enters as a single tariff-line item under the national tariff nomenclature. The bias introduced by this type of random weighting makes simple tariff-line averages inferior to import-value weighted tariff averages and, correspondingly, unweighted average-depth-of-cut estimates inferior to average-depth-of-cut estimates using import-value weights.[3]

Given that import-value weighting is appropriate in calculations of the average depth of tariff cut, the question is precisely what formulation of import weighting to apply. Two alternatives are conventionally used: the "tariff revenues forgone" approach, and a strict weighting of individual tariff depth of cut by tariff-line shares in total import value. These two

---

3. In principle, an alternative would be to weight by the value of total world trade in each category. World trade weights would be less biased downward for high-tariff categories than country import weights. In practice, because country categories are not compatible at the detailed level of individual tariff lines, it would be necessary to preaggregate to the level of four-digit BTN categories, for which compatible trade data are available. Although it would be possible to weight by country imports to obtain an average depth of tariff cut at the level of four-digit BTN categories, and to weight by world trade in arriving at a further aggregation up to the level of the total average depth of cut, we have not applied this procedure in view of computational costs.

measures are, respectively:

(1)
$$y_1 = \frac{\sum_i \Delta t_i M_i}{\sum_i t_i M_i},$$

(2)
$$y_2 = \sum_i \frac{M_i}{M} \frac{\Delta t_i}{t_i},$$

where y is average depth of tariff cut; subscript 1 is for the "tariffs forgone" approach; subscript 2 for the "individual import-value share weighting" approach; Δt_i is the change of tariff in tariff-line i; t_i is the original tariff in that line; M_i is the base level value of imports in the tariff-line item; and M is total import value.

Neither measure is strictly preferable on theoretical grounds. On practical grounds, the first is probably preferable because it represents a concept that is easily grasped—the total sacrifice in tariffs (assuming no change in import values excluding tariff changes) as a percentage of the base level of import tariff collections (hence, the name average tariffs forgone). The first measure tends to give more weight to higher tariffs, because they enter more forcefully in the aggregations of both the denominator and the numerator. By contrast, the second measure gives more weight to low tariffs. Considering the favoritism of the whole depth-of-cut approach to low tariffs, this divergence between the two measures provides another reason for choosing the approach of average tariffs forgone, or measure y_1.

Estimates of the Average Depth of Tariff Cut

Using the GATT trade data for 1971 and post-Kennedy Round tariffs for 1973, equation 1 above is used to compute the average depth of tariff cut for each of the twelve alternative tariff-cutting formulas discussed in chapter 3. For countries using f.o.b. evaluation of trade as the basis for applying tariffs (United States, Canada, and Australia), the tariffs are first converted to c.i.f. basis tariffs (that is, lowered by dividing the tariff by the ratio of c.i.f. prices to f.o.b. prices). Furthermore, for the case of the EEC the average depth of cut is based on values of imports from nonmembers, since tariffs are charged only on goods from countries outside the bloc.

Table A-1. *Average Depth of Tariff Cut*[a] *on All Dutiable Imports under Alternative Tariff-Cutting Formulas*
Percent

	Importer			
Formula[b]	*United States*	*Canada*	*Japan*	*EEC*
1	60.0	60.0	60.0	60.0
2	32.0	36.2	59.0	31.8
3	60.2	51.0	67.1	52.2
4	100.0	100.0	100.0	100.0
5	46.3	47.1	66.7	44.8
6	28.7	38.8	45.1	33.0
7	43.4	43.4	43.4	43.4
8	67.7	60.8	60.1	61.3
9	39.1	54.7	54.2	48.3
10	28.1	45.1	15.9	20.1
11	48.7	56.6	56.3	52.8
12	41.3	50.2	52.4	45.0

a. Average depth of tariff cut calculated as follows: tariff revenue forgone (based on original import values) divided by original hypothetical tariff revenue total. For EEC, computations involve imports from nonmembers only.
b. For a description of the formulas, see table 3-1.

Tables A-1 and A-2 show the calculations of the average depth of cut for the four major parties to the negotiations, for each of the twelve tariff-cutting formulas considered. Both tables exclude petroleum (BTN 2709 and 2710), as a product unaffected by tariff negotiations. Table A-2 also excludes textiles. Thus, because trade in textiles is controlled by a regime of voluntary export quotas, table A-2 is more meaningful than table A-1 as an indication of the "relevant" average depth of tariff cut for negotiation purposes.

Price Effect

It is not the depth of tariff cut that determines the response of imports to tariff liberalization; rather, it is the "price effect." This effect is the proportionate decline in import price, including the tariff, to the consumer, and it equals the change in tariff divided by unity plus the original tariff. It is important to consider the average price effect in addition to the estimates of average depth of tariff cut for alternative tariff-cutting formulas.

Table A-2. *Average Depth of Tariff Cut*[a] *on Dutiable Imports Excluding Textiles under Alternative Tariff-Cutting Formulas*
Percent

	Importer			
Formula[b]	United States	Canada	Japan	EEC
1	60.0	60.0	60.0	60.0
2	25.8	34.0	60.1	31.6
3	63.4	51.2	67.7	52.5
4	100.0	100.0	100.0	100.0
5	42.3	45.6	67.6	44.8
6	22.6	37.1	45.5	32.3
7	43.4	43.4	43.4	43.4
8	70.2	61.0	60.1	61.4
9	32.6	53.7	54.3	47.1
10	22.5	44.4	15.7	20.5
11	45.2	55.9	56.4	52.2
12	36.2	48.5	52.6	44.4

a. See note a, table A-1.
b. For a description of the formulas, see table 3-1.

The measure used for average price effect is the following:

$$(3) \qquad \dot{p} = \sum_i \left(\frac{\Delta t_i}{1 + t_i}\right)\left(\frac{M_i}{M}\right),$$

where $\dot{p}$ is average price effect, M is total imports (value), and the other variables are as before. Thus, the measure is a weighted average of tariff-line price effects, with weights equal to shares in import values.

Tables A-3 and A-4 report the estimates of "average price effect" for the four major negotiating parties. Table A-4 is the more meaningful because it excludes textiles.

A result that immediately stands out in table A-4 is that all of the price effects are relatively modest. Formula 4 is the complete elimination of tariffs, and even in this extreme case for dutiable imports the price to consumers would fall by only 7 percent in the United States, 9 percent in the EEC, 12 percent in Canada, and 13 percent in Japan. In fact, the results for this formula are a direct indication of the relative levels of tariffs among the four importing areas. Moreover, these results clearly indicate the point emphasized earlier: the price effect will be a more substantial price reduction for countries with higher average tariffs for a given average depth of tariff cut equally applied to all countries. These results

Table A-3. *Weighted Average Price Effect[a] on Dutiable Imports
of Alternative Tariff-Cutting Formulas*
Percent

	Importer			
Formula[b]	United States	Canada	Japan	EEC
1	4.30	7.10	7.62	5.63
2	2.15	4.21	5.89	2.88
3	4.38	6.05	7.49	4.89
4	7.17	11.83	12.69	9.39
5	3.22	5.52	7.18	4.13
6	1.92	4.52	5.03	3.01
7	3.11	5.14	5.51	4.07
8	4.91	7.21	7.64	5.76
9	2.66	6.41	6.53	4.45
10	1.89	5.31	2.80	1.94
11	3.41	6.66	6.93	4.91
12	2.85	5.87	6.23	4.15

a. Price effect equals change in tariff divided by unity plus tariff. Tariff-line price effects weighted by share in value of dutiable imports. Nondutiable imports are excluded from calculation.
b. For a description of the formulas, see table 3-1.

(which hold for the other linear cuts, formulas 1 and 7, as well as for complete tariff elimination) mean that, other things being equal, Canada and Japan can expect their dutiable imports to rise by greater proportions from tariff liberalization than will the dutiable imports of the United States and the EEC. The reason for this is that Canada and Japan have higher tariffs, on the average, on those goods that do not enter duty free.

Formula Rankings

One measure of preferred negotiating outcome that negotiators consider important is the average depth of tariff cut. The measure is easy to understand, and it requires no assumptions about, or estimation of, trade elasticities. Therefore, it is informative to consider the preference rankings of tariff-cutting formulas on the basis of the estimations of the average depth of tariff cut.

Negotiators typically will seek a low average depth of cut for their own tariffs and a high average depth of cut for tariffs of the other negotiating partners. That is, a country could reduce its own tariffs unilaterally, so

Table A-4. *Weighted Average Price Effect[a] on Dutiable Imports,*
Excluding Textiles, of Alternative Tariff-Cutting Formulas
Percent

	Importer			
Formula[b]	United States	Canada	Japan	EEC
1	3.66	6.66	7.70	5.48
2	1.48	3.71	6.06	2.77
3	3.92	5.70	7.64	4.78
4	6.10	11.10	12.84	9.13
5	2.51	5.02	7.35	4.01
6	1.29	4.06	5.12	2.86
7	2.65	4.82	5.57	3.96
8	4.33	6.78	7.73	5.62
9	1.89	5.91	6.61	4.21
10	1.30	4.92	2.84	1.93
11	2.71	6.17	7.02	4.71
12	2.14	5.33	6.32	3.97

a. See note a, table A-3.
b. For a description of the formulas, see table 3-1.

that negotiations are for the purpose of obtaining the maximum possible liberalization by other countries in exchange for reducing the home country's protection. A second consideration is the overall degree of liberalization. Representatives of countries in a strong competitive position may seek large overall cuts, and those from countries with poor competitive strength (an admittedly elusive concept) may seek low overall cuts. Finally, members of free-trade blocs may seek low overall cuts, both because the maintenance of a higher common external tariff can provide a needed source of ongoing unity for political objectives and because the "substitution effect" of "unwinding" trade diversion originally caused by the formation of the free-trade area will be more pronounced if the overall degree of tariff liberalization is greater.

Table A-5 presents an indicator of presumed preference by formula on the basis of the average-depth-of-tariff-cut results (excluding textiles) from table A-2. The table shows the weighted four-party average depth of cut for each of the twelve formulas considered. For example, the three-iteration harmonization formula (number 2) yields an average depth of cut of 32.5 percent for the United States, Canada, Japan, and the EEC combined. The weights of each area, listed in note b to the table, equal the area's share of total dutiable nontextile, nonpetroleum imports in 1971.

Table A-5. Relative Average Depth of Tariff Cut by Alternative Tariff Formulas for the Four Major Negotiating Areas, Excluding Textiles

Formula[a]	Weighted four-area average depth of cut[b] (percent)	United States		Canada		Japan		EEC	
		Ratio to four-area average	Rank	Ratio to four-area average	Rank	Ratio to four-area average	Rank	Ratio to four-area average	Rank
1	60.0	1.00	8.5	1.00	4.5	1.00	3.5	1.00	6.5
2	32.5	0.79	3	1.05	6	1.85	11	0.97	4
3	59.1	1.07	10	0.87	1	1.15	6	0.89	2
5	46.4	0.91	6	0.98	3	1.46	9	0.97	3
6	29.9	0.76	1	1.24	9	1.52	10	1.50	11
7	43.4	1.00	8.5	1.00	4.5	1.00	3.5	1.00	6.5
8	65.2	1.08	11	0.94	2	0.92	2	0.94	5
9	42.0	0.78	2	1.28	10	1.29	8	1.12	10
10	23.2	0.97	7	1.91	11	0.68	1	0.88	1
11	49.9	0.91	5	1.12	7	1.13	5	1.05	8
12	42.0	0.86	4	1.15	8	1.25	7	1.06	9

Source: Calculated from table A-2.
a. For a description of the formulas, see table 3-1.
b. Weights: United States, 0.454; Canada, 0.097; Japan, 0.115; EEC, 0.334. Based on shares of dutiable 1971 imports (excluding textile and petroleum imports as well as EEC imports from members for agricultural goods, and from members as well as EFTA countries for other goods).

The table also shows the ratio of each individual importing area's depth of cut to the four-area average. The lower this ratio, the greater the implied advantage for a given country.

The rankings shown in table A-5 are relatively close to those found under the trade-effect criterion (on the joint basis of trade balance effect and ratio of percentage increase in exports to percentage increase in imports; table 3-12). For example, the formula most favored by Canada on both criteria is number 3 (the formula similar to that submitted for discussion by Canada). Under both criteria, the formula least favorable to Japan is number 2 (three-iteration harmonization). However, the two criteria diverge more for the United States and for the EEC. Whereas the trade-effect criterion shows the three-iteration formula (number 2) as the most favorable for the EEC, the depth-of-cut criterion indicates that three other formulas rank higher for the EEC. A reason for this difference is that the trade-effect measure gives credit to formula 2 for its restrictively small degree of trade liberalization (thereby limiting the magnitude of the expected EEC deficit), whereas the average-depth-of-cut approach focuses only on tariff profiles and abstracts from the magnitude of trade effects.[4] Similarly, the most favorable formula for the United States on the depth-of-cut basis (number 6) is so restrictive in trade creation that it limits the size of trade balance increases and therefore ranks behind three other formulas on the trade-effect criterion.

More generally, formula rankings based on average depth of tariff cut provide some insight but, as a rule, they fail to capture the information provided by the more complete assessment of trade effects through the analysis presented in chapter 3. Therefore, despite its past popularity among negotiators, the average-depth-of-cut approach appears to be of limited usefulness. To the extent that it is of any use, the approach appears to be more relevant for Canada and Japan and less relevant for the United States and the EEC.[5]

4. Also note that, ironically, the average depth of tariff cut for the United States would be lower than that for the EEC under the three-iteration harmonization formula. Even when textiles are included, the average depth of cut for the United States would not be higher than that for the EEC under this formula (table A-1).

5. As an overall measure of the degree of correspondence between the relative average-depth-of-cut criterion and the trade-effect criterion, we may examine the sum of the absolute values of differences between the two sets of rankings over all eleven formulas. Out of a maximum possible index of divergence of 60 on this basis, the comparison yields an index of 28 for the United States, 20 for Canada, 13 for Japan, and 39 for the EEC.

Expansion of 1971 Results to 1974

DETAILED trade data at tariff-line levels, compiled by GATT, were available to this study for the base year 1971 only. Therefore, 1971 is the year used as the base for the estimates of trade effects of multilateral tariff negotiations. That year is not, however, satisfactory as a guide to results of liberalization under current circumstances for two reasons. First, real growth and price inflation were enormous in the years following 1971, so that 1971 values are seriously outdated. Second, the year 1971 was one of serious deficit in the trade balance of the United States. Any projections based on 1971 data alone are likely to overstate the reduction in the U.S. trade balance from liberalization and overstate the increase to other countries' trade balances, because the calculations apply to an abnormally high import base relative to the export base. This problem of trade balance disequilibrium became even more severe in 1972, so that liberalization estimates are likely to be even more misleading if they are based on 1972 trade data. Although the negotiators in the Tokyo Round expected a data base for 1974 to be available late in 1977, the 1974 data base was not available for the calculations of this study.

We have adopted the approach of obtaining the initial results using 1971 trade data at tariff-line levels, and then "updating" these results to 1974 levels by applying a relatively detailed set of expansion factors relating 1974 trade levels to 1971 levels. Data for 1975 are not yet available but, in view of the severe recession in 1975, the trade levels for 1974 are probably more representative than 1975 levels in any event.

The data used for 1974 trade levels are from the OECD publication, *Trade by Commodities: Country Summaries,* OECD Statistics of Foreign Trade, Series B. From this source 1971 and 1974 dollar values of trade are obtained, with the following detail. Supplier countries are the eighteen industrial countries directly examined in chapter 3 of this study, plus total world supply. Importing countries are, again, the eighteen industrial countries, although imports are then aggregated to obtain data for imports by the EEC as a bloc.[1] The commodity detail involves a breakdown of trade into nineteen categories.

The OECD data are used to obtain expansion factors indicating the ratio of 1974 to 1971 dollar values of trade, for each of the nineteen product categories and, within each category, from each of the eighteen industrial country suppliers (plus "total" as well as "rest of world") to each of the eleven importing areas examined in the study. These expansion factors are applied to the corresponding 1971 estimates of changes in trade flows from alternative tariff cuts to obtain the 1974 estimates desired. The correspondences between the OECD product groups, which are SITC categories, and the twenty-one two-digit BTN sections, for which results are obtained in our tariff reform model, are listed in table B-1.

For supplier countries other than the eighteen industrial countries considered directly, 1974 trade flows are estimated by applying to 1971 levels the overall expansion factor for rest-of-world countries on the basis of the OECD data (derived from total imports less imports from the eighteen industrial countries individually identified).

In principle, all trade effects originally estimated in 1971 values, at the level of aggregation of the twenty-one BTN sections, are merely expanded by the product- and supplier-specific expansion factors described above. However, for the case of the effects of tariff reform on imports into EEC and EFTA countries, the "substitution" component cannot be simply expanded in this way. This expansion depends not only on the terminal level of imports from a given supplier but also on the terminal share of bloc versus nonbloc suppliers within total imports of the good. The expansion method takes this factor into account, using the OECD data once again to determine the shares of bloc suppliers in 1971 and 1974 imports.

A formal statement of the expansion procedure is shown in equations

---

1. Imports into Australia (1971) and New Zealand (1971, 1974) were not available in the OECD data. These data were therefore approximated using data from United Nations, *Commodity Trade Statistics*, 1973, in addition to data on exports of OECD members to these countries. A similar procedure was required for 1974 imports by the Netherlands and Ireland because of the incomplete status of OECD data for 1974.

Table B-1. *Correspondences between BTN and SITC Categories Used for 1974/1971 Expansion Factors*

BTN categories		Corresponding SITC division
Section	Description	
1	Live animals, animal products	0, 1
2	Vegetable products	0, 1
3	Animal and vegetable fats and oils	4
4	Prepared foodstuffs, beverages, tobacco	0, 1
5	Mineral products (excluding petroleum)	2
6	Chemicals	5
7	Plastics, rubber	5
8	Hides, leather goods	2
9	Wood, cork articles	2
10	Paper, paper products	64
11	Textiles	65
12	Footwear, headgear	85
13	Stone, plaster, cement, ceramic, glass products	66
14	Precious stones, jewelry	66
15	Base metals, articles	67, 68, 69
16	Machinery, electrical equipment	71, 72
17	Transportation equipment	73
18	Precision instruments	86
19	Arms and ammunition	Total[a]
20	Miscellaneous manufactures, including furniture	8
21	Works of art	Total[a]

SITC categories used	
Division	Description
0	Food, live animals
1	Beverages and tobacco
2	Crude materials, except fuels
3	Mineral fuels, lubricants
4	Animal and vegetable oils and fats
5	Chemicals
64	Paper, paper products
65	Textile yarn, fabrics, made-up articles
66	Nonmetallic mineral manufactures, n.e.s.[b]
67	Iron and steel
68	Nonferrous metals
69	Manufactures of metal, n.e.s.[b]
71	Machinery, other than electric
72	Electrical machinery, apparatus and appliances
73	Transportation equipment

Table B-1 (*continued*)

SITC categories used	
Division	*Description*
8	Miscellaneous manufactured articles
85	Footwear
86	Professional, scientific instruments

a. No corresponding SITC category; expansion factor based on expansion for total trade from country supplier in question.
b. Not elsewhere specified.

1 through 9. A description of the variables and steps involved follows the formulas.

$$(1) \qquad \Delta M_{ij}^{74} = \Delta M_{ij}^{74,TC} + \Delta M_{ij}^{74,S}.$$

$$(2) \qquad M_{ij}^{74} = \lambda_{ij} M_{ij}^{71}.$$

$$(3) \qquad \Delta M_{ij}^{74,TC} = \eta \dot{T} M_{ij}^{74} = \eta \dot{T} M_{ij}^{71} \lambda_{ij} = \lambda_{ij} \Delta M_{ij}^{71,TC}.$$

$$(4) \qquad \Delta M_{ij}^{74,S} = M_{ij}^{74} \frac{\phi_B^{74} \sigma \dot{T}}{1 + \phi_{NB}^{74} \sigma \dot{T}} \qquad \text{for} \quad i \in NB,$$

$$= \lambda_{ij} M_{ij}^{71} \frac{\phi_B^{74} \sigma \dot{T}}{1 + \phi_{NB}^{74} \sigma \dot{T}}.$$

Let

$$(5) \qquad \gamma_j \equiv \frac{\dfrac{\phi_B^{74} \sigma \dot{T}}{1 + \phi_{NB}^{74} \sigma \dot{T}}}{\dfrac{\phi_B^{71} \sigma \dot{T}}{1 + \phi_{NB}^{71} \sigma \dot{T}}} = \frac{\phi_B^{74}}{\phi_B^{71}} \frac{1 + \phi_{NB}^{71} \sigma \dot{T}}{1 + \phi_{NB}^{74} \sigma \dot{T}};$$

$$(6) \qquad \Delta M_{ij}^{74,S} = \lambda_{ij} M_{ij}^{71} \frac{\phi_B^{71} \sigma \dot{T}}{1 + \phi_{NB}^{71} \sigma \dot{T}} (\gamma_j) = \gamma_j \lambda_{ij} \Delta M_{ij}^{71,S};$$

$$(7) \qquad \psi_j \equiv \gamma_j - 1;$$

$$(8) \qquad \Delta M_{ij}^{74} = \lambda_{ij} \Delta M_{ij}^{71,TC} + \lambda_{ij} \Delta M_{ij}^{71,S} + \psi_j \lambda_{ij} \Delta M_{ij}^{71,S}$$

$$= \lambda_{ij} \Delta M_{ij}^{71} + \psi_j \lambda_{ij} \Delta M_{ij}^{71,S};$$

$$(9) \qquad \Delta M_{ij}^{74,S} = - \frac{\phi_{NB}^{74} \sigma \dot{T}}{1 + \phi_{NB}^{74} \sigma \dot{T}} M_{ij}^{74} \qquad \text{for} \quad i \in B.$$

$$(10) \qquad \delta_j \equiv \frac{\phi_{NB}^{74}}{\phi_{NB}^{71}} \frac{1 + \phi_{NB}^{71} \sigma \dot{T}}{1 + \phi_{NB}^{74} \sigma \dot{T}},$$

$$\theta_j \equiv \delta_j - 1;$$

$$(11) \qquad \Delta M_{ij}^{74} = \lambda_{ij} M_{ij}^{71} + \theta_j \lambda_{ij} \Delta M_{ij}^{71,S}.$$

All of the above equations refer to a single product category, at the level of the twenty-one BTN sections. Equation 1 states that 1974 increased imports into country j from supplier i because of a hypothesized tariff reform equal the sum of two components, trade creation (TC) and substitution (S). Equation 2 shows that 1974 imports equal 1971 levels multiplied by the relevant expansion factor λ_{ij}, for supplier i and importer j, in this category. Equation 3 first states the basic estimation of trade creation as a function of import price elasticity (η) and change in tariff as a fraction of unity plus tariff ($\dot{T}$) multiplied by the import level.[2] The equation then replaces 1974 imports by their equivalent, the 1971 level times the expansion factor. Finally, consolidating the terms except for the expansion factor, the result is merely the 1971 estimate of trade creation times the expansion factor. Thus, the estimate of the 1974 level of trade creation equals the 1971 estimate directly multiplied by the expansion factor.

Equation 4, which applies to nonbloc (NB) suppliers only, develops the expression for the 1974 level of the substitution effect of trade liberalization. Equation 5 defines a ratio γ_j relating the 1974 share of bloc suppliers (ϕ_B^{74}) in total imports to that share in 1971 (also involving the corresponding shares of nonbloc suppliers). Equation 6 uses the expression γ_j to express the 1974 trade substitution effect in terms of the 1971 substitution effect as well as the basic expansion factor λ_{ij}. To facilitate the expression of the final 1974 estimate in terms of the 1971 estimate, equation 7 defines an auxiliary term (ψ_j). Finally, equation 8 expresses the total 1974 trade change estimate as two components: the first is merely the total 1971 trade change multiplied by the expansion factor λ_{ij}; the second is an additional term which takes account of the fact that the substitution effect depends not only on the expansion factor but also on changes in the overall bloc share of supply. Note that, when the bloc share of supply has fallen between 1971 and 1974, γ_j is smaller than 1 so that ψ_j is negative. As a result, the substitution term in the final equation 8 is negative. This result indicates that, when bloc share of supply falls, the remaining scope for further "substitution" export gains by nonbloc suppliers is lower than that which would have been expected on the basis of 1971 trade shares. Therefore, the trade effect is smaller than that predicted by the simple application of the expansion factor λ_{ij} to the 1971

2. See chapter 2.

result. This particular example is important in practice, because the main shift from 1971 to 1974 with respect to the substitution effect should have been a decline in bloc supplier shares in Europe relative to the share of U.S. supply, because of the devaluation of the dollar in the interim. Thus, the method here takes account of the fact that U.S. export gains to be expected from "substitution" of products of bloc suppliers would be expected to be smaller in 1974 than in 1971 relative to the trade creation effect (although almost certainly larger in absolute terms than the 1971 substitution effect, because of inflation and real growth).

Equations 9 through 12 develop the corresponding expansion estimates for trade changes from bloc suppliers. Equation 9 is based on the corresponding bloc-supplier case (see chapter 2).

Finally, it should be noted that, for importing areas other than the EEC or EFTA countries, the expansion estimate involves the trade creation term only (since there is no substitution among suppliers), and the expansion estimate is merely the first of the two terms in the final expression of equation 8 or, equivalently, the final expression in equation 3.

As discussed above, the empirical estimates of the parameters for the updating to 1974 are obtained from OECD data at aggregation levels comparable to the twenty-one BTN sections, and the parameters are applied to the 1971 results at this same level of aggregation. For trade creation, this procedure should yield results identical to those that would be obtained from expanding results at the individual tariff-line level. This conclusion follows from the fact that any calculations requiring tariff-line detail are already contained in the term $\Delta M_{ij}^{71,TC}$ for 1971, and the 1974 expansion involves only more aggregative trade sums.[3] In the case of the trade substitution estimates, however, some degree of aggregation bias is involved. The bloc shares as well as the "price effect" variable ($\dot{T}$) are obtained at the broad level of the twenty-one BTN sections, and yet a completely accurate expansion would require the availability of these parameters at the tariff-line level. The difficulty occurs because the term $\dot{T}$ should be tariff-line-specific, and this term interacts with the bloc share term. Yet, because of the unavailability of 1974 tariff-line trade data, it is necessary to use aggregative level data. In particular, the $\dot{T}$ term is ob-

---

3. Specifically, suppose that two tariff lines, 1 and 2, constitute a BTN section, and that the 1971 trade creation for each is x_1 and x_2, respectively. Let λ_1 and λ_2 be tariff-line-specific expansion factors. Then, it is easy to demonstrate that, if $x_1^{71} + x_2^{71} = x^{71}$ and $\lambda = x^{74}/x^{71}$, then $\lambda x^{71} = \lambda_1 x_1^{71} + \lambda_2 x_2^{71}$.

tained from the 1971 import-value-weighted "average price effect" for dutiable items for each of the twenty-one BTN sections.[4]

The direction and extent of any aggregation bias involved in the expansion of trade substitution estimates to 1974 are indeterminate on a priori grounds. It is highly unlikely that such bias substantially alters the overall results from those that would be obtained using fully detailed 1974 tariff-line trade data.

4. For results of this price effect aggregated to overall levels, see appendix A.

Disaggregated Import Demand Functions for Japan

by NOBORU KAWANABE

ALTHOUGH there exist a number of studies of import price elasticities for Japan, most are based on rather aggregated commodity classifications. Those studies with estimates for three-digit SITC commodities do not cover the bulk of Japan's imports. Accordingly, this study represents the first attempt to estimate Japanese import functions which include an explicit relative price term for finely disaggregated commodities which together account for a large part of the total imports of Japan.

Import demand functions were estimated for seventy-seven commodities. This selection of commodities depended on the availability of relevant data. Those commodities were selected for which import value, import price indexes, and domestic wholesale price indexes were available in the data sources described below.

Among the seventy-seven items, fourteen are aggregated commodities which have one or more disaggregated commodities as components which themselves were selected for estimation. The reason for including these aggregated commodities is that the estimates for these items could be used as substitutes for those products which are components of them and were not selected.

Altogether the selected seventy-seven items cover 91 percent of Japan's total import value as of 1972. Excluding one-digit SITC items, they cover 87 percent.

The basic specification of the import demand functions is as follows. Japan's imported commodities may be divided into three classes. The first class is competitive and final demand imports, the second is competitive and intermediate demand imports, and the third is noncompetitive and intermediate demand imports. Of course, there may be noncompetitive imports which are demanded as final goods. However, this class of commodities was ignored because, as far as Japan is concerned, it is difficult to isolate this kind of commodity without a very detailed commodity breakdown, using five or more classification digits.

The following standard forms of import demand equations were adopted. Although the estimation was performed in log linear form, for simplicity the functions are presented here in general form.

—Competitive and final:

$$M_i/PM_i = f(PM_i/PD_i, E_i),$$

where M_i is import value of commodity i; PM_i is import price of commodity i; PD_i is domestic price of commodity i or its close substitute; and E_i is relevant component of national expenditure, in constant prices.

—Competitive and intermediate:

$$M_i/PM_i = f(PM_i/PD_i, O_j, I_j),$$

where O_j is amount of production of industry j which uses commodity i; and I_j is amount of material inventory of industry j.

—Noncompetitive and intermediate:

$$M_i/PM_i = f(PM_i/PD_j, O_j, I_j),$$

where PD_j is domestic price of products of industry j.

The material inventory was included as an explanatory variable when the data for it was available and it raised the significance of estimates.

The polynomial distributed lag (Almon lag) was assumed in order to account for price effects taking place after a time period lag. For all items the second degree of the polynomial was chosen. The length of lag and the type of zero constraint differ from item to item.

After trying many different sets of lag length, type of zero constraint, and activity variable for each of the items, the equation which produced the best results was selected (in the absence of any theoretical basis for stating length of lag and zero constraint). Here, the term "best" means satisfaction of sign condition, higher t-statistic for price elasticity, and higher coefficient of determination corrected by degree of freedom. When the corrected coefficients of determination were not significantly different among several forms of equations, the equation which brought about the highest *t*-statistic for the price elasticity was adopted.

The estimation was performed using quarterly data. Data sources are presented below along with adjustments made upon original data. Data periods are from the first quarter of 1965 to the fourth quarter of 1972 for import value; from the third quarter of 1966 to the fourth quarter of 1972 for unit value; and from the first quarter of 1964 to the fourth quarter of 1972 for other variables. Data on import value were taken from *Gaikoku Boeki Gaikyo* [Summary Report of Trade of Japan] (Japan: Ministry of Finance). Import price index data came from Bank of Japan, *Yushutsunyu Bukka Shisu Nenpo* [Export and Import Price Index Annual].

The import price index given in this source is a weighted average of contract prices of specified sample brands. For seventy items, out of seventy-seven, this import price index was used.

Although the original data include three different base years during the period from 1964 to 1972, the base year was adjusted to 1965.

For most items, two or more original series were aggregated by weighted average using the weights given in the source in order to make them accord with the import-value classification. Since these weights are given only every five years, this adjustment may be a source of error.

For seven items[1] the import price index was available only from an alternative source, *Gaikoku Boeki Gaikyo,* on the basis of unit values calculated from import quantities and values.

The domestic wholesale price index was taken from Bank of Japan, *Orsohiuri Bukka Shisu Nenpo* [Wholesale Price Index Annual]. Original data were adjusted to base year and aggregated in the same way as for the import price index.

Expenditure data came from *Kokumin Shotoku Tokei Nenpo* [Annual Report of National Accounts] (Japan: Agency of Economic Planning). The expenditures are real values in 1965 prices.

The source for the production index and material inventory index was *Kokogyo Shisu Soran* [Summary of Industrial Indexes] (Japan: Ministry of International Trade and Industry). The indexes in this source are quantity indexes derived by averaging the quantities of component industries with value weights. The base year is 1970.

The resulting estimates are presented in table C-1. Those products

---

1. Essential oils; manufactures of rubber, wood, and paper; cotton fabrics; pumps and centrifuges; and transistors and diodes.

Table C-1. *Import Elasticities for Japan*
Negative sign is omitted for price elasticity and its *t*-statistic

Item	Price elasticity	*t*-statistic	Activity variable elasticity	*t*-statistic	$\bar{R}^2$	Degrees of freedom
Food	0.4716	1.9832	1.8491	15.8200	0.942	22
Meat	0.8028	2.1638	3.4154	8.3636	0.890	24
Beef	0.9819	1.2949	4.7676	7.3213	0.810	26
Mutton	0.5862	3.1539	1.5658	3.8323	0.747	26
Milk and cream	0.5217	2.7164	6.5442	7.5700	0.717	21
Cheese	1.9400	6.7417	2.0589	7.5745	0.930	25
Fish	1.2920	3.3609	3.5150	18.5150	0.930	25
Wheat	0.7628	1.9714	0.5539	1.5958	0.270	21
Feedingstuff	0.1575	1.6321	0.9992	5.1011	0.741	24
Beans	0.8255	1.2784	1.4033	1.9601	0.540	21
Sugar	0.7623	2.6179	2.8458	4.8166	0.631	22
Hide	0.2242	1.3567	0.6168	2.5633	0.409	26
Oil seeds	0.2419	2.4670	1.5427	18.2600	0.927	26
Soybeans	0.7263	2.9463	1.4356	9.4595	0.877	25
Crude rubber	0.1638	1.6877	0.8864	4.7338	0.842	25
			0.4905	5.0623		23
Wood	1.3071	3.7392	2.5354	10.3810	0.962	24
Pulp and paper	1.5561	3.6778	1.3602	3.3324	0.664	23
			0.6916	1.8663		
Textile fibers	1.0574	2.5547	1.2143	2.2132	0.778	18
			1.1249	2.1832		
Raw silk	2.1183	4.5711	6.0891	9.6724	0.845	26
Wool	1.1583	3.0862	1.6876	1.5105	0.580	
			1.8055	1.5078		

Commodity						n
Cotton	0.6790	2.1076	0.4015	1.1153	0.625	25
Crude minerals	0.9127	3.6650	-0.3651	-1.4838	0.976	27
Metalliferous ores and scrap	1.6671	8.1200	1.4685	34.1080	0.962	23
			3.3610	19.7630		
			-2.7233	-19.2910		
Iron ore	0.7323	1.9282	0.9567	8.7675	0.913	24
Iron scrap	2.0509	2.9822	2.9191	7.1014	0.683	21
			-2.2823	7.2411		
Nonferrous metal ore	1.2424	1.8129	1.6522	9.9381	0.932	26
Copper ore	2.7332	3.5226	1.9625	11.4930	0.889	26
Nickel ore	2.4586	3.0543	2.5987	7.5933	0.892	26
Bauxite	1.4462	1.8320	1.2426	11.4120	0.874	25
Zinc ore	1.1830	2.0782	1.3349	8.4165	0.844	24
Manganese ore	0.9679	0.9236	1.4706	5.8772	0.748	26
Nonferrous metal scrap	4.2136	3.2388	0.1364	4.8828	0.398	25
Coal	4.4477	7.0712	1.8932	5.2029	0.923	21
			-1.4054	-5.3835		
Petroleum	1.9359	2.5487	0.9864	10.3590	0.968	21
Crude petroleum	2.2602	4.0255	0.9228	8.5641	0.975	21
Motor spirit	1.0167	2.1665	1.2718	14.0150	0.930	25
Residual fuel oils	0.8983	2.0487	0.9915	5.4908	0.595	20
Gas	1.4293	3.2986	2.6259	29.7040	0.974	24
Animal oils	0.3219	1.9529	0.9513	4.8472	0.497	25
Vegetable oils	1.5108	3.1798	2.6800	7.1117	0.637	25
Chemicals	2.1881	3.7843	1.3773	22.0560	0.982	24
Chemical elements	1.0947	4.9797	1.2201	12.4560	0.882	24
Organic chemicals	1.4624	6.0822	1.6573	7.3212	0.688	24

Table C-1 (continued)

Item	Price elasticity	t-statistic	Activity variable elasticity	t-statistic	$\bar{R}^2$	Degrees of freedom
Inorganic chemicals	0.9160	10.0650	1.2865	11.3620	0.961	24
Dye stuff	4.9474	3.0421	2.8220	6.0647	0.796	24
Medical products	0.2051	2.0252	2.0452	4.0726	0.988	24
Essential oils	0.9010	8.7801	0.7330	5.6837	0.805	18
Fertilizer	0.3705	1.6432	0.4429	5.1833	0.674	25
Plastic materials	3.4829	1.9572	2.6747	6.8978	0.879	18
			−2.4171	−5.8777		
Chemicals, not elsewhere specified	1.3238	4.8664	1.3756	18.5690	0.953	24
Rubber manufactures	1.2256	8.9036	1.2574	6.7025	0.864	17
Wool manufactures	1.2241	5.3462	2.6618	6.7714	0.813	17
Paper manufactures	2.4442	9.8945	1.9984	8.0255	0.859	18
Cotton fabrics	1.5387	6.6255	8.5125	7.1682	0.891	20
Woolen fabrics	1.2218	2.1738	2.9763	2.7111	0.841	19
Iron and steel	5.2029	4.3521	3.9380	6.4645	0.654	22
			−3.9900	−7.4285		
Nonferrous metals	1.3788	3.6651	1.2543	0.1830	0.904	19
Copper	1.4533	3.2887	0.5615	3.4833	0.849	18
Aluminum	1.0109	3.2167	1.8691	8.4194	0.834	25
Tin	0.8985	1.8104	0.7501	3.2960	0.803	22
			−0.7383	−2.5881		

Manufactures of metals	5.2985	5.3742	0.6696	5.6781	0.973	24
Machinery	1.0102	2.6264	1.0521	19.7500	0.979	26
Power machinery	1.8887	1.7712	0.9467	6.6121	0.725	21
Office machines	1.6486	2.0794	1.5479	4.8170	0.904	21
Metalworking machinery	4.3705	2.5832	0.4654	0.9059	0.737	25
Textile machines	2.0670	2.7688	1.1260	18.9720	0.949	22
Pumps and centrifuges	1.0718	3.7438	0.3439	0.5836	0.831	17
Electrical machinery	1.1389	1.8633	1.9367	9.4232	0.960	24
Electric power machinery	6.8371	4.5021	0.7062	6.2098	0.718	24
Transistors and diodes instruments	1.0205	3.5644	0.8488	3.5141	0.856	20
Electrical measuring instruments	1.0616	2.2045	1.4167	9.5907	0.891	25
Transportation equipment	2.0161	0.6896	2.2020	4.7344	0.673	24
Passenger cars	1.2201	0.8871	1.4645	3.0123	0.821	24
Precision machines	1.6855	2.4326	1.2536	34.2510	0.978	24
Scientific instruments	2.8055	6.3929	0.7499	3.1744	0.899	24
Photographic supplies	0.9083	3.0030	1.6151	6.6087	0.943	23
Watches and clocks	5.0064	2.9886	1.9894	13.1610	0.878	24

showing two coefficients for the activity variable report the coefficient on domestic output of the using industry (O_j) first and the coefficient on material inventory (I_j) in the second row for the commodity in question. Further details on the functional form chosen for each product, the data used, and possible biases in the estimates,[2] are available on request.

2. Several commodities were under import quota during at least part of the estimation period. Beef, wheat and maslin, and beans were under import quota restrictions throughout the estimation period. Therefore, the import functions estimated for these items should be interpreted as representing the government's behavior rather than the consumer's import demand.

The items with a part of their components under quota restriction throughout the estimation period are meat, milk and cream, cheese and curd, fish, sugar, oil seeds, coal, and office machines.

The items with a part of their components under quota during a part of the estimation period are fish, sugar, oil seeds, feedingstuff, coal, organic chemicals, inorganic chemicals, medical products, woolen fabrics, power-generating machinery, office machines, metalworking machinery, textile machines, electrical power machinery, passenger cars, and photographic supplies. For coal, woolen fabrics, and metalworking machinery, a dummy variable for the import quota was used in the import demand equation. For the other commodities, no dummy variable was used because it lowered the significance of the estimates.

A Measurement of the Employment Effect of the Removal of Agricultural Import Quotas: The Case of Japan

by NOBORU KAWANABE

THIS APPENDIX reports measurements of potential employment effects of removing quotas on agricultural imports in Japan. The estimates here are based on the corresponding estimates of changes in imports presented in chapter 5.

Assuming that final demand for an industry declines by the amount of import increase and that the labor coefficient of the industry is constant through change in production and time, the direct decrease in employment caused by the import increase is equal to the labor coefficient times the amount of import increase.

Since, on the one hand, the available labor coefficient for a sector is man-years divided by amount of production of the sector evaluated by (preliberalization) domestic price and, on the other hand, the amount of import increase as reported in chapter 5 is evaluated at the given import price, we must revaluate the import increment at the domestic price. As the discrepancy between import price and domestic price is quite large in the case of quota-imposed commodities, this procedure is indispensable.

Accordingly,

$$\Delta DL_i = \alpha_i \Delta M_i \frac{Pd_i}{Pm_i},$$

where ΔDL_i, α_i, ΔM_i, Pd_i, and Pm_i stand, respectively, for direct change in employment, labor coefficient, change in import, domestic price, and import price of industry or commodity i.[1]

Under the additional assumptions that input-output coefficients are constant and that the proportion of domestically produced material to imported material is constant, the formula for the total (direct plus indirect) employment effect is

$$\Delta TL_s = D_L[I - A_d]^{-1}\Delta M_d,$$

where ΔTL_s and ΔM_d are vectors of total change in employment and import change (in domestic prices), respectively; D_L is a diagonal matrix of labor coefficients; and A_d stands for the input-output coefficient matrix with respect to domestically produced material only.

In the above formula, ΔTL shows the total employment effect caused in each sector. On the other hand, the following formula gives the total employment effect caused by each sector's commodity:

$$\Delta TL_c = D_m[I - A_d]^{-1}\gamma,$$

where ΔTL_c and γ are vectors of total employment effect and labor coefficients, respectively; and D_m is a diagonal matrix of the domestic price values of import changes.

The employment effects were calculated for import increases based on 1971 and 1974 import values. In both cases the 160-sector input-output and labor coefficients for 1970 were employed. For the 1971 base year, import changes in domestic prices were calculated using the same data sources as shown in chapter 5. For the 1974 base year, import changes in domestic prices were calculated from 1974 import values in *Nihon Boeki Geppyo* [Japan Exports and Imports] (Japan: Ministry of Finance, December 1974), using the elasticities and tariff-equivalents discussed in chapter 5.

The labor coefficients were calculated from "Employment Table" and "Output Table" in *1970 Input-Output Tables* (Government of Japan, 1974). The inverse of the input-output matrix, $[I - A_d]^{-1}$, was drawn from the same source. The correspondence between the industrial sectors

---

1. The labor coefficient is expressed in man-years per unit of gross output at domestic prices. Note that the final term in the equation essentially converts the labor coefficient into man-years per unit of output at import prices, for comparability with import-value change expressed in import prices. Note furthermore that labor coefficients are available only for more aggregative categories than trade change figures, so that the term for import increase in sector i refers to the sum of import change for all commodities belonging to the aggregate sector i.

and the trade commodity sectors was developed from the "Table of Correspondence between I-O Code and Trade Classification Code," in *1970 Input-Output Tables,* and *Genko Yunuy Seido Ichiran* [List of Current Import Regulations] (Japan: Tsusho Sangyo Chosakai, 1974).

The results of measurement of the direct employment effect (ΔD_L), the total employment effect in each sector (ΔTL_s), and the total employment effect caused by each commodity (ΔTL_c) are reported in tables D-1 through D-4.

The employment effect was measured for import increases based on 1971 and 1974 import values. In the case of the 1974 base, the results may be exaggerated. Tariff-equivalents based on 1970 prices were applied to 1974 import data to calculate the corresponding employment-decrease effect. However, tariff-equivalents might have been lowered between 1970 and 1974 because of the rapid reduction of quotas after the problem of the huge balance-of-payments surplus arose; moreover, labor coefficients might have been lowered because of improvement in productivity. On the other hand, in view of the possible underestimation of the import-increasing effect because of the use of import price elasticities estimated on the basis of past data, the 1974 base measurement might give results closer to the reality.

Since Japan's grain imports, especially imports of wheat, have been confronted with serious problems on the supply side, we measured the employment effect in three cases. The first case is to take import increases of all grains into account; the second is to exclude import increases of wheat; and the third is to exclude import increases of all grains.

Table D-1 shows the direct employment effect of the removal of agricultural import quotas and the corresponding percentage of total 1970 sectoral employment. Prominent decreases of employment (1 percent or more of total sector employment) occur in the sectors of grains, other field farming, butchery, dairy preparation, vegetable and fruit processing, and other food manufacturing (0111, 0112, 2011, 2020, 2030, and 2091) when based on 1971 import values. Except for vegetable and fruit processing, these sectors are subjected to still larger percentage employment decreases when the estimates are based on 1974 import values.[2]

2. Comparing the 1974-based employment decrease with the 1970 sectoral employment figures exaggerates the proportional employment effect for sectors with expanding labor forces. However, as far as the agricultural, fishery, and forestry sectors are concerned, we may safely say that the number of employed workers decreased between 1971 and 1974, and the comparison does not cause exaggeration.

Table D-1. *Direct Employment Decrease by Removal of Quota, 1971 Base and 1974 Base*
Employment figures in man-years

I-O code	Sector	1970 employment	Employment decrease, 1971 base	Rate of decrease (percent)	Employment decrease, 1974 base	Rate of decrease (percent)
0111	Grain	3,771,318	325,217[a] 62,046[b] 0[c]	8.64[a] 1.65[b] 0.00[c]	984,210[a] 210,657[b] 0[c]	26.10[a] 5.59[b] 0.00[c]
0112	Other field farming	2,097,873	24,887	1.19	31,864	1.52
0113	Fruit	967,287	1,253	0.13	3,562	0.37
0410	Saltwater fishery	542,060	1,856	0.34	5,133	0.95
2011	Butchery	19,941	768	3.85	1,838	9.22
2012	Meat preparing	25,783	87	0.34	398	1.54
2020	Dairy product preparing	67,176	3,913	5.82	13,090	19.49
2030	Vegetable and fruit processing	67,886	1,413	2.08	840	1.24
2040	Seafood processing	220,411	96	0.04	126	0.06
2050	Grain polishing and milling	28,312	14[a] 4[c]	0.05[a] 0.01[c]	245[a] 11[c]	0.87[a] 0.04[c]
2070	Sugar refining	14,992	120	0.80	1	0.00
2091	Other food manufacturing	330,413	5,523	1.67	13,413	4.06
2140	Soft drinks	48,504	76	0.16	137	0.28
	Total	8,201,956	365,823	4.46	1,054,857	12.86
	Total, excluding wheat	n.a.[d]	102,052	1.24[e]	281,305	3.43
	Total, excluding all grain	4,430,638	39,997	0.90	70,413	1.59

Source: See text of appendix D.
a. Including all grain.
b. Excluding wheat.
c. Excluding all grain.
d. Employment for wheat is inseparable.
e. Ratio to total of case including all grain.

The total (direct plus indirect) employment effects caused in agricultural and food manufacturing sectors are presented in table D-2 for 1971. (The corresponding table for the 1974 base is available on request.)

The sectors which are added to the list of prominent sectors with decreasing employment are cattlebreeding, agricultural services, sugar refining, and feedingstuff (0116, 0120, 2070, and 2092), in the case of the 1971 base; in the case of the 1974 base, industrial material farming, firewood and charcoal, saltwater fishery, meat preparation, and grain polishing and milling (0114, 0212, 0410, 2012, and 2050) are added.

Sectors which relate to grain, beef, and dairy products undergo the highest rates of employment decrease. This point is apparent in the estimates of total employment effects caused by import increases for each quota commodity, reported in table D-4.

One noteworthy point is that, although wheat remains the most influential commodity in the case of the total labor effect, the effect of its exclusion is smaller in this case than in the case of the direct labor effects only. Namely, in the case of the direct effect, the exclusion of wheat reduces the rate of total employment decrease of relevant sectors from 4.46 percent to 1.24 percent for the 1971 base and from 12.86 percent to 3.43 percent for the 1974 base. By contrast, in the case of the total effect, these reductions are from 4.06 percent to 1.77 percent and from 11.72 percent to 4.98 percent. This means that the indirect effect is larger for import increases of beef and dairy products than for wheat.

Although Japanese employment in agricultural sectors has declined year after year, the rates of decrease which could be expected from quota removal for the total of agricultural, fishery, and forestry sectors are considerable (4.42 percent, 1.85 percent, and 1.23 percent, respectively) compared to the 1965–70 actual decrease (2.4 percent).

However, alternative data show that the average annual rate of decrease in agricultural employment was 7.57 percent for the period between 1969 and 1973.[3] Taking this recent experience of decrease into account, the magnitude of the total employment effect measured here for quota removal might be considered to be moderate.

Tables D-3 and D-4 show the total employment effects (for 1971) caused in nonagricultural sectors which are subject to more than a 0.5 percent rate of decrease when all grains are included.

3. *Year Book of Labor Statistics* (Japan: Department of Labor, 1973).

Table D-2. *Total Employment Decrease in Agricultural and Food Manufacturing Sectors, 1971 Base*
Employment figures in man-years

I-O code	Sector	1970 employment	Total		Excluding wheat		Excluding grain		1965–70 percentage change in employment
			Employment decrease	Rate of decrease	Employment decrease	Rate of decrease	Employment decrease	Rate of decrease	
0111	Grain	3,771,318	345,666	9.17	76,980	2.04	12,695	0.34	⎫
0112	Other field farming	2,097,873	37,742	1.80	36,998	1.76	36,820	1.76	⎪
0113	Fruit	967,287	2,858	0.30	2,858	0.30	2,858	0.30	⎬ −3.12
0114	Industrial material farming	372,965	2,483	0.67	2,465	0.66	2,452	0.66	⎪
0115	Fiber material farming	58,248	180	0.31	56	0.10	26	0.04	⎭
0116	Cattlebreeding	2,367,680	81,843	3.46	176,178	3.21	74,882	3.16	⎫
0117	Cattlebreeding for fiber	588	2	0.40	2	0.40	2	0.40	⎪
0118	Sericulture	224,910	113	0.05	49	0.02	33	0.01	⎬ 93.97
0120	Agricultural service	97,035	4,073	4.20	1,607	1.66	1,018	1.05	⎪
0211	Forestry	142,563	100	0.07	69	0.05	62	0.04	⎭
0212	Firewood and charcoal	29,827	196	0.66	181	0.61	177	0.59	⎫
0220	Crude lumber	103,875	48	0.05	32	0.03	28	0.03	⎬ −32.11
0410	Saltwater fishery	542,060	2,418	0.45	2,388	0.44	2,381	0.44	⎫
0420	Whaling	3,929	1	0.04	1	0.03	1	0.03	⎬ 42.08
0430	Freshwater fishery	40,221	2	0.00	2	0.00	2	0.00	⎭

2011	Butchery	19,941	781	3.92	781	3.92	781	3.92	40.17
2012	Meat preparation	25,783	108	0.42	108	0.42	108	0.42	14.32
2020	Dairy product preparation	67,176	4,236	6.31	4,234	6.30	4,233	6.30	5.43
2030	Vegetable and fruit processing	67,886	1,441	2.12	1,441	2.12	1,441	2.12	21.67
2040	Seafood processing	220,411	163	0.07	161	0.07	160	0.07	35.62
2050	Grain polishing and milling	28,312	80	0.28	78	0.27	67	0.24	−0.62
2060	Pastry	329,134	0	0.00	0	0.00	0	0.00	19.30
2070	Sugar refining	14,992	210	1.40	210	1.40	209	1.40	−6.96
2091	Other food manufacturing	330,413	6,182	1.87	6,164	1.87	6,160	1.86	10.41
2092	Feedingstuff	21,407	659	3.08	613	2.86	602	2.81	−5.49
2110	Brewing and distilling	109,105	14	0.01	13	0.01	13	0.01	6.34
2140	Soft drinks	48,504	76	0.16	76	0.16	76	0.16	4.61
	Total	12,103,443	491,675	4.06	213,745	1.77	147,227	1.22	0.49
	Total of agriculture, fishery, and forestry	10,820,379	477,725	4.42	199,866	1.85	133,377	1.23	−2.14
	Total of food manufacturing	1,283,064	13,950	1.09	13,879	1.08	13,850	1.08	13.47

Source: See text of appendix D.

Table D-3. *Total Employment Decrease in Nonagricultural Sectors, 1971 Base*
Employment figures in man-years

I-O code	Sector	1970 employment	Total Employment decrease	Total Rate of decrease	Excluding wheat Employment decrease	Excluding wheat Rate of decrease	Excluding grain Employment decrease	Excluding grain Rate of decrease	1965–70 percentage change in employment
1990	Other nonmetallic minerals	6,195	34	0.54	15	0.23	10	0.16	−63.79
3111	Inorganic chemical	28,120	218	0.78	95	0.34	66	0.23	−17.63
3118	Chemical fertilizer	18,299	578	3.16	207	1.13	118	0.65	−21.43
3120	Oil and fat processing	14,050	282	2.01	286	1.89	262	1.86	−33.17
3192	Other chemicals	89,544	591	0.66	209	0.23	117	0.13	21.51
8800	Government academic institutions	49,269	573	1.16	461	0.94	434	0.88	n.a.[a]
	Total of nonagricultural sectors	42,912	28,412	0.07	17,490	0.04	14,833	0.03	...

Source: See text of appendix D.
a. For I-O sector 8800, rate of five years change in employment is unavailable because of different sector disaggregation between 1965 and 1970 data.

Table D-4. *Total Employment Decrease Caused by Each BTN Commodity,*
1971 Base and 1974 Base
Employment figures in man-years

BTN code	Commodity	Employment decrease, 1971 base	Employment decrease, 1974 base
0201	Beef	55,414	132,587
0301	Fish, fresh, chilled, or frozen	372	1,284
0302	Fish, salted, dried, or smoked	136	260
0303	Cuttlefish and scallops	1,340	4,134
0402	Milk and cream	15,785	49,679
0403	Butter	1,298	45,514
0404	Cheese and curd	27,169	58,499
0705	Peas and beans	23,136	28,075
0802	Oranges	1,354	3,850
1001	Wheat	288,851	847,105
1003	Barley	67,946	230,687
1006	Rice	1,230	29,950
1101	Cereal flour	34	120
1102	Cereal meals and groats	503	1,301
1107	Malt	16,238	36,177
1108	Starches and inulin	1,595	7,664
1201	Peanuts	5,059	8,025
1208	Laner and other seaweeds	685	900
1602	Prepared meat	800	3,659
1702	Sugar, except beet and cane	2,951	1,929
2005	Fruit purees and pastes	31	321
2006	Fruit pulp and prepared pineapple	6,743	3,706
2007	Tomato juice and fruit juice	198	357
2104	Tomato sauce and ketchup	1	87
2107	Food preparations containing sugar, milk, seaweeds, and cereals	1,218	2,398

Source: See text of appendix D.

There are six of these sectors when based on 1971 import value, in-creasing to twenty-one sectors when based on 1974 import values. Among these sectors, most strongly affected are the sectors which relate to chemical fertilizers.

Finally, table D-4 reports the change in employment resulting from the removal of quotas by the product to which the quota applies, based on trade categories rather than domestic industrial sectors. It is clear from the table that the employment effects are concentrated overwhelmingly in the following products: wheat, and (less importantly) barley and beef.

Statistical Tables

Table E-1. *Matrix of Trade Effects of Tariff Formula 3, 1974 Base*
Millions of dollars; excluding textiles and petroleum

Importer[a]	Exporter											Total
	USA	CND	JPN	EEC	ATA	FIN	NOR	SWD	SWZ	ALA	NWZ	
ALA	30	17	97	56	0	0	0	0	0	0	48	249
ATA	37	4	5	−33	0	−1	−1	−2	−3	2	1	8
BLX	105	15	10	−233	−1	−1	−1	−3	−2	5	1	−105
CND	333	0	64	177	1	1	2	5	2	15	4	603
DEN	22	6	9	−42	−1	−1	3	−4	−1	5	1	−3
FIN	7	4	3	−51	−1	0	0	−5	0	1	0	−41
FRA	338	30	35	−375	−2	−1	−1	−7	−4	9	6	28
GFR	430	60	114	−654	−20	−6	−7	−27	−19	57	18	−54
IRE	19	2	1	−31	0	0	0	0	1	1	0	−8
ITL	351	31	21	−260	−2	−1	−1	−3	−4	26	6	163
JPN	1,043	162	0	651	18	10	17	42	25	169	39	2,176
NLD	69	11	16	−368	−1	0	−1	−2	−1	5	3	−269
NWZ	4	3	11	21	0	0	0	0	0	16	0	55
NOR	13	2	8	−16	0	−1	0	−4	0	1	0	3
SWD	53	17	21	−116	−2	−6	−2	0	−2	12	2	−24
SWZ	53	10	60	−66	−3	−1	0	−3	0	5	4	62
UK	236	92	54	−221	−2	−4	−3	−12	−4	97	75	307
USA	0	898	515	1,073	15	13	50	76	35	104	51	3,460
SBT	3,144	1,363	1,044	143	0	2	54	49	21	530	259	6,610
ROW	629	68	639	1,778	30	19	0	59	14	−42	−23	3,170
EEC	1,570	246	260	−2,184	−29	−13	−11	−59	−35	205	110	60
TOT	3,773	1,431	1,683	1,921	30	21	55	108	35	488	235	9,781
BST	316	−760	1,131	−83	9	−43	−51	−73	40	−282	−204	0
BTW	−313	−828	493	−1,861	−21	−63	−51	−132	27	−239	−181	−3,170
TL2	4,014	1,462	1,627	2,067	36	23	70	117	47	564	262	10,288
RW2	872	99	496	1,917	36	20	15	68	25	34	4	3,587

a. For abbreviations, see table 3-4. Figures are rounded.

Table E-2. *Matrix of Trade Effects of Tariff Formula 6, 1974 Base*
Millions of dollars; excluding textiles and petroleum

Importer[a]	USA	CND	JPN	EEC	ATA	FIN	NOR	SWD	SWZ	ALA	NWZ	Total
ALA	13	14	63	18	0	0	0	0	0	0	40	149
ATA	19	3	3	-13	0	0	0	-1	-1	2	0	12
BLX	16	10	5	-127	-1	0	-1	-1	0	4	1	-94
CND	90	0	32	83	0	0	1	1	0	11	3	221
DEN	6	5	7	-21	-1	0	3	-1	0	4	1	2
FIN	2	3	1	-27	-1	0	0	-2	0	1	0	-22
FRA	235	21	25	-204	-1	0	-1	-1	1	8	5	88
GFR	140	43	71	-320	-16	-2	-3	-7	-2	51	16	-30
IRE	13	2	1	-20	0	0	0	0	0	1	0	-3
ITL	247	25	14	-159	-2	0	-1	0	0	24	5	151
JPN	372	123	0	383	15	4	9	10	2	158	29	1,106
NLD	34	8	10	-223	-1	0	0	0	0	5	3	-163
NWZ	1	1	7	17	0	0	0	0	0	14	0	39
NOR	2	1	6	0	0	-1	0	-1	0	1	0	9
SWD	13	12	12	-48	-1	-3	0	0	0	11	1	-2
SWZ	27	7	44	-24	-2	0	0	0	0	4	4	61
UK	102	69	35	-110	-2	-2	-1	-3	0	83	64	235
USA	0	624	316	838	11	5	26	14	3	88	42	1,966
SBT	1,332	971	652	43	0	0	32	9	3	470	214	3,724
ROW	307	52	342	988	22	11	1	17	7	-42	-18	1,687
EEC	739	182	167	-1,185	-23	-5	-4	-13	-1	180	95	186
TOT	1,639	1,023	994	1,031	22	11	32	26	10	427	196	5,411
BST	634	-749	454	143	12	-22	-23	-11	58	-321	-175	0
BTW	327	-802	112	-845	-10	-33	-24	-28	51	-279	-157	-1,687
TL2	1,776	1,048	975	1,103	28	11	41	30	11	499	217	5,739
RW2	445	78	265	1,059	28	11	10	21	8	30	3	1,957

a. For abbreviations, see table 3-4. Figures are rounded.

Table E-3. *Matrix of Trade Effects of Tariff Formula 11, 1974 Base*
Millions of dollars; excluding textiles and petroleum

| | | | | | Exporter | | | | | | | |
Importer[a]	USA	CND	JPN	EEC	ATA	FIN	NOR	SWD	SWZ	ALA	NWZ	Total
ALA	24	18	83	39	0	0	0	0	0	0	47	212
ATA	32	5	5	-28	0	-1	-1	-1	-2	2	1	12
BLX	54	16	9	-219	-1	-1	-1	-2	-1	6	1	-139
CND	203	0	55	153	1	0	2	3	1	15	4	436
DEN	15	7	9	-38	-1	-1	3	-3	0	5	1	-2
FIN	5	4	2	-47	-1	0	0	-3	0	1	0	-39
FRA	305	32	37	-343	-2	-1	-1	-4	-1	10	6	40
GFR	278	66	117	-580	-22	-5	-6	-17	-8	63	19	-96
IRE	17	3	1	-31	0	0	0	0	0	1	0	-9
ITL	319	35	21	-255	-3	0	-1	-2	-2	29	6	148
JPN	721	185	0	652	20	7	15	27	12	189	38	1,866
NLD	55	13	16	-360	-1	0	-1	-1	0	6	3	-271
NWZ	3	2	10	23	0	0	0	0	0	17	0	56
NOR	7	2	9	-8	0	-1	0	-3	0	1	0	7
SWD	32	18	20	-96	-2	-5	-1	0	-1	14	2	-19
SWZ	45	11	66	-54	-3	0	0	-1	0	5	5	74
UK	178	103	53	-198	-2	-3	-2	-9	-1	105	76	299
USA	0	968	513	1,526	17	10	44	43	13	108	51	3,294
SBT	2,292	1,487	1,028	139	-1	0	50	27	9	579	259	5,870
ROW	566	74	493	1,638	31	17	1	40	12	-49	-23	2,800
EEC	1,221	274	263	-2,022	-32	-10	-9	-37	-13	224	112	-30
TOT	2,858	1,561	1,521	1,777	31	17	51	67	21	529	236	8,670
BST	1,003	-1,051	839	-170	12	-39	-43	-46	65	-367	-203	0
BTW	437	-1,125	346	-1,808	-19	-56	-44	-86	53	-318	-180	-2,800
TL2	3,051	1,596	1,494	1,915	38	18	65	75	26	615	263	9,157
RW2	760	109	374	1,772	39	18	15	48	17	36	4	3,193

a. For abbreviations, see table 3-4. Figures are rounded.

277

Table E-4. Matrix of Trade Effects of Tariff Formula 1, Including Textiles, 1974 Base

Millions of dollars; excluding petroleum

Importer[a]	Exporter											Total
	USA	CND	JPN	EEC	ATA	FIN	NOR	SWD	SWZ	ALA	NWZ	
ALA	38	20	91	52	0	0	0	0	0	0	51	254
ATA	51	7	8	-49	0	-1	-1	-3	-4	3	1	11
BLX	106	26	12	-345	-2	-1	-2	-4	-2	8	2	-202
CND	311	0	64	198	1	1	2	5	1	19	4	605
DEN	25	8	11	-49	-1	-2	1	-7	-1	5	1	-9
FIN	8	5	2	-61	-1	0	-1	-9	0	2	0	-55
FRA	370	49	62	-477	-2	-1	-1	-6	-4	12	6	7
GFR	454	90	140	-801	-27	-6	-8	-25	-17	71	20	-110
IRE	34	3	1	-46	0	0	0	0	0	1	0	-6
ITL	401	59	43	-396	-4	-1	-2	-4	-4	36	6	135
JPN	1,324	242	0	842	22	11	20	41	23	224	50	2,800
NLD	77	19	19	-471	-1	0	-1	-2	-1	6	3	-352
NWZ	8	2	13	25	0	0	0	0	0	25	0	74
NOR	11	3	9	-16	0	-1	0	-4	0	1	0	2
SWD	51	21	24	-128	-2	-7	-4	0	-2	15	2	-31
SWZ	67	17	75	-88	-6	-1	-1	-3	0	7	5	74
UK	288	154	67	-260	-4	-5	-4	-14	-4	123	83	424
USA	0	1,185	594	1,951	20	14	57	66	27	126	56	4,095
SBT	3,624	1,911	1,235	-120	-9	-1	56	32	11	685	292	7,715
ROW	1,837	149	636	2,604	48	26	17	96	27	-31	-23	5,386
EEC	1,754	409	354	-2,845	-42	-16	-17	-62	-34	264	122	-133
TOT	5,461	2,061	1,872	2,483	39	25	73	128	37	655	269	1,310
BST	471	-1,306	1,565	7	20	-54	-53	-63	63	-432	-218	0
BTW	-1,366	-1,455	928	-2,597	-28	-80	-70	-159	37	-401	-195	-5,386
TL2	6,247	2,111	1,861	2,617	46	26	84	135	47	743	300	14,218
RW2	2,625	200	522	2,732	56	27	28	103	36	58	8	6,397

a. For abbreviations, see table 3-4. Figures are rounded.

Table E-5. *Comparison of Direct Effects of Alternative Tariff-Cutting Formulas on Trade Balance for Four Major Negotiating Areas, 1971 Base and 1974 Base*
Millions of dollars

	United States				Canada				Japan				EEC			
	1971		1974		1971		1974		1971		1974		1971		1974	
Formula[a]	Trade balance (direct)[b]	Rank	Trade balance (direct)[b]	Rank	Trade balance (direct)[b]	Rank	Trade balance (direct)[b]	Rank	Trade balance (direct)[b]	Rank	Trade balance (direct)[b]	Rank	Trade balance (direct)[b]	Rank	Trade balance (direct)[b]	Rank
1	−40	7	211	7	−504	9	−1,116	9	300	4	501	3	−1,106	10	−2,202	10
2	−58	8	−49	9	−316	1	−673	1	79	11	90	12	−378	1	−555	1
3	−303	12	−313	12	−356	2	−828	4	320	3	493	4	−935	9	−1,861	9
4	−89	9	303	6	−843	12	−1,864	12	493	1	815	1	−1,782	12	−3,549	12
5	−107	10	−63	10	−392	5	−855	5	176	7	263	8	−662	4	−1,165	4
6	−113	3	327	5	−382	4	−802	2	77	12	112	11	−487	3	−845	3
7	−25	6	163	8	−369	3	−817	3	222	5	371	6	−823	6	−1,637	7
8	−227	11	−112	11	−456	6	−1,041	8	378	2	624	2	−1,130	11	−2,280	11
9	266	2	716	2	−558	11	−1,174	11	124	10	201	10	−831	7	−1,571	6
10	352	1	778	1	−475	8	−1,002	7	165	8	392	5	−354	2	−674	2
11	104	4	437	3	−522	10	−1,125	10	212	6	346	7	−934	8	−1,808	8
12	85	5	340	4	−465	7	−993	6	157	9	243	9	−729	5	−1,350	5

Source: Table 3-7 and unpublished computations.
a. For description of formulas, see table 3-1.
b. Direct trade balance excludes exports induced by the respending effect; see text, chapter 3.

279

Comparison of Results with Those of Alternative Models of Tariff Liberalization

ROBERT BALDWIN has prepared a model of the tariff negotiations somewhat similar to the model in this study.[1] Another study of tariff liberalization is that by Deardorff, Stern, and Baum.[2]

The study by Baldwin examines only the case of the United States, so that comparisons of its results with those presented in this study are possible only for this country. The model used by Baldwin resembles that used in this study, although Baldwin's study goes into much greater detail in the examination of employment effects, considering questions such as the impact of liberalization by skill group and by state. In terms of general approach, however, the principal differences between the two models are the following. With respect to imports, the present study uses import elasticities estimated by Mordechai E. Kreinin in preference to those provided by Clopper Almon, Jr., and others (see chapter 2) for sectors in which the former are available,[3] whereas Baldwin applies the Almon and others

---

1. Robert E. Baldwin, "Trade and Employment Effects in the United States of Multilateral Tariff Restrictions" (Washington, D.C., 1975; processed).

2. Alan V. Deardorff, Robert M. Stern, and Christopher F. Baum, "A Multi-Country Simulation of the Employment and Exchange-Rate Effects of Post-Kennedy Round Tariff Reductions" (University of Michigan, 1976; processed).

3. See Mordechai E. Kreinin, "Disaggregated Import Demand Functions—Further Results," *Southern Economic Journal,* vol. 40 (July 1973), pp. 19–25; and

elasticities for all sectors. Second, the present study expands the results for 1971 to 1974 levels, whereas Baldwin's estimates refer to 1971 only.

On the export side, the approach used by Baldwin differs radically from that used in this study. Baldwin identifies a "price elasticity of exports" for each U.S. product (again from Almon and others). He then computes a weighted average of foreign tariffs facing the United States in the category and, applying the appropriate "price" change for a given tariff formula, calculates the increase in U.S. exports to be expected.[4] By contrast, this study obtains changes in U.S. exports by summing up individually the increases in other countries' imports from the United States, based on the application of the model to the other countries' tariff and import data.

Conceptually, one issue raised by the Baldwin approach is whether it is appropriate to use an export elasticity when the prices of all suppliers to a foreign market are changing, not just the price of the United States. That is, in the estimation and conceptual definition of an export elasticity, it is assumed that the exporter in question changes its price relative to the prices of all other export competitors in the same market. Yet, precisely the opposite happens in trade liberalization: the prices of the United States and all other export suppliers remain unchanged in relation to each other,[5] but all of these suppliers and the United States have their price lowered to consumers within the protected market.

A second major difference between this study and that by Baldwin, on the export side, is that in this study we explicitly estimate the effects of both substitution in the markets of free-trade blocs and the increased exports to rest-of-world countries induced by their additional export earnings through the "free-rider" effect. Although the study by Baldwin mentions both of these additional export effects, it contains no detailed empirical estimates of them.

Given these similarities and differences between the two studies, their results should be similar for imports. However, the results on the export side should be different. Aside from the "responding" export effect, how-

---

Clopper Almon, Jr., and others, *1985: Interindustry Forecasts of the American Economy* (Lexington Books, 1974).

4. That is, the increase in exports equals the base level of exports, times the export price elasticity, times the change in foreign tariff as a fraction of unity plus the foreign tariff.

5. Abstracting from the trade bloc "substitution" cases, discussed below.

Table F-1. *Alternative Estimates of Effects of a 50 Percent Tariff Cut on U.S. Trade and Employment, 1971 Base*
Millions of dollars; thousands of jobs; excluding trade in petroleum and textiles

	Baldwin (1)	This study[a] (2)	Column 1/ column 2 (3)
Imports	1,746	1,533.9	1.138
Direct exports			
Total	n.a.	1,503.2	n.a.
Trade creation	1,750	1,027.8	1.703
Trade substitution	n.a.	475.4	n.a.
Induced exports (respending effect)	n.a.	188.6	n.a.
Trade balance[b]	n.a.	157.9	n.a.
Increased employment (direct exports)	136.0	97.2	1.399
Decreased employment (import effect)	151.2	100.5	1.521
Net employment change	−15.2	−3.3	...

Source: Column 1, Robert E. Baldwin, "Trade and Employment Effects in the United States of Multilateral Tariff Restrictions" (Washington, D.C., 1975; processed), chapter 3, p. 1.
n.a. Not available.
a. Results interpolated between direct estimates for 60 percent and 43.4 percent tariff cuts, from unpublished employment effect estimates for 1971.
b. Direct exports plus induced exports minus imports.

ever, it is ambiguous whether our results would be expected to be higher or lower than those by Baldwin. On the one hand, since our estimates include the trade substitution effect, the direct export effects estimated in this study should be higher than those estimated by Baldwin. On the other hand, the use of an export price elasticity that is conceptually appropriate when only U.S. prices are falling, in a situation where all exporters' prices are falling simultaneously to the importing consumer, would tend to bias upward the export results obtained by Baldwin. Whether that upward bias would be expected to fall short of or exceed the additional components of export increase computed in this study—namely, the substitution and respending effects—is unclear.

Table F-1 shows the results obtained by Baldwin for U.S. exports and imports in 1971 from a 50 percent tariff cut, along with the corresponding estimates from this study with the export results separated by individual components for comparability with the Baldwin estimates. Our results are calculated by linear interpolation between the results for formulas 1 and 7, linear cuts of 60 percent and 43.4 percent, respectively.

The table shows that Baldwin's estimates are quite close to those of this study for imports, as expected. They exceed the comparable estimate (1971 increase in nonoil, nontextile imports) by 13.8 percent. However, the divergence between the two studies is much greater for the export estimate, at least when focusing on the appropriate corresponding concept rather than the total. For increased U.S. exports, under the concept of "trade creation," Baldwin's estimate exceeds that of this study by 70.3 percent. This discrepancy is consistent with the point discussed above. The use of an export elasticity (as done by Baldwin) for tariff reduction effects will tend to overstate the results because the tariff declines apply to all suppliers simultaneously, not to the United States in isolation.

For the remaining components of the export effect—the substitution effect and the respending effect—the Baldwin study contains no estimates for comparison.

If any direction of bias in our own estimates can be inferred from the comparison with the results obtained by Baldwin, it would be that our estimates for the United States are downward biased, slightly for imports and perhaps more substantially for exports. For the reasons given above, however, in the case of exports, it seems more likely that there is an upward bias in the Baldwin results rather than a downward bias in the results of the present study.

Finally, the Baldwin study contains estimates of the employment effects of tariff liberalization, which we may compare with those obtained in this study. As shown in table F-1, the Baldwin estimates are 52 percent higher than those of this study for the job loss attributable to liberalization. Considering the fact that the corresponding difference between import-value estimates is 13.8 percent, Baldwin's analysis appears to generate approximately 34 percent higher "labor intensity" per unit value of import change. This divergence is probably attributable in part to different procedures in the two studies for harmonizing the year of the job coefficient data base with the 1971 value estimates for trade changes.[6] However, the discrepancy is sufficiently limited that it does not challenge the fundamental conclusions in this study, that job losses from import liberalization would be almost imperceptibly small, at least in the aggregate.

6. In the present study, 1970 job coefficients were available from the 134-sector input-output table. However, these coefficients were stated in terms of jobs per $1 billion delivery to final demand specified in dollars of 1963. In order to apply the coefficients to 1971 trade values, the overall U.S. wholesale price index was applied to all coefficients to reduce jobs per $1 billion from the levels applicable to 1963 dollars to appropriate levels for 1971 dollars. By contrast, the Baldwin study worked with coefficients for 1967 from the 363-sector input-output table. The study deflated 1971 trade-value estimates back to 1967 prices in order to compute job changes expected from liberalization.

On the export side, Baldwin's employment estimates exceed those in this study by 40 percent, again not enough to alter the basic policy implications. (This divergence represents a direct export-value estimate 16 percent higher than that of this study, implying a labor intensity of exports 20 percent higher than that estimated in this study.)

Despite these differences, the central findings of the study by Baldwin are similar to those of this study: deep tariff cuts could be carried out with little or no serious threat of the dislocation of workers by increased imports. This same conclusion on the small size of employment effects is reached in the study by Deardorff, Stern, and Baum. Although that study has limitations on the policy information contained in its results (as discussed in chapter 2), it does obtain empirical estimates that support the central conclusions of the Baldwin study and our own: trade balance, employment, and exchange rate changes from liberalization would all be small.[7]

The employment estimates from the Baldwin study would be expected to be somewhat larger than those of this study because they apply real labor productivity levels of 1967, whereas this study applies labor productivity levels of 1970. This difference, as well as differing treatment of inflating and deflating nominal values, lies behind the different implied "labor intensity" of trade between the two studies.

7. The Deardorff-Stern-Baum study reports calculations based on 1970 trade values. The trade balance estimates for a 50 percent tariff cut are the following: United States, −$50.9 million; Canada, −$93.3 million; EEC, +$1,094 million; Japan, −$19.1 million. The corresponding estimates of this study for 1971 (excluding "responding" exports) are: United States, −$33 million; Canada, −$420 million; EEC, −$922 million; Japan, +$250 million. Both sets of estimates are extremely small compared to total trade values. Differences by area are pronounced only for the EEC. The positive trade balance effect for the EEC found in the Deardorff-Stern-Baum model appears to result from the failure of that study to take into account the trade substitution effect. The negative trade balance effect for Japan has no immediately obvious explanation.

Similarly, the exchange rate changes estimated in Deardorff-Stern-Baum are extremely small, like those estimated in this study. For all but one of eighteen industrial countries the exchange rate changes estimated in Deardorff-Stern-Baum are less than one-half of one percent; for two-thirds of the countries they are less than one-fifth of one percent. Finally, the Deardorff-Stern-Baum estimates of employment change from a 50 percent tariff cut are: United States, −20,400 jobs; Canada, −27,900; Japan, −43,100; and EEC, +24,400. The corresponding estimates of this study are: United States, +24,100; Canada, −42,200; Japan, +19,100; and EEC (direct jobs only), −93,500. (Calculated from table 3-14 as five-sixths of the effects for a 60 percent tariff cut; results refer to 1974 trade-value base.) Once again, the job effects are all so small, relative to total labor force, that differences between the Deardorff-Stern-Baum estimates and those of this study may be considered inconsequential.

A Note on Aggregation Bias

CHAPTER 2 states that the tariff-liberalization model of this study avoids aggregation bias by calculating trade effects at the level of industrial tariff-line commodities, and that calculations at broader trade-category levels using average tariffs would cause bias in the estimates. This appendix examines this bias.

Consider first the bias for a linear tariff cut. Consider the case of two tariff-line items in a broader category. A linear proportionate cut of α (for example, 0.5 for a 50 percent cut) would cause the following trade effect for the category as a whole:

$$(1) \qquad \Delta M = \eta \frac{\alpha t_1}{1 + t_1} M_1 + \eta \frac{\alpha t_2}{1 + t} M_2,$$

where ΔM is increase in the group's imports; η is the import elasticity (assumed equal for the two line items); t_1 and t_2 are tariffs on good 1 and good 2, respectively; M_1 and M_2 are import values of good 1 and good 2; $M_1 + M_2 = M$.

If calculations are made using an average tariff for the whole group, $\bar{t} = t_1(M_1/M) + t_2(M_2/M)$, then the estimate will be:

$$(2) \qquad \Delta M^a = \eta \frac{\alpha \bar{t}}{1 + \bar{t}} M,$$

where superscript a stands for aggregate-based estimate. The question is whether:

$$(3) \qquad \eta \frac{\alpha t_1}{1 + t_1} M_1 + \eta \frac{\alpha t_2}{1 + t_2} M_2 \overset{?}{=} \eta \frac{\alpha \bar{t}}{1 + \bar{t}} M,$$

285

and thus whether:

$$(4) \qquad \frac{t_1}{1+t_1} M_1 + \frac{t_2}{1+t_2} M_2 \overset{?}{=} \frac{t_1 \dfrac{M_1}{M} + t_2 \dfrac{M_2}{M}}{1+t_1 \dfrac{M_1}{M} + t_2 \dfrac{M_2}{M}} M.$$

This equality cannot hold true unless $t_1 = t_2$. Therefore, there exists a bias using preaggregated tariff and trade data even for a linear tariff cut. To examine the likely size and direction of this bias, consider the case where $t_1 = 10$ percent, $t_2 = 20$ percent, and $M_1 = M_2 = \frac{1}{2} M$. Then the detailed estimate (left-hand side of equation 4) gives a slightly smaller value than the aggregate-based estimate (right-hand side). The left-hand and right-hand sides are 0.1288 and 0.1304, respectively—meaning that the aggregate-based estimate would be 1.29 percent higher than the line-item-based estimate in this example.

A more serious bias from preaggregation occurs when tariff cutting is by a harmonization formula. In a harmonization formula of the type where percent cut in tariff equals a constant plus a coefficient times tariff, equation 3 becomes:

$$(5) \qquad \eta \frac{\alpha t_1 + \beta t_1^2}{1+t_1} M_1 + \eta \frac{\alpha t_2 + \beta t_2^2}{1+t_2} \overset{?}{=} \eta \frac{\alpha \bar{t} + \beta \bar{t}^2}{1+\bar{t}}.$$

It is clear in equation 5 that the aggregate-based right-hand side will be underestimated—smaller than the disaggregated left-hand side—because of the strength of the quadratic term in raising the numerator of the high tariff term on the left side. That is, the average of the sum of two squares of individual numbers will always exceed the square of their average.

To turn to a concrete example of the downward bias in import estimates using average tariff, for preaggregated commodity groups, consider the three-iteration harmonization formula (EEC-type) examined in chapter 3. By this formula, for a group of two commodities, each with equal import value in the base year, but one having a tariff of only 1 percent and the other a tariff of 50 percent (giving the cut to the lowest tariff allowed under our version of the formula), the disaggregated approach would yield an estimated proportionate price reduction of: $\frac{1}{2}$ (0.0003) + $\frac{1}{2}$ (0.2318) = 0.1161. The corresponding price effect of the formula on the group average tariff would be 0.0994. Therefore the detailed tariff-line-based estimate would give an import increase 16.8 percent higher than that calculated using the group average tariff.

Finally, as noted in chapter 2 an examination of our results for a few selected products indicates that, in practice, the use of aggregate data in evaluating the EEC harmonization formula could give rise to a downward bias in trade estimates by a magnitude on the order of 11 percent or more.

A Model of Optimal Tariff Negotiations

THE BASIC quantitative estimates of this study for tariff-liberalization effects appear in chapter 3. Those estimates assume that all industrial countries participating in the negotiations will adopt the same tariff-cutting formula (whichever formula that may be) and, furthermore, that they will apply the formula across all product sectors. However, an alternative approach may be considered, in which an "optimal" set of tariff reductions is chosen, with the possibility of different formulas applied across sectors and among countries. The purpose of this appendix is to explore the nature of an "optimal tariff negotiation" of this nature. The appendix develops a linear programming model in order to examine the question. Essentially, the model maximizes total welfare from tariff reduction subject to restraints placed on the permissible magnitudes of the resulting trade balance deficits of participating countries. The following section sets forth the model at the theoretical level. The reader unfamiliar with linear programming analysis may wish to skip to the subsequent section which presents and interprets the quantitative results.

Description of the Model

The problem we seek to solve is the following: select tariff-cutting formulas by country and product such that total welfare from liberalization is maximized, subject to constraints to be set on the acceptable deterioration of trade balance for each participant. The dimensions of the problem are potentially enormous. For each of eleven importing areas, there are approximately 5,000 tariff rates that may be varied in many conceivable ways. In order to simplify, we consider each of the twenty-one broad BTN sections of each of the eleven importing countries as the basic units of analysis. Information for the problem is available for tariff cuts following any of the twelve formulas for which trade and welfare effects are estimated (as reported in chapter 3). If we think of tariff cutting by a given rule in a certain sector for any country as an "activity," there are potentially 2,772 tools at our disposal.

For reasons of convenience and computational considerations, we use linear programming to analyze an "optimal" tariff reform. Although not purely appropriate, this approach probably gives a close approximation of an optimal solution. The discussion also considers the likely sizes and directions of bias in the analysis.

The objective function to be maximized is the sum of static welfare gains across all sectors and across all countries without weights. (For the purposes of this appendix, we deal with static welfare estimates, which are precisely specified, rather than the approximated total welfare effects including dynamic influences discussed in chapter 3.) Because all of the industrial countries are at comparable levels of per capita income, there is no reason to attach a higher utility per unit of welfare gain to any one country than to that for another. Were there no constraints on the tariff cuts, each country would of course cut all tariffs to zero. Welfare rises as imports increase, and maximum welfare gain (and import increase) would occur under complete elimination of tariffs. We chose to constrain this obvious first best economic solution in two ways. The first narrowing of options is to eliminate the 100 percent tariff cut as a tool on the ground that it is strictly unrealistic. Were this the only restriction, there would be no links connecting actions by the various countries within the various commodity sections. In this case, the solution would be to treat each country-commodity unit separately and to cut tariffs according to that rule which maximized welfare gain.[1]

However, a second basic restriction is necessary: a balance-of-payments restriction. Although it would be more elegant to specify a welfare

1. If there were no aggregation bias—as described below—that formula which yields the highest "average depth of cut" would be chosen, but because of the biases we must consult the welfare figure directly.

cost per unit of balance-of-trade deficit, there is no theoretical basis for specifying this cost. Therefore, the model contains, instead, an arbitrary limit upon the amount by which the balance of trade may deteriorate as the result of trade liberalization, for each negotiating country. This constraint links countries and commodities together and introduces a multitude of interaction terms. That is, increased imports by one country alleviate the balance-of-trade constraint on another country by increasing the second country's exports.

The model contains a third type of restriction as well: for any given country-sector, the sum of the "activity levels" for all of the different tariff-cutting formulas considered may be no greater than unity. The model then selects the optimizing "blend" of tariff-cutting rules for the country-sector. For example, if the model chooses the level 0.5 for a 60 percent tariff cut and 0.5 for the three-iteration harmonization rule, then the tariff will be cut to an intermediate point halfway between the two "after-reform" levels that would result from the two respective individual formulas.

Finally, in evaluation of the trade balance constraint, the model takes into account not only a country's increased imports, and increased exports to other liberalizing industrial countries, but also the country's increased exports to the less developed and communist countries through the "respending effect" (as discussed in chapter 3).

The specific formulation of the model is as follows:

(1) $$\text{Max } W^* = \sum_i \sum_j \sum_k \phi_{ijk} W_{ijk};$$

subject to:

(a) $0 \leq \sum_i \phi_{ijk} \leq 1$,

(b) $- \sum_i \sum_j \sum_h \phi_{ijk} M_{ijkh}$

$$+ \sum_{h=1}^{18} \sum_i \sum_j \phi_{ijh} M_{ijhk}$$

$$+ \sum_{h=19}^{132} \lambda_{hk} \sum_i \sum_j \sum_k \phi_{ijk} M_{ijkh} \geq B_k^*;$$

where:

W^* = total welfare;

W_{ijk} = welfare gain from complete application of tariff formula i in sector j of importing area k;

ϕ_{ijk} = fractional activity level at which tariff cut i in sector j of country k is to be operated;

M_{ijkh} = increased imports from supplier h into buyer k in sector j associated with complete application of tariff formula i;

λ_{hk} = proportion of increased export earnings of supplier h that will be respent on induced purchases from country k.

Note that suppliers $h = 1$ through 18 are the industrial countries directly considered (ten individual countries plus the EEC); suppliers $h = 19$ through 132 are the less developed and communist countries whose respending is taken into account.

The objective function states that total welfare equals the sum over "fractional" levels of each tariff-cutting policy applied (ϕ_{ijk}) multiplied by the full welfare effect associated with complete application of each policy. As discussed below, the measure involves a minor bias in that it treats nonlinear welfare effects as linear. Restraint (a) states that for a given sector and country, the "fractional" activity levels for all tariff-cutting options i may sum to no more than unity (allowing a blend of tariff-cutting formulas), although the sum may fall to zero (no cuts whatsoever). Restraint (b) is the balance-of-trade constraint, which must be larger than the arbitrary level B_k^* for importing country k. The first term in the constraint represents the trade balance loss because of increased imports. That is, M_{ijkh} is the increased import value under tariff formula i and good j in importing country k bought from supplier h. The sum over fractional activity levels (ϕ_{ijk}) multiplied by the full import value associated with each policy (M_{ijk}) constitutes total trade balance cost to country k through increased imports. The two final terms of restraint (b) are the offsetting export gains for country k. The first of these two represent country k's direct sales to other importing industrial countries, themselves liberalizing.[2] The second term represents country k's exports to the free-rider countries through the respending effect. That is, each free-rider h has an amount available for respending equal to its exports attributable to liberalization ($\sum_i \sum_j \sum_k \phi_{ijk} M_{ijkh}$); of this amount, each free-rider h spends the fraction λ_{hk} on purchases from industrial country k.

This model is capable of obtaining an optimal solution for tariff cuts by

---

2. Note that in this term the final two subscripts on the import element are reversed. Here, country k is the supplier and h is the buyer. It is the sequence of subscript dimensions that remains unchanged (formula, sector, buyer, supplier).

sector and by country subject to a limitation on trade balance deterioration. Before turning to the results obtained using the model, it is important to consider its basic properties and probable biases.

Neglecting for a moment all country interaction terms by assuming that there are only two countries, and assuming that the second country will react in the same way to additional trade balance gain regardless of the sector or source, as in fact would occur, then we can surmise the nature of the optimal pattern of liberalization. If a country's trade balance constraint is very "tight," it will choose for liberalization that product sector and that tariff-cutting rule that give the highest ratio of welfare gain to increased imports. It is probable that, were there no biases in looking at BTN section "averages," this conclusion would mean using a tariff-cutting rule that results in a small cut in a sector with a high tariff. That is, reducing the highest percentage tariff on a high-tariff sector provides the most powerful welfare gains per unit of increased imports. This would be true because the feedback effects on the country's trade balance and on world welfare depends only on the amount of increased imports, and not on the sector. This conclusion does not hold, however, with many countries with different constraints. If we call two other countries Japan (for which, suppose, the constraint is not relevant) and New Zealand (for which the constraint is relevant), this point can be demonstrated. Suppose that liberalization is carried out in a sector primarily supplied by Japan, and that the sector has a high ratio of direct (first-country) welfare gain to increased imports. In this case, since Japan is constrained by the maximum cuts allowed rather than by balance-of-trade considerations, there will be no indirect effects. However, if liberalization is carried out in a sector primarily supplied by New Zealand, New Zealand can liberalize more herself, importing more and releasing the first-country trade balance constraint, allowing still further liberalization in the first country. Thus, the gain achieved for the system as a whole may be greater through the liberalization of some sector other than that with the highest tariffs.

These types of considerations are considered by the linear programming approach. Were no sectors or rules "intensive" in their incidence on one country as opposed to another, these considerations would not matter and it would be possible to impute answers merely by examining the ratios of welfare gain to import increases. As the balance-of-trade constraint was relaxed, the model would move from using rules with mild tariff cuts to those with deeper cuts and would begin to include sectors with lower tariff levels.

There are certain biases associated with applying a linear programming analysis in the face of nonlinear characteristics of the problem. The welfare gain resulting from a tariff cut is not linear. The welfare cost of an existing tariff rises geometrically with the height of the tariff. Therefore, if we consider the relationship of welfare gain to percentage cut in tariff, then for a given tariff at a specified height the greatest welfare gain will be for the "first" percentage cut, and each successive percentage cut will add diminishing increments of welfare gain. Another area of nonlinearity concerns the trade balance effect. Although the effect is linear with respect to imports, it is nonlinear for members of the EEC or EFTA (because of the appearance of the tariff-cut term in the denominator of the substitution term; see chapter 2). However, we will ignore this second nonlinearity, which is quite small.

In deciding where to cut tariffs, there are two types of decisions: when to change from one tariff-cutting rule to another within a sector, and when to change sectors. What types of errors are likely to be introduced by considering the problem as linear? To obtain an idea of the answer it is helpful to consider problems simpler than the full programming model but similar in essence.

What errors will occur in the choice of the optimal combination of tariff-cutting rules for a given sector? We will argue that, since it is the total cut that matters for welfare and the balance of payments, it is unimportant how that total cut is determined. More specifically, consider a problem in which welfare is maximized subject to an import constraint, assuming feedback effects to depend only on the level of imports. We only have one sector; this makes the assumption relating feedback to the level of extra imports more likely. For simplicity, we assume three possible tariff-cutting rules characterized in figure H-1 by the combinations of welfare and imports they generate. If the import limit is K_1, we use a combination of relatively nonliberalizing rule one with a high ratio of extra welfare to extra imports but low total welfare and import increase; and a more liberal rule two having a lower ratio of welfare to imports but more abundant total welfare and import increases. Were the constraint more liberal (at K_2, for example), we would use rules two and three, since the need to conserve on imports implicit in policy one is reduced.

Figure H-1. *Model for Selecting "Optimal" Tariff-Cutting Formula within a Given Sector*

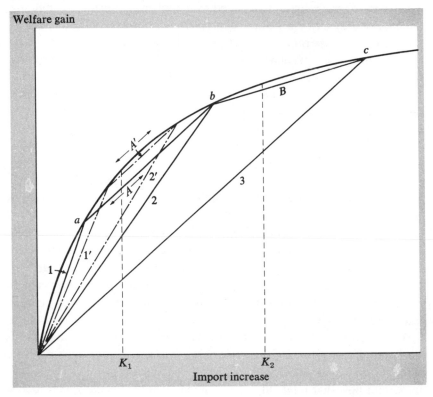

The only error here will be in the welfare attributed to the policy, which will be underestimated. This may be seen by the fact that the straight line segments *A* and *B* in the diagram lie underneath the curve showing actual welfare gain in relation to import increase (and it is from the "blend" of policies along the connecting line segments that the linear program computes the level of welfare achieved). In short, the import increase allowed (K_1 or K_2) determines the blend of tariff-cutting rules that is allowed.

If we now add policies 1' and 2', we will still end up with the same tariff cut but will have less error in measuring the actual welfare. What will be different in the optimizing problem between the solutions is the value of reducing the constraint and how that feeds into the rest of the problem. In our problem we have nine policies for each sector, which probably allows us to be rather close to the nonlinear curve. This conclusion would be particularly true when most of the rules are clustered with import values close to the constraint. In short, the systematic error involved in nonlinearity is to underestimate the welfare gain. However, not only is the degree of underestimation likely to be small, but also in selecting the combination of tariff rules to use in making a given cut the linear programming problem will choose the one that minimizes that error.[3] Thus, our conclusion is that, in choosing which rules to use and when to change from one combination to another, our formulation will not commit serious errors.

The same conclusion does not hold in choosing in which sector to cut tariffs if a choice is necessary. To explain the point simply, consider only two sectors and an import constraint. Figure H-2 shows the ratio of welfare gain to import increase on the vertical axis, and the total increase in imports on the horizontal axis. Lines W_1 and W_2 show the welfare gains in sectors one and two, respectively. Now, suppose a total of M^* increased imports is allowed. The obvious optimal policy is to arrange tariff cuts to equalize the marginal welfare gains in each sector to $\bar{W}$, causing $\bar{M}_1$ and $\bar{M}_2$ increased imports in each sector, respectively, where $\bar{M}_1$ and $\bar{M}_2$ sum to the permissible M^*. However, the linear program will instead choose the "best" sector for liberalizing on the "average"—which is sector 2—and liberalize it *completely* before making any liberalization whatsoever in the next sector. In the case shown in figure H-2, the linear program would choose only sector 2 and liberalize it to point C (full import constraint exhausted). At that point, there would be a welfare gain possible by reducing the liberalization in sector 2 by a unit of imports (losing welfare, W_{LP}) and replacing it by an initial unit liberalization in sector 1 (gaining initial welfare, W_1^0).

In practical terms, the sectoral problem amounts to the following: Ideally tariffs would be reduced in the highest tariff sector until the level of the next sector was reached; then tariffs in both sectors would be re-

3. That is, since (a) the model tends to understate welfare, and (b) the rules selected maximize estimated welfare, it follows that (c) the rules selected will minimize the error. Alternatively viewed, in figure H-1 the model would have the option of reaching import level K_1 by a combination along a line segment connecting points a and c—combining policies 1 and 3. The model will reject this option, which would yield lower welfare, and choose instead the line segment between a and b, thereby coming as close as possible to the real welfare level associated with import level K_1 (shown on the curve).

Figure H-2. *Model for Selecting "Best" Sector for Liberalization*

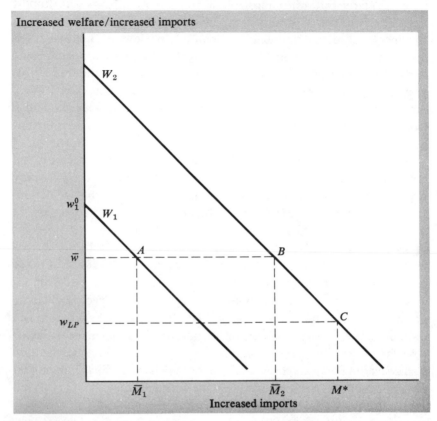

duced jointly until the lower level of a third sector was reached; and so forth. But, because the linear program deals in linear "averages" for each sector, it chooses the high tariff sector and reduces tariffs in that sector to well below the tariff level of a second (low initial tariff) sector. Essentially, the model fails to capture the fact that the welfare gain per unit liberalization falls as tariff level falls, and instead it applies a constant welfare/import ratio over all levels of tariff, given a sector's initial tariff level.[4]

4. This problem does not arise in the choice of which tariff rule to use within a sector, as opposed to which sector to choose. As illustrated in figure H-1, there is only one true marginal welfare gain curve which is a function of increased imports, regardless of which rule is used to proceed.

In short, the linear programming approach will tend to cut tariffs excessively in sectors with high initial tariffs, relative to sectors with low tariffs. Concentration of tariff cutting on sectors with high tariffs is, of course, desirable up to a point—where harmonization occurs. However, the linear programming model will "overdo" harmonization, leapfrogging sectors with high tariffs down to lower postreform tariffs than those resulting for sectors with lower initial tariffs.

The "sector choice" problem diminishes, however, as more tariff-cutting rules are introduced, because a new rule would break up the constant marginal welfare gain line into two gains of different magnitudes. If there are enough rules, it becomes possible to approach the nonlinear case results obtained by the combination of points *A* and *B* in figure H-2. It is unclear, however, how many rules are "enough."

The above discussion completes the considerations of properties and biases of the linear programming model, and we can now turn to the specifics of the model in actual application. In order to reduce the size of the problem, the model omits three of the twelve original tariff-cutting formulas as examined in chapter 3. The 100 percent cut is eliminated for two reasons. The primary reason is that of the political reality. (However, even though not realistic for political reasons, this rule could have been useful to add to possible combinations in the case where the trade balance constraint is not binding and a larger cut is needed.) Our general procedure has been to assume that formula 8 (full U.S. authority 60 percent tariff cut plus elimination of tariffs less than 5 percent) represents an upper limit of liberalization.

The model omits formula 10, the across-country harmonization rule, on two considerations. The formula generally results in low tariff cuts and with a large trade balance constraint it would probably not be used. Furthermore, since the tariff cuts do not depend on existing tariff levels but would vary by BTN categories, the presentation of results using the rule would be cumbersome. Finally, the 43.4 percent cut is eliminated in order to reduce the problem still further. The cut is at an intermediate level and of the remaining formulas it is the least different from basic cuts such as the 60 percent linear cut (although its inclusion would add information by presenting another break in a linear segment in what could be a sensitive range).

For the basic model we eliminate the petroleum sector. The model is estimated once excluding textiles and a second time including textiles.

In arriving at our balance-of-trade constraint figure, we have used merchandise exports for 1974 as the base, since exports for the country are somewhat analogous to income for the individual and represent earning power abroad or power to earn foreign exchange. For the developed countries, the model allows a deficit equal to 0.5 percent of this base vector. That is, we choose an extremely stringent trade balance constraint in order to force the model to exercise constraint maximization (rather than going immediately to maximum tariff cuts allowed, namely, full U.S. authority). Under most circumstances, a trade balance deterioration equal to 0.5 percent of export earnings would represent a very mild trade balance disruption, indeed. Furthermore, in the case of the EEC, for the purposes of the model, we consider the export base to include only exports to outside countries—or only a fraction of EEC member countries' total exports if intra-EEC trade is considered as well. Therefore, the model involves an acid test that should satisfy even the most nervous observer wary of possible trade balance deterioration resulting from trade liberalization.

To recapitulate, our linear programming problem has a welfare function, which is the sum of increased welfare for eleven importing areas. There are 1,996 activities: 1,881 tariff-cutting activities and 115 respending activities by free-rider countries. The free-rider problem is constrained by 115 equality constraints specifying that the balance-of-trade effects are zero. There are 11 inequality constraints specifying that the trade balance deficits of the negotiating countries must be no greater than 0.5 percent of their 1974 exports. There are also 204 constraints stating that the sum of activity levels across a sector by a country must be less than or equal to unity.

The two linear programming problems examined are identical except that the second allows tariff cutting in the textile industry while the first does not. From this addition we can draw two pieces of information. The difference between the total welfare value in the two cases gives the cost of not liberalizing textiles but liberalizing some other goods instead in the achievement of a given balance-of-payments deficit vector. Furthermore, adding textiles activity will cause other sectors to be eliminated in much the same way that tighter trade balance constraints would, and thus the second exercise provides some indication of those activities that would be eliminated were the trade balance constraints even more stringent.

Results

The results of the linear programming analyses are presented in tables H-1 (excluding textiles) and H-2 (including textiles).[5] The tables report the tariff-cutting formulas selected in the optimal solution for each BTN product sector in each importing area. Because the optimal solution in most cases assigns only one tariff-cutting formula to each sector (operated at the full possible "activity" level of "unity" rather than a lower fraction),[6] in most cases only one formula appears for each country-sector. In some cases, however, a "blend" of formulas is selected, and the secondary formula (along with the fractional level at which it is operated) appears in the lower portions of the tables. In these cases, the formula shown in the main part of the table also shows, in parentheses, the fractional level at which it is operated.

Before examining the results of tables H-1 and H-2, it is helpful to consider table H-3, which reports the "shadow price" on the trade balance constraint in the optimal solution. This "price" tells the premium of value associated with the per dollar relaxation of the trade balance constraint. For example, for Canada the solution shows that a $1 increase in the permissible level of trade deficit would allow increased liberalization that would raise welfare by $0.22. By contrast, for Japan the shadow price of the trade balance constraint is zero, indicating that the constraint is not "binding," so that the optimal welfare solution could not be further increased even if the constraint were relaxed.

The broad patterns evident for the results in the basic exercise excluding textiles (table H-1) are the following. First, the United States, Japan, Austria, and Switzerland tend to choose the most liberalizing tariff formula possible: number 8, full U.S. authority.[7] This tendency reflects the fact that for these countries the trade balance constraint is not binding (Japan, Austria, Switzerland—all of which have a zero shadow price for the constraint; see table H-3) or at least not seriously limiting (the

5. Note that the estimates apply our 1974-base measures of tariff-liberalization effects, not the 1971-base findings.

6. This result minimizes the practical significance of the bias in choice among tariff-cutting formulas, as discussed above. There is no error because of nonlinearity when only a single rule is applied, as opposed to a blend of rules.

7. In the one sector in which Japan chooses an alternative formula (number 5), the alternative is in fact more liberalizing than formula 8.

Table H-1. *Tariff-Cutting Formulas*[a] *Selected under Optimal Tariff Negotiations, by Importing Area, Excluding Textiles*
Figures in parentheses indicate fractional level of application of primary formula chosen, when less than 1.0.

BTN section	PRINCIPAL CUTS										
	United States[b]	Canada[b]	Japan[b]	EEC[b]	Aus-tria	Fin-land	Norway	Sweden	Switzer-land	Australia	New Zealand
1	8	8	8	8	8	6	5	1	8	...	6
2	8	6	8	11	8	6	5	8	8	6 (0.49)	...
3	1	...	8	9	8	...	11	8	8	...	...
4	8	5	5	5	5	6	5 (0.74)	8	5	2	6
6	8	2	8	1 (0.32)	8	6	9	1	8	6	...
7	5	2	8	11	8	2	9	8	8	...	...
8	8	2	8	9	8	...	1	8	8	6	...
9	8	...	8	5 (0.36)	8	...	...	9	8	6	...
10	8	2	8	8 (0.92)	9	...	12	...	8	6	...
12	8	2	8	2	8	...	5	1	8	6	...
13	8	2	8	1	8	6	3	8	3	...	...
14	8	2	8	1	8	2	...	1	1	6	...
15	8	2	8	12	8	...	9	9	1	6	...
16	1	2 (0.92)	8	11	5	...	9	1	1	6	...
17	12	...	8	6	8	...	9	3	8	...	6 (0.997)

18	9	...	8	9	1	...	6	1	8
19	8	6	8	1	8	...	...	1	8
20	9 (0.71)	2	8	5	12	...	6	8	9
21	8	5	...	...	...	...	...	8	8
									3

SECONDARY CUTS

Importing area	Sector	Formula	Weight
United States	20	1	0.29
EEC	6	9	0.18
EEC	9	2	0.14
EEC	10	1	0.08
Norway	4	1	0.26

a. For a description of the formulas, see table 3-1.

b. The following results are obtained in the maximization model for exports, imports, trade balance, and welfare, respectively (billions of 1974 dollars): United States, 3.10, 3.59, −0.49, 0.51; Canada, 0.60, 0.77, −0.17, 0.10; Japan, 2.13, 1.94, 0.19, 0.34; EEC, 2.66, 3.33, −0.67, 0.42.

Table H-2. *Tariff-Cutting Formulas*[a] *Selected under Optimal Tariff Negotiations, by Importing Area, Including Textiles*

Figures in parentheses indicate fractional level of application of primary formula chosen, when less than 1.0.

PRINCIPAL CUTS

BTN section	United States	Canada	Japan	EEC	Austria	Finland	Norway	Sweden	Switzerland	Australia	New Zealand
1	8	8	8	1	8	6	5	1	8	...	6
2	11	...	8	12	8	6 (0.44)	2	1	8	...	...
3	...	...	8	6	8	...	6	8	8	...	...
4	9	2	5	5	5	6	5	8	8	2	2
6	6	2	8	1	8	6	9	1	8	6 (0.94)	6 (0.06)
7	5	2 (0.39)	8	11	8	...	9	8	8	...	...
8	...	...	8	...	8	...	2	2 (0.51)	8	...	6
9	...	...	8	...	8	...	...	...	8	...	6
10	2	2	8	8	11	...	...	...	8	...	6
11	2	2	8	2	5	6	2	2	8	6	...
12	6	2 (0.53)	8	2	8	...	2	8	8	6	...
13	2	...	8	3	8	6	3	3	3	...	...
14	6	2	8	5	8	...	...	...	8	6	...
15	...	...	8	...	8	...	9	...	1	...	...
16	...	...	8	5	1	...	6 (0.65)	3	8	6	...
17	...	...	8	6 (0.25)	1	...	3	2	8	6	6
18	...	...	8	9	1	...	...	6	8	...	...
19	9	2	8	3	8	...	...	6	8	...	...
20	...	...	8	...	12	...	...	...	9	6	...
21	...	5	8	...	...	...	...	...	8	3	...

SECONDARY CUTS

Importing area	Sector	Formula	Weight
Norway	16	9	0.35
Sweden	8	6	0.43

a. For a description of the formulas, see table 3-1.

Table H-3. *Shadow Price Values for Trade Balance Constraints, Excluding and Including Textiles*[a]

	Excluding textiles		Including textiles	
Importing area	Value	Rank	Value	Rank
United States	0.108	5	0.250	6
Canada	0.217	8	0.351	8
Japan	0.000	1	0.000	1
EEC	0.134	6	0.222	5
Austria	0.000	1	0.000	1
Finland	0.447	10	0.571	11
Norway	0.149	7	0.297	7
Sweden	0.067	4	0.193	4
Switzerland	0.000	1	0.000	1
Australia	0.339	9	0.438	9
New Zealand	0.524	11	0.535	10

a. The shadow price of the trade balance constraint equals the increase in welfare attainable per unit increase in permissible trade balance deterioration.

United States). Second, New Zealand and Finland choose quite restrictive formulas (numbers 2 and 6, which have very low "depth of cut"; see appendix A, table A-1), or they do no liberalization whatsoever because of a seriously binding trade balance constraint (causing shadow prices as high as 0.45 for Finland and 0.52 for New Zealand; see table H-3). Third, Australia and Canada similarly tend to choose restrictive formulas (numbers 6 and 2, respectively), although they do cut tariffs somewhat in almost all sectors. Finally, the EEC and Sweden are in an "intermediate" situation in which for several sectors they make the deepest possible tariff cut but in others they choose more restrictive formulas. This intermediate position represents the intermediate severity of their trade balance constraints (see table H-3).

The broad thrust of these results is that even if exceedingly stringent limitations are set on the permissible decline in trade balance resulting from tariff reform, the most widespread optimal policy would still be the most liberalizing formula considered (full U.S. authority). The only exceptions among the four major negotiating areas would be for Canada (which would liberalize, but by a more restrictive formula) and the EEC (which would choose, in all but one sector, either the most liberal formula, number 8, or at least formulas much more liberal than its own iterative proposal, number 2).

Some specific features of the results in table H-1 warrant attention. Austria and Switzerland do not always adopt the most liberalizing formula, even though their trade balance constraints are not binding. The reason for this result lies in the substitution effect. For example, if Switzerland liberalizes, it may reduce purchases from EFTA partners with serious trade balance constraints (such as Finland) in the process of switching from partner to outside supply. This indirect effect would further limit the liberalization possible for Finland (say), so that an overall optimal solution recommends a less liberal rule for Switzerland (even though, if Switzerland were maximizing in isolation, it would choose the most liberal rules).

Another feature of the results is that the formulas chosen by countries under moderate or serious trade balance constraints tend to be harmonization-type rules. Moreover, as discussed in the previous section, the product sectors selected for liberalization tend to be those with the highest tariffs, causing a sort of harmonization across sectors in the results. These two forms of harmonization reflect the fact that countries with limiting trade balance constraints must concentrate on formulas and sectors that are the "best buys" in the sense of having high ratios of welfare gain to increased imports. These formulas economize on foreign exchange. By contrast, the countries with nonbinding trade balance constraints adopt the most liberalizing formula possible, and indeed that formula (number 8) is an "antiharmonization" formula (because it cuts tariffs under 5 percent by 100 percent, while cutting higher tariffs by only 60 percent).

As for the case that includes textiles in the analysis, the results of table H-2 show that—except for Japan, Switzerland, and Austria—the optimal solution changes to more restrictive tariff formulas. Countries do liberalize textiles (to obtain the corresponding welfare gains), but the resulting increased imports are sufficient to tighten their foreign exchange constraints and force them to less liberalizing tariff cuts in other sectors.[8]

Overall annual static welfare gains achieved amount to $1.51 billion in the first solution excluding textiles and to $1.87 billion in the second solution allowing textile liberalization. Thus, the liberalization of textiles would enable the industrial countries to raise their welfare gains from

8. The exception is New Zealand, which does not liberalize textiles (avoiding increased imports) but does gain extra textile export earnings, permitting it to adopt more liberal tariff cuts in other sectors.

trade liberalization by almost one-fourth over the level otherwise possible, with no increase in the total trade balance deterioration for those countries in which trade balance effects might be a constraint. Also, the overall welfare gain in the first problem (excluding textiles) is quite close to the maximum attainable if all countries adopted the most liberal formula, full U.S. authority ($1.686 billion; see table 3-2). Thus, our optimal solution succeeds in observing rigid trade balance constraints with very little sacrifice in the overall welfare achieved under liberalization.

Comparison of the results excluding and including textiles (tables H-1 and H-2, respectively) permits an examination of the sectors likely to be omitted under more serious trade balance constraints. In the United States, Canada, and the EEC, sectors 8, 9, 15, and 20 (leather, wood, base metals, and miscellaneous manufactures) completely drop out of the liberalization solution. In addition, sectors 3, 16, 17, and 18 (fats and oils, machinery and electrical equipment, transportation equipment, and precision instruments) drop out for the United States and Canada. The disappearance of these sectors would appear to represent their relatively low tariffs and, therefore, their lower priority for obtaining welfare gains once the trade balance constraint is made more severe by extra imports allowed under the solution including textiles.

These results would suggest that the first sectors that might be considered for "exemptions" would be within these broad BTN sections. However, this conclusion would hold only if the motive for exemptions were to conserve foreign exchange by avoiding trade balance loss. If, instead, avoiding domestic labor dislocation were the primary objective of any sectoral exemptions to general tariff-cutting rules, then these sectors would not necessarily be the "best" sectors for exemptions (and, in fact, because of their already low tariffs, it is likely that relatively more serious labor dislocation would be focused in other sectors with higher tariffs—as indeed would be the case of textiles).

Finally, it is useful to examine the "reciprocity" involved in the optimal solution to the programming problems. In one sense, the maximization problems automatically generate reciprocity by ensuring that no country experiences a trade balance loss in excess of a given percentage of its exports. In the more traditional sense, reciprocity may be examined by considering the "average depth of cut" of tariffs. Table H-4 presents the average-depth-of-cut estimates corresponding to the solutions of the two linear programming problems. As shown in the table, the countries without binding trade balance constraints (Japan,[9] Austria, Switzerland) make the deepest overall tariff cuts, while the countries with the most serious trade balance constraints (New Zealand, Finland, Australia, Canada) carry out more moderate cuts. (This may be seen by examining the ranking by depth of cut.) In general, most countries would cut tariffs by approximately 60 percent, although Australia, Canada, and New Zealand would cut them by as little as 34 percent, 28 percent, and 21 percent, respectively. The important case of the EEC shows a cut of 50 percent—well above the EEC depth of cut that would result under its favored three-iteration formula (32 percent; see table A-2, appendix A).

The overall reciprocity implications of the depth-of-cut results are that there could be some legitimate allowance for somewhat lower depth of cut for some countries—particularly Canada, Australia, and New Zealand—in a negotiation that nevertheless achieved a fundamental reciprocity for participants (as measured by welfare gains subject to a constraint on the maximum acceptable level of trade balance deterioration).

Table H-4 also shows average-depth-of-cut results when textile liberalization is allowed. These cuts are generally smaller than those in the problem excluding textiles (except for Austria and Switzerland). The reason is that, with a constraint on trade balance deterioration, less liberalization (proportional to the base) can be done when the base to be liberalized is expanded—especially considering the fact that the added sector is one that tends to generate relatively sizable trade balance losses.[10] It should be reiterated that the inclusion of textiles in liberalization raises total welfare gains substantially—so that the decline in measured "average depth of cut" is misleading for normative policy purposes. Also, when textiles are included, the rank of the United States drops from fifth most liberalizing to ninth—indicating the relatively high significance for the United States of the textile sector for increased imports under liberalization.

9. The high depth of cut for Japan, 75 percent, is somewhat overstated because it includes reduction of extremely high tariffs (355 percent) on government-controlled imports of tobacco (BTN 2401 and 2402). Yet, these imports are assumed not to increase in our basic trade-impact calculations because they are subject to a government trade monopoly. (Note that their import value in 1971 amounted to approximately $100 million.)

10. In addition, but less importantly, the column "including textiles" is lower than the column "excluding textiles" because of the increase in the measured "revenue base" to include textile revenue in the results for the former column.

Table H-4. *Average Depth of Tariff Cuts in the Linear Programming Solutions*

Importing area	Excluding textiles		Including textiles	
	Depth of cut[a]	Rank	Depth of cut[a]	Rank
United States	0.564	5	0.261	9
Canada	0.283	10	0.171	11
Japan	0.754	1	0.748	1
EEC	0.502	7	0.418	6
Austria	0.607	3	0.617	3
Finland	0.421	8	0.335	7
Norway	0.516	6	0.454	4.5
Sweden	0.599	4	0.454	4.5
Switzerland	0.636	2	0.655	2
Australia	0.342	9	0.312	8
New Zealand	0.205	11	0.209	10

a. Tariff revenue forgone as a fraction of base-level revenue. Refers to dutiable imports excluding oil. The column "excluding textiles" also excludes revenue on textile imports from the base.

Conclusion

The results of this appendix indicate that a rigorous mathematical optimization procedure comes to quite "liberalizing" conclusions when used to explore the "optimal" structure of tariff reform, subject to very restrictive requirements limiting the amount of trade balance deterioration allowed to occur to any negotiating country. The central thrust of the results is that, by and large, the most liberalizing practical formula— full U.S. authority (60 percent cut in tariffs and elimination of tariffs below 5 percent)—would be chosen for most sectors and most countries. The only systematic exceptions to this finding are the cases of Canada, Finland, Australia, and New Zealand, which would select more restrictive tariff-liberalization formulas (or else no liberalization at all in some sectors) because their trade balance restrictions turn out to be seriously binding constraints. For the EEC, quite liberal formulas would be chosen in the optimal solution even though the most liberal formula, U.S. authority, would be chosen in only two of twenty-one product sectors. Furthermore, the EEC results are, if anything, biased toward insufficient tariff cuts, because the trade balance constraint specified is 0.5 percent of extra-EEC exports rather than the larger, alternative concept,

0.5 percent of total exports of individual EEC countries regardless of destination.

In practical application, these results would appear to simplify to the following implication: the optimum tariff negotiation would involve full U.S. authority cuts by the three largest areas (the United States, Japan, and the EEC) as well as by all other participants, with the possible exception of Canada, Finland, Australia, and New Zealand. Once again simplifying, a possible modality for addressing this distinction within the negotiations could be to establish an alternative, more restrictive general formula (such as number 2 or number 6) to be applied by these four countries if negotiators judged that their prospective relative trade balance deteriorations did in fact warrant special treatment.

Index